OXFORD MONOGRAPHS IN INTERNATIONAL LAW

International Law and Corporate Actors in Deep Seabed Mining

OXFORD MONOGRAPHS IN INTERNATIONAL LAW

The aim of this series is to publish important and original pieces of research on all aspects of international law. Topics that are given particular prominence are those which, while of interest to the academic lawyer, also have important bearing on issues which touch the actual conduct of international relations. Nonetheless the series is wide in scope and includes monographs on the history and philosophical foundations of international law.

RECENT TITLES IN THE SERIES

The Concept of an International Organization in International Law
Lorenzo Gasbarri

Necessity and Proportionality and the Right of Self-Defence in International Law
Chris O'Meara

Neutrality in Contemporary International Law
James Upcher

Geographical Change and the Law of the Sea
Kate Purcell

Statehood and the State-Like in International Law
Rowan Nicholson

Confronting the Shadow State
Henri Decœur

Irresolvable Norm Conflicts in International Law
The Concept of a Legal Dilemma
Valentin Jeutner

International Law and Corporate Actors in Deep Seabed Mining

JOANNA DINGWALL

OXFORD
UNIVERSITY PRESS

OXFORD
UNIVERSITY PRESS

Great Clarendon Street, Oxford, OX2 6DP,
United Kingdom

Oxford University Press is a department of the University of Oxford.
It furthers the University's objective of excellence in research, scholarship,
and education by publishing worldwide. Oxford is a registered trade mark of
Oxford University Press in the UK and in certain other countries

First Edition published in 2021

Impression: 1

Published in the United States of America by Oxford University Press
198 Madison Avenue, New York, NY 10016, United States of America

British Library Cataloguing in Publication Data

Data available

Library of Congress Control Number: 2021933732

ISBN 978–0–19–289826–5

DOI: 10.1093/oso/9780192898265.001.0001

Printed and bound by
CPI Group (UK) Ltd, Croydon, CR0 4YY

General Editors' Preface

It is often said that we know less about the deep reaches of the ocean floor than we do about the Moon. Yet today humankind has moved beyond the vivid imaginings of Jules Verne and the epic journeys of his fictional *Nautilus* to active exploration of the resources of the deep seabed. Private corporations currently hold around 20% of the mining contracts granted for exploration – an increase from zero at the start of 2012. Dr Dingwall's seminal work acknowledges this increasing role and accordingly shifts the legal analysis from the predominantly state-centred perspective of the existing literature to focus on private commercial stakeholders. Her purpose is to analyse and critique the international legal framework applicable to private, non-State actors undertaking deep seabed mining activities beyond national jurisdiction. Part of this analysis inevitably focuses on the legal regime established by the 1982 United Nations Convention on the Law of the Sea (UNCLOS), where exploration for and exploitation of mineral resources in the deep seabed is regulated on behalf of the international community as a whole by the International Seabed Authority. This regime is underpinned by the central principle that the Area and its mineral resources constitute the 'common heritage of mankind'. This is the first study to analyse whether the UNCLOS regulatory regime can meet the challenge of reconciling this central principle with securing investment protection rights for commercial deep seabed miners. Many of the issues that this book considers also retain relevance for all deep seabed mining endeavours irrespective of whether these are carried out by States or non-State actors acting within or outside of the UNCLOS regime. And it does so at a critical juncture, as technological advances begin to outstrip legal developments but with commercial exploitation yet to take place.

While it will undoubtedly occupy a specialised niche on the reading list of any law of the sea course and should be addressed in any thorough treatment of the increasing role of non-State actors in international law, Dr Dingwall's work will also clearly be important for lawyers in government, corporate practice, and in international institutions and civil society lobbying in connection with commercial mining on the deep seabed.

CR, RO'K

Oxford and Milan
May 2021

Preface

For over ten years now, I have been considering the topic of this book in some form or another. In early 2008, while I was a public international lawyer in private practice, a client asked for my advice on deep seabed mining beyond national jurisdiction, and my fascination with this issue began. In the intervening decade, as my engagement with deep seabed mining has increased and intensified, so too has the international community's participation within the regime, exposing new legal tensions as deep seabed miners gear up for the anticipated exploitation phase.

The primary reason why the deep seabed mining regime captivates me is because it serves as a microcosm of so many of the issues that plague the international legal system. Can international law bind recalcitrant states (such as those outside of the UNCLOS regime)? What is the role of non-state actors, such as corporate entities, as participants on the international plane? Can international law mediate tensions between humanity's insatiable desire for more resources versus the compelling need to create a green economy and a more sustainable future? And, at a deeper level, can international law strike a workable balance between competing visions of world order: treading a middle way between liberal free market approaches and socialist communitarian ideals? This book aims to address some of these issues by focusing on the role of corporate actors within the deep seabed mining regime and the resultant implications of this on the realisation of the common heritage principle.

Many people have assisted me in this endeavour. This monograph is based on my PhD thesis, defended at the University of Glasgow in 2019. I am immensely grateful for the insightful advice and invaluable assistance of my supervisors, Professors Christian Tams and Irini Papanicolopulu, over the years. I also owe a debt of gratitude to my examiners, Professors Maria Gavouneli and Rosa Greaves, for their vigorous engagement with my work and for all of their helpful advice. In addition, I would like to thank the University of Glasgow's College of Social Sciences for funding my original research.

Working as a lawyer for the Scottish Government, advising on issues of law of the sea and marine environmental protection, has enhanced my practical understanding of these areas. Special thanks go to my colleagues and friends in SGLD and Marine Scotland. I am also indebted to the many former colleagues, near and far, who have worked alongside me in the field of international law, shaping and enriching my approach to the discipline: from my colleagues and friends at the ICTY and the International Criminal Court in The Hague; to those at Latham & Watkins, Volterra Fietta and SOAS in London; and from there to the thriving international law community at the University of Glasgow. I would like to give particular thanks to Dr Catriona Drew and Professor Iain Scobbie, for being there at the very start of my journey in international law, and for all of the enduring inspiration. I am grateful also for the unwavering support and encouragement of my family, loved ones and friends. My deepest thanks go to them, especially to my parents, Maria and Eric.

Finally, I would like to thank Oxford University Press and its delegates, especially Merel Alstein and Jack McNichol for their expert guidance and support throughout the publication process. I also extend my gratitude to the two anonymous referees who provided extremely useful comments and ideas. In addition, I am appreciative of the dedicated work of Alan O'Dowd in copy-editing this manuscript and Arokia Anthuvan Rani in preparing this book for publication. Many thanks also to Alan Evans at the National Oceanography Centre and to the International Seabed Authority for kindly providing me with the graphics used in Chapter 2 of this book.

I conducted the research for this monograph exclusively in my personal capacity. Therefore, the content expresses my personal views only and does not represent the views of the Scottish Government.

Joanna Dingwall

Glasgow, May 2021

Contents

Table of Cases xiii
Table of Treaties and Related Documents xvii
List of Abbreviations xxiii
Note on Method of Citation xxv

Introduction 1

1. A Methodological Approach to Deep Seabed Mining by Non-state Actors 11
    - 1.1 A Methodological Approach to Deep Seabed Mining 11
        - 1.1.1 Seeking Internal Coherence 11
        - 1.1.2 Evaluating Broader Context 16
        - 1.1.3 Concluding Remarks 20
    - 1.2 A Methodological Note on Non-state Actors: Conceptualising the Status of Corporate Entities within the Deep Seabed Mining Regime 20
        - 1.2.1 Terminology: Non-state Actors and Corporate Entities 21
        - 1.2.2 Nationality of Corporate Entities at International Law 23
        - 1.2.3 Corporate Entities within the International Legal System 32
        - 1.2.4 Initial Analysis of the Necessary Conditions for Corporate Rights and Obligations under International Law 36
    - 1.3 Conclusion 41

PART I UNCHARTED WATERS – DEEP SEABED MINING OF THE COMMON HERITAGE OF MANKIND BY CORPORATE ACTORS

Introduction to Part I 43

2. The Deep Seabed beyond National Jurisdiction and the Rise of Mining Activities within it by Non-state Actors 45
    - 2.1 The Scope of the Deep Seabed beyond National Jurisdiction 45
    - 2.2 Mineral Resources of the Area beyond National Jurisdiction 51
        - 2.2.1 Deep Seabed Mineral Resources 51
        - 2.2.2 Deep Seabed Mining for Rare Earth Elements 56
    - 2.3 Prospects for Deep Seabed Mining and Environmental Concerns 59
        - 2.3.1 Technological and Market-based Prospects for Deep Seabed Mining 59
        - 2.3.2 Environmental Challenges for Deep Seabed Mining 61
    - 2.4 Increasing Participation in Deep Seabed Mining Activities 65
    - 2.5 Conclusion 67

3. The Role of the Common Heritage Concept in Deep Seabed Mining 68
3.1 Deep Seabed Mineral Resources as the Common Heritage of Mankind 68
3.1.1 The Development of the Common Heritage Principle in the Deep Seabed Context 68
3.1.2 Situating the Common Heritage Concept within Broader International Law 73
3.1.3 The General Assembly's Application of the Common Heritage Principle to the Deep Seabed 77
3.1.4 The Difficult Road to the UNCLOS Deep Seabed Mining Regime 80
3.2 Key Features Underpinning the Modern Common Heritage Concept Applicable to Deep Seabed Mining 86
3.2.1 Component 1 – The Common Management Principle 87
3.2.2 Component 2 – The Prohibition of Unilateral Mining Activities 88
3.2.3 Component 3 – The Benefit-sharing Principle 89
3.2.4 Component 4 – The Principle of Marine Environmental Protection 91
3.2.5 Is Reservation for Peaceful Purposes a Component of the Common Heritage Concept? 93
3.2.6 Additional Components of the Common Heritage Concept? 94
3.2.7 The Common Heritage's Underlying Community/Autonomy Equilibrium 95
3.3 Conclusion: Devising an Analytical Framework to Evaluate Achievement of the Common Heritage Concept in Relation to Deep Seabed Mining Activities by Corporate Entities 95

PART II THE COMMON HERITAGE AS PROCESS – ANCHORING THE DEEP SEABED MINING REGIME APPLICABLE TO CORPORATE ACTORS WITHIN ITS INSTITUTIONAL CONTEXT

Introduction to Part II 101

4. Common Management through Institutional Architecture – What is the Scope of the UNCLOS Deep Seabed Mining Regime and the Role of the ISA within it? 103
4.1 Common Management through Common Rules: Overarching Principles of the UNCLOS Deep Seabed Mining Regime 103
4.1.1 Key Components of the Common Heritage Concept Captured by the UNCLOS Deep Seabed Mining Regime 104
4.1.2 Other Common Management Rules within the UNCLOS Deep Seabed Mining Regime 109
4.1.3 The UNCLOS Deep Seabed Mining Regime Implements a System of Common Management through Common Rules 110

4.2 Common Management through Institutional Power: The Role of the ISA 111
4.2.1 The ISA's Structure and Balance of Power 111
4.2.2 The ISA's Development of the Deep Seabed Mining Regime 116
4.2.3 The ISA's Licensing Process for Deep Seabed Mining Activities and Corporate Participation Therein 121
4.2.3.1 Introduction to the Licensing Process 121
4.2.3.2 Key Benefit-sharing Aspects within the Licensing Process 125
4.2.3.3 Corporate Participation within the Licensing Process 131
4.2.4 The UNCLOS Deep Seabed Mining Regime Implements a System of Common Management through Institutional Power 144
4.3 The Nature of Obligations for Corporate Actors Operating within the UNCLOS Deep Seabed Mining Regime 146
4.4 Conclusion 149

5. Preventing Unilateral Deep Seabed Mining Activities – To What Extent Does the UNCLOS Regime Constrain External Actors? 150
5.1 The Reach of the UNCLOS Deep Seabed Mining Regime as Treaty Law 151
5.1.1 Assessing the Extent of Third State Obligations within the UNCLOS Deep Seabed Mining Regime 151
5.1.2 Assessing the Extent to which the UNCLOS Deep Seabed Mining Regime Constitutes an Objective Regime 155
5.2 The Reach of the UNCLOS Deep Seabed Mining Regime as Customary Law 159
5.2.1 Methodological Note on the Formation of Customary Law 159
5.2.2 The Customary Law Status of the Common Heritage of Mankind Concept 161
5.2.3 The Customary Law Status of the UNCLOS Deep Seabed Mining Regime 162
5.2.3.1 Assessing Norm-creating Aspects of the UNCLOS Deep Seabed Mining Regime 165
5.2.3.2 Assessing State Participation and Conduct in Relation to the UNCLOS Deep Seabed Mining Regime 167
5.2.3.3 Assessing US Conduct in Relation to the UNCLOS Deep Seabed Mining Regime 175
5.2.3.4 Assessing the Role of the Persistent Objector Doctrine in Relation to the UNCLOS Deep Seabed Mining Regime 180
5.3 The Extent of Obligations Imposed by the UNCLOS Deep Seabed Mining Regime upon External Corporate Actors 183
5.3.1 Obligations upon External Corporate Actors as a Matter of Treaty Law 183
5.3.2 Obligations upon External Corporate Actors as a Matter of Customary Law 190
5.4 Conclusion 194

PART III THE COMMON HERITAGE'S SUBSTANTIVE CORE – NAVIGATING CONFLICT BETWEEN REGULATORY AUTHORITY AND CORPORATE PARTICIPATION

Introduction to Part III 197

6. Does the Regime Secure the Common Heritage's Benefit-sharing and Marine Environmental Protection Components? 199
   6.1 Developing the Regime's Benefit-sharing Aspects in Financial Terms 200
   6.2 Developing the Regime's Protection of the Marine Environment 208
   6.3 Developing the Regime through Ongoing Regulatory Adaptability 216
   6.4 Securing the Regime's Substantive Aspects in Practice: Implementation, Responsibility and Enforcement against Corporate Actors 223
      6.4.1 ISA Implementation Powers 223
      6.4.2 Responsibility for Deep Seabed Mining Activities 226
      6.4.3 Initial Note on Dispute Resolution in Respect of Deep Seabed Mining Activities 232
   6.5 Conclusion 234

7. Balancing Community and Autonomy – To What Extent Does the Regime Reconcile ISA Regulatory Authority and Investment Protection for Corporate Actors? 235
   7.1 Investment Protections for Deep Seabed Mining Contractors 236
      7.1.1 Protection against Unlawful Expropriation 239
      7.1.2 Entitlement to Fair and Equitable Treatment 242
      7.1.3 Protection against Impairment of Investment Activities by Unreasonable or Discriminatory Measures 244
      7.1.4 Entitlement to Full Protection and Security 245
      7.1.5 Reflections on the Deep Seabed Mining Investment Paradigm and its Opposability 246
   7.2 Deep Seabed Mining Disputes – Reconciling Corporate Rights and Obligations through Dispute Resolution 250
      7.2.1 The Seabed Disputes Chamber's Contentious Jurisdiction over Deep Seabed Mining Disputes Involving Corporate Contractors 251
      7.2.2 Resolution of Disputes between Corporate Contractors and other Actors aside from the International Seabed Authority 257
      7.2.3 Concluding Reflections: Can Corporate Rights and Obligations be Reconciled? 261

Concluding Remarks on Corporate Entity Involvement in Deep Seabed Mining 269

Appendix 1: Types of Contractors Participating in Exploration Activities in the Area 275
Appendix 2 : Status of Contracts for Exploration in the Area 281
Index 289

Table of Cases

For the benefit of digital users, table entries that span two pages (e.g., 52–53) may, on occasion, appear on only one of those pages.

INTERNATIONAL COURT OF JUSTICE (*ICJ*)

Ahmadou Sadio Diallo (Republic of Guinea v Democratic Republic of the Congo) (Preliminary Objections) [2007] ICJ Rep 582. . . . . 26n.92
Anglo-Norwegian Fisheries [1951] ICJ Rep 116. . . . . .160n.69, 180–81
Armed Activities on the Territory of the Congo (Democratic Republic of Congo v Uganda) (Judgment) [2005] ICJ Rep 168 . . . . 227n.190
Asylum Case [1950] ICJ Rep 266. . . . . 181n.182
Avena and other Mexican Nationals (Mexico v United States of America) (Judgment) [2004] ICJ Rep 12 . . . . .35 n.147, 36n.154, 185n.207
Barcelona Traction, Light and Power Company, Limited (Judgment) [1970] ICJ Rep 3 . . . . 24–26, 27n.101, 108n.34, 141n.285, 155n.28
Case Concerning Kasikili/Sedudu Island (Botswana/Namibia) (Judgment) [1999] ICJ Rep 1045. . . . . 14n.19
Case Concerning the Arrest Warrant of 11 April 2000 (Democratic Republic of the Congo v Belgium) (Joint Separate Opinion of Judges Higgins, Kooijmans and Buergenthal) [2002] ICJ Rep 63 . . . . 188n.233
Fisheries Jurisdiction Case (UK v Iceland) (Merits) [1974] ICJ Rep 3 180–81
International Status of South West Africa (Advisory Opinion) [1950] ICJ Rep 128 156
Interpretation of the Agreement of 25 March 1951 between the WHO and Egypt (Advisory Opinion) [1980] ICJ Rep 73 . . . . 190n.240, 190n.242
LaGrand Case (Germany v United States of America) (Judgment) [2001] ICJ Rep 466 . . . . 35n.147, 36n.154, 185
Legality of the Threat or Use of Nuclear Weapons (Advisory Opinion) [1996] ICJ Rep 226 . . . . 163–64, 169nn.129–30
Military and Paramilitary Activities in and against Nicaragua (Nicaragua v United States of America) (Merits) [1986] ICJ Rep 14. . . . . 160nn.68–69, 161n.73, 167–68n.115, 171n.137
North Sea Continental Shelf Cases [1969] ICJ Rep 3 . . . . 46n.8, 159–60, 161n.72, 161n.73, 164–65, 167–68, 181n.182
Nottebohm Case (Second Phase) [1955] ICJ Rep 4 . . . . 25n.83, 31n.121
Obligation to Negotiate Access to the Pacific Ocean (Bolivia v Chile) (Judgment) [2018] ICJ Rep 507 . . . . 262n.148
Oil Platforms (Islamic Republic of Iran v United States of America) (Preliminary Objection) [1996] ICJ Rep 803 . . . . 13n.14
Reparation for Injuries Suffered in the Service of the United Nations (Advisory Opinion) [1949] ICJ Rep 174 . . . . .32n.128, 111n.54, 156–57, 158
Territorial Dispute (Libya v Chad) (Merits) [1994] ICJ Rep 6 . . . . 13n.14

PERMANENT COURT OF INTERNATIONAL JUSTICE (*PCIJ*)

Case Concerning Certain German Interests in Polish Upper Silesia (Germany v Poland) (Merits Judgment) [1925] PCIJ Rep Series A No 7. . . . . 239n.22

Interpretation of Convention of 1919 Concerning Employment of Women During Night (Advisory Opinion) [1932] PCIJ Rep Series A/B No 50 152
Jurisdiction of the Courts of Danzig (Advisory Opinion) [1928] PCIJ Rep Series B No 15 185
Mavrommatis Palestine Concessions (Greece v United Kingdom) (Jurisdiction) [1924] PCIJ Rep Series A No 2 . . . . .36–37n.155
SS Lotus Case (France v Turkey) [1927] PCIJ Rep Series A No 10. . . . . 33n.130, 160n.65
SS Wimbledon Case [1923] PCIJ Rep Series A No 1 156

INTERNATIONAL TRIBUNAL FOR THE LAW OF THE SEA (*ITLOS*)

Delimitation of the Maritime Boundary in the Bay of Bengal (Bangladesh v Myanmar) (Judgment of 14 March 2012) ITLOS Reports 2012, 4. . . . . 46n.8
M/V 'SAIGA' (No 2) (Saint Vincent and the Grenadines v Guinea) (Judgment of 1 July 1999) ITLOS Reports 1999, 10 . . . . 31n.123, 227n.190
M/V 'Virginia G' Case (Panama v Guinea-Bissau) (Judgment of 14 April 2014) ITLOS Reports 2014, 1. . . . . 31n.123
Responsibility and Obligations of States Sponsoring Persons and Entities with Respect to Activities in the Area (Advisory Opinion of 1 February 2011) ITLOS Reports 2011, 10 (*ITLOS Advisory Opinion*) 13n.15, 30n.115, 108n.31, 108, 121n.139, 121n.141, 128, 135n.239, 137–39, 147n.320, 148n.330, 150, 209n.69, 212n.92, 217, 218n.128, 226–31, 232n.229, 238, 248n.76, 248n.79, 249n.84, 259–60

INTERNATIONAL ARBITRAL TRIBUNALS

International Centre for the Settlement of Investment Disputes (ICSID)

ADC Affiliate Limited and ADC & ADMC Management Limited v The Republic of Hungary (Award) ICSID Case No ARB/03/16 (2 October 2006) 239–40n.23
Aguas del Tunari SA v Republic of Bolivia (Decision on Jurisdiction) ICSID Case No ARB/02/3 (21 October 2005). 28, 142n.294
Amco Asia Corporation and others v Republic of Indonesia (Award on Merits) ICSID Case No ARB/81/1 (5 June 1990) 35n.147
Amco Asia Corporation and others v Republic of Indonesia (Decision on Jurisdiction) ICSID Case No ARB/81/1 (25 September 1983) 29n.113
Autopista Concesionada de Venezuela CA v Bolivarian Republic of Venezuela (Decision on Jurisdiction) ICSID Case No ARB/00/5 (27 September 2001) 142n.294
Azurix Corp v The Argentine Republic (Award) ICSID Case No ARB/01/12 (14 July 2006) 239–40n.23, 245n.54, 245n.56
Bear Creek Mining Corporation v Republic of Perú (Award) ICSID Case No ARB/14/21 (30 November 2017). 192–93n.260
Biwater Gauff (Tanzania) Ltd v United Republic of Tanzania (Award) ICSID Case No ARB/05/22 (24 July 2008) 239–40n.23, 245
Burlington Resources Inc v Republic of Ecuador (Decision on Counterclaims) ICSID Case No ARB/08/5 (7 February 2017) 253n.107
CMS Gas Transmission Company v The Argentine Republic (Award) ICSID Case No ARB/01/8 (12 May 2005) 242–45
David Aven et al v The Republic of Costa Rica (Final Award) ICSID Case No UNCT/15/3 (18 September 2018). 192–93n.260, 253n.107
El Paso Energy International Company v Argentine Republic (Award) ICSID Case No ARB/03/15 (31 October 2011). 36–37n.155

Enron Corporation Ponderosa Assets LP v Argentine Republic (Award) ICSID Case No ARB/01/03 (22 May 2007) 243n.41
Fireman's Fund Insurance Company v The United Mexican States (Award) ICSID Case No ARB(AF)/02/1 (17 July 2006) 264
LG&E Energy Corp and others v Argentine Republic (Decision on Liability) ICSID Case No ARB/02/1 (3 October 2006) 243n.39
Marvin Feldman v Mexico (Award) ICSID AF Case No ARB(AF)/99/1 (16 December 2002)) 241n.32
Metalclad Corporation v The United Mexican States (Award) ICSID Case No ARB(AF)/97/1 (30 August 2000) 239, 241n.32, 243n.39
Mondev International Ltd v United States of America (Award) ICSID Case No ARB(AF)/99/2 (11 October 2002) 239–40n.23
Pantechniki SA Contractors & Engineers v The Republic of Albania (Award) ICSID Case No ARB/07/21 (30 July 2009) 245n.57
Philip Morris Brands Sàrl, Philip Morris Products SA and Abal Hermanos SA v Oriental Republic of Uruguay (Award) ICSID Case No ARB/10/7 (8 July 2016) 265, 266n.172
PSEG Global Inc and Konya Ilgın Elektrik Üretim ve Ticaret Limited Şirketi v Republic of Turkey (Award) ICSID Case No ARB/02/5 (19 January 2007) 243n.39
Rumeli Telekom AS and Telsim Mobil Telekomunikasyon Hizmetleri AS v Republic of Kazakhstan (Award) ICSID Case No ARB/05/16 (29 July 2008) 242–43n.38, 243n.45
Siemens AG v The Argentine Republic (Award) ICSID Case No ARB/02/8 (6 February 2007) 239–40n.23, 245n.54
Société Ouest Africaine des Bétons Industriels v Senegal (Decision on Jurisdiction) ICSID Case No ARB/82/1 (1 August 1984) 29n.113
Técnicas Medioambientales Tecmed SA v The United Mexican States (Award) ICSID Case No ARB(AF)/00/2 (29 May 2003) 241n.32, 242n.37, 242–43n.38, 243n.45
Tenaris SA & Talta-Trading v Bolivarian Republic of Venezuela (Award) ICSID Case No ARB/11/26 (29 January 2016) 28n.103
Tokios Tokelės v Ukraine (Decision on Jurisdiction) ICSID Case No ARB/02/18 (29 April 2004) 27, 141
Urbaser and others v The Argentine Republic (Award) ICSID Case No ARB/07/26 (8 December 2016) 186n.217, 192, 193, 253n.107
Waste Management Inc v United Mexican States (Award) ICSID Case No ARB/(AF)/00/3 (30 April 2004) 242n.37

Other Arbitral Tribunals

Antaris GmbH and Dr Michael Göde v The Czech Republic (Award) PCA Case No 2014-01 (2 May 2018) 266n.172
BG Grp PLC v The Republic of Argentina (Final Award) UNCITRAL (24 December 2007) 243n.39
CME Czech Republic BV (The Netherlands) v The Czech Republic (Partial Award) UNCITRAL (13 September 2001) 239n.21, 239–40n.23, 245
Eureko BV v Republic of Poland (Partial Award) *Ad Hoc* Arbitration (19 August 2005) 239–40n.23, 242–43n.38
Frontier Petroleum Services Ltd v The Czech Republic (Final Award) UNCITRAL (12 November 2010) 243n.46, 245n.55
In the Matter of the South China Sea Arbitration (Philippines v China) (Award, 12 July 2016) PCA Case No 2013-19 . . . . 150n.5
International Thunderbird Gaming Corporation v The United Mexican States (Award) UNCITRAL (26 January 2006) 242–43n.38

Methanex Corporation v United States of America (Award) UNCITRAL (3 August 2005) 264–65
National Grid PLC v Argentine Republic (Award) UNCITRAL (3 November 2008) 243n.41, 245n.54
Norwegian Shipowners' Claims (Norway v United States) (Award) (1922) 1 RIAA 307 . . . . 239n.22
Occidental Exploration and Production Company v The Republic of Ecuador (Final Award) UNCITRAL, LCIA Case No UN 3467 (1 July 2004) 243n.39
Partial Award: Prisoners of War, Ethiopia's Claim 4 (Eritrea-Ethiopia Claims Commission, Decision of 1 July 2003) 26 RIAA 73 . . . . 169n.126, 171n.138
Phillips Petroleum v Iran (1989) 21 Iran-USCTR 79 . . . . 239n.22
Pope & Talbot Inc v The Government of Canada (Interim Award) UNCITRAL (26 June 2000) 241n.32
Rudloff Case (American-Venezuelan Commission) (Interlocutory Decision) (1905) 9 RIAA 244 . . . . 239n.22
Saluka Investments BV (The Netherlands) v The Czech Republic (Partial Award) UNCITRAL (17 March 2006) 27, 242–43n.38, 243n.40
Shufeldt Claim (Guatemala v US) (1930) 2 RIAA 1079 . . . . 239–40n.23
Steiner and Gross v Polish State (1927–28) 4 ADIL 291 187

REGIONAL DECISIONS

Banković and others v Belgium and others App no 52207/99 (ECtHR, 12 December 2001) 188n.231
Van Gend en Loos v Nederlandse Administratie der Belastingen ECJ Case 26-62 [1963] ECR 1 . . . . 185n.205
Velásquez Rodríguez Case (Judgment) Inter-American Court of Human Rights Series C No 4 (29 July 1988) 228n.198

OTHER INTERNATIONAL DECISIONS/PROCEEDINGS

Judgment of the Nuremberg International Military Tribunal 1946 (1947) 41 AJIL 172 . . . . 190–91n.246
Prosecutor v Sesay, Kallon and Gbao (Decision on Challenge to Jurisdiction: Lomé Accord Amnesty) SCSL-04-15-PT-060 (13 March 2004) 190n.243
Prosecutor v Tadić (Decision on Defence Motion for Interlocutory Appeal on Jurisdiction) ICTY-94-1 (2 October 1995) 191n.247
US v Carl Krauch et al (Judgment of 30 July 1948) VIII Trials of War Criminals before the Nuremberg Military Tribunals under Control Council Law no 10 191
WTO, *China: Measures Related to the Exportation of Rare Earths, Tungsten, and Molybdenum – Report of the Appellate Body* (7 August 2014) WT/DS431/AB/R / WT/DS432/AB/R / WT/DS433/AB/R 57n.69
WTO, *China: Measures Related to the Exportation of Rare Earths, Tungsten, and Molybdenum – Report of the Panel* (26 March 2014) WT/DS431/R and Add.1 / WT/DS432/R and Add.1 / WT/DS433/R and Add.1 . . . . 57n.69

NATIONAL DECISIONS

Canada, Supreme Court, *Nevsun Resources Ltd v Araya* 2020 SCC 5 191–92
US, Florida district court, *Glenn et al v Compania Cubana de Aviacion SA et al* 102 F Supp 631 (1952) 187–88

Table of Treaties and Related Documents

Note: References to tables are indicated by an italic *t* following the page numbers.

TREATIES

African Charter on Human and Peoples' Rights (adopted 27 June 1981, entered into force 21 October 1986) 1520 UNTS 217 75

Agreement Governing the Activities of States on the Moon and Other Celestial Bodies (adopted 5 December 1979, opened for signature 18 December 1979, entered into force 11 July 1984) 1363 UNTS 3 (*Moon Treaty*) 74–75

Agreement on Encouragement and Reciprocal Protection of Investments between —and the Kingdom of the Netherlands (March 2004) <https://investmentpolicy.unctad.org/international-investment-agreements/treaty-files/2859/download> (*Netherlands Model BIT*) 237nn.13–15, 250n.85

Agreement Relating to the Implementation of Part XI of the United Nations Convention on the Law of the Sea of 10 December 1982 (adopted 28 July 1994, entered into force provisionally 16 November 1994 and definitively 28 July 1996) 1836 UNTS 3 (*1994 Agreement*) 2n.8, 2nn.13–15, 3n.19, 3nn.20–21, 84–86, 91–92, 95n.173, 97*t*, 103–8, 110–18, 120, 121–22, 123–24, 125–28, 130–31, 141n.292, 145, 150n.3, 158, 163, 164, 167n.112, 169, 171–75, 173*t*, 175–76, 181–82, 200–4, 205–6, 209–10, 222, 223n.165, 225n.178, 238n.17, 244n.47, 244n.50, 251, 253n.109, 256n.123, 271–72, 282*t*

Antarctic Treaty (opened for signature 1 December 1959, entered into force 23 June 1961) 402 UNTS 71 75

Association of Southeast Asian Nations Comprehensive Investment Agreement (signed 26 February 2009, entered into force 29 March 2012) <www.asean.org/storage/images/2013/economic/aia/ACIA_Final_Text_26%20Feb%202009.pdf>. 237n.10

Consolidated Version of the Treaty on the Functioning of the European Union 2007 [2012] OJ C 326/47. . . . . 255n.117

Convention for the Protection of the Mediterranean Sea against Pollution (opened for signature 16 February 1976, amended 10 June 1995, entered into force 9 June 2004) 1102 UNTS 27 75

Convention on Biological Diversity (opened for signature 5 June 1992, entered into force 29 December 1993) 1760 UNTS 79. . . . . 76, 214

Convention on the High Seas (opened for signature 29 April 1958, entered into force 30 September 1962) 450 UNTS 11 (*High Seas Convention 1958*) 31n.121, 70n.11

Convention on the Legal Status of the Caspian Sea (signed 12 August 2018) <http://en.kremlin.ru/supplement/5328> 173*t*

Convention on the Settlement of Investment Disputes between States and Nationals of Other States (concluded 18 March 1965, entered into force 14 October 1966) 575 UNTS 159 (*ICSID Convention*) 29, 250n.85, 253n.107, 261n.145

Energy Charter Treaty (adopted 17 December 1994, entered into force 16 April 1998) 2080 UNTS 95 236–37
General Agreement on Tariffs and Trade (adopted 15 April 1994, entered into force 1 January 1995) 1867 UNTS 187 130
North American Free Trade Agreement (adopted 17 December 1992, entered into force 1 January 1994) (1993) 32 ILM 289 (*NAFTA*) 237n.10, 264
Paris Agreement (adopted 12 December 2015, entered into force 4 November 2016) <http://unfccc.int/files/essential_background/convention/application/pdf/english_paris_agreement.pdf> 76
Reciprocal Investment Promotion and Protection Agreement between the Government of the Kingdom of Morocco and the Government of the Federal Republic of Nigeria (signed on 3 December 2016) <https://investmentpolicy.unctad.org/international-investment-agreements/treaty-files/5409/download> 185–86
Treaty on Principles Governing the Activities of States in the Exploration and Use of Outer Space, including the Moon and Other Celestial Bodies (adopted 19 December 1966, opened for signature 27 January 1967, entered into force 10 October 1967) 610 UNTS 205 (*Outer Space Treaty*) 74
Treaty on the Prohibition of the Emplacement of Nuclear Weapons and Other Weapons of Mass Destruction on the Sea-bed and the Ocean Floor and in the Subsoil Thereof (adopted 11 February 1971, entered into force 18 May 1972) 955 UNTS 115 . . . . . 93n.164
United Nations Convention on the Law of the Sea (adopted and opened for signature 10 December 1982, entered into force 16 November 1994) 1833 UNTS 3 (*UNCLOS or Convention*) 1–3, 5–6, 9–10, 13, 14, 15, 16, 17–18, 21, 23–24n.74, 29–32, 45–48, 49–51, 68, 69–70, 77, 78, 80, 81n.78, 83–85, 86, 87, 88–89, 92–93, 95–99, 101, 103–18, 121–24, 125–28, 130, 131, 134–36, 137–39, 141, 142, 144–47, 147nn.321–22, 148n.328, 148–49, 150–52, 153–55, 157–58, 159, 161, 162–64, 165–68, 169–72, 173*t*, 175–80, 181–84, 186–87, 188–90, 193–94, 195*t*, 197–98, 199–201, 201n.12, 202n.17, 202, 203n.26, 203n.33, 205–6, 208, 208n.62, 209, 210n.82, 215n.108, 216–17, 218n.130, 222–24, 225, 225n.178, 226–29, 230–31, 232–33, 235–36, 238–39, 240, 241–42, 243–46, 248–50, 251–56, 257–62, 265–66, 270–72, 273, 282*t*
United Nations Framework Convention on Climate Change (adopted 9 May 1992, entered into force 21 March 1994) 1771 UNTS 107 76
Vienna Convention on Diplomatic Relations (opened for signature 18 April 1961, entered into force 24 April 1964, 500 UNTS 95) (*VCDR*) 36n.154, 185
Vienna Convention on the Law of Treaties (adopted 22 May 1969, opened for signature 23 May 1969, entered into force 27 January 1980) 1155 UNTS 331 (*VCLT*) 13–14, 28n.106, 104n.7, 105nn.12–13, 137–38, 141, 152–55, 156n.37, 157, 158, 161n.74, 164n.94, 182, 185n.205, 187n.221

COURT AND ARBITRAL RULES

International Tribunal for the Law of the Sea Rules of the Tribunal (as amended on 25 March 2021) ITLOS/8 . . . . . 252–53, 262n.147
Statute of the International Court of Justice (opened for signature 26 June 1945 as annex to UN Charter, entered into force 24 October 1945) UKTS 67 (1946) (*ICJ Statute*) 13, 153n.16, 159

United Nations Commission on International Trade Law Arbitration Rules (1976) 15 ILM 701 (*UNCITRAL Arbitration Rules*) 250n.85, 254–55, 261–62

INTERNATIONAL LAW COMMISSION DRAFT RULES AND COMMENTARIES

ILC, 'Draft Articles on Diplomatic Protection' in 'Report of the International Law Commission on the Work of its 58th Session' (1 May to 9 June and 3 July to 11 August 2006) UN Doc A/61/10 (*ILC DP Draft Articles*) 24n.76, 24nn.80–81, 25, 26n.90, 26nn.92–95

ILC, 'Draft Articles on Diplomatic Protection with Commentaries' in 'Report of the International Law Commission on the Work of its 58th Session' (1 May to 9 June and 3 July to 11 August 2006) UN Doc A/61/10 (*ILC DP Commentaries*) 25n.83, 25–26

ILC, 'Identification of Customary International Law – Text of the Draft Conclusions and Commentaries Thereto' in 'Report of the International Law Commission of the Work of its 70th Session' (30 April to 1 June and 2 July to 10 August 2018) UN Doc A/73/10 (*ILC CIL Commentaries*) 160nn.65–66, 161n.73, 161n.75, 163n.86, 167–68n.115, 168n.119, 168n.120, 169, 171n.138, 175n.151, 181n.183, 181nn.184–86

ILC, 'Identification of Customary International Law – Text of the Draft Conclusions as Adopted by the Drafting Committee on Second Reading' (17 May 2018) UN Doc A/CN.4/L.908 (*ILC CIL Conclusions*) 159n.60, 160nn.65–67, 161nn.75–76, 163n.86, 163n.87, 164n.94, 167–68n.115, 180–81

ILC, 'State Responsibility – Draft Commentaries' in 'Report of the International Law Commission on the Work of its 53rd Session' (23 April to 1 June and 2 July to 10 August 2001) UN Doc A/56/10 (*ILC Commentaries*) 39, 40n.186, 227n.193, 228nn.197–98

ILC, 'State Responsibility – Text of the Draft Articles on Responsibility of States for Internationally Wrongful Acts' in 'Report of the International Law Commission on the Work of its 53rd Session' (23 April to 1 June and 2 July to 10 August 2001) UN Doc A/56/10 (*ILC Draft Articles*) 39n.172, 227, 228n.202

ILC, 'Text of the Draft Articles on the Responsibility of International Organizations' in 'Report of the International Law Commission on the Work of its 63rd Session' (26 April to 3 June and 4 July to 12 August 2011) UN Doc A/66/10 . . . . 39n.173, 227n.194

INTERNATIONAL SEABED AUTHORITY REGULATIONS AND RECOMMENDATIONS

'Draft Regulations on Exploitation of Mineral Resources in the Area' (22 March 2019) ISBA/25/C/WP.1 (*DERs*) 119–20, 121–24, 125, 130n.210, 135, 139–40, 141, 143, 147, 150n.2, 176n.156, 201–2, 208n.62, 210–13, 214, 215, 216–18, 219–20, 221–23, 224–25, 229n.204, 231n.222, 235n.3, 240–41, 241n.31, 242, 243–44, 253n.109, 259, 261n.143, 262–63, 266

'Financial Regulations of the International Seabed Authority' <www.isa.org.jm/files/documents/EN/Regs/FinRegs.pdf> (*ISA Financial Regulations*). 202nn.21–24

'Recommendations for the Guidance of Contractors for the Assessment of the Possible Environmental Impacts Arising from Exploration for Marine Minerals in the Area' (30 March 2020) ISBA/25/LTC/6/Rev.1 . . . . . 119n.119, 210n.81, 219n.134
'Regulations on Prospecting and Exploration for Cobalt-Rich Ferromanganese Crusts in the Area' (adopted 27 July 2012) ISBA/18/A/11 (as amended by ISBA/19/A/12 (25 July 2013)) (*Cobalt Regulations*). 118n.118, 121–24, 125, 127–29, 130, 135, 139–40, 141, 147, 150n.2, 201n.16, 208, 209–11, 216–17, 218–19, 221–22, 223–24, 229n.204, 240–41, 241n.31, 242, 243–44, 245, 248n.75, 253n.109, 254, 256n.124, 259, 260–61, 262–63, 281
'Regulations on Prospecting and Exploration for Polymetallic Nodules in the Area' (adopted 13 July 2000) ISBA/6/A/18, (updated 22 July 2013) ISBA/19/C/17 (as amended by ISBA/19/A/12 (25 July 2013) and ISBA/20/A/9 (24 July 2014)) (*Nodules Regulations*). 118n.118, 121–24, 125, 127–28, 129–30, 135, 139–40, 141, 146–47, 150n.2, 201n.16, 208, 209–11, 216–17, 218–19, 221–22, 223–24, 229n.204, 240–41, 241n.31, 242, 243–44, 245, 248n.75, 253n.109, 254, 256n.124, 259, 260–61, 262–63, 281
'Regulations on Prospecting and Exploration for Polymetallic Sulphides in the Area' (adopted 7 May 2010) ISBA/16/A/12/Rev.1 (as amended by ISBA/19/A/12 (25 July 2013) and ISBA/20/A/10 (24 July 2014)) (*Sulphides Regulations*) 208, 118n.118, 121–24, 125, 127–29, 130, 135, 139–40, 141, 147, 150n.2, 201n.16, 209–11, 216–17, 218–19, 221–22, 223–24, 229n.204, 240–41, 241n.31, 242, 243–44, 245, 248n.75, 253n.109, 254, 256n.124, 259, 260–61, 262–63, 281

UNITED NATIONS GENERAL ASSEMBLY RESOLUTIONS

UNGA Res 47/65 (11 December 1992) UN Doc A/RES/47/65 (*1992 Resolution*) 84n.102, 85n.104, 86n.111, 95n.174
UNGA Res 48/263 (28 July 1994) UN Doc A/RES/48/263 . . . . 172n.147
UNGA Res 69/292 (19 June 2015) UN Doc A/RES/69/292. 49–51n.35
UNGA Res 70/1 (25 September 2015) UN Doc A/RES/70/1 . . . . 208n.64
UNGA Res 72/249 (24 December 2017) UN Doc A/RES/72/249 . . . . 51n.36
UNGA Res 73/203 (20 December 2018) UN Doc A/RES/73/203 . . . . 159n.60
UNGA Res 2340 (XXII) (18 December 1967). 77n.53
UNGA Res 2467 (XXIII) (21 December 1968). 77n.54
UNGA Res 2574 (XXIV) (15 December 1969) (*Moratorium Resolution*). 78
UNGA Res 2749 (XXV) (17 December 1970) (*1970 Seabed Declaration*). 78–80, 82, 86–88, 89n.133, 91n.146, 105n.16, 153–54, 163
UNGA Res 2750 (XXV) (17 December 1970). 79n.70
UNGA Res 3029 (XXVII) (18 December 1972) 79n.70
UNGA Res 3067 (XXVIII) (16 November 1973) 79n.70
UNGA Res 3201 (S-VI) (1 May 1974) 81n.77
UNGA Res 3202 (S-VI) (1 May 1974) 81n.77

DOMESTIC LEGISLATION

United States

Alien Tort Claims Act 28 USC §1350 193

Deep Seabed Hard Mineral Resources Act 30 USC §§ 1401–1473 (*US Act*) 170, 176–77, 178, 179
'Deep Seabed Mining Regulations for Exploration Licenses' 15 Code of Federal Regulations § 970.100 2016 . . . . 176n.157
'Executive Order 13914 of April 6, 2020; Encouraging International Support for the Recovery and Use of Space Resources' (10 April 2020) vol 85, issue 70 FR 20381 . . . . 75n.39
US Constitution 175n.154

List of Abbreviations

APEI	area of particular environmental interest
ASEAN	Association of Southeast Asian Nations
BBNJ	marine biodiversity beyond national jurisdiction
BGR	Federal Institute for Geosciences and Natural Resources of Germany
BIT	bilateral investment treaty
BMJ	Blue Minerals Jamaica Limited
CCAMLR	Commission for the Conservation of Antarctic Marine Living Resources
CCZ	Clarion-Clipperton Fracture Zone
CIIC	Cook Islands Investment Corporation
CLCS	Commission on the Limits of the Continental Shelf
COMRA	China Ocean Mineral Resources Research and Development Association
DEME	Dredging, Environment and Marine Engineering NV
DERs	Draft Exploitation Regulations
DOALOS	United Nations Division for Ocean Affairs and the Law of the Sea
DORD	Deep Ocean Resources Development Company Ltd
ECS	extended continental shelf
EEZ	exclusive economic zone
EIA	environmental impact assessment
EIC	English East India Company
EU	European Union
FET	fair and equitable treatment
FPS	full protection and security
G77	Group of 77 coalition of developing states
GA	United Nations General Assembly
GSR	Global Sea Mineral Resources NV
ICC	International Criminal Court
ICJ	International Court of Justice
ICSID	International Centre for Settlement of Investment Disputes
IFREMER	Institut Français de Recherche pour L'Exploitation de la Mer
IOM	Interoceanmetal Joint Organization
IHL	international humanitarian law
ILC	International Law Commission
ISA	International Seabed Authority
ITLOS	International Tribunal for the Law of the Sea
JOGMEC	Japan Oil, Gas and Metals National Corporation
LTC	Legal and Technical Commission
MIT	Massachusetts Institute of Technology
NAFTA	North American Free Trade Agreement 1992
NAIL	New Approaches to International Law

NGO	non-governmental organisation
NIEO	New International Economic Order
nm	nautical miles
NOAA	US National Oceanic and Atmospheric Administration
NORI	Nauru Ocean Resources Inc.
NSP	Non-State Party to UNCLOS
OECD	Organisation for Economic Co-operation and Development
OEIGWG	Intergovernmental Working Group on Transnational Corporations and Other Business Enterprises with Respect to Human Rights
OEWG	Open-Ended Working Group of the ISA Council on Financial Terms of Contracts
OMA	Ocean Mining Associates
OMCO	Ocean Minerals Company
OMI	Ocean Management Inc.
OMS	Ocean Mineral Singapore Pte Ltd
PCIJ	Permanent Court of International Justice
PCZ	Prime Crust Zone
REE	rare earth element
REMP	regional environmental management plan
TOML	Tonga Offshore Mining Limited
UKSRL	UK Seabed Resources Ltd
UN	United Nations
UNCITRAL	United Nations Commission on International Trade Law
UNCLOS	United Nations Convention on the Law of the Sea 1982
UNCLOS I	First United Nations Conference on the Law of the Sea, 1958
UNCLOS II	Second United Nations Conference on the Law of the Sea, 1960
UNCLOS III	Third United Nations Conference on the Law of the Sea, 1973–82
UNCTAD	United Nations Conference on Trade and Development
UNEP	United Nations Environment Programme
US	United States of America
VCDR	Vienna Convention on Diplomatic Relations 1961
VCLT	Vienna Convention on the Law of Treaties 1969
VOC	Verenigde Oost-Indische Compagnie (the Dutch East India Company)
WTO	World Trade Organization

Note on Method of Citation

This book is divided into seven chapters, which form separate units with regard to citation and footnote numbering. Citations predominantly follow the OSCOLA referencing style. However, when citing different works by the same author, subsequent citations provide author surname and year of work, together with a cross-reference to previous citation (e.g. Pardo (1979) (n 1)). Where necessary, different entries published by the same author in the same year are distinguished by 'a', 'b' or 'c' (e.g. Pardo (1967a), Pardo (1967b)).

Unless otherwise defined, International Seabed Authority documents with document numbers are cited in full at first appearance and by document number alone, thereafter.

Because of frequency of use, the following sources are cited in abbreviated form throughout this book, except at first appearance:

- *Responsibility and Obligations of States Sponsoring Persons and Entities with Respect to Activities in the Area* (Advisory Opinion of 1 February 2011) ITLOS Reports 2011, 10 (cited as *ITLOS AO*);
- Myron H Nordquist and others (eds), *United Nations Convention on the Law of the Sea 1982: A Commentary*, vol VI (Martinus Nijhoff Publishers 2002) (cited as Virginia Commentary);
- Alexander Proelss (ed), *The United Nations Convention on the Law of the Sea: A Commentary* (Beck Hart Nomos 2017) (cited as Proelss Commentary).

This book takes account of developments until 1 May 2021, and all weblinks are correct as at that date.

[A]ll law, despite its apparent veneration for the past, its concern with precedent and its almost obsessive quests for the ultimate "sources" of authority, is really about making decisions for the future: about maintaining an appropriate constitutive structure within which all decisions are taken, about maintaining, and hopefully enhancing minimum order and, within those constraints, about identifying the most efficient ways of shaping all the productive processes of social life and about the ways of sharing their fruits within a sustainable ecology.

(W Michael Reisman, *The Quest for World Order and Human Dignity in the Twenty-First Century* (Brill 2013) 22)

The challenge is to develop an exploitation regime, including a fiscal framework, that fosters commercially viable exploitation and at the same time benefits mankind as a whole.

(Nii Allotey Odunton, ISA Secretary-General 'Statement to the Twenty-Third Meeting of the States Parties to the United Nations Convention on the Law of the Sea' (10 June 2013))

Introduction

The deep seabed beyond national jurisdiction (the *deep seabed* or the *Area*) is home to a wealth of mineral resources, including a variety of valuable metals and rare earth elements.[1] Deep seabed minerals await discovery on volcanic ridges, seamounts and amongst the sediment of the ocean floor, typically at depths of up to around 5,000 metres.[2] In the coming decades, deep seabed mining beyond national jurisdiction may well become a commercial reality. The mining industry is looking increasingly seawards due to developments in subsea technology compounded by rising material consumption and anticipated scarcity of terrestrial mineral resources.[3] As the Secretary-General of the International Seabed Authority (*ISA* or the *Authority*) has predicted, the commercialisation of deep seabed minerals beyond national jurisdiction is 'well within reach' and 'attainable in the foreseeable future'.[4]

Within this context, this book analyses and critiques the international legal framework applicable to private, non-state actors undertaking deep seabed mining activities beyond national jurisdiction.[5] Exploration for, and exploitation of, mineral resources in the deep seabed is regulated on behalf of the international community as a whole by the ISA. The ISA is an autonomous international organisation headquartered in Jamaica, and it was established by the United Nations Convention on the Law of the Sea of 1982 (*UNCLOS* or the *Convention*).[6] UNCLOS has 168 States Parties, including the European Union (*EU*).[7] Part XI of

[1] ISA, 'Marine Mineral Resources' (2003) <www.isa.org.jm/files/documents/EN/Brochures/ENG6.pdf>; Jim Hein, 'ISA Briefing Paper 02/12 – Prospects for Rare Earth Elements from Marine Minerals' (May 2012) <www.isa.org.jm/files/documents/EN/Pubs/BP2.pdf>; Yves Fouquet and Denis Lacroix, 'Study Summary' in Yves Fouquet and Denis Lacroix (eds), *Deep Marine Mineral Resources* (Springer 2014) 3–4.

[2] ISA 'Marine Mineral Resources' (n 1).

[3] Fouquet and Lacroix (n 1) 3–5; see also Julie Packard and Chris Scholin, 'The Deep Sea May Soon Be Up for Grabs' *New York Times* (New York, 8 June 2018) <www.nytimes.com/2018/06/08/opinion/the-deep-sea-may-soon-be-up-for-grabs.html>; David Shukman, 'Electric Car Future May Depend on Deep Sea Mining' (*BBC News Online*, 13 November 2019) <www.bbc.co.uk/news/science-environment-49759626>.

[4] ISA Press Release, 'Commercialization of Marine Minerals in Deep Seabed Well Within Reach, ISA Secretary-General States as He Introduces Annual Report' (19 July 2016) SB/22/11.

[5] For a definition of such actors, and consideration of their methodological status within the international legal system, see Chapter 1, Section 1.2.

[6] United Nations Convention on the Law of the Sea (adopted and opened for signature 10 December 1982, entered into force 16 November 1994) 1833 UNTS 3, art 156.

[7] United Nations Division for Ocean Affairs and the Law of the Sea (*DOALOS*), 'Chronological List of Ratifications of, Accessions and Successions to the Convention and the Related Agreements' (9 March 2020) <www.un.org/Depts/los/reference_files/chronological_lists_of_ratifications.htm>.

International Law and Corporate Actors in Deep Seabed Mining. Joanna Dingwall, Oxford University Press. © Joanna Dingwall 2021. DOI: 10.1093/oso/9780192898265.003.0001

the Convention creates a unique legal regime to regulate the Area: the most ambitious and comprehensive regime ever devised to govern any global commons.[8] The regime is underpinned by the central principle that the Area and its mineral resources constitute the 'common heritage of mankind'.[9] No state or commercial entity can unilaterally claim sovereignty over them.[10] Deep seabed mining in the Area may be carried out only 'for the benefit of mankind as a whole'.[11] The regime aims also to promote the effective participation of developing states, and to take their particular interests into account.[12]

The ISA plays the instrumental role in bringing this vision to life: as custodian, developer, regulator and enforcer of the deep seabed mining regime. The ISA possesses broad powers to control access to minerals in the Area,[13] to progressively develop a regulatory regime for deep seabed mining (in the form of a Mining Code),[14] and to exercise supervisory authority to ensure that participants obey the regime.[15] Two of the most fundamental aspects of this regime (which the ISA is charged with developing) are the protection of the marine environment, and the equitable sharing of financial and other economic benefits derived from deep seabed mining activities.[16]

To control access to minerals in the Area, the ISA maintains a contract-based licensing regime for the exploration and exploitation of the Area's resources.[17] Pursuant to this regime, activities in the Area may be carried out either by States Parties to UNCLOS, or by 'state enterprises or natural or juridical persons which possess the nationality of States Parties or are effectively controlled by them or their nationals, when sponsored by such States'.[18] These actors may

[8] See, generally, UNCLOS, Part XI; see also UNCLOS, Annex III (containing basic conditions for mining activities in the Area). Various aspects of this regime were modified by the Agreement Relating to the Implementation of Part XI of the United Nations Convention on the Law of the Sea of 10 December 1982 (adopted 28 July 1994, entered into force provisionally 16 November 1994 and definitively 28 July 1996) 1836 UNTS 3 (*1994 Agreement*).

[9] UNCLOS, art 136. The Area comprises 'the sea-bed and ocean floor and subsoil thereof, beyond the limits of national jurisdiction' (UNCLOS, art 1(1)(1)). Unless otherwise indicated, references throughout this study to the deep seabed and the Area both refer to the 'Area' as defined in UNCLOS, art 1(1)(1).

[10] UNCLOS, art 137.

[11] UNCLOS, art 140(1).

[12] UNCLOS, arts 148, 150 and 152(2).

[13] UNCLOS, arts 137(2), 153 and 157(1); 1994 Agreement, Annex, s 1(1).

[14] UNCLOS, arts 140(2), 145, 160(2)(f), 162(2)(o), 165(2)(f) and Annex III, art 17; 1994 Agreement, Annex, s 1(1), (5)(f)–(g) and (15). The Mining Code 'refers to the whole of the comprehensive set of rules, regulations and procedures issued by ISA to regulate prospecting, exploration and exploitation … together with recommendations … for the guidance of contractors'; ISA, 'The Mining Code' <www.isa.org.jm/mining-code>.

[15] See, e.g. UNCLOS, art 153(4)–(5), 157, 160, 162 and 165; Annex III, art 18; 1994 Agreement, Annex, s 1(1).

[16] See, e.g. UNCLOS, arts 145 and 140(2), respectively.

[17] See, generally, UNCLOS, Part XI and Annex III. In relation to the Area, 'resources' are 'all solid, liquid or gaseous mineral resources *in situ* in the Area at or beneath the sea-bed, including polymetallic nodules' (UNCLOS, art 133(a)). Once extracted from the Area, such resources are referred to as 'minerals' (UNCLOS, art 133(b)).

[18] UNCLOS, art 153(2)(b).

submit a plan of work to the ISA, which, if approved, will form a contract with the ISA, granting exclusive rights over a particular area of the deep seabed for a fifteen-year term.[19]

The regime also envisages that the ISA will become a direct participant in deep seabed mining activities in similar terms, through its mining organ, the Enterprise (which is yet to become operational).[20] This planned parallel system should see states and state-sponsored entities being licensed by the ISA to explore for, and exploit, seabed resources alongside the Enterprise. To facilitate this approach, and aid participation by the Enterprise and developing states, UNCLOS provides for a system of reserved areas. When applying to conduct mining activities, prospective miners from developed states must propose two mining sites of equal value, and the ISA will allocate one area to the miner, while reserving the other area for activity by the Enterprise and developing states.[21]

The UNCLOS regime distinguishes between three types of deep seabed mining activities: prospecting, exploration and exploitation.[22] Prospecting is an initial search for resources in the Area, akin to marine scientific research. Although a prospector must inform the Authority of the details of its search, prospecting activities do not require state sponsorship and a formal contract from the ISA (unlike the more intensive exploration and exploitation stages).[23] So far, activities in the Area remain at the exploration stage and have not progressed to exploitation (which will involve extraction of minerals from the seabed for commercial production).

Much of the existing legal structure applicable to mining in the deep seabed has yet to be applied in practice, and many legal rules have still to be developed (particularly as regards marine environmental protection, forthcoming exploitation activities, and eventual distribution of economic benefits from exploitation). Indeed, the ISA Secretary-General has noted that key challenges to commercialisation of deep seabed mining include proving that it can be conducted in an environmentally sustainable way, and ensuring adoption of a transparent and flexible code for mineral exploitation.[24]

Despite the lack of a completed legal framework, deep sea mining technology is racing ahead. After decades of anticipation and exploration, deep seabed mining beyond national jurisdiction is set to begin in the coming years. The ISA has entered a total of thirty-one mining contracts with a range of states, state enterprises

[19] See UNCLOS, art 153(3) and Annex III, arts 3 and 16; 1994 Agreement, Annex, s 1(9).

[20] See, e.g. UNCLOS, arts 153(2)(a), 158(2) and 170; 1994 Agreement, Annex, s 2.

[21] See UNCLOS, Annex III, arts 8 and 9; 1994 Agreement, Annex, s 1(10). As Chapter 4 of this book will address, the ISA has, through the Mining Code, modified application of the system of reserved areas to certain mineral types.

[22] See UNCLOS, art 1(1)(3) (defining 'activities in the Area' as 'all activities of exploration for, and exploitation of, the resources of the Area'), and Annex III, art 2 (addressing prospecting).

[23] UNCLOS, Annex III, art 2(1)(b); cf Annex III, art 3. As prospecting activities are not subject to ISA contracts, they are beyond the scope of this book.

[24] SB/22/11.

and private entities to allow exploration of large swathes of the deep seabed.[25] To date, China, Russia and South Korea are the only states to hold exploration contracts relating to all three types of mineral for which exploration is currently permitted (polymetallic nodules, polymetallic sulphides and cobalt-rich ferromanganese crusts).

Commercial interest in the resources of the deep is growing amongst a range of private actors. Key industry players such as Belgium's Dredging, Environment and Marine Engineering NV (*DEME*), a world leader in dredging, marine engineering and environmental remediation, and US defence conglomerate Lockheed Martin Corporation, are already undertaking exploratory activities in the Area through subsidiary companies. Deep seabed prospects are also enticing the attention of relative newcomers, such as Canadian mining start-up company, DeepGreen Metals Inc (*DeepGreen*), which has attracted investment from established figures like British commodity trading and mining giant Glencore, Danish offshore marine services company Maersk Supply Service A/S, and Swiss offshore engineering company Allseas Group SA. At present, DeepGreen is in the process of a merger, and it plans to trade as The Metals Company.

Against this backdrop, this book will evaluate the role of non-state actors as participants in the legal regime regulating deep seabed mining in the Area, with a focus on the activities of corporate entities. To set the scene for this analysis, the remainder of this introduction will set out the purpose of this book and the contribution that it makes to the field, followed by an outline of its structure and scope.

Purpose of this Study

Commercial investment by private actors in deep seabed mining is increasing. Despite continued caution and uncertainty as regards the future viability of deep seabed mining, experts predict that '[t]he hydrosphere is the new frontier in mining'.[26] Industry prospects will be dependent on many factors, such as the speed of technological advancements, and fluctuations in global metal market prices. However, one key determinant of the industry's future feasibility will be the exact shape of the regulatory regime governing extraction of deep seabed minerals beyond national jurisdiction.

[25] For a detailed overview of the existing ISA contractors, and details of their contracts, see Appendices 1 and 2 to this book, respectively.

[26] Cole Latimer, 'Seabed Mining: Plunging into the Depths of a New Frontier' (*Australian Mining*, 10 August 2011) <www.australianmining.com.au/features/seabed-mining-plunging-into-the-depths-of-a-new-fr> (quoting Mike Woodbourne, former CEO of Australian mining company Bonaparte Diamonds); see also Packard and Scholin (n 3); Matthew Taylor, 'Deep-Sea Mining to Turn Oceans Into "New Industrial Frontier"' *The Guardian* (London, 3 July 2019) <www.theguardian.com/environment/2019/jul/03/deep-sea-mining-to-turn-oceans-into-new-industrial-frontier>.

The international legal regime applicable to deep seabed mining is complex, fragmentary and incomplete. A product of its history, the UNCLOS deep seabed mining regime is an unlikely hybrid of capitalist and communist values, embracing the role of private actors while enshrining principles of resource distribution.[27] At the heart of the regime is the undefined normative concept mentioned above: the notion that deep seabed resources are the 'common heritage of mankind'.[28] On this basis, deep seabed mining in the Area must be carried out only 'for the benefit of mankind as a whole'.[29] Given the potential for conflict between the values underpinning the regime, how will it perform when mining by non-state actors, such as corporations, commences? What legal challenges or contradictions, if any, will private actor mining activities present for the operation of the regime, particularly in terms of the realisation of the common heritage?

In light of the complex interaction between these unresolved matters, deep seabed mining is truly an area that 'sits on the boundaries of existing international law'.[30] But despite these many unsettled issues, academic literature has been largely confined to addressing the historical development of UNCLOS and the common heritage principle, the regime's mechanics (including functioning of the ISA and important issues of environmental protection), and the scope of the ISA's existing regulations. Commentary has provided limited consideration of the extent to which deep seabed mining by non-state actors, such as corporations, poses specific legal challenges.

Therefore, this book offers a unique contribution to the field. It is the first study to analyse whether upcoming commercial mining activities in the Area by corporate actors may serve to further, or hinder, realisation of the common heritage of mankind. As technological advances begin to outstrip legal developments, this study seeks to advance the discourse by addressing squarely the extent of any tension between corporate commercial activity in the Area and achievement of the common heritage. Indeed, addressing this issue at the present time takes advantage of a rare window of opportunity, currently open, before mining commences in earnest. Of course, given that the ISA's regulatory regime governing deep seabed exploitation is still under construction, this book can offer only an interim assessment. However, this interim assessment will perform a vital check on the extent to which the regime is currently developing in a way that balances its overriding common heritage goal with the facilitation of corporate activity.

Broadly speaking, many of the issues considered by this book retain relevance for all commercial operators in deep seabed mining endeavours, irrespective of

[27] See, e.g. Martti Koskenniemi and Marja Lehto, 'The Privilege of Universality: International Law, Economic Ideology and Seabed Resources' (1996) 65 Nordic J Int'l L 533, 553–554.

[28] UNCLOS, art 136.

[29] UNCLOS, art 140(1).

[30] Jan-Stefan Fritz, 'Deep Sea Anarchy: Mining at the Frontiers of International Law' (2015) 30 Int'l J Marine Coastal L 445, 448.

whether those participants are states or non-state actors, acting within or outside of the Convention's regime. For example, this book's analysis of the development, status and operation of the Convention regime has universal application for all deep seabed mining participants. However, the focus of this book is directed on the role of non-state actors (and corporations specifically) within deep seabed mining, for reasons that I will now set out.

From its inception, the UNCLOS deep seabed mining regime envisaged direct participation by private corporate actors. The common heritage principle is a finely poised balance between liberal free market approaches (enshrining commercial capitalist activity) and communitarian ideals (embodied in the primary aim of realising a benefit for all of humanity from deep seabed mining). In practice, this underlying tension is heightened because of the increasingly significant role that private actors are playing in deep seabed mining. Commentators have remarked upon this 'new trend', which evidences 'an increased interest from the private sector'.[31] Private corporate actors now hold over 20% of the mining contracts that the ISA has granted, up from zero at the start of 2012.[32] By including contracts that are held by state enterprises but performed by private corporations (through partnership arrangements), this reveals that private actors are currently conducting well over a quarter of ISA contracts (at just over 29%).[33]

The success, or otherwise, of private-sector involvement may have a bearing on the future feasibility of the deep seabed mining industry. Deep seabed mining in the Area is in its formative stages. The transition from initial exploration to sustained commercial production will require the outlay of considerable capital and technical resources.[34] Arguably, 'some form of private ownership is necessary to provide the capital needed to manage the resources in the Area'.[35] Notwithstanding the predominant role played by states and state enterprises, whether the industry becomes viable and self-sustaining in the longer term will be heavily dependent on market conditions and the facilitation of private investment.[36] Therefore, for deep

[31] Gwenaëlle Le Gurun, 'Annex III' in Alexander Proelss (ed), *The United Nations Convention on the Law of the Sea: A Commentary* (Beck Hart Nomos 2017) 2131 (this book will herein be referred to as Proelss Commentary).

[32] Seven of the ISA's thirty-one mining contracts are held by private corporate actors; for details, see Appendix 2.

[33] For details of the two contracts held by state enterprises of the Cook Islands and Kiribati, respectively, but performed through partnership arrangements with private corporations, see Appendices 1 and 2.

[34] Michael Lodge, ISA, 'Keynote Address: Plotting the Path to Commercial Reality' (Offshore and Deep Sea Mining Conference, London, 9 December 2015) (describing that the move from initial exploration to sustained exploitation will require substantial capital investment, as well as a high degree of operational and financial risk).

[35] Fritz (n 30) 461–462 (summarising this view as forming 'the current trend in positioning the Common Heritage of Mankind').

[36] See, e.g. ISA Secretary-General's comment that 'until the private sector gets involved, the prospects for commercial mining of minerals from the deep seabed will remain uncertain': UNGA '71st Plenary Meeting' (61st Session) (8 December 2006) UN Doc A/61/PV71 at 5. See also comments to ISA by Japan (an active deep seabed participant via two ISA contracts held by state enterprises), acknowledging that 'realization of the exploitation of the resources in the Area, which mankind has been longing for,

seabed mining to get off the ground, the common heritage must be realised in such a way as to foster and encourage private commercial mining activity within the system (while also securing communitarian, benefit-of-mankind aspects).

Notably, private actor involvement in deep seabed mining activities is leading to various forms of collaboration between corporate entities and developing states that are seeking to become active in the industry. This could also have an impact on common heritage concerns. As the ISA has observed, the consequences of such alliances upon 'key features at the heart of the common heritage regime' remain to be seen.[37] In practical terms, joining forces with private actors may provide developing states that lack the technical capabilities and resources with one of the only 'realistic' means by which to become active in deep seabed mining (thereby furthering aspects of the common heritage that seek equal opportunities for deep seabed mining participation).[38] One such developing state, which is participating as a state sponsor of a private contractor, has described this method of participation as being akin to the manner in which 'some developing countries require foreign direct investment'.[39] However, non-governmental organisations (*NGOs*) and other participants in civil society have been critical of the increasing corporatisation of deep seabed mining, sounding the alarm that the industry may be falling prey to the process of 'corporate capture'.[40]

Finally, and crucially, the involvement of corporations as direct actors in deep seabed mining poses a number of additional conceptual legal challenges as

presupposes the entry of ample number of companies to the deep-sea mining industry in the Area' and, therefore, requires 'provision of sufficient [commercial] incentives for companies to engage in deep-sea exploitation in light of the technical and economic difficulties they face in exploiting mineral resources in the Area': Japan, 'Comments on the Draft Regulations on Exploitation of Mineral Resources in the Area (ISBA/25/C/WP1)' (October 2019) 1 <https://isa.org.jm/files/files/documents/201910%20Japan%27s%20comments%20on%20draft%20regulations.pdf>. See also, generally, Catherine Danley, 'Diving to New Depths: How Green Energy Markets Can Push Mining Companies Into the Deep Sea, and Why Nations Must Balance Mineral Exploitation with Marine Conservation' (2019–20) 44 Wm & Mary Env L & Pol'y Rev 219.

[37] ISA LTC, 'Report of the Chair of the Legal and Technical Commission on the Work of the Commission at its Session in 2016' (13 July 2016) ISBA/22/C/17, para 56.

[38] Helmut Tuerk, 'The International Seabed Area' in Malgosia Fitzmaurice and Norman A Martinez Gutierrez (eds), *The IMLI Manual on International Maritime Law*, vol I (OUP 2014) 301.

[39] ISA Council, 'Submission by the Delegation of Nauru: Proposal to Seek an Advisory Opinion from the Seabed Disputes Chamber of the International Tribunal for the Law of the Sea on Matters Regarding Sponsoring State Responsibility and Liability' (5 March 2010) ISBA/16/C/6, para 1.

[40] See, e.g. Deep Sea Mining Campaign, London Mining Network, MiningWatch Canada, 'Why the Rush? Seabed Mining in the Pacific Ocean' (July 2019) 15–18 <https://miningwatch.ca/sites/default/files/why_the_rush.pdf>; Catherine Coumans, 'Mining the Deep Sea' (*Arena Magazine*, October 2019) <https://arena.org.au/mining-the-deep-sea-by-catherine-coumans/>; Greenpeace, 'Deep Trouble: The Murky World of the Deep Sea Mining Industry' (December 2020) 3, 27–29 <www.greenpeace.org/static/planet4-international-stateless/c86ff110-pto-deep-trouble-report-final-1.pdf>. The phenomenon of corporate capture has been described as 'the means by which an economic elite undermine the realization of human rights and the environment by exerting undue influence over domestic and international decision-makers and public institutions': International Network for Economic, Social and Cultural Rights, 'About Corporate Capture' (ESCR-Net) <www.escr-net.org/corporateaccountability/corporatecapture/about>.

compared to, for example, the status of state participants. These challenges relate to the broader international legal framework concerning the role and status of corporations within international law, including issues of applicability to corporations of treaty and customary law, international responsibility and dispute resolution options.

For all of these reasons, this study will concentrate on the role of corporate actors in deep seabed mining, constituting, as it does, the thorniest, least explored and most interesting potential tension point for the common heritage, in international legal terms. Given that deep seabed mining is due to begin in the coming years, and that the involvement of private actors in the Area looks set to continue and expand, this consideration of the implications of private actor involvement is both timely and necessary.

Outline and Scope of the Study

Consideration of the impact of commercial deep seabed mining activities on the realisation of the common heritage raises three key preliminary issues. Firstly, to begin to address this question, one must root it within an overarching methodological framework: both in terms of determining the most suitable method to approach the deep seabed, and also in recognition of the nuanced role of non-state actors within international law. Chapter 1 will explain this study's methodology. Given that the role of non-state actors is pivotal to this study, Chapter 1 offers a preliminary methodological note on non-state actors in international law. Its emphasis will be on private corporate entities, and it will include assessment of the key elements of corporate obligations under international law. Particular legal complexities raised by corporate actor involvement in deep seabed mining will then be revisited throughout this work.

Part I will then progress to its second strand of preliminary evaluation: to achieve an understanding of the deep seabed, and why the role of corporate actors within it is increasing. Accordingly, Chapter 2 will assess four key questions: where is the deep seabed? What mineral resources can be found there? Why is this important, in terms both of the industry prospects and environmental challenges? And, finally, what is the extent of the activities being undertaken there, thus far?[41] This examination is pivotal, in order to determine the real-life, practical content of the common heritage.[42]

[41] Further details on this are included in the two appendices to this book, which address the types of contractors currently participating in exploration activities in the Area (Appendix 1), and the status of existing contracts for exploration in the Area (Appendix 2).

[42] This book does not include examination of certain extraneous issues, such as purely domestic law issues, labour law and safety issues and the legal position as regards marine genetic resources.

Chapter 3 will then address the third, and final, preliminary conceptual issue. What is the role of the common heritage principle within the deep seabed mining regime? As Chapter 3 will reveal, in the modern-day deep seabed mining context, the common heritage concept comprises four central components: the common management principle, the prohibition of unilateral mining activities, the benefit-sharing principle and the principle of marine environmental protection. This book must assess the extent to which these components are operationalised within the UNCLOS regime, and the means by which they apply to corporate actors. In addition, inherent within the common heritage concept is a balance between securing benefits for humankind while also fostering commercial participation in line with market principles. The regime must satisfy both of these objectives in order to fulfil its common heritage goal.[43]

Against this backdrop, Parts II and III of this book will seek to reconcile commercial deep seabed mining activity and common heritage goals. The focus of Part II will be to determine whether the UNCLOS deep seabed regime creates a common management system that is binding on actors both inside and outside of the regime. As Chapter 4 will assess, UNCLOS creates a procedural architecture for the pursuit of deep seabed mining activities, and corporate actors are participating within it. Moreover, as Chapter 5 will establish, this procedural framework has a global reach, as it prohibits external actors from conducting unilateral mining activities outside of the Convention regime.

Part III will consider the key material goals of the common heritage ideal, namely benefit sharing and marine environmental protection. As Part III will address, the realisation of the substantive core of the common heritage concept will, in large part, be dependent on the ISA's effective institutional workings, for example through enactment and enforcement of appropriate regulations. Accordingly, Chapter 6 will provide an interim assessment of the extent to which the ISA's developing regulatory framework (and accompanying implementation and enforcement powers) may foster benefit sharing and marine environmental protection in the longer term. Thereafter, Chapter 7 will evaluate whether the UNCLOS deep seabed mining regime strikes an appropriate regulatory balance between realising benefits for humanity and securing investment protection rights for deep seabed miners.

On the basis of the analysis, in Parts II and III, of the interface between corporate mining activities and the key components of the common heritage concept, this book will conclude by assessing whether the UNCLOS regime is sufficient to accommodate increasing corporate involvement without riding roughshod over the common heritage concept. The conclusion will recognise that the UNCLOS

[43] Chapter 3, Section 3.3 sets out this framework of analysis in detail, and includes a table laying out these key elements and the steps of analysis that this book will undertake.

deep seabed mining regime may be adaptable enough to accommodate the shifting actors in the Area while allowing deep seabed resources to be exploited for the benefit of all humanity. However, to achieve this end, the ISA must work comprehensively to expand and implement its body of regulations, which form the Mining Code.

1

A Methodological Approach to Deep Seabed Mining by Non-state Actors

Deep seabed mining activities by non-state actors may raise challenges for the realisation of the common heritage of mankind. To address this, this book must firstly ground this study within its broader methodological framework on two levels. Firstly, Section 1.1 of this chapter will provide a method of analysis for evaluating the deep seabed regime. Secondly, Section 1.2 will offer a preliminary methodological note on non-state actors in international law, with an emphasis on private corporate entities, to facilitate detailed analysis of this issue in the deep seabed mining context.

1.1 A Methodological Approach to Deep Seabed Mining

1.1.1 Seeking Internal Coherence

> [L]egal theories are no more than tools; different islands and zones and the varied legal functions performed within them, present very different problems and types of law 'jobs' for which different tools and even toolboxes may be required.[1]

International law is a system in which certain areas of the law are more developed and effective than others. Leading theorist and commentator Reisman describes international law as being 'more "archipelagic" than other legal systems'.[2] Viewing international law from an archipelagic perspective, Reisman depicts a range of 'islands' within which law is applied fairly effectively, 'off-shore zones' which suffer from much more intermittent and case-specific legal application, and 'anomic' zones in which behaviour is either normless or carried out in accordance with another code, at variance from international law.[3]

In many ways, the law of the sea affords a well-regulated and comprehensive normative system, perhaps akin in some respects to the law on Reisman's

[1] W Michael Reisman, *The Quest for World Order and Human Dignity in the Twenty-first Century* (Brill 2013) 23–24 (citations omitted).

[2] Reisman (n 1) 19; see also 20 ('international law is dramatically, sometimes maddeningly, archipelagic').

[3] Reisman (n 1) 20.

International Law and Corporate Actors in Deep Seabed Mining. Joanna Dingwall, Oxford University Press. © Joanna Dingwall 2021. DOI: 10.1093/oso/9780192898265.003.0002

well-functioning and highly developed 'islands'. Indeed, pre-eminent international lawyer Brownlie notes that, in certain key areas of international affairs, 'the terms and categories of international law provide the syntax, the very fabric, of the subjects concerned'.[4] Brownlie identifies the law of the sea as one such category, in which 'the law, so to speak, sets the scene and provides the contours of the landscape of decision-making. The law is therefore not external, coercive and alien but internal, logically necessary and familiar.'[5] Thus, international legal rules are 'stitched into' the subject of the law of the sea.[6]

Within the well-developed body of the law of the sea, sits the regime applicable to deep seabed mining. Due to the detailed nature of the existing legal rules on deep seabed mining and their 'internal' character, underpinning and defining the activity, a formalist approach lends itself well to evaluation of the regime. On similar grounds, Bederman concludes that a formalist approach is well suited to analysis of the law of the sea in general.[7]

As Weinrib explains, '[t]he formalist … regards law as understandable from within, not as an alien language that requires translation into the terminology of another discipline'.[8] Formalism offers an opportunity 'to make sense of juristic thinking and discourse in their own terms'.[9] In order to engage fully with, and determine whether corporate mining activities are likely to undermine the concept of the common heritage, this book will employ a predominantly formalist perspective. This analysis will provide the framework required to highlight and attempt to solve the conflicts in the deep seabed mining regime within that regime's own terms, where possible.

One of the hallmarks of the formalist approach is its focus on the letter of the law.[10] Ordinarily, this approach may exclude consideration of the origins or policy issues behind the letter of the law. However, perhaps more so in relation to international law than any other branch of law, formalism can, in fact, engender a dynamic and creative approach that moves beyond purely black letter considerations.

4 Ian Brownlie, 'The Reality and Efficacy of International Law' (1981) 52 BYIL 1, 5.

5 Brownlie (n 4) 5.

6 Brownlie (n 4) 5.

7 David J Bederman, *The Spirit of International Law* (University of Georgia Press 2002) 168–169 (determining that the law of the sea, 'where many rules seem to be structured around what may appear to be arbitrary and peculiar distinctions', is dependant 'on a formal construct of rights and duties' (at 168 and 169, respectively)). Bederman notes that '[f]ormal doctrines … serve to mediate [state] disputes by imposing, almost literally, lines in the water that reflect different legal regimes' (at 169) (this particular issue will be considered further in Chapter 2 of this book).

8 Ernest J Weinrib, 'The Jurisprudence of Legal Formalism' (1993) 16 Harv JL & Pub Pol'y 583, 592.

9 Weinrib (1993) (n 8) 592.

10 See, e.g. Frederick Schauer, 'Formalism' (1988) 97 Yale LJ 509, 510 ('[a]t the heart of the word "formalism", in many of its numerous uses, lies the concept of decisionmaking according to *rule*' (emphasis in original)). On formalism as a 'vision of law as an autonomous body of ascertainable rules', see Lyrissa Barnett Lidsky, 'Defensor Fidei: The Travails of a Post-realist Formalist' (1995) 47 Fla L Rev 815, 819 (citations omitted); see also 816, fn 2; and, generally, 819–822 (for a 'sympathetic portrait' of key traits inherent in modern formalism).

One reason for this is because any formalist analysis of international law must be based on sources doctrine.

Unlike the sources of, for example, domestic law, international law sources incorporate a variety of elements and considerations. Article 38(1) of the Statute of the International Court of Justice (*ICJ*) sets out the traditional list of sources of international law. It lists four categories: treaties; custom; general principles of law; and, as a subsidiary source, judicial decisions and writings of distinguished jurists.[11] The positivistic 'quasi-scientific formula' contained in Article 38(1) belies the true nature of the sources of international law, assessment of which requires a multifaceted process.[12] For example, determination of customary international law involves examining a broad range of practice by states and other actors, including state policy actions and statements. Therefore, to provide a formal perspective on the procedural reach and customary status of the deep seabed regime, Chapter 5 of this book will consider various evidential and contextual considerations, in an attempt to ascertain and pin down the parameters of the law.

Similarly, as this study will demonstrate, a formalist approach to the UNCLOS deep seabed regime must be grounded in the rules of treaty interpretation. Interpretation of treaties is governed by the default rules contained in Articles 31 to 33 of the Vienna Convention on the Law of Treaties (*VCLT*).[13] These rules have the status of customary law,[14] and are applicable to the deep seabed regime contained in UNCLOS.[15]

The cardinal rule of treaty interpretation is that '[a] treaty shall be interpreted in good faith in accordance with the ordinary meaning to be given to the terms of the treaty in their context and in the light of its object and purpose'.[16] Pursuant to this approach, formalistic interpretation of a treaty must frequently include evaluation of various strands that go beyond the mere letter of the law, such as the context of the treaty and its object and purpose. Together with context, other relevant factors that one must take into account are 'any subsequent agreement between

[11] Statute for the International Court of Justice (opened for signature 26 June 1945 as annex to UN Charter, entered into force 24 October 1945) UKTS 67 (1946), art 38(1) (*ICJ Statute*). On the pervasive, enduring impact of Article 38(1) of the ICJ Statute, see Hilary Charlesworth, 'Law-making and Sources' in James Crawford and Martti Koskenniemi, *The Cambridge Companion to International Law* (CUP 2012) 188–189 (noting that, although Article 38(1) merely constitutes a list of principles for the ICJ to use when deciding cases, it 'has achieved an almost canonical status as a codification of the sources of international law'). cf Jean d'Aspremont, *Formalism and the Sources of International Law: A Theory of the Ascertainment of Legal Rules* (OUP 2011) (arguing that international lawyers must move away from the Article 38 approach and apply an alternative formalist approach towards the ascertainment of international legal rules).

[12] Charlesworth (n 11) 189.

[13] Vienna Convention on the Law of Treaties (adopted 22 May 1969, opened for signature 23 May 1969, entered into force 27 January 1980) 1155 UNTS 331 (*VCLT*).

[14] See, e.g. *Territorial Dispute (Libya v Chad)* (Merits) [1994] ICJ Rep 6, para 41; *Oil Platforms (Islamic Republic of Iran v United States of America)* (Preliminary Objection) [1996] ICJ Rep 803, para 23.

[15] *Responsibility and Obligations of States Sponsoring Persons and Entities with Respect to Activities in the Area* (Advisory Opinion of 1 February 2011) ITLOS Reports 2011, 10 (*ITLOS AO*) para 58.

[16] VCLT, art 31(1).

the parties regarding the interpretation of the treaty or the application of its provisions', 'any subsequent practice in the application of the treaty which establishes the agreement of the parties regarding its interpretation' and any other relevant rules of international law applicable between the parties.[17] As a supplementary means of interpretation, one may also rely upon the preparatory works of the treaty, which is the record of negotiations, known as the *travaux préparatoires*.[18] In addition, in certain circumstances, subsequent party conduct may also constitute a supplementary means of interpretation, under Article 32 of the VCLT.[19]

Moreover, to appraise the development of the UNCLOS treaty regime on deep seabed mining, this book must also take into account certain comparative and historical elements. For example, as will be demonstrated (in Chapters 3 to 5), a certain degree of historical analysis is required to understand the present scope of the UNCLOS regime, and the modern ambit of the common heritage concept within that regime. Furthermore, both comparative and historical analyses are indispensable for this book's consideration of the role of state practice in formation of customary rules on deep seabed mining (in Chapter 5).

By adopting a dynamic formalist perspective, this study seeks to ascertain whether the deep seabed regime can be synthesised to support sustainable commercial participation by non-state actors in deep seabed mining, while realising a benefit to mankind as a whole. In that sense, deployment of a formalist methodology will afford an opportunity to search for coherence and order within the terms of the regime itself.[20] At the peak of its endeavour, '[f]ormalism provides a coherent and elegant theory that philosophically unifies and politically legitimizes law, and formalism empowers human actors by making the legal system not only comprehensible but an outgrowth of human reason'.[21] However, formalism as a methodological approach has been subject to much criticism. In particular, formalism has often had a bad name in the field of international law.[22] Nevertheless, there are two main conceptual reasons why it is particularly apposite for application in this study.

[17] VCLT, art 31(3)(a)–(c).

[18] VCLT, art 32.

[19] See, e.g. *Case Concerning Kasikili/Sedudu Island (Botswana/Namibia)* (Judgment) [1999] ICJ Rep 1045, paras 78–80 (in which the ICJ relied upon subsequent practice by treaty parties concerning the Botswana–Namibia boundary as a supplementary means of interpretation, despite the fact that this practice did not amount to an agreement between the parties in terms of VCLT, art 31(3)(b)). See also Rahim Moloo, 'When Actions Speak Louder Than Words: The Relevance of Subsequent Party Conduct to Treaty Interpretation' (2013) 31 Berkley J Int'l L 39, 46–47.

[20] Ernest J Weinrib, 'Legal Formalism: On the Immanent Rationality of Law' (1988) 97 Yale LJ 949, 950–951: Weinrib argues that 'formalism, properly understood ... embodies a profound and inescapable truth about law's inner coherence', and that one of the reasons lawyers are attracted to the formalist approach is because it constitutes an 'effort to make sense of the lawyer's perception of an intelligible order' (at 950 and 951, respectively). See, further, Weinrib (1993) (n 8) 592–593.

[21] Barnett Lidsky (n 10) 832.

[22] See, e.g. Martti Koskenniemi, 'What is International Law for?' in Malcolm D Evans (ed), *International Law* (5th edn, OUP 2018) 39 ('[t]he almost uniformly pejorative use of the term "formalism" in international law reflects the predominance of the instrumentalist mindset in diplomacy and international politics'); see also Bederman (2002) (n 7) 163.

Firstly, it may be only through reliance on a formal approach that the true power of the UNCLOS deep seabed regime can be realised: as a means by which to regulate behaviour and provide a coherent global structure for deep seabed mining. As Koskenniemi observes, 'there is a reason to defend a legal "formalism" against a "pragmatism" that views international law only in terms of the immediate objectives it serves'.[23] Specifically, adoption of a formalist perspective that assesses the law on the basis of its stated content, rather than as a mere instrument for achievement of (often competing) objectives, may afford the only way to pin down the law's substantive content and thereby restrain powerful actors.[24]

As Koskenniemi and Lehto note, in relation specifically to the deep seabed mining regime, it is by virtue of the 'substantive emptiness' of the medium of law that a version of the common heritage could be agreed within UNCLOS that satisfied various opposing objectives and a range of state ideologies (from capitalist to communist).[25] And it is this modern common heritage concept, as captured within the UNCLOS system, that this study must evaluate, in formal terms, for its compatibility with corporate participation in deep seabed mining.

The second advantage afforded by a formalist approach to deep seabed mining is structural in nature. Reliance on a formal perspective towards the UNCLOS deep seabed regime affords a 'shared surface' on which to engage with ramifications upon the regime of corporate participation, including analysis of implications for non-States Parties and their nationals.[26] As Koskenniemi explains:

> [I]t is international law's formalism that brings political antagonists together as they invoke contrasting understandings of its rules and institutions.... the pure form of international law provides the shared surface – the *only* such surface – on which political adversaries recognize each other as such and pursue their adversity in terms of something shared, instead of seeking to attain full exclusion – 'outlawry' – of the other.[27]

[23] Koskenniemi (2018) (n 22) 34.

[24] Koskenniemi (2018) (n 22) 34: 'there is often a reason to adopt a "formalist" view on international law that refuses to engage with the question of its objectives precisely in order to constrain those in powerful positions'. See also Weinrib (1993) (n 8) 593 (arguing that 'formalism is evaluative and not merely descriptive'. Hence, 'formalism asks what law would look like if it were true to [its] claim [to be a justificatory enterprise]'. Therefore, within formalism is a 'critical standpoint, but one that emerges from law's own aspirations').

[25] Martti Koskenniemi and Marja Lehto, 'The Privilege of Universality: International Law, Economic Ideology and Seabed Resources' (1996) 65 Nordic J Int'l L 533, 555 (see also 554: '[t]he combination of pragmatism and universalism was possible precisely because of the materially empty character of the principles in which the supranational rhetoric of the law of the sea (common heritage, universality) was encapsulated').

[26] Koskenniemi (2018) (n 22) 46.

[27] Koskenniemi (2018) (n 22) 46.

In this respect, what Koskenniemi terms as 'international law's value and its misery' is its capacity to provide a structure within which we can begin the debate.[28] By creating at least an illusion of structure, as Barnett Lidsky explains, 'formalism's promise of stability and order may be essential to the effective functioning of the legal system, even if this promise can never be realized'.[29] In that sense, 'what formalism promises may be as important as what it delivers'.[30] Consequently, regardless of whether the often lofty aspirations of international law can be achieved and adhered to, it may still be a triumph of sorts for the discipline that opponents can argue their differences using a common language: that of international legal discourse.[31]

As this study will demonstrate, the international legal regime applicable to deep seabed mining is one in which a 'shared surface' is particularly manifest, by virtue of the structure and process provided by the body effectively in charge of the Area: the ISA. The deep seabed mining regime – more so than many other areas of international law – is unusually centralised. The ISA is a unique, and potentially dynamic, body at the helm of deep seabed mining activities, with far-ranging regulatory powers at its disposal. Therefore, formal analysis of the rules provided by the UNCLOS regime, and the institutional architecture constituted by the ISA and its law-making process, will be critical components in determining whether corporate activities may conflict with the common heritage ideal.

1.1.2 Evaluating Broader Context

The impending wholesale involvement of non-state actors, such as private corporate entities, may be the key test of the legal architecture for deep seabed mining.[32] In practice, private actors are likely to play a crucial role in driving forward the mining process.[33] Thus, the degree to which these private actors can participate competitively, while ensuring realisation of benefits for humanity, may be

[28] Koskenniemi (2018) (n 22) 46. In this regard, one can draw a comparison with Parlett's approach in determining the role of the individual in international law: Kate Parlett, *The Individual in the International Legal System* (CUP 2011). Parlett, in adopting a predominantly formalist, 'rules-based approach' (see 7), acknowledges the importance of the international legal system – irrespective of its flaws – in affording an underlying structure within which to engage in her evaluation (see 9, where she notes that '[t]he enterprise of international law may be flawed, even radically flawed, but that it is an enterprise in its own terms does not seem open to doubt').

[29] Barnett Lidsky (n 10) 818; see also 832, 836.

[30] Barnett Lidsky (n 10) 832.

[31] Similarly, see Rosalyn Higgins, 'Final Remarks' (2005) 16 EJIL 347, 353 ('I share much of Philip [Allot]'s view on what international law *can't* do. But I take such small comfort as I can muster in believing that, if it can help at the margin in our wretched world, then the effort must be made and is worthwhile.' (emphasis in original)).

[32] See Section 1.2 below for a definition of non-state actors, including private corporate entities, and analysis of their methodological status within the international legal system.

[33] See discussion in the introduction to this book, text to nn 31–39.

the acid test in determining whether the international community will ultimately be able to 'cite the establishment of the [ISA] as the first true internationalist venture'.[34] As emphasised by the ISA Secretary-General in one of the quotations that open this book, the critical challenge facing the industry is 'to develop an exploitation regime, including a fiscal framework, that fosters commercially viable exploitation and at the same time benefits mankind as a whole'.[35] This study aims to contribute towards the resolution of this challenge by assessing the extent to which these two, sometimes competing, aims can be reconciled.

In order to do so, although this study will necessarily be rooted in the law of the sea, it will also place the deep seabed regime firmly within its broader international law framework. There is an enduring doctrinal debate about the issue of fragmentation of international law.[36] As noted at the start of this chapter, international law can be viewed as a series of islands and offshore zones.[37] This archipelagic metaphor illustrates aptly the way in which certain facets of the international legal system are now remarkably self-contained and self-sufficient. The modern era has witnessed a proliferation of sophisticated and increasingly disparate spheres within the international legal system, such as investment law, trade law, human rights law, international humanitarian law and environmental law. In many respects, law of the sea is one such stand-alone system.

Some actors embrace the prospect of a fragmented international legal order.[38] Others seek a pluralistic approach in which diverse specialisations within international law are grounded in the international legal system as a whole.[39] Thorough engagement with this wider debate is beyond the scope of this book. However, this study, while cognisant of the well-developed nature of the law of the sea and the *sui generis* character of the deep seabed mining regime, will employ a critique that is grounded robustly in general international law.

The deep seabed mining regime, although a highly technical and detailed subdiscipline, is part of the larger international legal system, with all the customary laws and treaty rules which that entails.[40] In order to navigate conflicts in the deep

[34] Koskenniemi and Lehto (n 25) 552.

[35] Nii Allotey Odunton, ISA Secretary-General 'Statement to the Twenty-Third Meeting of the States Parties to UNCLOS' (10 June 2013) <www.isa.org.jm/files/documents/EN/SG-Stats/SPLOS-SGStat-23Meet.pdf>.

[36] See, e.g. International Law Commission (*ILC*), 'Fragmentation of International Law: Difficulties Arising from the Diversification and Expansion of International Law – Report of the Study Group of the International Law Commission Finalized by Martti Koskenniemi' (13 April 2006) UN Doc A/CN4/L682.

[37] Reisman (n 1) 20.

[38] See, e.g. Eyal Benvenisti and George W Downs, 'The Empire's New Clothes: Political Economy and the Fragmentation of International Law' (2007) 60 Stan L Rev 595, 610ff (analysing pursuit of fragmentation by powerful states to protect dominance).

[39] See, e.g. Jonathan I Charney, 'The Implications of Expanding International Dispute Settlement Systems: The 1982 Convention on the Law of the Sea' (1996) 90 AJIL 69.

[40] In the same vein, see, e.g. Richard A Barnes, 'Consolidating Governance Principles for Areas beyond National Jurisdiction' (2012) 27 Int'l J Marine Coastal L 261, 274 (recalling that 'the law of the sea is part of international law and is subject to the same systemic requirements that constrain and shape

seabed regime, this study will draw on the existing body of international law to provide guidance as to how these conflicts could – or should – be mitigated. Beyond the specific terms of the regime found in UNCLOS, other areas of international law must be brought to bear on the issue of non-state actor involvement and the realisation of the common heritage. These other areas include, of course, analysis of custom formation and treaty interpretation, together with consideration of certain implications under laws of international responsibility, international environmental law, investment protection law, and the law on non-state actors, such as it is.

The main advantages to grounding analysis of the UNCLOS regime in general international law are twofold. First, locating the regime within the scheme of international law as a whole avoids normative dissonance and the trap of false universalisation, with all the 'normative and jurisdictional conflicts' that can engender.[41] Second, to reach a more holistic perspective, one must understand that the ISA forms part of a larger network of international bodies and institutions. Only by doing so can one begin to assess the scope of the ISA's role, and its ability to address the challenges of widespread private actor participation in deep seabed mining.[42]

Therefore, adoption of a formal approach rooted within the law of the sea and general international law will provide the key framework for this book's analysis. However, although formalism is an indispensable starting point, this study will also evaluate the deep seabed mining regime in its broader context on two levels. Firstly, to understand the functioning of the regime fully, one must have some appreciation of certain scientific and technological elements of deep seabed activities, including the extent of current advancement in both fields. Consequently, where necessary, this book will draw on a literature base that includes scientific papers, technical analyses and news reports, in order to augment its legal appraisal.

Secondly, adoption of a formal approach is a prerequisite for engaging with the deep seabed mining regime, but it alone is insufficient. In evaluating whether mining activities by corporate actors will impinge upon the common heritage, much of the answer will lie in effective further regulation of deep seabed mining. That regulation will, in turn, be dependent on the activities of the ISA, and its entire process of decision-making and secondary law-making, including input by various actors, such as those participating in ongoing stakeholder consultations. To assess

general international law' (citing Alan Boyle, 'Further Development of the 1982 Convention on the Law of the Sea' in David Freestone, Richard Barnes and David Ong (eds), *Law of the Sea – Progress and Prospects* (OUP 2006) 40)).

[41] Koskenniemi (2018) (n 22) 45.

[42] cf Jan-Stefan Fritz, 'Deep Sea Anarchy: Mining at the Frontiers of International Law' (2015) 30 Int'l J Marine Coastal L 445, 466–467 (noting that aspects of the ISA's role may exemplify 'a general trend' towards fragmentation or decentralisation of international law, citing specifically the lack of a dialogue between the ISA and the Commission on the Limits of the Continental Shelf (at 466), and the disconnect between issues of deep seabed mining and other matters connected to the deep seabed, such as biodiversity issues (at 467)).

the prospects for the success of the regime, this study will be open to certain considerations of a more socio-legal nature.

Elements of the socio-legal approach, such as rule-scepticism and rejection of formalist assumptions concerning law, are present in key theoretical approaches to international law, such as New Approaches to International Law (*NAIL*)[43] and the New Haven approach.[44] For New Haven theorists, rules are simply the formal articulation of past decisions: societal context is all-important to their application. For example, as stated by Rosalyn Higgins, former ICJ President, and proponent of the New Haven approach, '[i]nternational law is not rules'.[45] Rather, international law is a continuing process of authoritative and controlling decisions taken in context.[46] Viewed from this perspective, far from being a static body of rules, international law is the entire decision-making process, considered within its overall context.

Reisman summarises the appeal and utility of such a process-orientated approach in endeavouring to connect the operative parts of the international legal process to the contexts in which they are applied, be they social, political or economic.[47] As Reisman identifies, this affords the opportunity to spot any disjuncture between the stated goals of international law and their achievement on the ground, and 'insofar as there is a discrepancy ... to propose realistic and feasible alternatives that can recommend themselves for their practicability and not merely for their moral appeal'.[48]

Consequently, this study will apply a form of process-orientated approach that marries formalism with a more contextual strand. This approach will acknowledge

[43] See, e.g. key NAIL works: David Kennedy, 'Theses about International Law Discourse' (1980) 23 GYIL 355; David Kennedy, *International Legal Structures* (Nomos Verlagsgesellschaft 1987); David Kennedy, 'A New Stream of International Law Scholarship' (1988) 7 Wis Int'l LJ 1; Martti Koskenniemi, 'The Politics of International Law' (1990) 1 EJIL 4; David Kennedy, 'The Disciplines of International Law and Policy' (1999) 12 LJIL 9; Martti Koskenniemi, *From Apology to Utopia: The Structure of International Legal Argument* (CUP 2005); Martti Koskenniemi, 'The Politics of International Law – 20 Years Later' (2009) 20 EJIL 7. See, further, David Kennedy and Chris Tennant, 'New Approaches to International Law: A Bibliography' (1994) 35 Harv Int'l LJ 417; José María Beneyto and others (eds), *New Approaches to International Law: The European and The American Experiences* (TMC Asser Press 2013); Ntina Tzouvala, 'New Approaches to International Law: The History of a Project' (2016) 27 EJIL 215.

[44] For leading examples of the New Haven approach, see, e.g. Harold D Lasswell, Myres S McDougal and W Michael Reisman, 'Theories about International Law: Prologue to a Configurative Jurisprudence' (1968) 8 Va J Int'l L 188; Rosalyn Higgins, *Problems & Process – International Law and How We Use It* (Clarendon Press 1994); Reisman (n 1). See, further, Harold Hongju Koh, 'Is There a "New" New Haven School of International Law?' (2007) 32 Yale J Int'l L 559. For a useful overview of the genesis of this approach, see Harold Hongju Koh, 'Why Do Nations Obey International Law?' (1996–7) 106 Yale LJ 2599, 2618–2624. On the New Haven approach as a form of 'socio-legal realism', see Paul Schiff Berman, 'A Pluralist Approach to International Law' (2007) 32 Yale J Int'l L 301, 305.

[45] Higgins (1994) (n 44) 1.

[46] Higgins (1994) (n 44) 1–2; Rosalyn Higgins, 'Policy Considerations and the International Judicial Process' (1968) 17 ICLQ 58, 58–59.

[47] Reisman (n 1) 23.

[48] Reisman (n 1) 23.

the importance of rules and the core of certainty typically contained within them,[49] while recognising that an understanding of other elements, such as overall context, and decision-making and law-making processes, may be vital in allowing one to determine how rules will develop and be applied, in practice.

1.1.3 Concluding Remarks

The blended approach contained within this book is defensible. Arguably, it is the only way in which one can accurately address the question as to whether deep seabed mining activities by non-state actors are compatible with common heritage concerns, given the important role of the ISA secondary law-making and decision-making processes in any answer to this question. Indeed, as Koskenniemi cautions, a formalist approach may be viable only if it is also grounded in pragmatism, to some extent.[50] As part of Koskenniemi's broader critique of international law as a series of binary oppositions,[51] he argues that without recognition of the political, 'law becomes pure positivity, its violence a mere fact of power'.[52] However, at the other extreme, if law is entirely based upon politics, it becomes a mere apology for the activities of dominant actors.[53] Only by treading a path that takes account of both the form of the law and its operation in practice, can one seek to arrive at a true understanding of the functioning of the deep seabed regime.[54]

Now that this section has established this book's overall method of inquiry, Section 1.2 will provide a brief methodological perspective on one of the key strands underpinning this study: the role of non-state actors (specifically, corporations).

1.2 A Methodological Note on Non-state Actors: Conceptualising the Status of Corporate Entities within the Deep Seabed Mining Regime

The role of non-state actors in deep seabed mining raises a host of issues. This section will address the following four key queries: what constitutes a non-state actor for the purposes of this book's analysis (Section 1.2.1), and how may its

[49] HLA Hart, *The Concept of Law* (3rd edn, OUP 2012), 123: Hart famously distinguished between 'clear central cases' at the core of a general rule and other cases falling within the rule's penumbra, in relation to which application of the rule could be argued either way. He concluded that '[n]othing can eliminate this duality of a core of certainty and a penumbra of doubt when we are engaged in bringing particular situations under general rules' (also at 123).

[50] Koskenniemi (2018) (n 22) 47.

[51] See, e.g. Koskenniemi (2005) (n 43) 60, 165–168.

[52] Koskenniemi (2018) (n 22) 47.

[53] Koskenniemi (2005) (n 43) 159, 167.

[54] As Hart has cautioned, '[f]ormalism and rule scepticism . . . are great exaggerations, salutary where they correct each other, and the truth lies between them'(Hart (n 49) 147).

nationality be established, as a matter of international law (Section 1.2.2)? More generally, to what extent are such actors capable of participating within the international legal system (Section 1.2.3)? Specifically, what are the conditions under which a corporate entity can gain rights or incur obligations pursuant to international law (Section 1.2.4)? This analysis will provide the necessary conceptual backdrop against which this book can evaluate the role of corporate activities within deep seabed mining.

1.2.1 Terminology: Non-state Actors and Corporate Entities

Turning to the first issue, the concept of non-state actors is an amorphous term, encompassing various different entities. Clapham defines the term as including 'any entity that is not actually a state, often used to refer to armed groups, terrorists, civil society, religious groups or corporations'.[55] As Noortmann et al explain, '[n]on-State actors cover a broad range of entities, from intergovernmental organisations ... to non-governmental organisations (NGOs), multinational corporations (MNCs), and individuals'.[56] One must exercise caution when assessing international legal consequences for varying types of non-state actors because there may be 'significant differences between the rules applicable to specific categories of non-state actors'.[57]

Currently, an array of participants are involved in deep seabed mining in the Area, including both state and non-state actors. These participants comprise various states, an inter-state consortium formed by several States Parties to UNCLOS (Interoceanmetal Joint Organization), and many state enterprises, public institutions or state-controlled corporations (including Russia's Yuzhmorgeologiya, the China Ocean Mineral Resources Research and Development Association, the French Research Institute for Exploitation of the Sea, Germany's Federal Institute for Geosciences and Natural Resources, and Japan's Deep Ocean Resources Development Company (*DORD*)), together with several private corporations.[58] In addition, some state-controlled contractors in the Area are conducting mining activities in tandem with private corporations, through joint venture or partnership arrangements.[59]

[55] Andrew Clapham, *Human Rights Obligations of Non-state Actors* (OUP 2006) 211. See also Crawford's analysis of the various potential subjects of international law, ranging from more 'established legal persons' (such as states and international organisations) through to 'special types of personality', including corporations: James Crawford, *Brownlie's Principles of Public International Law* (9th edn, OUP 2019) Chapter 4 (at 106 and 111, respectively).

[56] Math Noortmann, August Reinisch and Cedric Ryngaert, 'Introduction' in Math Noortmann, August Reinisch and Cedric Ryngaert (eds), *Non-state Actors in International Law* (Hart Publishing 2015) 2.

[57] Parlett (n 28) 5.

[58] For details of all contractors currently participating in the Area, see Appendix 1.

[59] See Appendices 1 and 2 for details of contracts held by state enterprises of the Cook Islands and Kiribati, respectively, but performed in conjunction with private corporations.

Despite the range of participants in deep seabed mining, this book will focus primarily on the role of private corporate entities as ISA contractors, for the reasons already set out in the introduction. Indeed, increasing attention is being paid to the role of the private sector within international law more generally, given the economic heft and quasi-governmental functions exercised by various titans of industry.[60] Within the international law context, commentators have attempted to categorise corporate actors varyingly as 'multinational' or 'transnational' 'corporations' or 'entities', focusing on factors such as exercise of control by entities of various nationalities or the existence of cross-border operations, in order to distinguish and define them.[61]

However, as Karavias acknowledges, such an approach may be unnecessarily limiting.[62] Although corporate actors on the international plane typically possess corporate structures crossing countries, and often continents, there is no compelling reason why national corporations should be 'excluded from the reach of potential international law obligations'.[63] As will be explained below, rather than focusing on the precise form of a corporation, in terms of whether it has, within its corporate structure, entities of 'diverse nationalities',[64] or whether it is conducting activities in more than one state, it may be more instructive to assess whether the corporation in question is subject to rights and obligations on the international plane.

Consequently, this study will endorse Karavias's useful, if 'untechnical',[65] assessment that a corporation is 'an organization of persons and material resources, with a distinct legal personality, of limited liability and licensed by the state for the purpose of conducting profit-seeking business activity'.[66] An important further condition to add to this definition is that, for the purposes of this book's enquiry, a corporate entity must be a private actor rather than under the control of a state. As

[60] See, e.g. Jonathan I Charney, 'Transnational Corporations and Developing Public International Law' (1983) 32 Duke LJ 748; Markos Karavias, *Corporate Obligations under International Law* (OUP 2013); Jan Wouters and Anna-Luise Chané, 'Multinational Corporations in International Law' in Math Noortmann, August Reinisch and Cedric Ryngaert (eds), *Non-state Actors in International Law* (Hart Publishing 2015); Jay Butler, 'The Corporate Keepers of International Law' (2020) 114 AJIL 189; Doreen Lustig, *Veiled Power: International Law and the Private Corporation 1886–1981* (OUP 2020).

[61] On 'terminological indeterminacy' concerning categorisation of corporations under international law, see Wouters and Chané (n 60) 226, citing varying definitions of multinational and transnational corporations used by the UN, the Organisation for Economic Co-operation and Development (*OECD*), and within international legal scholarship (at 226–228); see also Charney (1983a) (n 60) 749, fn 1 and Karavias (n 60) 3.

[62] Karavias (n 60) 3.

[63] Karavias (n 60) 3–4.

[64] Detlev F Vagts, 'The Multinational Enterprise: A New Challenge for Transnational Law' (1970) 83 Harv L Rev 739, 740 (relying on the definition of multinational enterprises provided by Raymond Vernon, 'Economic Sovereignty at Bay' (1968) 47 Foreign Aff 110, 114); see also Karavias (n 60) 3, fn 19.

[65] Karavias ((n 60) 4) caveats his definition thus, quoting I Seidl-Hohenveldern, 'Public International Law Influences on Conflicts of Law Rules on Corporations' (1968) 123 RdC 1, 7.

[66] Karavias (n 60) 4; similarly, see analysis of defining features of a corporation in Peter T Muchlinski, 'Corporations in International Law' in Rüdiger Wolfrum (ed), *The Max Planck Encyclopedia of Public International Law* (OUP 2014) paras 1–2 (listing 'five main elements' of a corporation as 'legal personality, transferable shares, limited liability, centralized management, and investor ownership').

Crawford notes, it is 'not always easy to distinguish ... a private or public corporation under some degree of state control from the state itself'.[67] Determining this can be difficult, and may be a matter of degree.[68] For the purposes of this book, a corporation which is wholly owned or majority-controlled by a state will be considered to be a state-controlled corporation.[69] Such state-controlled corporations are outwith this book's scope of analysis.[70] Rather, this study will focus on analysing the role of private, corporate entities within the deep seabed mining regime.[71]

1.2.2 Nationality of Corporate Entities at International Law

When establishing a definition of corporate actors, another important element to consider is the means by which corporations acquire a nationality. Nationality is the legal bond of attachment between an individual or a corporation and a given state. The rules concerning nationality are primarily regulated at the domestic level: '[i]n principle ... it is not for international law but for the internal law of each state to determine who is, and who is not, to be considered its national'.[72] However, in order to create effects on the international plane, a state's grant of nationality must be consistent with international law.[73] In international legal terms, nationality is of particular importance as a ground for establishing the scope of a state's personal jurisdiction,[74] as a means for requiring a state to readmit its nationals to

[67] Crawford (2019) (n 55) 116.

[68] This issue arises across many areas of international law, including when determining state responsibility at international law.

[69] Similarly, Vázquez defines 'private corporations' as 'those that are not owned or operated by governments', but includes, within the term, publicly traded corporations: Carlos M Vázquez, 'Direct vs Indirect Obligations of Corporations under International Law' (2004–05) 43 Colum J Transnat'l L 927, 929, fn 9. Equally, when addressing private corporate actors, this study will include consideration of public companies (such as public limited companies and publicly traded companies, which tend to be listed on a recognised stock exchange, with publicly traded stock), as well as privately held companies (such as private limited companies), provided that they are not wholly or majority state-controlled.

[70] For example, ISA contractor DORD, which is over 75% majority-owned by Japanese state enterprise Japan Oil, Gas and Metals National Corporation (*JOGMEC*), is a state-controlled corporation, beyond the scope of the present analysis. For classification of each of the entities currently involved in deep seabed mining, see Appendix 1, which categorises these actors as either states, consortiums, state enterprises, state institutions, other state-controlled entities or private corporate actors.

[71] Within this book, terms such as 'private actor', 'corporate actor', 'corporate entity' and 'corporation' will be used interchangeably, and sometimes in combination to refer to a private corporate entity as defined in this section (although, as noted in the introduction to this study, many of the issues considered retain relevance for all commercial operators in deep seabed mining endeavours, irrespective of whether those participants are states, state entities or private actors).

[72] Robert Jennings and Arthur Watts, *Oppenheim's International Law: Vol 1, Peace, Pts 2–4* (9th edn, Longman 1996) 852.

[73] Jennings and Watts (n 72) 853.

[74] Oliver Dörr, 'Nationality' in Rüdiger Wolfrum (ed), *The Max Planck Encyclopedia of Public International Law* (OUP 2006) paras 43–49; see, further, Bernard H Oxman, 'Jurisdiction of States' in Rüdiger Wolfrum (ed), *The Max Planck Encyclopedia of Public International Law* (OUP 2007) paras 11, 18–20. Personal jurisdiction includes the jurisdiction of a state to bring its nationals within the personal scope of a particular treaty, where the scope of that treaty is based on nationality (e.g. typically, entitlement to investment treaty protection is premised upon nationality, which forms the basis of

its territory,[75] and as a basis on which a state can exert diplomatic protection in respect of its nationals.[76]

In what circumstances is international law likely to accept that a corporation has acquired the nationality of a given state? Determining corporate nationality 'is not always easy'.[77] The key problem is in establishing the appropriate criteria for ascertaining the nationality of a corporation, especially in the face of somewhat 'contradictory and incomplete principles'.[78] Factors that have been suggested to have relevance for corporate nationality include a corporation's location of incorporation, the seat of its registered office, the nationality of its controlling shareholders and the presence of a close connection between a corporation and a particular state.[79]

The particular international legal context determines the extent to which nationality may be established, as a matter of international law, and the consequences that flow from it. To inform this book's subsequent discussion of the nationality requirements for corporations to participate within the deep seabed mining regime, which have significant implications for the operation of the regime, the following analysis will briefly introduce three contrasting international legal contexts, in which corporate nationality may feature: firstly, the field of diplomatic protection; secondly, international investment law; and, finally, the UNCLOS system itself.

Turning to the first of these categories, nationality forms the essential link between a person (natural or legal) and a state, in the exercise of diplomatic protection, providing the home state with standing to pursue a claim on its subject's behalf against a foreign state.[80] The applicable rules differ depending on whether the national is an individual or a corporation.[81] As regards corporations, the ICJ

jurisdiction *ratione personae* for the purposes of investor–state disputes). As will be addressed further herein, UNCLOS uses nationality as a condition for participation within deep seabed mining by actors other than States Parties: UNCLOS, art 153(2)(b).

[75] Dörr (n 74) paras 50–51.

[76] See, generally, ILC, 'Draft Articles on Diplomatic Protection' in 'Report of the International Law Commission on the Work of its 58th Session' (1 May to 9 June and 3 July to 11 August 2006) UN Doc A/61/10 (*ILC DP Draft Articles*); see also Chittharanjan F Amerasinghe, *Diplomatic Protection* (OUP 2008); John Dugard, 'Diplomatic Protection' in Rüdiger Wolfrum (ed), *The Max Planck Encyclopedia of Public International Law* (OUP 2009).

[77] Muchlinski (n 66) para 18 (see also para 14, noting that the issue of nationality 'causes particular difficulties where the claimant is [a multinational enterprise], given the possibility of its being linked to more than one country by reason of the international character of its operations, and given the differing nationalities of the parent company and its overseas subsidiaries'). See, further, Vaughan Lowe, 'Corporations as International Actors and International Law Makers' (2004) XIV Italian YB Int'l L 23, 34 ('[t]here are considerable problems relating to the concept of corporate nationality').

[78] Phoebe Okowa, 'Issues of Admissibility and the Law on International Responsibility' in Malcolm D Evans (ed), *International Law* (5th edn, OUP 2018) 462.

[79] *Barcelona Traction, Light and Power Company, Limited* (Judgment) [1970] ICJ Rep 3, para 70.

[80] This nationality of claims rule is reflected in ILC DP Draft Articles (n 76) art 3; the other essential precursor to exercise of diplomatic protection is contained in art 14 (exhaustion of local remedies).

[81] ILC DP Draft Articles (n 76) arts 4–8 (nationality of natural persons) and arts 9–13 (nationality of legal persons, particularly corporations).

acknowledged in *Barcelona Traction* that '[t]he traditional rule attributes the right of diplomatic protection of a corporate entity to the State under the laws of which it is incorporated and in whose territory it has its registered office'.[82] In that case, the ICJ applied these two criteria cumulatively, and also endorsed the presence of some 'close and permanent connection' between corporation and state.[83]

The International Law Commission (*ILC*) developed the position further in its Draft Articles on Diplomatic Protection.[84] As a general rule, in accordance with Article 9, a corporation will acquire the nationality of the state in which it is incorporated.[85] Incorporation constitutes 'the most important criterion', and 'it is incorporation that confers nationality on a corporation for the purposes of diplomatic protection'.[86] However, Article 9 admits an exception to this rule, designed to cater for circumstances in which the corporation has a closer connection to another state. Thus, incorporation alone may not always be sufficient.[87] Rather, a corporation may qualify as a national of another state (other than the state of its incorporation) when the following three conditions are satisfied: (1) 'the corporation is controlled by nationals of another State or States'; (2) the corporation 'has no substantial business activities in the State of incorporation'; and (3) 'the seat of management and the financial control of the corporation are both located in another State'.[88] Therefore, pursuant to the ILC's approach, '[t]he State of nationality with the right to exercise diplomatic protection is *either* the State of incorporation *or*, if the required conditions are met, the State of the seat of management and financial control of the corporation'.[89]

On the whole, shareholder nationality is of limited relevance in the determination of corporate nationality for the purposes of diplomatic protection. As the ILC has affirmed, '[t]he most fundamental principle of the diplomatic protection

[82] *Barcelona Traction* (n 79) para 70.

[83] *Barcelona Traction* (n 79) para 71. Despite endorsing a 'close and permanent connection' between the corporation and state of nationality, the ICJ rejected the application to corporations of a *Nottebohm* requirement of a 'genuine connection' (see para 70, 'in the particular field of the diplomatic protection of corporate entities, no absolute test of the "genuine connection" has found general acceptance'); cf *Nottebohm Case* (Second Phase) [1955] ICJ Rep 4, 23 (requiring evidence of a 'genuine connection' between an individual and a state, in order to allow diplomatic protection in respect of an individual upon whom nationality was conferred by naturalisation). Arguably, *Nottebohm* is limited to the facts of the particular case and does not establish 'a general rule applicable to all States': ILC, 'Draft Articles on Diplomatic Protection with Commentaries' in 'Report of the International Law Commission on the Work of its 58th Session' (1 May to 9 June and 3 July to 11 August 2006) UN Doc A/61/10 (*ILC DP Commentaries*) 30 (citation omitted).

[84] See ILC DP Draft Articles (n 76), much of which codifies customary law, with some elements of progressive development; Dugard (n 76) para 6.

[85] See ILC DP Draft Articles (n 76) art 9 (providing that, inter alia, 'the State of nationality means the State under whose law the corporation was incorporated'; this reflects the central premise of *Barcelona Traction* (n 79) para 70).

[86] ILC DP Commentaries (n 83) 37 and 38 (respectively).

[87] Javier García Olmedo, 'Nationality of Claim: Investment Arbitration' in Rüdiger Wolfrum (ed), *The Max Planck Encyclopedia of Public International Law* (OUP 2019) para 15.

[88] ILC DP Draft Articles (n 76) art 9.

[89] ILC DP Commentaries (n 83) 38 (emphasis in original).

of corporations is that a corporation is to be protected by the State of nationality of the corporation and *not* by the State or States of nationality of the shareholders in a corporation'.[90] There are three narrow exceptions to this, whereby international law may pierce the corporate veil, allowing shareholders' state of nationality to claim diplomatic protection on their behalf.[91] The first is where shareholders have suffered direct injury to their rights.[92] Secondly, the state of nationality may exercise diplomatic protection for shareholders in relation to corporate injury (as opposed to direct injury of shareholder rights) if the corporation no longer exists, for reasons unrelated to the injury.[93] Thirdly, and again in relation to corporate injury, the state of nationality of shareholders may be permitted to exercise diplomatic protection for them if the state of incorporation caused the injury, and 'incorporation in that state was required by it as a precondition for doing business there'.[94]

Therefore, for the purposes of diplomatic protection, corporate nationality is determined based on the state of incorporation or, in certain circumstances, the state of the seat of management and financial control, with shareholder nationality having less significance. While a body of customary law has coalesced around the requirements for the recognition of corporate nationality for the purposes of diplomatic protection, in other contexts – such as international investment law – the rules governing the nationality of an investor will be determined by the particular terms of the relevant treaty.[95]

Given that there are well over 3,000 international investment agreements, the scope of their application and the precise terms of their protections vary.[96] However, investment agreements are premised on a 'nationality of claims' rule, protecting investors from one contracting state (the home state) against harm to their investments located in the territory of another contracting state (the host state). Both natural and legal persons are usually covered by the scope of protection. As

[90] ILC DP Commentaries (n 83) 38 (emphasis in original); see ILC DP Draft Articles (n 76) art 11. This is also reflected in *Barcelona Traction* (n 79) para 44.

[91] See Dugard (n 76) para 35, drawing on *Barcelona Traction* (n 79) and other jurisprudence. See, generally, *Barcelona Traction* (ibid) para 58.

[92] ILC DP Draft Articles (n 76) art 12; see also *Barcelona Traction* (n 79) para 47 ('[w]henever one of his direct rights is infringed, the shareholder has an independent right of action'); see, further, *Ahmadou Sadio Diallo (Republic of Guinea v Democratic Republic of the Congo)* (Preliminary Objections) [2007] ICJ Rep 582 (reaffirming the right to diplomatic protection for shareholders in respect of direct injury to their rights).

[93] ILC DP Draft Articles (n 76) art 11(a). Similarly, see *Barcelona Traction* (n 79) para 66.

[94] ILC DP Draft Articles (n 76) art 11(b). See also ILC DP Commentaries (n 83) 41–42 and citations therein (citing support for this approach); Dugard (n 76) paras 39–43; Okowa (n 78) 464–465.

[95] The ILC acknowledged this in ILC DP Draft Articles (n 76) art 17 ('[t]he present draft articles do not apply to the extent that they are inconsistent with special rules of international law, such as treaty provisions for the protection of investments'). In practice, reliance on investment agreements has supplanted resort to diplomatic protection as the most common modality for foreign investors to pursue claims against host states for interference with investments Okowa (n 78) 465.

[96] For current figures on the volume of such agreements, see UN Conference on Trade and Development (*UNCTAD*), 'International Investment Agreements Navigator' <https://investmentpolicy.unctad.org/international-investment-agreements>.

compared to diplomatic protection, investment agreements generally adopt a less restrictive, more investor-friendly approach.[97] Most investment treaties include some combination of three particular requirements that a corporation must meet in order to qualify as a protected investor.

Firstly, and most commonly, an investment treaty will require a corporate investor to be incorporated in its home state (thus replicating the primary criterion for diplomatic protection of corporations).[98] Most bilateral investment treaties (*BITs*) are premised on this requirement. Absent further limitations contained expressly within the investment treaty text, investment tribunals have been reluctant to infer any additional requirement of a real or substantial connection between the corporation and the state in which it is incorporated, preferring to focus on corporate form.[99]

For example, the arbitral tribunal in *Saluka*, while expressing 'some sympathy for the argument that a company which has no real connection with a State party to a BIT, and which is in reality a mere shell company controlled by another company which is not constituted under the laws of that State' should not be entitled to protection under that BIT, held that it was 'not open to the Tribunal to add other requirements [to the BIT's definition of investor] which the parties could themselves have added but which they omitted to add'.[100] Equally, as regards the scope of its jurisdiction *ratione personae*, the *Tokios Tokelės* tribunal found that 'it is not for tribunals to impose limits on the scope of BITs not found in the text', even in circumstances where relying solely on an incorporation criterion rendered a Lithuanian entity (which was, in fact, 99% owned by Ukrainian nationals) eligible to bring a claim against Ukraine under the Lithuania–Ukraine BIT.[101]

[97] García Olmedo (n 87) para 2.

[98] García Olmedo (n 87) para 22. See also Zachary Douglas, *The International Law of Investment Claims* (CUP 2009) 22–23 (listing examples of such treaties at fn 96).

[99] See, e.g. Douglas (2009) (n 98) 314–318; Patrick W Pearsall and David Manners-Weber, 'Covered Investors' in Barton Legum (ed), *The Investment Treaty Arbitration Review* (4th edn, Law Business Research Ltd 2019) 21–22.

[100] *Saluka Investments BV (The Netherlands) v The Czech Republic* (Partial Award) UNCITRAL (17 March 2006) paras 240–241.

[101] *Tokios Tokelės v Ukraine* (Decision on Jurisdiction) ICSID Case No ARB/02/18 (29 April 2004) para 36 (see also paras 53–56, finding no need to lift the corporate veil on grounds of abuse of legal personality and acknowledging the ICJ's approach in this regard in *Barcelona Traction* (n 79)); cf dissenting opinion of Prosper Weil (adopting an 'origin of capital' approach and urging that the 'economic reality' of the investment be taken into account when determining jurisdiction (paras 20 and 23, respectively)). Conversely, some investment treaties do require a 'bond of economic substance' between a corporation and its home state, or the presence of 'genuine economic activity', in order for a corporation to attain the status of a protected investor: Pearsall and Manners-Weber (n 99) 22–23 (and citations therein); see also Douglas (2009) (n 98) 23, at fn 97, for examples of such 'exceptional' provisions, and, generally, 317–318. Such a requirement may also take the form of a denial of benefits clause, pursuant to which contracting states reserve the right to deny BIT protection to certain categories of investors (such as corporations without substantial business activities in their state of incorporation). However, enforceability of such clauses can be contentious: see case law analysis in García Olmedo (n 87) paras 49–56; Pearsall and Manners-Weber (ibid) 23–24.

Secondly, as an additional requirement, some investment treaties require a corporation to have its seat (*siège social*) or place of administration in the home state in order to qualify as an investor.[102] These types of requirement may be 'susceptible of *either* a formal or substantive meaning', and investment tribunals have adopted differing approaches.[103]

Thirdly, some investment treaties use an element of control to define corporate investors, and 'on some occasions, this element is incorporated in the treaty with the aim of expanding its coverage even further'.[104] Depending on the wording of the treaty, the control element may expand the treaty's reach by allowing a corporation to qualify for protection if it was constituted in a third state, but is controlled by nationals of the home state.[105] When assessing provisions of this type, in determining whether the element of control is satisfied by formal ownership or requires evidence of actual substantive control, arbitral tribunals have generally been satisfied by the presence of formal ownership alone. For example, in *Aguas del Tunari* the arbitral tribunal found that 'one entity may be said to control another entity (either directly, that is without an intermediary entity, or indirectly) if that entity possesses the legal capacity to control the other entity'.[106] Notably, this 'does not require actual day-to-day or ultimate control as part of the "controlled directly or indirectly" requirement'.[107] In contrast to diplomatic protection claims, a shareholder may be entitled to direct recourse under an investment treaty in respect of injuries suffered by a company in which it has invested.[108]

[102] García Olmedo (n 87) para 22. See also Douglas (2009) (n 98) 23 (listing, at fn 97, examples of treaties with such a requirement).

[103] *Tenaris SA & Talta-Trading v Bolivarian Republic of Venezuela* (Award) ICSID Case No ARB/11/26 (29 January 2016) para 144 (emphasis in original). See also Markus Perkams, 'Protection for Legal Persons' in Marc Bungenberg and others (eds), *International Investment Law: A Handbook* (Nomos/Hart 2015) 644–646; Pearsall and Manners-Weber (n 99) 22.

[104] García Olmedo (n 87) para 23.

[105] See Douglas (2009) (n 98) 302 (listing, at fn 61, examples of treaties which extend investment protection to investors that have 'direct or indirect' ownership or control over an investment).

[106] *Aguas del Tunari SA v Republic of Bolivia* (Decision on Jurisdiction) ICSID Case No ARB/02/3 (21 October 2005) para 264; see, generally, paras 225–323 for thorough analysis of the meaning of the BIT's control requirement (finding, on the basis of the Netherlands–Bolivia BIT, as interpreted in accordance with the VCLT rules of treaty interpretation, that formal ownership is sufficient for the purposes of establishing control (as opposed to the actual exercise of control), so that any corporate entity that owns the investment vehicle (either directly or indirectly) may qualify for BIT protection if it is a national of a contracting Party); cf dissenting declaration of José Luis Alberro-Semerena (arguing that the BIT requires actual control and that the claimant had not met this test). See also analysis in Christoph H Schreuer and others, *The ICSID Convention: A Commentary* (2nd edn, CUP 2009) 326–327; Perkams (n 103) 648–649.

[107] *AdT* (n 106) para 264 (see also para 237, finding that '[t]he phrase, "directly or indirectly," in modifying the term "controlled" creates the possibility of there simultaneously being a direct controller and one or more indirect controllers. The BIT does not limit the scope of eligible claimants to only the "ultimate controller." ').

[108] For example, a majority shareholder may qualify as a protected investor on the basis of its formal control over the injured corporation. Even a minority shareholder may qualify as a protected investor on the basis of control, if it possesses 'the legal capacity to control an entity [which] may exist by reason of the percentage of shares held, legal rights conveyed in instruments or agreements such as the articles of incorporation or shareholders' agreements, or a combination of these' (*AdT* (n 106) para 264). Moreover, the broad definition of 'investment' within most investment treaties extends to cover the

Nationality requirements may also serve as a precondition for submission of an investment dispute to a particular venue for dispute settlement. For example, a preferred means of investor–state dispute settlement, often included as an option within investment treaties, is recourse to the International Centre for Settlement of Investment Disputes (*ICSID*).[109] Adopting a 'generous' approach,[110] Article 25(2)(b) of the ICSID Convention extends protection both to corporations that are nationals of a state party other than the state in which they are investing (i.e. home state nationals), and also to corporations which are nationals of a state party in which they are investing (i.e. host state nationals) 'and which, because of foreign control, the parties have agreed should be treated as a national of another Contracting State for the purposes of this Convention'.[111]

The latter 'foreign control' exception was included to address the frequent host state requirement that investments must be made through locally incorporated companies. This means that such companies may be entitled to instigate a claim at ICSID against their own state of nationality, where 'foreign control' of the company belongs to nationals in another contracting state. The term 'foreign control' is undefined within the ICSID Convention. However, in determining the objective presence of 'foreign control', ICSID tribunals have taken various elements into account, including shareholdings, voting rights and managerial control.[112] Certain ICSID tribunals have pierced the corporate veil to extend protection up the chain of corporate command, to include the ultimate corporate investors with indirect control of a locally incorporated company.[113]

Other contexts, aside from diplomatic protection and international investment law, shed light upon international law's treatment of corporate nationality. The final

shareholding itself, affording shareholders independent standing against a host state for losses occurring from reduction in value of the shareholding as a result of injury to the company. See, generally, David Gaukrodger, 'Investment Treaties and Shareholder Claims – Analysis of Treaty Practice' (2014) OECD Working Paper on International Investment 2014/03 <www.oecd.org/investment/investment-policy/WP-2014-3.pdf>.

109 ICSID was established by the Convention on the Settlement of Investment Disputes between States and Nationals of Other States (concluded 18 March 1965, entered into force 14 October 1966) 575 UNTS 159 (*ICSID Convention*).

110 García Olmedo (n 87) para 24.

111 ICSID Convention, art 25(2)(b) (although this provision does not provide a definition of the concept of nationality, '[t]he overwhelming weight of the authority … points towards the traditional criteria of incorporation or seat for the determination of corporate nationality of claimants under Art. 25(2)(b)'; Schreuer and others (n 106) 283).

112 See, e.g. Schreuer and others (n 106) 327.

113 See, e.g. *Société Ouest Africaine des Bétons Industriels v Senegal* (Decision on Jurisdiction) ICSID Case No ARB/82/1 (1 August 1984) paras 35–38 (going beyond the direct control which a Panamanian corporation exercised over the locally incorporated claimant to recognise the indirect control of Belgian nationals, in order to allow jurisdiction). cf *Amco Asia Corporation and others v Republic of Indonesia* (Decision on Jurisdiction) ICSID Case No ARB/81/1 (25 September 1983) para 14(iii) (recognising the immediate control exercised by the claimant's parent company (controlled by a US national) as sufficient to qualify for jurisdiction, thereby ignoring further layers of indirect control beyond this first level). On this issue of indirect control, see Schreuer and others (n 106) 320–323.

example to introduce briefly here is the UNCLOS system itself. For example, as will be examined in more detail in Chapter 4, UNCLOS includes nationality as a precondition for participation within deep seabed mining. To be eligible to apply to the ISA for a mining contract, a corporate actor (or other entity) must obtain sponsorship from the State Party (or States Parties) of which it is a national, together with sponsorship from any other State Party that effectively controls it.[114] Thus, nationality and effective control become the crucial parameters for corporate participation within the deep seabed mining system. The purpose of these parameters is to ensure that the sponsoring state will, in fact, be in a position to exercise direct regulatory control over the entity that it sponsors.[115] Accordingly, in evaluating whether a corporation is eligible to participate in the regime, the ISA places faith in the sponsoring state to certify, as part of the application process, that the sponsored corporation possesses its nationality and/or is under its effective control.

In practice, the ISA has deemed the effective control requirement to be satisfied where a corporation exhibits the nationality of a state (e.g. through incorporation), and that state pledges that the corporation has its nationality and is under its effective control.[116] The ISA supports this approach even in circumstances where the corporation in question is a wholly owned subsidiary, under the 'complete commercial and financial domination' of a parent company that is the national of another state.[117] In distinction to the approach to corporate nationality for diplomatic protection (in which closeness of connection between state and corporation may be relevant, and the seat of management and financial control of the corporation may determine nationality), the ISA adopts a formal approach to nationality and effective control (more akin to the international investment law approach to determining protected investors), seeking to establish merely that the sponsoring state exhibits appropriate regulatory control, rather than requiring any more substantial link between state and corporation (such as a substantive or economic connection).[118]

Before concluding this consideration of nationality within the UNCLOS system, the legal regime of the high seas also affords an interesting point of comparison, with its system of 'flag state nationality' of ships. As Article 91(1) of UNCLOS provides, '[s]hips have the nationality of the State whose flag they are entitled to fly'. This provision gives states discretion to set conditions for grant of nationality to

[114] UNCLOS, art 153(2)(b).

[115] See UNCLOS, arts 139(1)–(2), 153(4) and Annex III, art 4(4). See also ITLOS AO, paras 74–75; see, further, Jule Siegfried, 'Article 153' in Proelss Commentary 1084.

[116] This will be addressed further in Chapter 4, Section 4.2.3.3.

[117] See, generally, ISA Secretariat, 'Analysis of Regulation 11.2 of the Regulations on Prospecting and Exploration for Polymetallic Nodules and Polymetallic Sulphides in the Area' (5 June 2014) ISBA/20/LTC/10, para 22.

[118] Indeed, in considering the nationality/effective control requirements within the deep seabed mining regime, the ISA Secretariat expressly distinguished the application of the diplomatic protection approach, on the basis that it would not necessarily ensure that the sponsoring state has the requisite regulatory control over the sponsored corporation: see ISBA/20/LTC/10, para 17.

ships, ship registration, and the right to sail under a given state flag. Given that the high seas, like the Area, are beyond the national jurisdiction of states, the requirement of flag state jurisdiction for ships is the key route to maintaining order on the high seas.[119] By granting nationality, the flag state incurs certain duties, including the duty to 'effectively exercise its jurisdiction and control' over flag ships.[120]

In principle, in order for flag state nationality to attach, '[t]here must exist a genuine link between the State and the ship'.[121] In practice, the application of the genuine link concept has posed problems. Some states have ignored it, favouring an 'open registry' or 'flag of convenience' approach, with vessels flying the flag of a state to which they have 'very little or virtually no link'.[122] The International Tribunal for the Law of the Sea (*ITLOS*) has clarified matters to some extent, emphasising that the genuine link serves as a basis to ensure effective regulatory control by the flag state, by establishing a permanent legal link between the flag state and the ship, evidenced by appropriate documentation, irrespective of beneficial ownership of economic interest in the vessel.[123] Therefore, similarly to the ISA's approach to the requirement of effective control for the purposes of participation in deep seabed mining, effective control for the application of flag state nationality is satisfied by regulatory control. This is achieved, in practice, through registration of a vessel (akin to incorporation of a corporation): 'it is the act of registration that conveys nationality to a ship and provides the basis for jurisdiction over the vessel, irrespective of ownership or financial interest in the vessel or its operations'.[124]

In conclusion, as the preceding analysis has demonstrated, when determining the extent to which corporate nationality may be established as a matter of

[119] This echoes the approach, within the deep seabed mining regime, of requiring sponsoring state nationality/effective control for an entity's participation, to ensure that the sponsoring state possesses regulatory control over the sponsored entity.

[120] UNCLOS, art 94(1).

[121] UNCLOS, art 91(1). This 'genuine link' requirement for flag state nationality was introduced, originally, in Article 5(1) of the Convention on the High Seas (opened for signature 29 April 1958, entered into force 30 September 1962) 450 UNTS 11 (*High Seas Convention 1958*). In formulating this provision, the drafters of that treaty were 'strongly influenced' by the 'then recent' *Nottebohm* case: Robin R Churchill and A Vaughan Lowe, *The Law of the Sea* (3rd edn, Manchester UP 1999) 258; cf *Nottebohm* (n 83) 23.

[122] Churchill and Lowe (n 121) 258 (see also 259, noting the danger that such flag states of convenience may be 'unwilling or unable to exercise effective jurisdiction over their ships in matters of pollution control and shipping safety'). See, generally, Doris König, 'Flags of Convenience' in Rüdiger Wolfrum (ed), *The Max Planck Encyclopedia of Public International Law* (OUP 2008); see, further, Douglas Guilfoyle, 'Article 91' in Proelss Commentary 694.

[123] See, e.g. *M/V 'SAIGA' (No 2) (Saint Vincent and the Grenadines v Guinea)* (Judgment of 1 July 1999) ITLOS Reports 1999, 10, para 83 (finding that 'the purpose of the provisions of [UNCLOS] on the need for a genuine link between a ship and its flag State is to secure more effective implementation of the duties of the flag State, and not to establish criteria by reference to which the validity of the registration of ships in a flag State may be challenged by other States'.); reaffirmed in *M/V 'Virginia G' Case (Panama v Guinea-Bissau)* (Judgment of 14 April 2014) ITLOS Reports 2014, 1, paras 112–113. See also discussion by Douglas Guilfoyle, 'Article 91' in Proelss Commentary 694–695 and 699 (noting that, with regard to establishment of a genuine link, 'ITLOS has been unwilling to look past compliance with conditions of registration under national law' (699)).

[124] ISBA/20/LTC/10, para 14.

international law, the underlying context is a decisive factor. Certain parameters, such as incorporation, have significance in all contexts. Other factors, such as location of the seat, may also have relevance, depending on the broader circumstances. However, while the field of diplomatic protection has required evidence of a close connection between a corporation and a state for the latter to bring a claim on the former's behalf, other areas of international law, like international investment law, have eschewed the need for a substantive or economic connection between a corporate investor and its home state (absent contrary provisions in the treaty text), instead favouring a more formal approach to corporate nationality. UNCLOS echoes this more formalistic approach to the issues of nationality and effective control, accepting regulatory control as being sufficient, both as regards the participation of corporations in deep seabed mining (as Chapter 4 will consider further), and in relation to the nationality of flag state vessels.[125]

1.2.3 Corporate Entities within the International Legal System

Now that the relevant definition is settled, and issues of nationality have been assessed, the even thornier matter to which this section now turns is the third issue: by what means are corporate entities brought within the international legal system? To what extent are they capable of participating, as overt actors, in a web of legal relations on the international plane? Specifically, how does international law filter down to bind corporate entities in the deep seabed mining context?

The previous section has already addressed the important role that nationality may play as an essential link between a corporation (or an individual) and international law.[126] However, moving beyond considerations of nationality alone, the extent to which various non-state actors, including corporations, constitute subjects of international law more generally, and can be construed as having international legal personality, is contentious.[127] As set out by the ICJ, an 'international person ... is a subject of international law and capable of possessing international rights and duties' and 'has capacity to maintain its rights by bringing international claims'.[128] Pursuant to the traditional approach to international law, states were

[125] As Chapter 4, Section 4.2.3 will address, the formal approach to nationality/effective control within the deep seabed mining regime has implications for the operation of some substantive aspects of the regime, such as the system of reserved areas.

[126] See also Jennings and Watts (n 72) 859 (noting that 'it is often necessary, in order that international law can apply in relation to a corporation, to attribute it to a state').

[127] Terms such as subjecthood, legal personality and international personality are essentially synonyms: Roland Portmann, *Legal Personality in International Law* (CUP 2010) 1, 8. These terms will be used interchangeably herein.

[128] *Reparation for Injuries Suffered in the Service of the United Nations* (Advisory Opinion) [1949] ICJ Rep 174, 179. For key literature on international legal personality, see works cited in Portmann (n 127) 1–2, fns 3 and 8, fn 2; for detailed historical analysis, see Janne Elisabeth Nijman, *The Concept of International Legal Personality: An Inquiry into the History and Theory of International Law* (TMC Asser Press 2004).

deemed to be the primary actor on the international plane ('States solely and exclusively are the subjects of international law').[129] The Permanent Court of International Justice (*PCIJ*) encapsulated this state-centric, Westphalian approach when it stated that '[i]nternational law governs relations between independent States'.[130]

However, despite 'controversy' concerning the exact scope of legal personality at international law,[131] it is evident that non-state actors have long had some capacity in the international sphere.[132] For example, during the seventeenth and eighteenth centuries, chartered companies played a dominant role in international trade, shaping the development of the modern state system and international law itself.[133] Corporations such as the Dutch East India Company (Verenigde Oost-Indische Compagnie or *VOC*) and the English East India Company (*EIC*) fused elements of private control and state influence, going so far as to act as 'de facto State[s]' in entering into treaties, conquering overseas territories and waging wars.[134]

As noted by Charney, '[e]mphasis upon relations between States, to the exclusion of individuals, is, in fact, of relatively recent origin, a product of nineteenth century positivism'.[135] Indeed, as Lauterpacht recognised in 1927:

> Gradually a consensus of opinion is evolving to the effect that although it is States which are the normal subjects of international law, there is nothing in

[129] L Oppenheim, *International Law: A Treatise, vol 1* (2nd edn, Longmans, Green and Co 1912) 19; see also Crawford (2019) (n 55) 106 ('[i]n spite of the complexities, it is as well to remember the primacy of states as subjects of the law'). Pursuant to this 'traditional doctrinal approach', corporations were not capable of acting on the international plane 'and so their claims would be limited to the field of diplomatic protection' (which, as addressed in Section 1.2.2, involves a claim brought by their home state on their behalf, on the basis of nationality): Muchlinski (n 66) para 6.

[130] *SS Lotus Case (France v Turkey)* [1927] PCIJ Rep Series A No 10, 18. For historical analysis of the emergence of states as the primary actors in international law, in the wake of the Peace of Westphalia of 1648, see Antonio Cassese, 'States: The Rise and Decline of the Primary Subjects of the International Community' in Bardo Fassbender and Anne Peters (eds), *The Oxford Handbook of the History of International Law* (OUP 2015) 49ff; see also Charney (1983a) (n 60) 758–759.

[131] *Reparation* (Advisory Opinion) (n 128) 178.

[132] Lowe (n 77) 23 ('[n]on-sovereign entities have always participated in international legal relations'). See, generally, Lustig (n 60) (charting the role of the international legal order in facilitating the operation of private corporations during a hundred-year period, from 1886 to 1981).

[133] See, generally, Eric Wilson, *Savage Republic: De Indis of Hugo Grotius, Republicanism and Dutch Hegemony with the Early Modern World-system (c 1600–1619)* (Martinus Nijhoff 2008), especially ch 4; see also Koen Stapelbroek, 'Trade, Chartered Companies, and Mercantile Associations' in Bardo Fassbender and Anne Peters (eds), *The Oxford Handbook of the History of International Law* (OUP 2015) 339.

[134] Stapelbroek (n 133) 351 (as Stapelbroek analyses (at 346), these entities would 'autonomously modulate between the positions of being a "mere merchant" and an "independent sovereign", without needing to feign *imperium*' (quoting Philp J Stern, *The Company State: Corporate Sovereignty and the Early Modern Foundations of the British Empire in India* (OUP 2011) 13)). See also Philip C Jessup, *A Modern Law of Nations* (The Macmillan Company 1948) 22 (describing how the VOC and the EIC 'had the power to make war and peace and to conclude treaties on which their states relied as the basis of rights').

[135] Charney (1983a) (n 60) 753, fn 9 (citing the Catholic Church as '[p]erhaps the oldest example of the applicability of international law to a non-state'). See also Higgins (1994) (n 44) 49.

> international law which is fundamentally opposed to individuals and other legal persons becoming subjects of international rights and duties.[136]

This uncertainty concerning the scope of international personality has led scholars to devise sophisticated and varying conceptions and approaches to the issue. Some commentators have sought to depart from the concepts of subjects and legal persons altogether, condemning them as a Procrustean bed, and focusing instead on 'participants' and 'actors', which can be assessed by virtue of the extent of their effective participation, rather than their formal status.[137]

In his comprehensive analysis of legal personality in international law, Portmann identifies five different conceptions present within international legal discourse: 'the "states-only conception", the "recognition conception", the "individualistic conception", the "formal conception" and the "actor conception"'.[138] These respective approaches range from reserving international personality to states (consistent with the traditional, state-centric approach); allowing other entities to derive international personality based on state recognition; presuming in favour of the international personality of individuals, with international responsibility as a consequence; opening international personality to all addressees of international legal norms; and rejecting international personality in favour of a focus on effective participation.[139]

Today, there is arguably a sliding scale of certainty as regards the extent to which various types of non-state actors possess international personality. The spectrum ranges from international organisations at one end, which are accepted subjects of international law,[140] through to 'non-governmental organisations (NGOs),

[136] Hersch Lauterpacht, *Private Law Sources and Analogies of International Law* (Longmans, Green and Co Ltd 1927) 79 (see also 51). Similarly, see Charney (1983a) (n 60) 762 ('there is no systematic reason why non-state entities may not participate in the international legal system'). See also Jan Klabbers, *An Introduction to International Institutional Law* (2nd edn, CUP 2009) 52 ('personality is by no means a threshold which must be crossed before an entity can participate in international legal relations; instead, once an entity does participate, it may be usefully described as having a degree of international legal personality'); and Karavias (n 60) 9–10 (particularly citations at fns 27–28).

[137] See, e.g. Higgins (1994) (n 44) 49–50 (denouncing the 'subject/object' distinction in international law, arguing that '[w]e have erected an intellectual prison of our own choosing and then declared it to be an unalterable constraint' (at 49)). This focus on the participant, by Higgins and other New Haven theorists such as Myres McDougal and Harold Lasswell, is a hallmark of the New Haven approach, and it influenced John Dugard's approach as the ILC's Special Rapporteur on diplomatic protection: ILC, 'First Report on Diplomatic Protection by Mr John R Dugard, Special Rapporteur' (7 March 2000) UN Doc A/CN4/506, para 24 ('[t]he debate over the question whether the individual is a mere "object" of international law (the traditional view) or a "subject" of international law is unhelpful. It is better to view the individual as a participant in the international legal order'); see also Portmann (n 127) 209; Jose E Alvarez, 'Are Corporations "Subjects" of International Law?' (2011) 9 Santa Clara J Int'l L 1, 8; Wouters and Chané (n 60) 229–230.

[138] Portmann (n 127) 2 (see, further, ch 2 therein (for an overview of each of these conceptions) and ch 5–9 (for analysis of each)).

[139] Portmann (n 127) 13–14. As Portmann addresses in ch 9, the latter approach (the 'actor conception') is epitomised by Higgins et al (as discussed already in this section at text to n 137).

[140] *Reparation* (Advisory Opinion) (n 128) 179. See also Klabbers (n 136) ch 3, especially 46–52 and Portmann (n 127) 22. For analysis of theories underpinning international personality for international organisations, see Charney (1983a) (n 60) 760, fn 26.

multinational corporations (MNCs), and individuals whose status under international law is far more uncertain'.[141] The issue of international personality for corporations, in particular, is marked by a lack of consensus.[142] This study has sympathy with Lowe's view of corporations as 'hybrids, with features of both subjects and objects'.[143] On this basis, 'they are best approached by looking at the ways in which corporations function in particular contexts'.[144]

Significant as the debate concerning international personality of non-state actors continues to be, more detailed engagement with it is beyond the scope of this book. For a corporation to constitute an international legal person, it must have capacity to incur obligations at international law. However, it is important to recognise that these two issues are 'not identical'.[145] As Karavias emphasises, '[t]he question of the applicability of international law to the corporation is not to be equated with the question of its personality under international law'.[146]

In order to assess the impact of private actor activity on the deep seabed mining regime, this book need not determine conclusively if such actors have international legal personality. Rather, the relevant question for this study must be framed more narrowly: to what extent does the deep seabed mining regime create rights and obligations directly upon corporate entities?[147] Although this issue is a necessary

[141] Noortmann, Reinisch and Ryngaert (n 56) 2; see also Charney (1983a) (n 60) 760–761. For the argument that a paradigm shift is occurring and individuals are now supplanting states as the primary subject in international law, see Anne Peters, *Beyond Human Rights – The Legal Status of the Individual in International Law* (CUP 2016); see also Parlett (n 28). On the argument that international investment law provides investors with 'at least some degree of international legal personality' see August Reinisch, 'Investors' in Math Noortmann, August Reinisch and Cedric Ryngaert (eds), *Non-state Actors in International Law* (Hart Publishing 2015) 260 (and citations at fns 38–39).

[142] For an overview of the 'heated debate' concerning international personality of corporations, see Karavias (n 60) 1; Merja Pentikäinen, 'Changing International "Subjectivity" and Rights and Obligations under International Law – Status of Corporations' (2012) 8 Utrecht L Rev 145, 147; Wouters and Chané (n 60) 228–230. See also Charney (1983a) (n 60) 753 (fns 8–10 and accompanying text) and 762 (citing evidence that transnational corporations 'have had international legal personality and have participated in the international legal system for some time'). For an extensive listing of leading literature on this topic, see Noortmann, Reinisch and Ryngaert (n 56) 1, fns 1–2. See also American Law Institute, *Restatement of the Law, Third: The Foreign Relations Law of the United States*, vol 1 (1987), Introductory Note ('[i]n principle ... individuals and private juridical entities can have any status, capacity, rights, or duties given them by international law or agreement, and increasingly individuals and private entities have been accorded such aspects of personality in varying measures').

[143] Lowe (n 77) 26.

[144] Lowe (n 77) 26; see also 38.

[145] Karavias (n 60) 7.

[146] Karavias (n 60) 7.

[147] Notably, adopting an approach to international personality focusing on rights and obligations that an entity possesses under international law, instead of the form and nature of that entity, is akin to what Portmann styles as the 'formal conception' of legal personality: Portmann (n 127) ch 8. International courts and tribunals have endorsed this conception when determining direct effect of treaties on individuals (including corporations): Portmann, 197ff citing the ICJ's approach in *LaGrand* and *Avena* and, in the ICSID context, analysing *Amco v Indonesia*: see *LaGrand Case (Germany v United States of America)* (Judgment) [2001] ICJ Rep 466; *Avena and other Mexican Nationals (Mexico v United States of America)* (Judgment) [2004] ICJ Rep 12; *Amco Asia Corporation and others v Republic of Indonesia* (Award on Merits) ICSID Case No ARB/81/1 (5 June 1990). While acknowledging the evolving terms of this broader debate, it is beyond the scope of this book to take a definitive position on the correct conception for international personality.

precursor to a determination of international legal personality, it is a line of enquiry in its own right, and this book will deal with it as such. Other commentators have adopted a similarly defined frame of analysis when addressing comparable issues.[148] As noted by Karavias, this type of approach may reflect a broader shift within international discourse towards a functional assessment of activities of corporations on the international stage.[149] A key advantage of such an approach is that it prevents analysis from faltering at the first hurdle.[150] In keeping with this book's basis of enquiry, Section 1.2.4 will provide a preliminary evaluation of the extent to which corporate entities may benefit from rights and incur obligations under international law.

1.2.4 Initial Analysis of the Necessary Conditions for Corporate Rights and Obligations under International Law

Although corporations are increasingly active on the international plane, there is 'ambivalence' concerning this interaction, with the international legal system '[continuing] to approach the question of corporate obligations in a piecemeal fashion'.[151] Nevertheless, as this section will address, corporate actors can be subject to rights and obligations under international law in certain circumstances.

Corporations are perhaps closer to the form of a state than to that of an individual, in terms of structure and power.[152] However, there is more overlap between the treatment of the status of individuals and corporations within international legal discourse.[153] There is growing consensus that individuals and corporations may possess rights under international law,[154] and that these rights are not held merely as beneficiaries of their home state.[155] This has been most evident in fields

[148] See, e.g. Alvarez (n 137) 31 (Alvarez argues strongly that '[i]nternational lawyers should spend their time addressing which international rules apply to corporations rather than whether corporations are or are not "subjects" of international law' (at 31); he dismisses protracted debates on personality or subjecthood for corporations as 'mislead[ing]' (at 34) and 'at best a distraction' (at 3)); similarly, see Lowe (n 77) 24, 26; Karavias (n 60) 7; Wouters and Chané (n 60) 230.

[149] Karavias (n 60) 2.

[150] For example, as emphasised by Wouter and Chané, to focus solely on international personality of corporations excludes valuable analysis of the extent to which such entities are in fact participating on the international plane: Wouter and Chané ((n 60) 250–251).

[151] Karavias (n 60) 6.

[152] Vázquez (n 69) 944, 957; Karavias (n 60) 2, 7.

[153] Karavias (n 60) 7 ('no distinction has been drawn in theory between the corporation and the individual in the context of rights and obligations derived from international law. It could be argued that the individual-based analysis should *a fortiori* apply to the corporation'. (citations omitted)).

[154] See, e.g. the ICJ's finding in *LaGrand* (n 147, para 77) that Article 36(1)(b) of the Vienna Convention on Diplomatic Relations (opened for signature 18 April 1961, entered into force 24 April 1964, 500 UNTS 95) 'creates individual rights' (affirmed by the ICJ in *Avena* (n 147) para 40). See also Higgins (1994) (n 44) 53–54; Steven R Ratner, 'Corporations and Human Rights: A Theory of Legal Responsibility' (2001) 111 Yale LJ 443, 488; Vázquez (n 69) 932; Alvarez (n 137) 31; Pentikäinen (n 142) 148; Wouters and Chané (n 60) 230 and literature cited at fn 42 therein.

[155] For example, contrast PCIJ approach in *Mavrommatis Palestine Concessions (Greece v United Kingdom)* (Jurisdiction) [1924] PCIJ Rep Series A No 2, 12, setting forth the famous *Mavrommatis*

such as international human rights law, international humanitarian law and international investment law.[156]

More divisive and conceptually challenging is the issue of whether corporations (or individuals) can be the subject of obligations under international law. Wouters and Chané exemplify what they describe as the 'prevailing view' that corporations do not have binding obligations under international law.[157] However, although it is evident that 'for the most part, the obligations imposed by international law are obligations of states',[158] there are certain circumstances in which international law may impose obligations on corporations directly. Regulation of non-state actors under international law may be 'far less common', but there is 'no conceptual obstacle to an agreement among states to impose obligations directly on private parties'.[159] That being said, some commentators, engaging with a 'voluntaristic' conception of international law, have questioned whether international law can legitimately bind entities which do not have a role in the law-creation process.[160] However, this conception does not hold: although to some extent international law rests on a 'consensualist paradigm, there are universally accepted examples of international legal norms binding on entities which did not consent to them'.[161]

In this regard, it is important firstly to distinguish between 'direct' and 'indirect' obligations.[162] Most frequently, an international norm which addresses non-state actor conduct will do so by indirect means. Before an indirect obligation will bind

formula ('[b]y taking up the case of one of its subjects and by resorting to diplomatic action or international judicial proceedings on his behalf, a State is in reality asserting its own rights'), with ICSID decisions rejecting the diplomatic protection paradigm in the investment law context (e.g. *El Paso Energy International Company v Argentine Republic* (Award) ICSID Case No ARB/03/15 (31 October 2011). See, further, Douglas (2009) (n 98) 32–35; Reinisch (n 141) 261; Portmann (n 127) 204.

[156] For analysis of corporate rights in fields of international human rights law and international investment law, see Wouters and Chané (n 60) 230–236. On international investment law rights, see also Reinisch (n 141) 260–263.

[157] Wouters and Chané (n 60) 236 (see also fn79 citations and further analysis at 251).

[158] Vázquez (n 69) 932.

[159] Vázquez (n 69) 932 and 930, respectively; Vázquez admits (at 930) that although there may be no 'conceptual challenge' to direct corporate obligations under international law, on the basis of the current international legal system, there remain significant challenges for implementation and enforcement of such obligations.

[160] cf Anthea Roberts and Sandesh Sivakumaran, 'Lawmaking by Nonstate Actors: Engaging Armed Groups in the Creation of International Humanitarian Law' (2012) 37 Yale J Int'l L 107, 109, 112–113, 122; Peters (n 141) 51–54, 72–74.

[161] Marko Milanovic, 'Is the Rome Statute Binding on Individuals? (And Why We Should Care)' (2011) 9 JICJ 25, 39. Evaluation of this strand of analysis is beyond the scope of this book. For arguments that non-state actors may play a role in the creation of international law, see, e.g. Anthony Clark Arend, *Legal Rules and International Society* (OUP 1999) 176–177; Robert McCorquodale, 'An Inclusive International Legal System' (2004) 17 LJIL 477, 479–480; and, generally, Christiana Ochoa, 'The Individual and Customary International Law Formation' (2007) 48 Va J Int'l L 119; Roberts and Sivakumaran (n 160). cf Clapham (2006) (n 55) 28 (arguing for broad international law rights and obligations for non-state actors, but stopping short of recognising a role for them in the law-creation process); and Parlett (n 28) 371 (arguing that '[i]ndividuals have no capacities to enter into treaties, or to create or to contribute to the creation of customary international law').

[162] See, generally, Vázquez (n 69).

non-state actors, the state that is the primary addressee of the obligation must take steps at the domestic level to implement and enforce the obligation vis-à-vis non-state actors within its jurisdiction.[163] Nevertheless, 'the existence of a corporate obligation under international law is theoretically conceivable'.[164] Although less common, international law does not preclude the possibility of a direct obligation upon corporate conduct.

What conditions must be present for an international norm to regulate a corporate entity directly? Identifying direct obligations upon corporate conduct 'is not an easy task'.[165] Such an evaluation should be undertaken on a case-by-case basis. Karavias distils the identification of direct corporate obligations at international law down to three essential elements, which are instructive here.[166] First, one must be able to point to an international law rule that regulates corporate conduct directly, without the need for resort to municipal legislation.[167] As this book will consider in more detail subsequently, the underlying international law rule may take various forms, such as treaty or customary law,[168] or other means, such as 'internationalised functional contracts'.[169]

The second element is, in many respects, a flipside of the first. With obligation comes responsibility for violation. As emphasised by Karavias, '[i]nternational responsibility cannot be separated from the international obligation'.[170] In the event

[163] Vázquez (n 69) 932–936. See also Ratner (n 154) 488 (regarding the indirect obligations which international law has imposed on corporations 'by prescribing international labor law, environmental law, anti-corruption law, and economic sanctions'). Such 'indirect' obligations are beyond this book's scope of analysis; this book will not engage in consideration of domestic application and incorporation of the Convention's deep seabed mining regime.

[164] Karavias (n 60) 6; see also Ratner (n 154) 488 ('[i]f states and international organizations can accept rights and duties of corporations in some areas, there is no theoretical bar to recognizing duties more broadly'); see, further, Harold Hongju Koh, 'Separating Myth from Reality About Corporate Responsibility Litigation' (2004) 7 J Int'l Econ Law 263, 265 ('[i]f corporations have rights under international law, by parity of reasoning, they must have duties as well').

[165] Vázquez (n 69) 940.

[166] Karavias (n 60) 11–15. cf Peters (n 141) 113 (arguing, in the context of direct international law obligations for individuals, that two conditions must be satisfied: first, 'a need for global regulation in that regard' and, second, respect for the principle of legality).

[167] Karavias (n 60) 11–13. This echoes Vázquez's insistence that a norm which requires domestic implementation before it regulates corporate conduct is an indirect rather than direct obligation: Vázquez (n 69) 940. However, Karavias urges terminological caution, emphasising that so-called 'indirect' corporate obligations are merely obligations upon states alone to regulate conduct of private actors; therefore, indirect obligations remain 'typical obligations binding on States according to the traditional international law doctrine': Karavias (n 60) 12. They are wholly distinct from direct obligations that bind corporate entities without recourse to municipal law. In order for an obligation to directly regulate corporate conduct, it must be of the latter variety.

[168] This book will assess the extent to which UNCLOS imposes direct treaty/customary obligations upon corporate actors, in Chapter 5, Section 5.3.

[169] On 'internationalised functional contracts' as a means of imposing direct obligations on corporations, see, generally, Karavias (n 60) ch IV. The present book will consider this medium in the deep seabed mining context in Chapter 4, Section 4.3.

[170] Karavias (n 60) 144, citing B Graefrath, 'Responsibility and Damages Caused: Relationship Between Responsibility and Damages' (1984) 185 RdC 9, 21.

that a corporate entity commits a wrongful act or omission that violates a rule of international law applicable to it, such violation must engage the international legal responsibility of that corporation.[171]

This second condition is consistent with one of the underpinnings of the international legal system: that an internationally wrongful act attracts international responsibility.[172] The principle of international responsibility has been applied to international organisations,[173] and to armed opposition groups.[174] Karavias takes this further, submitting that 'it is properly applicable to all subjects of international obligations'.[175] As Karavias argues convincingly, the existence of corporate obligations under international law must go hand in hand with the attribution of international responsibility in the event of breach. Indeed, as the ILC has noted, '[i]t may be that the notion of responsibility for wrongful conduct is a basic element in the possession of international legal personality'.[176] To restate this from the perspective of obligations (rather than personality), if a corporation is subject directly to international obligations, it is axiomatic that, in the event of a breach of those obligations attributable to that corporation, the corporation is internationally responsible. If such circumstances are present, the second element for the existence of corporate obligations under international law is satisfied.

Finally, the corporate entity's responsibility should be capable of being implemented pursuant to the application of international law.[177] Karavias also describes this element as 'the standing of corporations before international dispute settlement bodies'.[178] To similar effect, Vázquez notes that establishment

[171] Karavias (n 60) 14–15, 143–144.

[172] For the customary law formulation of this principle as regards responsibility of states, see ILC, 'State Responsibility – Text of the Draft Articles on Responsibility of States for Internationally Wrongful Acts' in 'Report of the International Law Commission on the Work of its 53rd Session' (23 April to 1 June and 2 July to 10 August 2001) UN Doc A/56/10, art 1.

[173] See, generally, ILC, 'Text of the Draft Articles on the Responsibility of International Organizations' in 'Report of the International Law Commission on the Work of its 63rd Session' (26 April to 3 June and 4 July to 12 August 2011) UN Doc A/66/10.

[174] Leisbeth Zegveld, *Accountability of Armed Opposition Groups in International Law* (CUP 2002) 133. See also Veronika Bílková, 'Armed Opposition Groups and Shared Responsibility' (2015) 62 NILR 69; Jordan J Paust, 'Responsibilities of Armed Opposition Groups and Corporations for Violations of International Law and Possible Sanctions' in Noemi Gal-Or, Cedric Ryngaert and Math Noortmann (eds), *Responsibilities of the Non-state Actor in Armed Conflict and the Market Place* (Brill 2015).

[175] Karavias (n 60) 14. See also Ratner (n 154) 492–496 (focusing on human rights law, and arguing for a form of corporate responsibility under international law on the basis of the existing general international law of responsibility); cf Alvarez (n 137) 24–26 (for conceptual analysis of implications of extending 'personhood' to corporations in terms of state responsibility rules). See also Peters (n 141) ch 5 (on international responsibility of the individual).

[176] ILC, 'State Responsibility – Draft Commentaries' in 'Report of the International Law Commission on the Work of its 53rd Session' (23 April to 1 June and 2 July to 10 August 2001) UN Doc A/56/10 (*ILC Commentaries*) 34. This takes us back full circle to issues of international personality: on which, see Section 1.2.3.

[177] Karavias (n 60) 15.

[178] Karavias (n 60) 118, 156.

of an international enforcement mechanism against a non-state actor is a clear indication that a direct obligation of international law applies to that actor.[179] However, as Vázquez cautions, '[s]cholars have stressed … that the absence of such a mechanism does not necessarily establish the opposite'.[180] Karavias initially frames this final element as a 'condition' that has to be met for the existence of a corporate obligation under international law.[181] However, he later refers to the characterisation of a dispute as 'international' merely as good 'evidence' of the international status of the underlying corporate obligation.[182] In doing so, he points to various factors that should be taken into account in this regard, including whether the corporation has direct rights of access to international dispute settlement fora, and whether the law applicable to the dispute is international law.[183]

Broadly consistent with the approaches of Karavias and Vázquez, the present author submits that the ability to use international law to enforce corporate responsibility constitutes overwhelming proof of the international nature of the underlying corporate obligation. However, one must be careful not to assume that the converse is automatically true. To do so, and to assume that lack of ability to enforce corporate responsibility at international law negates the existence of a corporate obligation under international law, would be to give credence to 'the realist charge that international law is not really law, because it cannot be enforced'.[184] If the existence of international obligation is rendered contingent on the existence of international mechanisms for enforcement, the international legal system, as we know it, would collapse.[185] Therefore, while Karavias's final element – enforcement of corporate responsibility via international law – is good evidence of the international character of the underlying corporate obligation, the lack of enforcement mechanisms is not determinative.[186]

[179] Vázquez (n 69) 940.

[180] Vázquez (n 69) 940 (see citations therein).

[181] Karavias (n 60) 16.

[182] Karavias (n 60) 156.

[183] Karavias (n 60) 156.

[184] Koh (1996–7) (n 44) 2602 (see also citations therein).

[185] On the dangers of making the existence of an international norm coterminous with the availability of enforcement mechanisms, see Higgins (1994) (n 44) 53 (where she notes wryly that '[a]s international lawyers, all too familiar with the realities of power, we have long had a vested interest in rejecting the Austinian and Kelsenian precept of the dependence of international law upon the existence of an effective sanction').

[186] Similarly, when assessing the extent to which international law imposes responsibility on corporations, Ratner advocates a careful approach, to avoid 'confus[ing] the existence of responsibility with the mode of implementing it': Ratner (n 154) 481. See also ILC Commentaries (n 176) 117 ('State responsibility arises under international law independently of its invocation by another State' and, in order to invoke responsibility, 'some more specific entitlement is needed'). See, further, Peters (n 141) 65 (noting that 'the existence of individual obligations (substantive legal level) should be distinguished from their enforceability (procedural legal level). An individual may be subject to an international obligation independently of the possibility and form of enforcement.').

1.3 Conclusion

Now that the scene has been set in methodological terms for this study's analysis, Part I will provide an introductory assessment of deep seabed mining in the Area, and the rise of activity therein (Chapter 2). It will also evaluate the principle that underpins the deep seabed mining regime – the common heritage of mankind – reconceptualising this ideal and breaking it down into its modern-day components (Chapter 3).

PART I

UNCHARTED WATERS – DEEP SEABED MINING OF THE COMMON HERITAGE OF MANKIND BY CORPORATE ACTORS

[A]ll of us have in our veins the exact same percentage of salt in our blood that exists in the ocean, and, therefore, we have salt in our blood, in our sweat, in our tears. We are tied to the ocean. And when we go back to the sea, whether it is to sail or to watch it, we are going back from whence we came.

(John F Kennedy, 'Remarks at the America's Cup Dinner Given by the Australian Ambassador' (Newport, Rhode Island, 14 September 1962))

Introduction to Part I

Part I will provide the essential toolbox for this study's enquiry, by evaluating both the parameters of deep seabed mining and the rise of such mining activities by non-state actors, including corporations, in the Area, (Chapter 2) and the vital role of the common heritage concept in the deep seabed mining context (Chapter 3). Against this backdrop, the remainder of the study will critically assess the concept of the common heritage of mankind in deep seabed mining, and the extent to which corporate mining activities may jeopardise it, or assist in its achievement.

2
The Deep Seabed beyond National Jurisdiction and the Rise of Mining Activities within it by Non-state Actors

In order to assess the growth in mining activities in the Area, by corporate entities in particular, one must firstly understand the scope of the deep seabed beyond national jurisdiction, the types of mineral resources that it contains, the likely viability of deep seabed mining and the current extent of mining activities. This chapter addresses each of these issues, incorporating scientific, geological and technological analysis, where appropriate, to place deep seabed mining in its broader context.[1] The following four sections will answer these questions, in turn: where is the deep seabed (Section 2.1)? What mineral resources can be found there (Section 2.2)? Why is the presence of these minerals important, both in terms of the industry prospects and the environmental challenges (Section 2.3)? And, finally, to what extent are activities already being undertaken in the deep seabed (Section 2.4)?

2.1 The Scope of the Deep Seabed beyond National Jurisdiction

The deep seabed is composed of 'the sea-bed and ocean floor and subsoil thereof, beyond the limits of national jurisdiction'.[2] To assess the extent of the Area, one must understand the scope of national jurisdiction. UNCLOS provides that national jurisdiction extends through a series of maritime zones: the territorial sea, the contiguous zone, the exclusive economic zone (*EEZ*) and the continental shelf.[3] Depending on the topography of their continental shelves, certain coastal states may be entitled to assert an outer continental shelf going beyond 200 nautical miles (*nm*) from their coastlines.[4]

Throughout the zones of national jurisdiction and the Area, definitions of resources vary. The form of a resource and the zone within which it is located have a

[1] Elements of this chapter are also addressed in Joanna Dingwall, 'The International Legal Regime Applicable to the Mineral Resources of the Deep Seabed' (2018) 9 Eur YB of Int'l Econ L 261.
[2] UNCLOS, art 1(1)(1).
[3] UNCLOS, arts 3 (territorial sea), 33 (contiguous zone), 57 (EEZ) and 76 (continental shelf).
[4] UNCLOS, art 76(4)–(6).

International Law and Corporate Actors in Deep Seabed Mining. Joanna Dingwall, Oxford University Press. © Joanna Dingwall 2021. DOI: 10.1093/oso/9780192898265.003.0003

decisive impact on the applicable legal regime. Within the territorial sea, a coastal state's resources rights are equivalent to those that it exercises in respect of its land territory, with state sovereignty extending to the airspace above the territorial sea, as well as to the seabed and subsoil below.[5] Seawards of the territorial sea lie the contiguous zone and EEZ.[6] Within a state's EEZ, it has sovereignty over 'natural resources, whether living or non-living, of the waters superjacent to the sea-bed and of the sea-bed and its subsoil'.[7]

The continental shelf lies beyond the territorial sea, overlapping partially with the contiguous zone and the EEZ. The continental shelf is composed of the seabed and subsoil extending beyond the territorial sea and forming a 'natural prolongation' of the coastal state's land mass below the sea.[8] Typically, this submerged prolongation of the coastal state's land mass comprises three distinct parts, and each of these parts has different resource implications. First, there is the continental shelf itself: this is an area of abundant sediment in comparatively shallow waters.[9] Second, there is the continental slope, which is where the shelf gives way to a steep descent. Thirdly, and finally, there is the continental rise. The rise is the more gradual descent immediately beyond the slope, which is created by sediment from the shelf and slope tumbling downwards. Taken together, the shelf, the slope and the rise form the 'continental margin'.[10] Pursuant to UNCLOS, the regime

[5] UNCLOS, art 2(2). The territorial sea may extend up to twelve nm from coastal state baselines (art 3). Determination of baselines is critically important, because it is from these baselines that coastal states establish the extent of their maritime zones under national jurisdiction. Default baselines are 'low-water line along the coast as marked on large-scale charts officially recognized by the coastal State' (UNCLOS, art 5). However, subject to certain limitations, straight baselines may be used if the coastline under consideration is 'deeply indented and cut into, or if there is a fringe of islands along the coast in its immediate vicinity' (ibid, art 7). UNCLOS also details the method to use when baselines are measured from reefs (art 6), mouths of rivers (art 9), bays (art 10), low-tide elevations (art 13), archipelagos (art 47), or by a combination of methods (art 14).

[6] The contiguous zone extends from the outer limit of the territorial sea up to twenty-four nm from coastal state baselines (UNCLOS, art 33(2)). Partially overlapping with the contiguous zone, the EEZ also extends from the outer edge of the territorial sea, but spans up to 200 nm from coastal state baselines (ibid, arts 55 and 57).

[7] UNCLOS, art 56(1)(a). As the contiguous zone is subsumed within the larger EEZ, this definition of natural resources applies there too.

[8] UNCLOS, art 76(1). On the concept of 'natural prolongation', see also *North Sea Continental Shelf Cases* [1969] ICJ Rep 3, paras 19, 31, 43–44, 95–96; *Delimitation of the Maritime Boundary in the Bay of Bengal (Bangladesh v Myanmar)* (Judgment of 14 March 2012) ITLOS Reports 2012, 4, paras 428–437; Philip A Symonds and others, 'Characteristics of Continental Margins' in Peter J Cook and Chris M Carleton (eds), *Continental Shelf Limits – The Scientific and Legal Interface* (OUP 2000) 27–29; Ted McDorman, 'The Continental Shelf' in Donald R Rothwell and others (eds), *The Oxford Handbook on the Law of the Sea* (OUP 2015) 185–186.

[9] Michael Pidwirny, 'Physiography of the Ocean Basins' in *Fundamentals of Physical Geography* (2nd edn, 2006) <www.physicalgeography.net/fundamentals/10p.html>.

[10] UNCLOS, art 76(3). In practice, continental margins exhibit significant variance in attributes and features: Chris M Carleton and others, 'The Practical Realization of the Continental Shelf Limit' in Peter J Cook and Chris M Carleton (eds), *Continental Shelf Limits – The Scientific and Legal Interface* (OUP 2000) 270–271. For example, many 'Pacific-type margins' consist only of a shelf and a slope bottoming into a deep trench: Symonds and others (n 8) 29, and see also 25, 31–32.

applicable to what it styles as the 'continental shelf' in fact extends to encompass the entire continental margin (comprising shelf, slope and rise).[11]

A coastal state has inherent sovereign rights in respect of its continental shelf up to 200 nm from its baselines, subject to any competing claims by littoral states.[12] If scientific and technical data verifies that the outer edge of a coastal state's continental margin in fact extends beyond 200 nm from that state's baselines, that state is entitled to an 'outer' or 'extended' continental shelf (*ECS*).[13] A state seeking to establish an opposable ECS must do so by way of submission to the Commission on the Limits of the Continental Shelf (*CLCS*).[14] The CLCS is a highly specialised body of twenty-one scientific experts, and is best described as 'a hybrid: a scientific-administrative institution'.[15] Once a coastal state establishes the outer limits of its ECS, in accordance with CLCS recommendations, such outer limits become 'final and binding'.[16] Currently, CLCS determination of coastal state ECS claims is ongoing.[17] By facilitating coastal state entitlement to areas of ECS, the Convention reduces the geographical scope of the Area by around 30 million square kilometres.[18]

Within its continental shelf, including any area of ECS, a coastal state has exclusive sovereign rights for the purposes of exploring and exploiting its natural resources.[19] In contrast to the position regarding the EEZ, where a coastal state

[11] UNCLOS, art 76(1). In geological terms, the continental shelf does not include the slope and the rise. Therefore, 'the [continental shelf] legal doctrine as it is used today would be better called the *continental margin doctrine*': Symonds and others (n 8) 26 (emphasis in original).

[12] UNCLOS, arts 76(1), (10) and 77(3).

[13] UNCLOS, art 76(1). UNCLOS sets out a complicated process, in Article 76(4)–(7), for determining the outer edge of the continental margin. Article 76(5) permits the line of fixed points establishing the outer limits of the ECS to extend up to whichever is further offshore of either: (i) 350 nm from the coastal state's baselines; or (ii) 100 nm from the 2,500 metre isobath (a line connecting the depth of 2,500 metres).

[14] UNCLOS, art 76(8).

[15] Øystein Jensen, 'The Commission on the Limits of the Continental Shelf: An Administrative, Scientific, or Judicial Institution?' (2014) 45 OD Int'l L 171, 182.

[16] UNCLOS, art 76(8). Notably, a coastal state's right to establish the outer limits of its ECS is an inherent entitlement, not dependent on procedural requirements in UNCLOS, art 76, such as submission of a claim to the CLCS: *Bangladesh v Myanmar* (n 8) para 408. As McDorman explains, 'a State has an inherent right to a shelf beyond 200 nm (where it physically exists), and [UNCLOS] provides a procedural opportunity to establish the outer limits of that shelf that will enhance the opposability of those limits vis-à-vis other States': McDorman (n 8) 192.

[17] Originally, when UNCLOS was drafted, it was anticipated that only around thirty or so states would be entitled to claim an ECS: DOALOS, *The Law of the Sea: Definition of the Continental Shelf* (United Nations 1993) 6; see also Suzette V Suarez, *The Outer Limits of the Continental Shelf, Legal Aspects of their Establishment* (Springer 2008) 234; Helmut Tuerk, 'The International Seabed Area' in Malgosia Fitzmaurice and Norman A Martinez Gutierrez (eds), *The IMLI Manual on International Maritime Law*, vol I (OUP 2014) 278. In fact, thus far, the CLCS has received eighty-eight submissions from various coastal states (including some joint submissions): see DOALOS webpage on CLCS submissions <www.un.org/depts/los/clcs_new/commission_submissions.htm>.

[18] Michael W Lodge, ISA Secretary-General, 'Statement to the Open Meeting of the Commission on the Limits of the Continental Shelf', United Nations (New York, 10 March 2017) 4 <www.isa.org.jm/files/documents/EN/SG-Stats/2017/CLCS-10Mar17.pdf>.

[19] UNCLOS, arts 77(1)–(2) and 81; see also art 82 (pursuant to which a portion of any coastal state revenues generated by exploitation of non-living ECS resources must be distributed equitably by the ISA).

has sovereignty over living and non-living natural resources throughout the entire water column, in the continental shelf, coastal state resource rights are defined in narrower terms.[20] In relation to the continental shelf, the definition of 'natural resources' encompasses only mineral and other non-living resources located in the seabed and subsoil, together with bottom-dwelling sedentary species.[21] These contrasting definitions of natural resources are of greatest import in any areas of ECS (i.e. beyond the 200 nm limit of the EEZ), where only the narrower definition of natural resources applies.

Beyond these zones of national jurisdiction lies the Area, which constitutes the 'common heritage of mankind'.[22] The Area is composed primarily of abyssal plains, usually spanning depths of between 3,000 and 6,000 metres, but it may include other features such as seamounts, deep oceanic trenches, submarine ridges and hydrothermal vents.[23]

When trying to determine the precise extent of the Area, a key challenge is the difficulty in delineating a boundary between the Area and the ECS. Pending final determination of ECS outer limits in any given area, there will necessarily be a margin of uncertainty in establishing such a boundary. This difficulty is compounded by the lack of defined timescales for determination of the Area/ECS boundary,[24] the absence of a formal relationship between the ISA and the CLCS[25] and the lack of dispute resolution procedures to govern this process.[26] One could query whether the boundaries of the Area will ever be fully defined, given that

[20] cf UNCLOS, arts 56(1)(a) (EEZ) and 77(4) (continental shelf).

[21] UNCLOS, art 77(4).

[22] UNCLOS, arts 1(1)(1) and 136.

[23] See overview by Eva Ramirez-Llodra, 'Deep-Sea Ecosystems: Biodiversity and Anthropogenic Impacts' in Catherine Banet (ed), *The Law of the Seabed: Access, Uses, and Protection of Seabed Resources* (Brill 2020) at 44–49.

[24] See, e.g. Robert W Smith and George Taft, 'Legal Aspects of the Continental Shelf' in Peter J Cook and Chris M Carleton (eds), *Continental Shelf Limits – The Scientific and Legal Interface* (OUP 2000) 20–21; McDorman (n 8) 192. See also Erik Franckx, 'The International Seabed Authority and the Common Heritage of Mankind: The Need for States to Establish the Outer Limits of their Continental Shelf' (2010) 25 Int'l J Marine Coastal L 543, 555–556 (critiquing the 'flexible' approach of UNCLOS States Parties to ECS claim deadlines).

[25] Lodge (2017) (n 18) 4 (noting that the ISA and the CLCS work in 'apparent isolation'). See also Franckx (2010) (n 24) 557–558. For example, no formal process is in place to allow ISA/CLCS coordination on issues of delineation, or in relation to disputes concerning the Area/ECS boundary. See, e.g. Jan-Stefan Fritz, 'Deep Sea Anarchy: Mining at the Frontiers of International Law' (2015) 30 Int'l J Marine Coastal L 445, 466–467 (noting that aspects of the ISA's role may exemplify 'a general trend' towards fragmentation or decentralisation of international law, citing specifically the lack of a dialogue between bodies such as the ISA and the CLCS (at 466)).

[26] Lodge (2017) (n 18) 3. For example, there is no formal process by which the ISA can challenge coastal state ECS claims for impinging upon the Area. See John E Noyes, 'The Common Heritage of Mankind: Past, Present, and Future' (2012) 40 Denv J Int'l L & P 447, 467–468; see also John E Noyes, 'Judicial and Arbitral Proceedings and the Outer Limits of the Continental Shelf' (2009) 42 Vand J Transnat'l L 1211, 1239–1240; see further Franckx (2010) (n 24) 554, 560–561. cf Alan Boyle, 'Dispute Settlement and the Law of the Sea Convention: Problems of Fragmentation and Jurisdiction' (1997) 46 ICLQ 37, 46 (fn 23). See generally Erik Franckx, 'The 200 Mile Limit: Between Creeping Jurisdiction and Creeping Common Heritage?' (2007) 39 Geo Wash Int'l L Rev 467.

several states with territorial claims over Antarctica have elected not to submit data to the CLCS concerning the outer limits of their ECS in that region. In any event, the CLCS has indicated that, in light of disputes concerning the Antarctic, it is not permitted to consider parts of the continental shelf appurtenant to Antarctica.[27] Consequently, the boundaries of the Area remain 'fluid'.[28]

However, to put the size of the Area into perspective, it constitutes almost three quarters of the entire global seabed. The 'best estimate' of its surface area is approximately 260 million square kilometres[29] (or around 72% of the total surface area of the oceans[30]). The oceans themselves cover over 70% of the earth's surface.[31] This means that mineral access rights to around half of the globe's surface may fall within the regime which applies to deep seabed mining in the Area. The size of the Area is illustrated in the following figure (Figure 2.1), as the area depicted in white.

In contrast to definitions of natural resources within maritime zones of national jurisdiction, the definition of 'resources' in the Area is narrower again, excluding living resources of any description, whether sedentary or otherwise. For the purposes of deep seabed mining in the Area, the Convention defines 'resources' as 'all solid, liquid or gaseous mineral resources *in situ* in the Area at or beneath the sea-bed, including polymetallic nodules'.[32] Upon extraction from the Area, such resources are classified as 'minerals'.[33]

As the UNCLOS deep seabed regime is not applicable to living resources, there has been some controversy over the extent to which marine genetic resources (materials from marine plants, animals or microbes) form part of the common heritage.[34] In light of this, the UN General Assembly voted, in 2015, to develop a treaty to complement UNCLOS on the conservation and sustainable use of marine biological diversity of areas beyond national jurisdiction (also known as *BBNJ*).[35] Amidst growing realisation of the scientific importance and commercial value of

[27] Commission on the Limits of the Continental Shelf, 'Statement by the Chairman of the Commission on the Limits of the Continental Shelf on the Progress of Work in the Commission' (1 October 2009) CLCS 64, para 77.

[28] Lodge (2017) (n 18).

[29] Michael W Lodge, 'Satya Nandan's Legacy for the Common Heritage of Mankind' in Michael W Lodge and Myron H Nordquist (eds), *Peaceful Order in the World's Oceans* (Brill 2014) 290, fn 22.

[30] BW Eakins and GF Sharman, 'Volumes of the World's Oceans from ETOPO1' (National Oceanic and Atmospheric Administration (NOAA), National Geophysical Data Center, 2010) <www.ngdc.noaa.gov/mgg/global/etopo1_ocean_volumes.html> (the surface area of the oceans is 361.9 million square kilometres).

[31] Eakins and Sharman (n 30) (the surface area of the oceans is approximately 70.9% of the total surface area of the earth).

[32] UNCLOS, art 133(a).

[33] UNCLOS, art 133(b).

[34] See, e.g. Konrad Jan Marciniak, 'Marine Genetic Resources: Do They Form Part of the Common Heritage of Mankind Principle?' in Lawrence Martin and others (eds), *Natural Resources and the Law of the Sea: Exploration, Allocation, Exploitation of Natural Resources in Areas under National Jurisdiction and Beyond* (Juris Publishing 2017); Tullio Scovazzi, 'Article 133' in Proelss Commentary 940–942.

[35] UNGA Res 69/292 (19 June 2015) UN Doc A/RES/69/292 (establishing a Preparatory Committee (*PrepCom*) to make recommendations on substantive elements of the draft treaty text); see also Tullio Scovazzi, 'Negotiating Conservation and Sustainable Use of Marine Biological Diversity in Areas

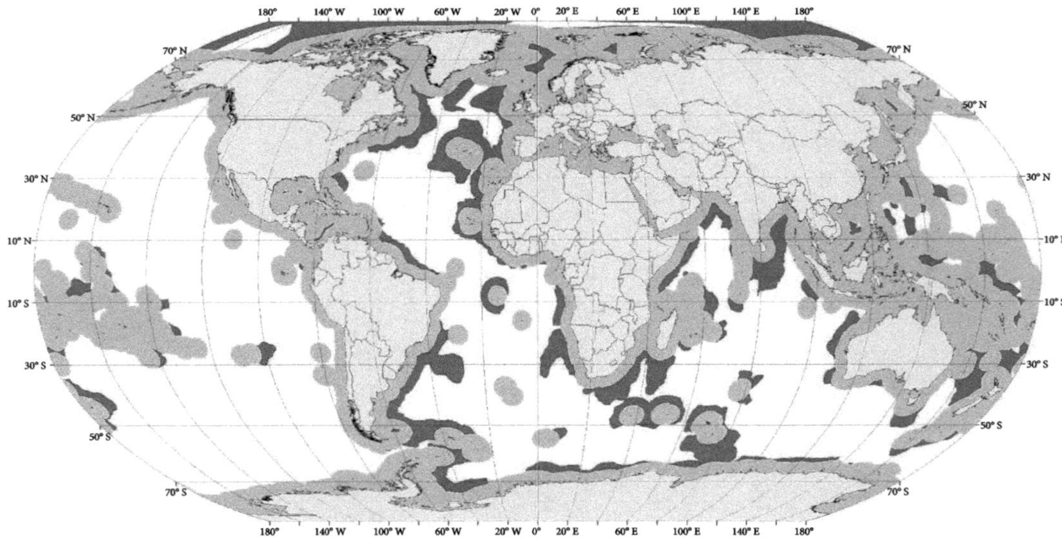

Depiction of submissions for areas of continental shelf beyond 200 nautical miles, as submitted to the UN Division for Ocean Affairs and the Law of the Sea
January 2021

Figure 2.1 World Map Indicating the Approximate Size of the Deep Seabed*

*Graphic by Alan Evans, National Oceanography Centre, Southampton, UK (January 2021).

the microfauna and bacteria of the deep seabed, work on this treaty is under way at present.[36]

Therefore, both the location of a resource and its form are crucial factors for determining the applicable legal regime. If a resource is present within the maritime zone of a coastal state, and if it is included within the definition of natural resources for that zone, sovereignty over the resource lies with the coastal state. An actor seeking to explore for, or exploit, such natural resources must secure coastal state permission. Conversely, mineral resources within the deep seabed fall within the remit of the ISA and can be explored or exploited only with ISA authorisation. The following section will now consider the mineral resources typically present in the deep seabed.

2.2 Mineral Resources of the Area beyond National Jurisdiction

2.2.1 Deep Seabed Mineral Resources

Differences in the underlying geology of the various maritime zones have significant ramifications upon resultant resource distribution throughout the oceans. A product of its history, the continental shelf is rich in organic matter and sediment. Plate tectonic theory explains that the continents moved apart through the process of seafloor spreading.[37] Historically, much of the land which now constitutes the continental shelf was located above sea level. However, the continental shelf became submerged, due to rising sea levels at the end of the glacial period.[38] In contrast, the deep seabed Area was formed as a result of hardening lava, as the continents moved apart.[39] As the Area formed, molten rock from the earth's mantle extinguished most organic matter. Much of the resultant Area is composed of heavy,

Beyond National Jurisdiction: Prospects and Challenges' (2015) 24 Italian YB Int'l L 61. For an overview of PrepCom's work, and relevant documents, see <www.un.org/depts/los/biodiversity/prepcom.htm>.

[36] In accordance with PrepCom's recommendations, the UN General Assembly (*GA*) established an intergovernmental conference on BBNJ: UNGA Res 72/249 (24 December 2017) UN Doc A/RES/72/249. This conference held three sessions during 2018–19. Its fourth session, due to be held in March 2020, was postponed due to the COVID-19 pandemic. The latest draft treaty text on BBNJ is contained in 'Revised Draft Text of an Agreement under the United Nations Convention on the Law of the Sea on the Conservation and Sustainable Use of Marine Biological Diversity of Areas Beyond National Jurisdiction' (18 November 2019) UN Doc A/CONF.232/2020/3. See also UN webpage for the intergovernmental conference <www.un.org/bbnj/>.

[37] The British Geographer, 'Plate Tectonic Theory' (The British Geographer Blog) <http://thebritishgeographer.weebly.com/plate-tectonic-theory.html>; see also Paul R Pinet, *Invitation to Oceanography* (7th edn, Jones and Bartlett Publishers 2014) 54–73.

[38] Pinet (n 37) 97.

[39] Alvar Braathen and Harald Brekke, 'Characterizing the Seabed: A Geoscience Perspective' in Catherine Banet (ed), *The Law of the Seabed: Access, Uses, and Protection of Seabed Resources* (Brill 2020) 22–26.

rock-based material, which is why it sits much deeper than the shelf. Due to the heavier, rock-based structure of much of the deep ocean floor, its resources differ from those present on the continental margin. Deep sea resource types are dominated by metallic minerals, such as polymetallic nodules, polymetallic sulphides and cobalt-rich ferromanganese crusts.

Continental shelf exploration and exploitation activities have progressed to a far more advanced stage than comparable activities within the Area. Although the size and composition of continental margins varies, they tend to yield various non-living resource types. Resources commonly found on the shelf include sand, gravel and placer deposits of various minerals (such as diamonds, gold, ilmenite and tin), together with industrial minerals such as phosphorites.[40] Hydrocarbons, including natural gas and petroleum, may be present on the continental shelf, and may also be found on the slope and the rise.[41]

The presence of frozen natural gas in certain subsea areas is attracting increasing attention. These methane hydrates (or clathrates) are pockets of natural gas trapped in a crystallised structure with a consistency similar to ice.[42] Typically found only in very deep and very cold water, retrieval of methane from gas hydrates is challenging, as exposing them to an increase in temperature causes their cage-like structure to melt, releasing the gas. Such deposits have been discovered in various global locations, concentrated mainly on the continental slope and rise.[43] The resource potential of methane hydrate deposits worldwide is immense. These deposits are 'conservatively estimated to hold over twice the total combustible carbon known from all other fossil fuels on the planet'.[44] Recently, certain states, such as China and Japan, have successfully extracted methane hydrates from locations within their national jurisdiction for the first time.[45]

[40] Victor Prescott, 'Resources of the Continental Margin and International Law' in Peter J Cook and Chris M Carleton (eds), *Continental Shelf Limits – The Scientific and Legal Interface* (OUP 2000) 77–79; ISA, 'Marine Mineral Resources' (2003) 1–2 <www.isa.org.jm/files/documents/EN/Brochures/ENG6.pdf>; Tim Schröder (ed), *World Ocean Review: Marine Resources – Opportunities and Risks*, vol 3 (Maribus 2014) 54, 64–65 ('WOR3').

[41] As Prescott notes, 'continental slopes may offer better hydrocarbon prospects than the rises as they receive more organic matter from the land . . . By comparison, the rises normally receive comparatively low amounts of terrestrial organic matter': Prescott (n 40) 75–76. See also ISA, 'Marine Minerals' (n 40) 1.

[42] Prescott (n 40) 77; ISA, 'Marine Minerals' (n 40) 1; Tim Schröder (ed), *World Ocean Review: Living with the Oceans*, vol 1 (Maribus 2010) 147 ('WOR1') 48–49; WOR3 (n 40) 96ff.

[43] Prescott (n 40) 77; WOR1 (n 42) 152.

[44] Adrian G Glover and Craig R Smith, 'The Deep-Sea Floor Ecosystem: Current Status and Prospects of Anthropogenic Change by the Year 2025' (2003) 30 Env Conservation 219, 229. Similarly, see also WOR1 (n 42) 49–50; WOR3 (n 40) 116.

[45] Matthew Brown, 'Japan and China Successfully Extract "Combustible Ice" from Seafloor in Potential Energy Breakthrough' *The Independent* (London, 19 May 2017) <www.independent.co.uk/news/science/japan-china-combustible-ice-frozen-fossil-fuel-extract-seafloor-energy-methane-hydrate-a7744456.html>. See also Kathryn A Miller and others, 'An Overview of Seabed Mining Including the Current State of Development, Environmental Impacts, and Knowledge Gaps' (2018) 4(418) Frontiers Marine Sci 1, 11.

The overwhelming majority of the deep ocean floor is located within the Area. However, as a result of varying continental shelf attributes, some states have swathes of deep ocean floor within their inherent 200 nm continental shelf entitlement. This is a more common phenomenon as regards various small oceanic islands which possess shallow continental shelves in geomorphical terms.[46] As a result of this, there have been some moves to commence mining for metallic minerals on the deep ocean floor within the national jurisdiction of certain territories, such as Papua New Guinea. For example, Nautilus Minerals Inc (*Nautilus*) had been due to start mining for sulphides within deep waters off Papua New Guinea in 2019. This project, named Solwara 1, would have been the world's deepest mining venture yet, at depths of 1,600 metres. However, this project folded, following Nautilus's financial collapse.[47] Certain other Pacific island nations have not been deterred by this, and are pressing ahead with plans to authorise deep water exploration within their national jurisdictions.[48]

Already, Japan has become (in 2017) the first nation to successfully trial large-scale deep water mining activities, at a depth of 1,600 metres within its EEZ, off the coast of Okinawa.[49] In the wake of increasing interest in deep sea resources, Saudi Arabia and Sudan have revived a project, within their national waters, to retrieve sulphides from deep sea mud on the ocean floor of the Red Sea.[50]

In contrast to mining within national waters, exploration and exploitation for mineral resources within the Area is governed by the ISA's contract-based licensing regime (as Chapter 4 will address). The ISA's regulatory role in relation to deep seabed mining includes the power to develop, progressively, a Mining Code with a comprehensive scope, regulating exploration and exploitation for all forms of mineral resources within the Area. Presently, the ISA's Mining Code addresses exploration activities in relation to three particular categories of metallic

[46] Prescott (n 40) 79.

[47] Ben Doherty, 'Collapse of PNG Deep-Sea Mining Venture Sparks Calls for Moratorium' *The Guardian* (London, 15 September 2019) <www.theguardian.com/world/2019/sep/16/collapse-of-png-deep-sea-mining-venture-sparks-calls-for-moratorium>.

[48] See, e.g. Monica Evans, 'Cook Islands to Grant Seabed Mining Exploration Licenses Within a Year' (*Mongabay*, 17 June 2020) <https://news.mongabay.com/2020/06/cook-islands-to-grant-seabed-mining-exploration-licenses-within-a-year/> (reporting that the Cook Islands plans to licence seabed mining operators to conduct exploration of the deep waters within its EEZ). The position of the Cook Islands can be contrasted with that of other Pacific Island Forum members, such as Fiji, Vanuatu and (now) Papua New Guinea, who support a moratorium on seabed mining within national waters: see overview in A Chin and K Hari, 'Predicting the Impacts of Mining Deep Sea Polymetallic Nodules in the Pacific Ocean – A Review of Scientific Literature' (Deep Sea Mining Campaign and MiningWatch Canada, May 2020) 48 <www.deepseaminingoutofourdepth.org/wp-content/uploads/Nodule-Mining-in-the-Pacific-Ocean.pdf>.

[49] See, e.g. 'Japan Successfully Undertakes Large-Scale Deep-Sea Mineral Extraction' *Japan Times* (Tokyo, 26 September 2017) <www.japantimes.co.jp/news/2017/09/26/national/japan-successfully-undertakes-large-scale-deep-sea-mineral-extraction/#.W9xafOQ5Pcs>.

[50] For further details of this Atlantis II Deep project, which would take place at depths of 2,000 metres, see, e.g. Louise Murray, 'Deep-Sea Mining: Plundering the Seafloor's Minerals' (*E&T*, 18 February 2019) <https://eandt.theiet.org/content/articles/2019/02/deep-sea-mining-plundering-the-seafloor-s-minerals/>.

minerals: polymetallic nodules, polymetallic sulphides and cobalt-rich crusts. As depicted in Figure 2.2, these three resource types occur throughout the Area, although they tend to be most heavily concentrated in certain locations, depending on the nature of their formation.

Polymetallic nodules are potato-sized rock deposits found on the deep ocean floor, typically at depths below 3,500 metres.[51] They comprise manganese, iron and other metals, such as copper, nickel, titanium and cobalt, in varying concentrations, plus traces of other commercially important metals such as platinum and tellurium.[52] Nodules form through an accretion process, commonly involving the gradual precipitation of dissolved metals onto a hard core, such as the tooth of a prehistoric shark.[53] The process of nodule formation happens extremely slowly, with increases in nodule diameter that may be measured in millimetres per million years.[54]

Although nodules are present in various global locations, they are clustered most heavily in four particular regions.[55] The largest of these, the Clarion-Clipperton Fracture Zone (*CCZ*), is a region of the deep seabed approximately the size of Europe, situated west of Mexico and towards Hawaii. Two other nodule hotspots, also within the Area, are found in the Peru Basin and the central Indian Ocean. Finally, there is an area rich in nodules in the central western Pacific Ocean: the Penrhyn Basin, predominantly falling within the Cook Islands EEZ. Taken as a whole, the volume of certain metals that are present within deep seabed nodules, such as manganese, may surpass known volumes of terrestrial reserves.[56]

Unlike nodules, which are present on the floor of the deep ocean, sulphides emanate from hydrothermal vents on the mid-ocean ridge, where tectonic plates meet.[57] In these locations, volcanic activity can produce distinctive chimneys (including black smokers) spewing forth dark billowing clouds of mineral-rich seawater; the minerals then accumulate gradually on the ocean floor as sulphide deposits.[58] Sulphides have also been found within iron-rich deep sea mud.[59] Typically found at depths of anywhere between 500 and 4,000 metres, sulphides contain various

[51] WOR3 (n 40) 63, and also 66 (nodules may be found as deep as around 6,500 metres). See, further, ISA, 'Marine Minerals' (n 40) 2.

[52] WOR1 (n 42) 147; WOR3 (n 40) 66–67, 70; see also Miller and others (n 45) 2.

[53] Glover and Smith (n 44) 229; WOR3 (n 40) 66, 68–69.

[54] For example, Schröder cites a growth rate of 'only about one to 3 millimetres per million years' in respect of certain types of polymetallic nodules: WOR1 (n 42) 146; see also WOR3 (n 40) 68.

[55] WOR3 (n 40) 66–67.

[56] WOR3 (n 40) 66.

[57] Polymetallic sulphides are also known as massive sulphides or seafloor massive sulphides. Consistent with the ISA approach, this book will refer to these minerals as polymetallic sulphides or sulphides.

[58] ISA, 'Marine Minerals' (n 40) 2; WOR1 (n 42) 148; WOR3 (n 40) 82.

[59] Glover and Smith (n 44) 231–232; WOR1 (n 42) 151; WOR3 (n 40) 91; one such occurrence of metalliferous mud lies 2,000 metres deep in the Red Sea (this is the intended target of the Atlantis II Deep project within the national waters of Saudi Arabia and Sudan, as discussed in this section at text to n 50).

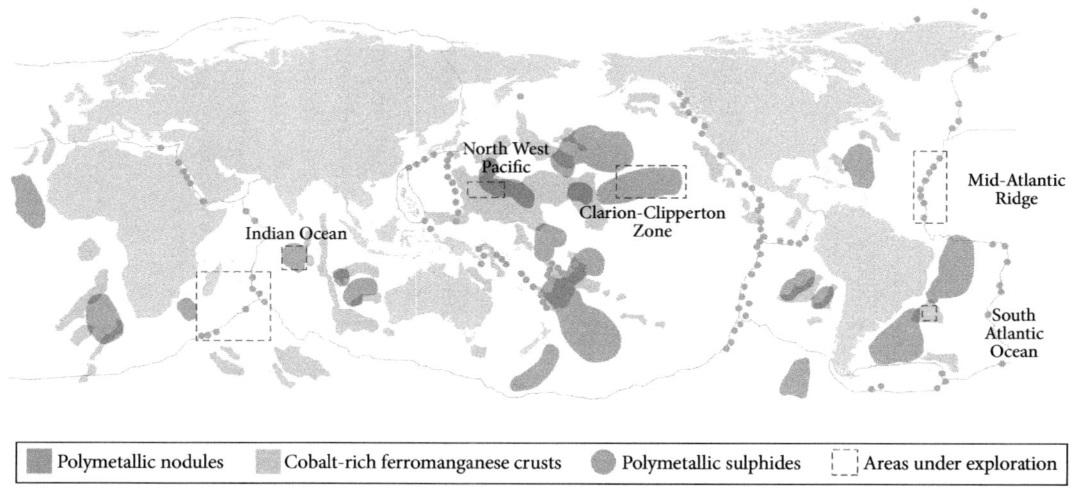

Figure 2.2 Global Distribution of Main Categories of Deep Seabed Mineral Resources (Nodules, Sulphides and Cobalt Crusts)*

*Graphic by the ISA (2021).

chemical elements, including iron, copper and zinc, and may contain quantities of gold and silver.[60] As with the other types of deep seabed minerals, the exact composition of sulphide deposits may vary depending on the location of their discovery.[61]

Cobalt-rich crusts are the final category of mineral resources which the ISA's regulatory regime covers. These crusts may form on seamounts, and rocky outcrops and ridges in the seafloor, and can contain elements such as manganese and iron, together with some quantities of cobalt, copper, nickel and titanium, plus a wide array of trace metals like platinum and tellurium.[62] Found at depths of anywhere between 600 to 7,000 metres (with those richest in resources tending to be located between 800 and 2,500 metres deep), these crusts take many millions of years to form, through a similar process to nodule formation.[63] Cobalt crusts occur globally, but are present in their highest volumes within the Pacific Ocean, particularly in an area, south-west of Japan, known as the Prime Crust Zone (*PCZ*).[64]

2.2.2 Deep Seabed Mining for Rare Earth Elements

Piquing commercial interest is the fact that deep seabed minerals may contain traces of rare earth elements (*REEs*). These are highly coveted commodities: fundamental in the manufacturing of green energy technologies, including solar panels, wind turbines and electric cars. These metals are also essential in weapons manufacturing, and in the electronics industry.

Amidst growing global calls for sustainable energy, and the increasing movement away from fossil fuels, there is an emerging narrative that elements derived from deep seabed minerals could play an important role in the drive to lower carbon emissions. Some commentators have argued that this poses one of the key conundrums inherent within the prospect of deep seabed mining.[65] Delivery of 'green energy' requires sufficient raw materials to produce the necessary technology. As terrestrial sources decline, does the quest for sustainable, clean energy justify the potential environmental impact of extracting these raw materials from the deep seabed?[66] That question may have no straightforward answer.

[60] WOR1 (n 42) 146, 148; WOR3 (n 40) 87; see also ISA, 'Marine Minerals' (n 40) 2.

[61] WOR1 (n 42) 148; WOR3 (n 40) 87.

[62] Glover and Smith (n 44) 231; WOR3 (n 40) 74–75.

[63] Glover and Smith (n 44) 231; see also WOR1 (n 42) 148; WOR3 (n 40) 76; see, further, ISA, 'Cobalt-Rich Crusts' (March 2008) <www.isa.org.jm/files/documents/EN/Brochures/ENG9.pdf>.

[64] WOR3 (n 40) 74–75.

[65] See, e.g. Daniele La Porta Arrobas and others, 'The Growing Role of Minerals and Metals for a Low Carbon Future' (World Bank Group, June 2017) especially at 7-25 <http://documents1.worldbank.org/curated/en/207371500386458722/pdf/117581-WP-P159838-PUBLIC-ClimateSmartMiningJuly.pdf>.

[66] On this apparent 'conundrum', see, e.g. David Shukman, 'Renewables' Deep-Sea Mining Conundrum' (*BBC News*, 11 April 2017) <www.bbc.co.uk/news/science-environment-39347620>;

In recent years, China has benefited from an almost total monopoly on worldwide REE production. During 2009 and 2010, China produced over 97% of the global supply of REEs.[67] However, in 2010, taking its trading partners by surprise, China imposed strict export restrictions on its domestically produced REEs. Due to these export limits, global demand for REEs came to significantly outstrip supply.[68] After successful challenge by the EU, the US and Japan, the World Trade Organisation directed China to relax its export restrictions.[69] Thereafter, the price of REEs stabilised.[70] Nevertheless, the international community remains concerned about the security of the REE supply chain,[71] and the market continues to be vulnerable to flaring inter-state tensions.[72]

Due to these geopolitical uncertainties, investors are increasingly attracted to the deep seabed as a potential source of REEs and other critical metals.[73] As discussed in Section 2.2.1, deep seabed minerals have varying compositions, depending on factors such as location and formation process. Various samples of deep seabed minerals have been found to include traces of REEs. For example, REEs may be

Damian Carrington, 'Is Deep Sea Mining Vital for a Greener Future – Even if it Destroys Ecosystems?' *The Guardian* (London, 4 June 2017) <www.theguardian.com/environment/2017/jun/04/is-deep-sea-mining-vital-for-greener-future-even-if-it-means-destroying-precious-ecosystems>. See also Aline Jaeckel, 'Benefitting from the Common Heritage of Humankind: From Expectation to Reality' (2020) 35 Int'l J Marine Coastal L 660, 674–675 (noting that, in this regard, '[w]hile the jury is still out, some regard seabed mining as a necessary compromise, whereas others consider this choice to be a false one' (citations omitted)).

67 US Department of the Interior and US Geological Survey, 'Mineral Commodity Summaries 2011' (2011) <http://minerals.usgs.gov/minerals/pubs/mcs/2011/mcs2011.pdf>.

68 Justin Rowlatt, 'Rare Earths: Neither Rare, Nor Earths' (*BBC News*, 23 March 2014) <www.bbc.co.uk/news/magazine-26687605>.

69 WTO, *China: Measures Related to the Exportation of Rare Earths, Tungsten, and Molybdenum – Report of the Panel* (26 March 2014) WT/DS431/R and Add.1/WT/DS432/R and Add.1/WT/DS433/R and Add.1, adopted 29 August 2014; upheld by Appellate Body Reports: WTO, *China: Measures Related to the Exportation of Rare Earths, Tungsten, and Molybdenum – Report of the Appellate Body* (7 August 2014) WT/DS431/AB/R/WT/DS432/AB/R/WT/DS433/AB/R.

70 Rowlatt (n 68).

71 Parliamentary Office of Science and Technology, *Deep-Sea Mining* (UK Houses of Parliament, POSTnote 508, September 2015) 2 <http://researchbriefings.files.parliament.uk/documents/POST-PN-0508/POST-PN-0508.pdf>.

72 See, e.g. Sharon Chen and others, 'China Rare Earth Stock Rally Returns Along With US Tensions' (*Bloomberg News*, 31 May 2020) <www.bloomberg.com/news/articles/2020-05-31/trump-s-sparring-with-china-revives-rare-earths-stock-trade> (reporting on the intermittent surge of Chinese rare earth stocks, amidst oscillating tensions between China and the US). See also Henry Sanderson, 'Lockheed Subsidiary Calls for Global Agreement on Deep Sea Mining Code' *Financial Times* (London, 10 September 2019) <www.ft.com/content/e18a3aa7-76d2-429a-b9c8-ec70d24b9700> (describing managing director of UK Seabed Resources Ltd Chris Williams as pointing to the 'need to build mineral supply chains that were less reliant on China').

73 Ian Coles, 'Rare Earth Elements: Deep Sea Mining and the Law of the Sea' (2014) 14 Pratt's Energy L Rep 4, 8–10; Luz Danielle O Bolong, 'Into the Abyss: Rationalizing Commercial Deep Seabed Mining through International Law' (2016) 25 Tul J Int'l & Comp L 127, 134–135. See, generally, Catherine Danley, 'Diving to New Depths: How Green Energy Markets Can Push Mining Companies Into the Deep Sea, and Why Nations Must Balance Mineral Exploitation with Marine Conservation' (2019–20) 44 Wm & Mary Env L & Pol'y Rev 219.

extracted as by-products during the mining of both nodules and sulphides,[74] and cobalt crusts may offer an especially promising source of REEs.[75]

Recent discoveries evidence the wealth of REEs on the deep seabed, both within national jurisdictions and the Area. For example, experts have discovered several sites containing deep sea mud with high concentrations of REEs, by sampling various areas on the ocean floor.[76] Estimates indicate that an area in the Pacific Ocean of only one square kilometre may have the potential to satisfy one-fifth of current annual world consumption of REEs.[77] Another site in the central north Pacific, measuring around five square kilometres, could have the potential to supply almost the entire global annual REE consumption.[78]

Certain states, including oceanic islands such as the Cook Islands, have areas of deep ocean floor within their inherent 200 nm continental shelf entitlement. Experts estimate that the polymetallic nodules present within Cook Islands national jurisdiction (which consist of a relatively high REE content in comparison to other nodules samples) boast 'significant resource potential'.[79] Equally, Japan has detected high concentrations of REEs within its EEZ, near the island of Minami-Torishima.[80] Japan accounts for over half of global consumption of REEs, which are used in its environmental, electronics and car industries.[81] On the basis of the discovery near Minami-Torishima, Japanese scientists estimate that the contents of a single vessel, mining in this area, could yield 60% of Japan's annual REE requirements.[82] Another finding which highlights the REE

[74] James R Hein and others, 'Deep-Ocean Mineral Deposits as a Source of Critical Metals for High- and Green-Technology Applications: Comparison With Land-Based Resources' (2013) 51 Ore Geology Rev 1, 2. See also Jim Hein, 'ISA Briefing Paper 02/12 – Prospects for Rare Earth Elements from Marine Minerals' (May 2012) 1–2 <www.isa.org.jm/files/documents/EN/Pubs/BP2.pdf>; Yves Fouquet and Bruno Martel-Jantin, 'Rare and Strategic Metals' in Yves Fouquet and Denis Lacroix (eds), *Deep Marine Mineral Resources* (Springer 2014) 63ff; see, generally, Sang-Joon Pak and others, 'Rare Earth Elements and Other Critical Metals in Deep Seabed Mineral Deposits: Composition and Implications for Resource Potential' (2019) 9 Min 3.

[75] See citations at n 74; see also ISA, 'Cobalt-Rich Crusts' (n 63) 2; WOR3 (n 40) 74–76 (noting that 'in the southern area of the PCZ, comparatively high elements of rare earth elements are found in crusts').

[76] Yasuhiro Kato and others, 'Deep-Sea Mud in the Pacific Ocean as a Potential Resource for Rare-Earth Elements' (2011) 4 Nat Geoscience 535, 535 (noting that REE-rich mud appears to be concentrated mainly in two regions: the eastern South Pacific and the central North Pacific).

[77] Kato and others (n 76) 535.

[78] Kato and others (n 76) 538.

[79] James R Hein and others, 'Critical Metals in Manganese Nodules from the Cook Islands EEZ, Abundances and Distributions' (2015) 68 Ore Geology Rev 97, 97.

[80] University of Tokyo, Graduate School of Engineering, 'Discovery of Rare Earths Around Minami-Torishima' (*Research News*, 2 May 2013) <www.u-tokyo.ac.jp/focus/en/articles/a_00145.html>. See, further, Yutaro Takaya, 'The Tremendous Potential of Deep-Sea Mud as a Source of Rare-Earth Elements' (2018) 8(5763) Sci Rep 1 (on resource potential of REEs near Minami-Torishima island).

[81] Ambrose Evans-Pritchard, 'Japan Breaks China's Stranglehold on Rare Metals with Sea-Mud Bonanza' *The Telegraph* (London, 24 March 2013) <www.telegraph.co.uk/finance/comment/ambroseevans_pritchard/9951299/Japan-breaks-Chinas-stranglehold-on-rare-metals-with-sea-mud-bonanza.html>.

[82] Evans-Pritchard (n 81).

potential of deep seabed resources has been made within the Atlantic Ocean, on Tropic Seamount, an underwater mountain 270 nm from Tenerife.[83]

Altogether, the volume of REEs within the deep seabed has the potential to exceed global land reserves.[84] Deep seabed mining may prove a tenable means by which to secure a dependable supply chain of REEs and other critical metals, protected from possible geopolitical ruptures. Moreover, some experts maintain that deep seabed mining for REEs could be preferable from an environmental perspective, in comparison to equivalent processes for terrestrial mining of such metals. They claim that the process for deep seabed mining for REEs may be comparatively less intrusive, in that it could impact a smaller area and be achieved without the toxic waste products generated by land-based mining.[85] In this context, there is an increasing focus on the potential to mine the seafloor for REEs and other critical metals, in both national jurisdictions and the Area.

2.3 Prospects for Deep Seabed Mining and Environmental Concerns

2.3.1 Technological and Market-based Prospects for Deep Seabed Mining

At the turn of this century, deep seabed mining in the Area seemed, to some extent, to be 'further off than ever before'.[86] Interest in polymetallic nodules appeared to have 'dwindled to the point where commercial exploitation of these resources [seemed], at best, a remote possibility'.[87] However, the tide may now be turning. Although the challenges to commercial operation remain substantial, it may soon be both economically feasible and technologically viable to extract mineral resources from the Area.[88] Indeed, Michael Lodge, the current ISA Secretary-General, previously described the scale of deep seabed mineral deposits

[83] Tropic Seamount is rich in crusts containing REEs and other elements attractive for use in green energy technology, such as tellurium: Shukman (2017) (n 66). Both Spain and Morocco have claimed sovereignty over this area; see James Badcock, 'Spain Rejects Morocco's Claim on Mineral-Rich Undersea Volcano' *The Telegraph* (London, 23 January 2020) <www.telegraph.co.uk/news/2020/01/23/spain-rejects-moroccos-claim-mineral-rich-undersea-volcano/>.

[84] Kato and others (n 76) 538.

[85] Hein (n 74) 3; Kato and others (n 76) 535; Coles (n 73) 8. On environmental impacts of deep seabed mining more generally, see Section 2.3.2 below.

[86] Michael W Lodge, 'International Seabed Authority's Regulations on Prospecting and Exploration for Polymetallic Nodules in the Area' (2002) 20 J Energy Nat Res L 270, 294.

[87] Lodge (2002) (n 86) 294.

[88] SB/22/11; see also UN Environment Programme (*UNEP*), 'Wealth in the Oceans: Deep Sea Mining on the Horizon?' (Global Environmental Alert Service, May 2014) <https://wedocs.unep.org/bitstream/handle/20.500.11822/8903/-UNEP%20global%20environmental%20alert%20service%3a%20May%202014-2014GEAS_May2014_DeepSeaMining.pdf?sequence=3&isAllowed=y>.

as 'staggering'.[89] As Lodge has remarked, there are 'thousands of years' worth of minerals in the seabed'.[90] By 2050, deep seabed mining of critical metals could constitute 15% of the entire global supply.[91]

Thus far, contracts for exploration relate to three particular types of minerals: polymetallic nodules, polymetallic sulphides and cobalt-rich crusts. Each of these seabed deposits comprise relatively high concentrations of valuable metals as compared to equivalent terrestrial minerals.[92] As availability of land-based metal stocks continues to decline because of rising material consumption, commentators expect that corresponding costs will continue to rise.[93] Recent attempts to identify critical raw minerals that are important for industry and subject to high supply risk have included several minerals available from deep seabed resources. These include cobalt, platinum and REEs (identified as critical minerals by both the EU and the US), as well as manganese, tellurium and titanium (included on the US critical minerals list).[94] In this context, some experts anticipate that seabed metals will increasingly be in demand.[95]

The necessary technology to mine for these three types of deep seabed minerals is at varying stages of development. As sulphides mining in deep waters within national jurisdiction has been on the cusp of commencing, development of the requisite technology is well under way.[96] Polymetallic nodules can, in theory, be removed from the seafloor 'relatively easily' and collected using 'underwater vehicles similar to a potato harvester'.[97] However, the key challenge will be bringing the nodules to the surface of the water in a manner which minimises risks to the marine environment. In contrast, the technology which will be required for miners

[89] Michael Lodge, 'Deep Sea Mining: The New Frontier in the Struggle for Resources?' (*World Economic Forum*, 10 November 2014) <https://agenda.weforum.org/2014/11/deep-sea-mining-the-new-frontier-in-the-struggle-for-resources/>.

[90] As quoted in Greg Walters, 'World's First Deep-Sea Mining Venture Set to Launch in 2019' (*Seeker*, 24 March 2017) <www.seeker.com/worlds-first-deep-sea-mining-venture-set-to-launch-in-2019-2327856967.html>.

[91] See estimates by US Geological Survey, as quoted in Henry Sanderson, 'Electric Vehicles Spur Race to Mine Deep Sea Riches' *Financial Times* (London, 14 November 2018) <www.ft.com/content/00b2e3c8-e2b0-11e8-a6e5-792428919cee>.

[92] Hein and others (2013) (n 74).

[93] UNEP (n 88) 1; Yves Fouquet and Denis Lacroix, 'Study Summary' in Yves Fouquet and Denis Lacroix (eds), *Deep Marine Mineral Resources* (Springer 2014) 5; Parliamentary Office of Science and Technology (n 71) 1–2; WOR3 (n 40) 54–61, 63.

[94] Commission, 'Critical Raw Materials Resilience: Charting a Path towards Greater Security and Sustainability' COM (2020) 474 final; US Department of the Interior, 'Final List of Critical Minerals 2018' (18 May 2018) Vol 83, Issue 97 FR 23295.

[95] UNEP (n 88) 1; Parliamentary Office of Science and Technology (n 71) 1–2; Bolong (n 73) 130–132; Pak and others (n 74) 1; Commission, 'The EU Blue Economy Report 2020' COM (2020) 132 <https://ec.europa.eu/maritimeaffairs/sites/maritimeaffairs/files/2020_06_blueeconomy-2020-ld_final.pdf>.

[96] For example, before its collapse, Nautilus had developed machinery for sulphides mining. See 'ISA Secretary-General gets First Look at Nautilus Minerals Polymetallic Sulphides Mining Technology' (*ISA News*, September 2014) <www.isa.org.jm/news/isa-secretary-general-gets-first-look-nautilus-minerals-polymetallic-sulphides-mining>.

[97] WOR3 (n 40) 66, and see also 71–73.

to extract cobalt crusts is still at the conception stage.[98] Commercial mining of cobalt crusts is likely to pose the most technological challenges. Such endeavours will require cobalt crusts to be 'laboriously separated and removed from the underlying rocks'.[99]

As the technological prospects and market appetite for deep seabed mining both increase, concerns for the marine environment intensify. The following section will outline key challenges which deep seabed mining activities pose for the marine environment.

2.3.2 Environmental Challenges for Deep Seabed Mining

Putting issues of technology and market forces aside, the overwhelming challenge to the deep seabed industry is in environmental terms. One of the most significant features of the deep seabed is its rare and often uncharted ecological life. The deep seabed is home to a vast array of species. The oceans also play an important role in global sustainability, for example in regulating temperature, absorbing carbon dioxide emissions and providing other ecosystem services.

Deep seabed mining faces vehement opposition from various quarters.[100] The Deep Sea Mining Campaign is seeking a moratorium on all deep seabed mining in both international and national waters.[101] Greenpeace also condemns deep seabed mining, highlighting concerns for sensitive and unexplored deep seabed ecosystems.[102] Against this backdrop, the European Parliament has called for a moratorium on deep seabed mining until the marine environmental impacts are understood, and certain major corporate groups, such as BMW, Volvo, Samsung and Google, have vowed to exclude deep seabed minerals from their supply chains until the environmental consequences are clear.[103]

98 WOR3 (n 40) 77; see also WOR1 (n 42) 146–148.

99 WOR3 (n 40) 74.

100 See overview in Bolong (n 73) 141–146 and citations therein.

101 Deep Sea Mining Campaign, London Mining Network, MiningWatch Canada, 'Why the Rush? Seabed Mining in the Pacific Ocean' (July 2019) <https://miningwatch.ca/sites/default/files/why_the_rush.pdf>. On the growing impetus across civil society for some form of moratorium on deep seabed mining, see Deep Sea Conversation Coalition, 'Deep-sea Mining: Growing Support for a Moratorium' (June 2020) <www.savethehighseas.org/wp-content/uploads/2020/06/DSCC_FactSheet3_DSM_moratorium_4pp_web.pdf>.

102 Greenpeace, 'In Deep Water: The Emerging Threat of Deep Sea Mining' (2019) <www.greenpeace.org/international/publication/22578/deep-sea-mining-in-deep-water/>.

103 European Parliament, 'International Ocean Governance: An Agenda for the Future of our Oceans in the Context of the 2030 Sustainable Development Goals' (16 January 2018) P8_TA(2018)0004 <www.europarl.europa.eu/sides/getDoc.do?pubRef=-//EP//TEXT+TA+P8-TA-2018-0004+0+DOC+XML+V0//EN&language=EN>. On recent corporate opposition to deep seabed mining, see Henry Sanderson, 'BMW, Volvo and Google Vow to Exclude Use of Ocean-mined Metals' *Financial Times* (London, 31 March 2021) <www.ft.com/content/e618a555-2d21-4f33-b6b5-46564197f834>; see also David Shukman, 'Companies Back Moratorium on Deep Sea Mining' (*BBC News*, 4 April 2021) <www.bbc.co.uk/news/science-environment-56607700>.

It is beyond the parameters of this book to provide a thorough assessment of the dangers to the marine environment posed by deep seabed mining activities. Various other commentators are already undertaking valuable analysis in both scientific and legal contexts.[104] However, this section will note key risks to the marine environment which deep seabed mining may entail. Deep seabed exploitation, in particular, presents certain common concerns irrespective of the type of mineral being exploited. These common concerns include direct destruction of fauna and habitats, together with marine degradation through plumes of seafloor sediments generated by mining activities, discharge of waste and tailings, and other resultant effects such as underwater noise, vibration and light pollution.[105] A key challenge presented by extraction of all mineral types is the depth at which exploitation activities are likely to occur. The extreme depth of mining activities in the Area will intensify the risks that these activities pose, and hamper rectification of problems, in the event that accidents do occur.

In addition to these common concerns, to some extent the challenges to protection of the marine environment will vary depending on the type of deep seabed resource being extracted.[106] For example, compared to other mineral or natural resource types, polymetallic nodules tend to be spread over a considerable area. Commercial extraction of nodules could potentially lead to destruction of large swathes of the marine environment.[107] Conversely, cobalt crusts may cover a

[104] For scientific assessment of environmental concerns posed by deep seabed mining, see Rahul Sharma, 'Environmental Issues of Deep-Sea Mining' (2015) 11 Procedia Earth & Planetary Sci 204; Ann Vanreusel and others, 'Threatened by Mining, Polymetallic Nodules are Required to Preserve Abyssal Epifauna' (2016) 6(26808) Sci Rep 1; CL Van Dover and others, 'Biodiversity Loss from Deep-Sea Mining' (2017) 10 Nat Geoscience 464; Miller and others (n 45); Holly J Niner and others, 'Deep-Sea Mining With No Net Loss of Biodiversity – An Impossible Aim' (2018) 5(53) Frontiers Marine Sci 1; Pippa Howard and others, 'An Assessment of the Risks and Impacts of Seabed Mining on Marine Ecosystems' (Fauna & Flora International, March 2020) <https://cms.fauna-flora.org/wp-content/uploads/2020/03/FFI_2020_The-risks-impacts-deep-seabed-mining_Report.pdf>; Chin and Hari (n 48). For detailed legal consideration of the balance between commercial mineral exploitation and protection of the Area's marine environment, see Aline L Jaeckel, *The International Seabed Authority and the Precautionary Principle – Balancing Deep Seabed Mineral Mining and Marine Environmental Protection* (Brill 2017); see also Kristina M Gjerde, 'Challenges to Protecting the Marine Environment beyond National Jurisdiction' (2012) 27 Int'l J Marine Coastal L 839.

[105] Sharma (2015) (n 104) 205; WOR3 (n 40) 73; Jaeckel (2017) (n 104) 11–14; Miller and others (n 45) 15–17; Ramirez-Llodra (n 23) 57–58. See also, generally, ISA Council, 'Submission by the Delegation of the Netherlands: Development of Environmentally Responsible Mining Technologies: Towards an Approval Process for Mining Equipment' (1 June 2017) ISBA/23/C/5. For detailed results of EU-funded projects researching impacts of deep seabed mining see, e.g. Ecorys, 'Study to Investigate the State of Knowledge of Deep-Sea Mining – Final Report to the European Commission' (19 November 2014) 93–119 <https://webgate.ec.europa.eu/maritimeforum/en/node/3732>; MIDAS, 'Implications of MIDAS Results for Policy Makers: Recommendations for Future Regulations' (December 2016) 7ff <www.eu-midas.net/sites/default/files/downloads/MIDAS_recommendations_for_policy_lowres.pdf>.

[106] For thorough assessment of potential impacts of deep seabed mining in relation to each resource type, see Howard and others (n 104) 178–275.

[107] See, e.g. WOR1 (n 42) 147 (noting that the projected consequences of excavation of polymetallic nodules 'would affect about 120 square kilometres of ocean floor per year, an area the size of the city of Kiel. Huge amounts of sediment, water, and countless organisms would be dug up with the nodules, and

smaller surface area, but they require a more intensive process of extraction from the underlying rock substrate, meaning that the potential for species extinction may be significant.[108] As the growth rates of both nodules and cobalt crusts are amongst the slowest formation rates of all known minerals, the speed of regeneration of mined areas would likely be extremely slow.

Extraction of polymetallic sulphides poses varying concerns and challenges. In the Area, sulphides tend to be concentrated within smaller areas than on land. On the deep seabed, sulphides typically form on marine features, such as hydrothermal vents and mid-oceanic ridges, which are accustomed to undergoing volcanic and seismic eruptions. Consequently, both sulphides and the habitats around them may be better suited to regenerating within what is often already a volatile environment.[109] Nevertheless, experts urge caution as regards sulphides exploitation, in light of the variety of life forms in and around hydrothermal vents, especially given the importance of the microfauna and bacteria of the deep seabed in scientific and commercial terms.[110]

Perversely, by virtue of the increase in deep seabed exploration, scientists are, for the first time, gaining a fuller picture of deep seabed habitats and ecosystems. Many deep seabed miners are working with the scientific community in order to obtain greater insight into the marine environment of the Area. If commercial extraction of deep seabed minerals does proceed, miners could strive towards developing certain tailored measures aimed at lessening the environmental impact. For example, measures such as incorporating cowls on relevant machinery and installing sophisticated pipe systems may reduce sediment plumes and related

the destruction of the sea-bed habitat would be substantial'). See also Vanreusel and others (n 104) (reporting on lack of recovery of fauna at experimental nodule mining sites in the CCZ, up to thirty-seven years after activities ceased, suggesting that nodule mining may have an irreversible impact on fauna that have habitats on nodules, given the slow rate of nodule growth). See, further, Glover and Smith (n 44) 230–231.

[108] Glover and Smith (n 44) 231 (noting greater potential for species extinction from cobalt crusts extraction, as compared to nodules, 'due to the high diversity and endemic nature of seamount biota ... and because the hard substrate lying under the crust may not be equally suitable for sessile faunal colonization' (citations omitted)).

[109] Glover and Smith (n 44) 232; Ramirez-Llodra (n 23) 56–57.

[110] See, e.g. Ramirez-Llodra (n 23) 56 and citations therein. Recent scientific discoveries indicate that the origin of life may be traced back to tiny organisms which escaped from within hydrothermal vents. The last universal common ancestor (or LUCA) may have been an aquatic microorganism created within a hydrothermal vent, which evolved to survive outside of it, forming the building block for all known life on earth: Nick Lane and William F Martin, 'The Origin of Membrane Bioenergetics' (2012) 151 Cell 1406; see also Ed Yong, 'How Life Emerged From Deep-Sea Rocks' (Nature: News, 20 December 2012) <www.nature.com/news/how-life-emerged-from-deep-sea-rocks-1.12109>. Microbes from vents already play an important role in biotechnology. For example, PCR tests used to diagnose COVID-19, and other viruses like AIDS and SARS, were developed using an enzyme isolated from a vent-based microbe: see Elise Hugus, 'Finding Answers in the Ocean' (*Woods Hole Oceanographic Institute*, 9 November 2020) <www.whoi.edu/oceanus/feature/finding-answers-in-the-ocean/>.

marine degradation.[111] Equally, one means of facilitating habitat regeneration may be to replace minerals removed from the ocean floor (such as nodules) with artificial substrates.[112]

Despite mounting opposition to deep seabed mining on environmental grounds, there is some evidence that deep seabed mining could pose less of a threat than land-based mining, perhaps resulting in a reduced 'footprint' of damage.[113] For example, Nautilus, which prior to its financial collapse was the entity closest to commencing deep seabed mining operations at significant depths, claimed that its intended mining activities would have had the 'potential to significantly reduce social and environmental impacts compared to terrestrial copper mines'.[114] Likewise, DeepGreen, a Canadian mining company, which holds two ISA contracts (through wholly owned subsidiaries sponsored by Nauru and Tonga, respectively), and has an interest in one further ISA contract (through partnership arrangements between its subsidiary and a Kiribati-sponsored state enterprise),[115] has emphasised the perceived environmental advantages of mining the deep seabed rather than the land. It has also highlighted other benefits such as avoiding human rights abuses associated with some land-based operations, like child labour.[116] DeepGreen maintains that deep seabed mining will produce lower carbon dioxide emissions than are generated by producing metals from land ores, and that it will allow for the possibility of generating no toxic waste or tailings, again in contrast to terrestrial mining.[117] However, critics accuse proponents of deep seabed mining of engaging in 'greenwashing', in an attempt to render the associated environmental challenges

[111] MIDAS (n 105) 19–20; WOR3 (n 40) 73; Niner and others (n 104) 5.

[112] MIDAS (n 105) 19.

[113] See, e.g. James R Hein, Andrea Koschinsky and Thomas Kuhn, 'Deep-Ocean Polymetallic Nodules as a Resource for Critical Materials' (2020) 1 Nat Rev Earth & Env 158, 162–163.

[114] Nautilus Minerals Inc, 'Nautilus Minerals' Solwara 1 Project has the Potential to Significantly Reduce Social and Environmental Impacts Compared to Terrestrial Copper Mines' (1 June 2015) <www.globenewswire.com/news-release/2015/06/01/1093475/0/en/Nautilus-Minerals-Solwara-1-Project-Has-the-Potential-to-Significantly-Reduce-Social-and-Environmental-Impacts-Compared-to-Terrestrial-Copper-Mines.html>. Nautilus's findings were based on the conclusions of an NGO (Earth Economics) which Nautilus commissioned to conduct independent analysis on environmental implications of the Solwara 1 project.

[115] For details, see overview of contractors in Appendix 1.

[116] For analysis underlying these assertions, see report commissioned by DeepGreen: Daina Paulikas and others, 'Where Should Metals for the Green Transition Come From? Comparing Environmental, Social and Economic Impacts of Supplying Base Metals from Land Ores and Seafloor Polymetallic Nodules' (April 2020) <https://3421n927z6wq3ktzng37wbqk-wpengine.netdna-ssl.com/wp-content/uploads/2020/04/LCA-White-Paper_Where-Should-Metals-for-the-Green-Transition-Come-From_FINAL_low-res.pdf>.

[117] See, e.g. Gerard Barron, CEO and Chairman of DeepGreen Metals, appearing as a Member of Nauru Delegation, 'Address to the ISA Council' (27 February 2019) 5–6 <https://isa.org.jm/files/files/documents/nauru-gb.pdf> (portraying deep seabed mining as the most sustainable route to obtain metals needed for green energy technology and to slow down global warming, and describing DeepGreen as being 'in the transition business – we want to help the world transition away from fossil fuels with the smallest possible climate change and environmental impact' (at 8)).

more palatable in political terms and call for alternatives to deep seabed mining to be explored fully, including recycling of existing materials, reduction of demand and improvement of terrestrial mining methods, in pursuit of a more sustainable, circular economy.[118]

Environmental controversy notwithstanding, the exploitation phase of deep seabed mining may begin in the coming years.[119] As the ISA's Secretary-General remarked recently, '[a]t a time when some appear to want to enter into an existential debate about whether deep sea mining should be permitted to go ahead or not, we do well to remember that the international community passed that point already many years ago'.[120] In light of this, the following section will provide a brief snapshot of the extent of current activities within the deep seabed.

2.4 Increasing Participation in Deep Seabed Mining Activities

Industry experts remain cautious about deep seabed mining prospects due to the sheer costs involved, together with other factors such as fluctuating metal prices.[121] However, contractors in the Area have already made significant investments, and the industry is showing signs that it may be commercialised in the future.[122]

As of 1 May 2021, the ISA had entered into thirty-one mining contracts, with a range of contractors, for exploration in relation to the three categories of mineral resource which it regulates (nodules, sulphides and cobalt crusts).[123] The ISA approved the latest exploration application in December 2020, which was signed as a contract in March 2021.[124] In recent years, there has been a notable spike in the number of exploration applications and contracts granted by the ISA. As recently

118 See, e.g. Greenpeace (2019) (n 102) 17 (critiquing the manner in which '[t]he deep sea mining industry appears to have resolved to gain political acceptability for its significant environmental costs by framing the industry as essential for the development of a low-carbon, high-tech future'); see also Catherine Coumans, 'Mining the Deep Sea' (*Arena Magazine*, October 2019) <https://arena.org.au/mining-the-deep-sea-by-catherine-coumans/>. For analysis of strategies that corporate actors may use to 'legitimise' deep seabed mining pursuits, see John Childs, 'Greening the Blue? Corporate Strategies for Legitimising Deep Sea Mining' (2019) 74 Pol Geography 102060.

119 SB/22/11.

120 Michael Lodge, ISA Secretary-General, 'Statement at the Workshop on the Draft Regulations for the Exploitation of Mineral Resources in the Area: Policy, Legal and Institutional Considerations' (London, 12–13 February 2018) 1 <https://isa.org.jm/files/documents/EN/SG-Stats/12-13_February_2018.pdf>.

121 Rahul Sharma, 'Deep-Sea Mining: Economic, Technical, Technological, and Environmental Considerations for Sustainable Development' (2011) 45(5) Marine Tech Soc J 28, 28–31.

122 See citations in introduction at n 26.

123 For an overview of the contractors and key details of their contracts, see Appendices 1 and 2, respectively.

124 ISA Council, 'Decision of the Council of the ISA Relating to an Application for Approval of a Plan of Work for Exploration for Polymetallic Nodules Submitted by Blue Minerals Jamaica Ltd' (10 December 2020) ISBA/26/C/27/Rev1; ISA Press Release, 'Blue Minerals Jamaica Limited and ISA Sign Exploration Contract for Polymetallic Nodules in the CCZ' (22 April 2021) <www.isa.org.jm/news/blue-minerals-jamaica-limited-and-isa-sign-exploration-contract-polymetallic-nodules-ccz>.

as early 2011, the ISA had approved only eight applications for exploration; by the end of 2015, that figure had more than tripled. The total area of deep seabed which the ISA has approved for exploration now totals nearly 1.5 million square kilometres.[125] Although this approved area may seem vast, in fact it represents only around 0.6% of the entire deep seabed beyond national jurisdiction that is open to licensing by the ISA.

The ISA has most commonly granted contracts to explore for polymetallic nodules, having entered nineteen such contracts. All but two nodules contracts are in respect of areas of the seabed in the CCZ.[126] The remaining two nodules contracts relate to areas in the Central Indian Ocean Basin and the Western Pacific Ocean, respectively. Of all the mining activities in the Area, nodules exploration has been undertaken for the longest duration. Seven contracts for nodules exploration were due to expire between 2016 and 2017, having reached the end of their respective fifteen-year terms. In 2015, the ISA adopted procedures and criteria to allow for extension of approved plans of work for exploration.[127] Thereafter, the ISA extended the contracts that had been due to expire, each for a period of five years.[128] With seven contracts due to expire in 2021, the ISA is considering whether to grant further five-year extensions.[129]

The ISA has agreed seven contracts for sulphides exploration. Of these, four concern areas in the Indian Ocean (including areas on the Central Indian Ridge and the Southwest Indian Ridge). The remaining three contracts involve areas on the Mid-Atlantic Ridge, on the floor of the Atlantic Ocean. In addition, the ISA has granted five contracts for cobalt crusts exploration. Four of these contracts concern areas in the Western Pacific Ocean. The fifth contract relates to an area on the Rio Grande Rise, which is located in the South Atlantic Ocean.

[125] This total includes all areas subject to exploration contracts, excluding reserved areas not currently under contract. For a detailed breakdown of the underlying figures, see Appendix 2, which includes size/location of exploration sites covered by ISA contracts.

[126] For discussion of the CCZ, see Section 2.2.1 at text following n 55. As considered further in Chapter 4, Section 4.2.3.3, when considering corporate participation, all ISA contracts with private corporate actors concern nodules exploration in the CCZ (see also Appendix 2 for an overview of these contracts).

[127] ISA Council, 'Decision of the Council Relating to the Procedures and Criteria for the Extension of an Approved Plan of Work for Exploration Pursuant to Section 1, Paragraph 9, of the Annex to the Agreement Relating to the Implementation of Part XI of UNCLOS' (24 July 2015) ISBA/21/C/19*.

[128] ISA Press Release, 'Seabed Council Puts Forward Two Candidates for Election of Secretary-General; Approves Six Exploration Contract Extensions; Begins LTC Election Debate' (18 July 2016) SB/22/9; for the draft decisions by the Council to approve the first six extensions, see ISA Council, 'Draft Decisions' (all dated 14 July 2016) ISBA/22/C/L4–L9. For the Council's approval of the seventh extension, see ISA Council, 'Decision of the Council Relating to an Application by the Government of India for Extension of a Contract for Exploration for Polymetallic Nodules between the Government of India and the Authority' (10 August 2017) ISBA/23/C/15.

[129] For details, see ISA Secretariat, 'Applications for the Extension of an Approved Plan of Work for Exploration Pursuant to Section 1, Paragraph 9, of the Annex to the Agreement Relating to the Implementation of Part XI of UNCLOS' (8 March 2021) ISBA/26/LTC/6.

Various actors are engaged in exploratory activities in the Area, including states, state enterprises and private actors (with state sponsorship). The thirty-one existing contracts are held by the following actors: one international consortium of states (exploring for nodules);[130] four states (holding eight contracts between them to explore for a mixture of nodules, sulphides and cobalt crusts);[131] eleven state enterprises, state institutions or state-controlled corporations (holding fifteen contracts, in total, to explore for nodules, sulphides or cobalt crusts)[132] and six private corporations (holding seven contracts between them to explore for nodules).[133] As noted in the introduction to this book, private corporate actors now hold over one-fifth of ISA mining contracts and, in fact, are conducting well over a quarter of all such contracts (when joint venture activities are taken into account).[134] The trend towards increasing private-sector activity in the Area looks set to expand and continue, given that the ISA's latest contract is with a private corporate actor seeking to explore for polymetallic nodules in the CCZ.[135]

2.5 Conclusion

This chapter has brought vital scientific, geological and technological analysis to bear on the Area's mineral resources. Specifically, it has evaluated the boundaries of the Area in both geological and legal terms, to gain clarity on the physical limits of the deep seabed mining regime. As well as addressing the geographical and geological extent of the deep seabed beyond national jurisdiction, and its common resources, this chapter has analysed the likely viability of deep seabed mining and noted the current extent of mining activities, including those being carried out by non-state actors, especially corporations. As this chapter has demonstrated, the deep seabed mining industry appears to be on the cusp of moving towards commercial exploitation. Within the last decade, investment by private actors in deep seabed mining ventures beyond national jurisdiction has grown considerably. Against this important contextual background, Chapter 3 will now begin to deconstruct and reconceptualise the notion of the common heritage of mankind within the present-day deep seabed mining context.

[130] This contractor is the Interoceanmetal Joint Organization (comprising Bulgaria, Cuba, Czech Republic, Poland, Russia and Slovakia).

[131] These four states are India, Poland, Russia and South Korea.

[132] These eleven entities possess eight nationalities between them, with Chinese entities holding five contracts; French, German and Japanese entities holding two contracts each; and entities controlled by Brazil, the Cook Islands, Kiribati and Russia holding one contract each.

[133] For an overview of these private corporations, see Appendix 1; see also detailed consideration of participation by these corporate actors within the licensing system in Chapter 4, Section 4.2.3.3.

[134] See introduction, text to nn 32–33. See also Appendix 1 (for details concerning state enterprises of the Cook Islands and Kiribati, respectively, which hold ISA contracts performed through partnership arrangements with private corporations).

[135] ISBA/26/C/27/Rev1.

3

The Role of the Common Heritage Concept in Deep Seabed Mining

This chapter will evaluate the backbone of the UNCLOS deep seabed mining regime: the common heritage concept.[1] It aims to determine the common heritage's modern content within the deep seabed mining context. In order to do so, this chapter must, firstly, gauge the lineage of the common heritage within the deep seabed mining context and within international law more generally, while charting the historical developments that led to the common heritage's inclusion within UNCLOS (Section 3.1).

As historical evaluation will reveal, the common heritage concept contained, from inception, a number of central elements that still form the roots of its key features today. On this basis, as Section 3.2 will demonstrate, the modern-day parameters of the common heritage in the deep seabed context can be distilled down to four central components. In light of this, Section 3.3 will establish the appropriate framework for analysis that this study must apply when appraising the impact that increasing corporate activities in the Area are having upon realisation of the modern-day common heritage concept.

3.1 Deep Seabed Mineral Resources as the Common Heritage of Mankind

3.1.1 The Development of the Common Heritage Principle in the Deep Seabed Context

In the late 1800s, the HMS Challenger expedition discovered the existence of polymetallic nodules on the deep ocean floor.[2] Only in the mid twentieth

[1] Throughout this book, the common heritage of mankind will be described interchangeably as a 'concept', 'principle' or 'ideal'; no specific legal consequences should be ascribed from these differing designations. cf Kemal Baslar, *The Concept of the Common Heritage of Mankind in International Law* (Martin Nijhoff Publishers 1998) 2–6. Although some commentators prefer to describe the common heritage principle as the common heritage of *humanity* or *humankind* (see, e.g. John E Noyes, 'The Common Heritage of Mankind: Past, Present, and Future' (2012) 40 Denv J Int'l L & P 447), this book will remain consistent with the UNCLOS regime, which refers to it as the 'common heritage of mankind' (see, e.g. UNCLOS, art 136).

[2] John Murray and Alphonse François Renard, *Report on Deep-sea Deposits Based on the Specimens Collected during the Voyage of HMS Challenger in the Years 1872 to 1876* (Neill & Co for HM Stationary Office 1891).

International Law and Corporate Actors in Deep Seabed Mining. Joanna Dingwall, Oxford University Press. © Joanna Dingwall 2021. DOI: 10.1093/oso/9780192898265.003.0004

century did the economic prospects of deep seabed resources begin to catch the international community's imagination. During the 1960s, the prospective riches of the deep seabed began to seem within humanity's grasp.[3] As technology advanced, the untold wealth of the seabed appeared, for the first time, tantalisingly close.[4]

At this time, the key quandary confronting the international community was how to determine the appropriate international law approach to exploitation rights over deep seabed resources.[5] During this period there were three dominant interpretations of the law, and all of them had the practical consequence that 'the main benefit of mining would accrue to a handful of developed States'.[6] The first of these conceptions was the extensive delimitation approach. This interpretation epitomised the fear of landlocked and otherwise geographically disadvantaged states that coastal states would extend their continental shelf claims continually outwards until the entire ocean was divided between them.[7] This position did not gain traction.[8] This left two other interpretations: the freedom of the high seas (or *res communis*) approach and the *res nullius* interpretation.

The prevalent Western interpretation was the freedom of the high seas approach.[9] The antecedents to this approach hail from private corporate actor activities in the 1600s. Throughout the seventeenth and eighteenth centuries, private

[3] See, e.g. John L Mero, *The Mineral Resources of the Sea* (Elsevier 1965).

[4] UNGA First Committee (22nd Session) 'Speech by Arvid Pardo' (1 November 1967, 3 pm) UN Doc A/C1/PV1516, para 9. For a critique of economic assumptions underlying assessments of both Pardo (ibid) and Mero (n 3), see Surabhi Ranganathan, 'Global Commons' (2016) 27 EJIL 693, 711–713.

[5] Generally, on historical development of the deep seabed mining regime, see, e.g. Martti Koskenniemi and Marja Lehto, 'The Privilege of Universality: International Law, Economic Ideology and Seabed Resources' (1996) 65 Nordic J Int'l L 533, 536–552; Robin R Churchill and A Vaughan Lowe, *The Law of the Sea* (3rd edn, Manchester UP 1999) 224–229; ED Brown, *Sea-bed Energy and Minerals: The International Legal Regime*, vol 2 (Martin Nijhoff Publishers 2001), ch 2; Erkki Holmila, 'Common Heritage of Mankind in the Law of the Sea' (2005) 1 Acta Societatis Martensis 187; Noyes (2012) (n 1) 459–460; Helmut Tuerk, 'The International Seabed Area' in Malgosia Fitzmaurice and Norman A Martinez Gutierrez (eds), *The IMLI Manual on International Maritime Law*, vol I (OUP 2014) 280–282; Jan-Stefan Fritz, 'Deep Sea Anarchy: Mining at the Frontiers of International Law' (2015) 30 Int'l J Marine Coastal L 445, 450–452.

[6] Churchill and Lowe (n 5) 224. On the historical distinction between so-called 'developed' or 'industrialised' states and 'developing' states, which endured until the post-decolonisation era, see Antonio Cassese, 'States: The Rise and Decline of the Primary Subjects of the International Community' in Bardo Fassbender and Anne Peters (eds), *The Oxford Handbook of the History of International Law* (OUP 2015) 53–55 (noting that 'from the inception of the world community until the end of the decolonization process (1970s) there have existed two categories of States, those endowed with full sovereignty (European countries, plus the United States, and later on China, Japan, the Soviet Union, and so on), and those that were subjected to European countries').

[7] Churchill and Lowe (n 5) 224–225. See also Antonio Cassese, *International Law in a Divided World* (Clarendon Press 1986) 379.

[8] Koskenniemi and Lehto (n 5) 538. As assessed in Chapter 2, coastal state ECS limits can extend no further than the underlying geological extent of their continental margins: UNCLOS, art 76(1), (4)–(7).

[9] Churchill and Lowe (n 5) 226; Malgosia Fitzmaurice, 'Third Parties and the Law of Treaties' (2002) 6 Max Planck YB UN L 37, 110.

corporate actors, such as the VOC, led ocean resource exploration and exploitation. The behaviour of these dominant corporate actors shaped and influenced the evolution of international law in this area. Grotius wrote his influential work *Mare Liberum* as a defence of the freedom of the seas, while acting as counsel to the VOC in relation to a dispute concerning the VOC's seizure of a Portuguese merchant ship.[10] The doctrine of freedom of the high seas has applied since that period, and today it is codified within UNCLOS.[11]

During the 1960s, Western states sought to apply freedom of the high seas to the deep seabed. They 'usually presented [it] as giving to the deep seabed the status of *res communis*'.[12] Pursuant to the Roman property law principle of *res communis*, areas of global commons do not belong to any individual state. Rather, '[a]ll states, their citizens, and international legal entities are free to explore, use, and exploit the commons and its resources'.[13] In accordance with this approach, Western states argued that, although no individual state or states could claim title to the underlying deep seabed, all states were free to explore for, and exploit, the deep seabed's mineral resources and thereby attain title to those resources, in much the same way as they could enjoy other high seas freedoms, such as fishing rights. The *res nullius* approach was, in turn, a variant of that interpretation. As with *res communis*, the deep seabed itself was classified as belonging to no individual state or states. However, in a divergence from *res communis*, under the *res nullius* conception, states could acquire title to portions of the deep seabed by occupation through use.[14]

Against the backdrop of decolonisation, entitlement to deep seabed resources became an ideological battleground, split into broadly two camps. In one camp were the industrialised states, favouring freedom for all states to exploit the resources of the deep on a 'first come, first served' basis. In the other camp were the developing states, fighting for a contrary system whereby deep seabed resources could be exploited only for the benefit of humanity. The latter camp were motivated by the realisation that to allow freedom for all to exploit deep seabed resources

[10] Hugo Grotius, *Mare Liberum* (Elzevier 1609); see also Rosalyn Higgins, *Problems & Process – International Law and How we Use It* (Clarendon Press 1994) 129–130.

[11] UNCLOS, art 87 (freedom of the high seas) and Part VII generally. The freedom of the high seas concept was first codified from customary law in the High Seas Convention 1958.

[12] Churchill and Lowe (n 5) 225; see also Baslar (n 1) 40–41; Scott J Shackelford, 'The Tragedy of the Common Heritage of Mankind' (2008) 27 Stan Env LJ 101, 116; Edwin Egede, *Africa and the Deep Seabed Regime: Politics and International Law of the Common Heritage of Mankind* (Springer 2011) 56–60.

[13] Shackelford (n 12) 116 (citations omitted).

[14] Churchill and Lowe (n 5) 225. For comparison of these two approaches in the deep seabed mining context, see Shackelford (n 12) 115–116. See also Edward Guntrip, 'The Common Heritage of Mankind: An Adequate Regime for Managing the Deep Seabed?' (2003) 4 Melb J Int'l L 376, 388–389 (on rejection of *res nullius* in practice).

would not be as egalitarian as it appeared.[15] A 'free-for-all' system would, in fact, preserve deep seabed mining as the domain of the small number of wealthy states possessing the relevant technical expertise, who would be in prime position to carve up the spoils between them.[16] This concern was compounded for developing states that were land-based exporters of metals that were also present on the deep seabed. Such states feared that a boom in deep seabed mining could impact on their economies by undermining their domestic mining industries.[17]

In 1967, in the wake of these growing concerns, Malta's ambassador, Arvid Pardo, articulated to the UN General Assembly the notion that the deep seabed beyond national jurisdiction should be classified as the common heritage of mankind.[18] Pardo's proposal that the deep seabed beyond national jurisdiction should constitute a global commons, regulated and controlled for the good of all mankind, proved controversial and was met with 'some astonishment, if not suspicion'.[19] Notwithstanding the controversy provoked by Pardo's proposals, his common heritage conception met with general acclamation by the international community. During the late 1960s, the common heritage conception quickly began to gain popularity amongst a large swathe of the international community, particularly within the coalition of developing states forming the Group of 77 (*G77*).[20]

Pardo's position was itself a variant of *res communis* (albeit with distinct legal consequences[21]). As with the *res communis* conception set out above in relation to freedom of the high seas, under Pardo's alternative vision, the deep seabed was similarly to be treated as a commons over which no state could claim title. Equally, under either approach, the international community would be free to explore and exploit deep seabed resources. Therefore, both conceptions were 'buttressed ... with communitarian rhetoric'.[22]

[15] Higgins (1994) (n 10) 130–131.

[16] Higgins (1994) (n 10) 130–131; Koskenniemi and Lehto (n 5) 540; Churchill and Lowe (n 5) 225; Noyes (2012) (n 1) 459–460.

[17] Churchill and Lowe (n 5) 223.

[18] UNGA First Committee (22nd Session) 'Speech by Arvid Pardo' (1 November 1967, 10.30 am) UN Doc A/C1/PV1515. For discussion of precursors to Pardo's speech by nineteenth century jurists, see Myron H Nordquist and others (eds), *United Nations Convention on the Law of the Sea 1982: A Commentary*, vol VI (Martinus Nijhoff Publishers 2002) (this volume will herein be referred to as the *Virginia Commentary*) 6–7 (the commentary by Nordquist et al, which runs to seven volumes, provides an article-by-article analysis and drafting history of UNCLOS. As noted by Churchill and Lowe (n 5) at 27, '[i]n view of the relative paucity of *travaux préparatoires* of the Convention and the distinction of the contributors to that series, it enjoys an unusual authority on the subject'). See also Michael W Lodge, 'International Seabed Authority's Regulations on Prospecting and Exploration for Polymetallic Nodules in the Area' (2002) 20 J Energy Nat Res L 270, 271, fn 5; Baslar (n 1) 80–81.

[19] Pardo (1967b) (n 18) para 4.

[20] Higgins (1994) (n 10) 131; see also Baslar (n 1) 82.

[21] On the 'distinct legal effect' of *res communis* and common heritage conceptions, see Egede (2011) (n 12) 56–57.

[22] Koskenniemi and Lehto (n 5) 537.

However, fundamentally, Pardo's construction of *res communis* predicated common use upon common management: deep seabed resources would become 'a property whose uses could be decided only through a supranational decision-process'.[23] This element is captured in Pardo's call for 'establishment of an international agency which will ensure that national activities undertaken in the deep seas and on the ocean floor will conform to the principles and provisions incorporated in the proposed treaty [to govern deep seabed mining]'.[24] From the outset of Pardo's vision of the common heritage, common management of deep seabed resources was a key feature.

Flowing from this is one of the most fundamental aspects of the common heritage principle. On the basis that 'any exploitation of the Area should be collective and regulated', the common heritage concept precludes state appropriation of the deep seabed and also 'excludes unilateral exploitation'.[25] As will be discussed further below, the limitation of unilateral deep seabed mining activities can be construed as a crucial consequence of the common heritage's common management requirement.[26]

Another central strand of Pardo's vision was that the deep seabed 'should be used and exploited for peaceful purposes and for the exclusive benefit of mankind as a whole', with the needs of 'poor countries' to be given 'preferential consideration'.[27] Other key aspects included that deep seabed mining activities should be conducted in accordance with the UN Charter 'and in a manner not causing unnecessary obstruction of the high seas or serious impairment of the marine environment'.[28]

Therefore, from the outset, certain central elements of the common heritage concept were clearly evident within Pardo's vision. For example, as Pardo describes:

> [T]he common heritage concept has five basic implications. First, the common heritage of mankind could not be appropriated; it was open to use by the international community but was not owned by the international community. Second, it required a system of management in which all users have a right to share. Third, it implied an active sharing of benefits, not only financial but also benefits derived

[23] Koskenniemi and Lehto (n 5) 537; Baslar (n 1) 92.
[24] Pardo (1967a) (n 4) para 15.
[25] Egede (2011) (n 12) 57. See also Pardo (1967a) (n 4) para 10(a) (arguing that the deep seabed should 'not [be] subject to national appropriation in any manner whatsoever') and para 14 (calling for a freeze on all sovereignty claims to the seabed beyond national jurisdiction); the extent to which this common heritage element goes beyond a prohibition on unilateral appropriation and prohibits unilateral mining activities more generally will be discussed further in Section 3.2.
[26] Baslar (n 1) 92. cf the *res communis* approach, pursuant to which '[a] territory that is deemed *res communis*, though [it] cannot be appropriated by any State, is nevertheless open to unilateral exploitation by all. In other words, it is owned by none but open to unilateral exploitation by all' (citations omitted): Egede (2011) (n 12) 57.
[27] Pardo (1967a) (n 4) para 13; see also para 10(b) and (d).
[28] Pardo (1967a) (n 4) para 10(e).

> from shared management and transfer of technology, thus radically transforming the conventional relationships between states and traditional concepts of development aid. Fourth, the concept of common heritage implied reservation for peaceful purposes, insofar as politically achievable, and, fifth, it implied reservation for further generations, and thus had environmental implications.[29]

Other leading commentators acknowledge these aspects as forming core elements of Pardo's original common heritage conception.[30] The common heritage ideal, therefore, had a number of clear features from its inception. In order to understand the impact of this common heritage conception within the deep seabed mining context, the following section will briefly place it within its wider context in international law.

3.1.2 Situating the Common Heritage Concept within Broader International Law

To determine the common heritage's implications in the deep seabed mining context, one must also recognise the concept's broader relevance within international law.[31] Proponents have argued for application of common heritage principles to other areas beyond national jurisdiction (such as the moon and outer space), and in relation to certain uninhabited or remote locations (such as Antarctica).

[29] Arvid Pardo, 'Law of the Sea Conference – What Went Wrong' in Robert L Friedheim (ed), *Managing Ocean Resources: A Primer* (Westview Press 1979) 139; see also Baslar (n 1) 81. For a critique of Pardo's speech and its underlying assumptions, see Ranganathan (2016) (n 4) 709–714.

[30] See Mary Victoria White, 'The Common Heritage of Mankind: An Assessment' (1982) 14 Case W Res J Int'l L 509, 535; LFE Goldie, 'A Note on Some Diverse Meanings of "The Common Heritage of Mankind"' (1983) 10 Syracuse J Int'l L & Com 69; Michael W Lodge, 'The Common Heritage of Mankind' (2012) 27 Int'l J Marine Coastal L 733; Tuerk (n 5) 280; Silja Vöneky and Anja Höfelmeier, 'Article 136' in Proelss Commentary 954.

[31] There is a wealth of literature on the common heritage concept more broadly, e.g. see Rüdiger Wolfrum, 'The Principle of the Common Heritage of Mankind' (1983) 43 Heidelberg J Int'l L 312; Christopher C Joyner, 'Legal Implications of the Concept of the Common Heritage of Mankind' (1986) 35 ICLQ 190; Barbara Ellen Heim, 'Exploring the Last Frontiers for Mineral Resources: A Comparison of International Law Regarding the Deep Seabed, Outer Space, and Antarctica' (1990–91) 23 Vand J Transnat'l L 819; Baslar (n 1); Graham Nicholson, 'The Common Heritage of Mankind and Mining: An Analysis of the Law as to the High Seas, Outer Space, the Antarctic and World Heritage' (2002) 6 New Zealand J Int'l L 177; Jennifer Frakes, 'The Common Heritage of Mankind Principle and the Deep Seabed, Outer Space, and Antarctica: Will Developed and Developing Nations Reach a Compromise?' (2003) 21 Wis Int'l LJ 409; Guntrip (2003) (n 14); Christopher Garrison, 'Beneath the Surface: The Common Heritage of Mankind' (2007) 1 KEStudies <www.kestudies.org/wp-content/uploads/2019/06/chrisg_21-144-3-PB.pdf>; Rüdiger Wolfrum, 'Common Heritage of Mankind' in Rüdiger Wolfrum (ed), *The Max Planck Encyclopedia of Public International Law* (OUP 2009); Noyes (2012) (n 1) 447. For helpful overviews of key sources, see Prue Taylor and Lucy Stroud, *Common Heritage of Mankind: A Bibliography of Legal Writings* (Fondation de Malte 2013); Edwin Egede, 'Common Heritage of Mankind' in Anthony Carty (ed), *Oxford Bibliographies* (12 May 2017) <www.oxfordbibliographies.com/view/document/obo-9780199796953/obo-9780199796953-0109.xml>.

However, as the following analysis will demonstrate, reliance on the common heritage concept has been limited outside of the deep seabed context.[32]

The common heritage approach does have some application in relation to the moon. The Outer Space Treaty 1967 designates outer space, including the moon and other celestial bodies, as 'the province of all mankind', and 'not subject to national appropriation by claim of sovereignty, by means of use or occupation, or by any other means'.[33] The Outer Space Treaty further provides that 'exploration and use of outer space, including the Moon and other celestial bodies, shall be carried out for the benefit and in the interests of all countries'.[34]

In 1979, the Moon Treaty developed this further by specifically designating the moon and its natural resources as 'the common heritage of mankind'.[35] In contrast to the ultimate position as regards deep seabed mining, the Moon Treaty did not establish a common management regime for the exploitation of the moon's natural resources. Instead, States Parties to the Moon Treaty pledged to establish an appropriate international regime, at a time when 'such exploitation is about to become feasible'.[36] Within the intended purposes of any such international regime, the Moon Treaty includes 'equitable sharing by all States parties in the benefits derived from [moon] resources', with 'special consideration' for the interests of developing states and states that have contributed (directly or indirectly) to moon exploration activities.[37] Ratification of the Moon Treaty has been limited, especially amongst spacefaring states. Yet, Schrijver argues that 'the agreement is still important because it clearly delegitimises any unilateral action by interested states'.[38]

[32] Maria Gavouneli, *Functional Jurisdiction in the Law of the Sea* (Martinus Nijhoff Publishers 2007) 137.

[33] Treaty on Principles Governing the Activities of States in the Exploration and Use of Outer Space, including the Moon and Other Celestial Bodies (adopted 19 December 1966, opened for signature 27 January 1967, entered into force 10 October 1967) 610 UNTS 205 (*Outer Space Treaty*), arts I and II, respectively.

[34] Outer Space Treaty, art I.

[35] Agreement Governing the Activities of States on the Moon and Other Celestial Bodies (adopted 5 December 1979, opened for signature 18 December 1979, entered into force 11 July 1984) 1363 UNTS 3 (*Moon Treaty*), art 11(1). Although see critique by Lyall and Larsen (demonstrating that the Moon Treaty's common heritage provisions 'pale by comparison' with the Convention's deep seabed mining regime and are 'obscure to the point of meaninglessness'); Francis Lyall and Paul B Larsen, *Space Law: A Treatise* (Routledge 2016) 195.

[36] Moon Treaty, art 11(5).

[37] Moon Treaty, art 11(7)(d); for a critique of the 'complete failure' of this provision to strike an appropriate balance, with the result that '[t]he concept of "common heritage" hinders rather than encourages development' and renders 'future commitment to it by space-faring states unlikely', see Lyall and Larsen (n 35) 196.

[38] Nico Schrijver, 'Managing the Global Commons: Common Good or Common Sink?' (2016) 37 Third World Q 1252, 1257. But see also Jinyuan Su, 'Legality of Unilateral Exploitation of Space Resources under International Law' (2017) 66 ICLQ 991 (arguing that the principle of non-appropriation does not prohibit unilateral exploitation of space resources, and that such unilateral activity is consistent with the freedom of use for common benefit and interests, provided that it does not exclude exploitation by other users or aggravate inequality within the international community); cf Zachos A Paliouras, 'The Non-appropriation Principle: The Grundnorm of International Space Law' (2014) 27 LJIL 37 (arguing that the principle of non-appropriation is the 'Grundnorm of international

Nevertheless, some states, such as the US, have been vehement in rejecting a 'global commons' approach to outer space, reserving the right of unilateral action.[39]

In contrast to this (albeit limited) application of the common heritage concept in relation to the moon, the legal regime for Antarctica does not follow the common heritage approach. Rather, the Antarctic Treaty 1959, while reserving Antarctica for peaceful purposes, including scientific research, and freezing state territorial claims,[40] stops short of 'permanently internationali[sing] the area' or proclaiming it as a common heritage of mankind.[41] By operation of the Antarctic Treaty, state claims to Antarctica are suspended but preserved. However, as Jaeckel notes, the common heritage concept has been employed in certain other contexts, including in the Convention for the Protection of the Mediterranean Sea against Pollution 1976, and in the African Charter on Human and Peoples' Rights 1981.[42]

Wider visions of the common heritage ideal also feed, more generally, into the prevailing notion of the global commons, which includes 'spaces beyond national jurisdictions, essential resources and concerns such as biodiversity conservation and climate change'.[43] Global commons now include 'the high seas and their living resources, the deep seabed, outer space (including the Moon and other celestial bodies), the two polar regions and the atmosphere (in particular the ozone layer and the climate system)'.[44]

space law'); see, further, Lyall and Larsen (n 35) 195, fn 85. See, more generally, Carl Q Christol, 'The Moon Treaty and the Allocation of Resources' (1997) 22 Annals of Air Space L 31; Heim, Nicholson, Frakes (all n 31); Baslar (n 1), ch 5; Guntrip (2003) (n 14); Shackelford (n 12).

[39] US President, 'Executive Order 13914 of April 6, 2020; Encouraging International Support for the Recovery and Use of Space Resources' (10 April 2020) Vol 85, Issue 70 FR 20381.

[40] Antarctic Treaty (opened for signature 1 December 1959, entered into force 23 June 1961) 402 UNTS 71, arts I (peaceful purposes), II (freedom of scientific investigation) and IV (reserving state territorial claims in relation to Antarctica).

[41] Gerhard Hafner, 'The Division of the Commons? The Myth of the Commons: Divide or Perish' in H Hestermeyer and others (eds), *Law of the Sea Dialogue* (Springer 2011). See also Federica Mucci and Fiammetta Borgia, 'The Legal Regime of the Antarctic' in Malgosia Fitzmaurice and Norman A Martinez Gutierrez (eds), *The IMLI Manual on International Maritime Law*, vol I (OUP 2014); Heim, Nicholson, Frakes (all n 31); Baslar (n 1) ch 7; Guntrip (2003) (n 14); Shackelford (n 12); Schrijver (n 38).

[42] Aline L Jaeckel, *The International Seabed Authority and the Precautionary Principle – Balancing Deep Seabed Mineral Mining and Marine Environmental Protection* (Brill 2017), 80–81 citing Convention for the Protection of the Mediterranean Sea against Pollution (opened for signature 16 February 1976, amended 10 June 1995, entered into force 9 June 2004) 1102 UNTS 27, preamble; African Charter on Human and Peoples' Rights (adopted 27 June 1981, entered into force 21 October 1986) 1520 UNTS 217, art 22(1) (linking the common heritage with the right to development). See also Baslar (n 1) 108–110.

[43] Ranganathan (2016) (n 4) 693 (providing a critical account of the origins of both the common heritage concept (as conceptualised by Pardo) and the concept of the 'tragedy of the commons' (pioneered by biologist Garrett Hardin), as aspects of the 'global commons'; Garrett Hardin, 'The Tragedy of the Commons' (1968) 162 Science 1243).

[44] Schrijver (n 38) 1262. On the concept of the global commons, see also Susan J Buck, *The Global Commons: An Introduction* (Island Press 1998). For analysis of necessary factors to successfully achieve common management of finite resources such as grazing land, forests and irrigation waters, see the Nobel Prize-winning approach of Elinor Ostrom, *Governing the Commons: The Evolution of Institutions for Collective Action* (CUP 1990); Elinor Ostrom and others, *The Drama of the Commons* (National

In the context of this global commons, general focus has moved away, within the last three decades, from the common *heritage* of mankind, and on to the newer concept of the common *concern* of humankind.[45] While the common heritage principle applies to particular *locations* beyond national jurisdiction (namely the deep seabed and the moon), the 'common concern' concept applies to certain *issues* such as the conservation of biological diversity and the effects of climate change.[46] At present, the effects of climate change are recognised as a 'common concern of humankind' in both the UN Framework Convention on Climate Change 1992 and the Paris Agreement 2015.[47] The conservation of biological diversity is also classified as a 'common concern of humankind' in the Convention on Biological Diversity 1992.[48] It remains to be seen whether the new treaty being negotiated to regulate BBNJ beyond national jurisdiction will endorse the common heritage concept or designate regulation of BBNJ as a common concern.[49]

Academy Press 2002). See also Hafner (n 41) (evaluating whether international legal regimes governing global commons satisfy Ostrom's parameters for successful common management regimes). Finally, see Eric A Posner and Alan O Sykes, 'Economic Foundations of Law of the Sea' (2010) 104 AJIL 569 (for an economic perspective on management of common pool resources both in the context of the law of the sea (571–577) and in relation to the Convention's deep seabed mining regime in particular (587–592)).

[45] cf Dinah Shelton, 'Common Concern of Humanity' (2009) 39 Env L Pol'y 83 (tracing the historical antecedents of today's international environmental law concept of common concern back to international humanitarian law and human rights law). On the common concern concept generally, see Antônio Augusto Cançado Trindade, *International Law for Humankind* (3rd edn, Brill 2020) 327–352; Friedrich Soltau, 'Common Concern of Humankind' in Kevin R Gray, Richard Tarasofsky and Cinnamon Carlarne (eds), *The Oxford Handbook of International Climate Change Law* (OUP 2016). See also Baslar (n 1) 107ff (arguing for the common concern of mankind as a new element of the common humanity of mankind).

[46] Schrijver (n 38) 1258. See also Shelton (n 45) 85; Chelsea Bowling, Elizabeth Pierson and Stephanie Ratté, 'The Common Concern of Humankind: A Potential Framework for a New International Legally Binding Instrument on the Conservation and Sustainable Use of Marine Biological Diversity in the High Seas' (White Paper submitted to the Preparatory Committee on BBNJ, 2016) <www.un.org/depts/los/biodiversity/prepcom_files/BowlingPiersonandRatte_Common_Concern.pdf>.

[47] United Nations Framework Convention on Climate Change (adopted 9 May 1992, entered into force 21 March 1994) 1771 UNTS 107, preamble; Paris Agreement (adopted 12 December 2015, entered into force 4 November 2016), preamble <http://unfccc.int/files/essential_background/convention/application/pdf/english_paris_agreement.pdf>.

[48] Convention on Biological Diversity (opened for signature 5 June 1992, entered into force 29 December 1993) 1760 UNTS 79, preamble. Arguably, designation of conservation of biological diversity as a common concern applies both within and outwith areas of national jurisdiction (see Convention on Biological Diversity, arts 3, 4(b) and 5; see also analysis by Bowling, Pierson and Ratté (n 46) 9).

[49] For details of the intergovernmental conference on BBNJ, see Chapter 2, nn 35–36. The present draft treaty text includes the common heritage of mankind as a general principle (see draft art 5(c) of 'Revised Draft Text of an Agreement under the United Nations Convention on the Law of the Sea on the Conservation and Sustainable Use of Marine Biological Diversity of Areas Beyond National Jurisdiction' (18 November 2019) UN Doc A/CONF.232/2020/3). However, this provision is bracketed, to indicate divergence of views (evidenced most recently by comments in 'Article-by-Article Compilation of Textual Proposals for Consideration at the Fourth Session' (UN Intergovernmental Conference on BBNJ, 15 April 2020) <www.un.org/bbnj/sites/www.un.org.bbnj/files/textual_proposals_compilation_article-by-article_-_15_april_2020.pdf>). See also Vito De Lucia, 'A Very Quick Look at the Revised Draft Text of the new Agreement on Marine Biodiversity in Areas beyond National Jurisdiction' (*EJIL: Talk!*, 23 January 2020) <www.ejiltalk.org/a-very-quick-look-at-the-revised-draft-text-of-the-new-agreement-on-marine-biodiversity-in-areas-beyond-national-jurisdiction/>.

As Gavouneli highlights, this movement from common heritage to common concern is part of the trend towards common management over common ownership: '[o]verall … it seems that the world has moved away from novel concepts of common or joint ownership or jurisdiction towards new concepts of management'.[50] One can view this trend towards common management as part of the broader drive for the development of governance principles for areas beyond national jurisdiction more generally, including in relation to the deep seabed.[51]

Now that this section has placed the common heritage concept within its wider context, the following sections will briefly assess the way in which the General Assembly developed Pardo's conception of the common heritage principle in relation to deep seabed mining, setting the international community on a path towards agreement of the deep seabed mining regime, in the form of UNCLOS. As this examination will reveal, the overriding component of the common heritage concept, pervading all other elements, is that deep seabed resources must be subject to a system of common management. Therefore, as the ensuing analysis will demonstrate, Gavouneli's recognition of the shift in emphasis from ownership to management holds true within the deep seabed mining context also.[52]

3.1.3 The General Assembly's Application of the Common Heritage Principle to the Deep Seabed

Acting rapidly upon Pardo's vision, the UN General Assembly adopted its first resolution on the deep seabed a mere six weeks after Pardo's speech.[53] This established an ad hoc committee to consider the matter. Just over a year later, following the ad hoc committee's consideration and further debate, the General Assembly established a standing Committee on the Peaceful Uses of the Sea-Bed and the Ocean Floor Beyond the Limits of National Jurisdiction (*Seabed Committee*).[54]

As the common heritage concept became further imbued with life during these processes, it retained the central elements of Pardo's original vision.[55] The Seabed

[50] Gavouneli (n 32) 141, citing Harry N Schreiber (ed), *Law of the Sea: The Common Heritage and Emerging Challenges* (Kluwer Law International 2000) and Guntrip (2003) (n 14).

[51] See, generally, Richard A Barnes, 'Consolidating Governance Principles for Areas beyond National Jurisdiction' (2012) 27 Int'l J Marine Coastal L 261; David Freestone, 'International Governance, Responsibility and Management of Areas beyond National Jurisdiction' (2012) 27 Int'l J Marine Coastal L 191; Alex G Oude Elferink, 'Governance Principles for Areas beyond National Jurisdiction' (2012) 27 Int'l J Marine Coastal L 205.

[52] Similarly, see Joyner (1986) (n 31) 194 (recognising that, pursuant to the common heritage concept, 'the key consideration [is] *access* to the region, rather than ownership of it' (emphasis in original) (citations omitted)). See, further, Baslar (n 1) 91 (arguing that the common heritage is not a 'territorial concept' and is instead a 'functional concept'). cf Egede (2011) (n 12) 61–66 (concluding that, from an African perspective, the common heritage concept is founded upon joint ownership rather than merely common management).

[53] UNGA Res 2340 (XXII) (18 December 1967). cf Pardo (1967b) (n 18); Pardo (1967a) (n 4).

[54] UNGA Res 2467 (XXIII) (21 December 1968).

[55] Baslar (n 1) 81.

Committee's Legal Sub-Committee, in its report of its 1969 session, described the common heritage of mankind as providing the 'basis' for all rules concerning the Area.[56] As the Legal Sub-Committee described, 'the concept of "common heritage of mankind" implies an international machinery for the regulation and management of the sea-bed and ocean floor beyond the limits of national jurisdiction on behalf of the international community'.[57] Integral to the common heritage notion was some form of prohibition of unilateral appropriation of the Area, although there was disagreement as to the specifics.[58] The Legal Sub-Committee also considered issues concerning protection of the Area's marine environment, noting that there was general consensus on the need to safeguard the deep seabed from pollution and protect its living resources.[59]

Nevertheless, despite recognition of these common elements, industrialised and developing states continued, throughout this period, to hold differing visions for the overall thrust of deep seabed regulation.[60] This division culminated in late 1969, when developing states used their numerical majority in the General Assembly to secure a controversial resolution imposing a moratorium on deep seabed mining. On 15 December 1969, the General Assembly adopted Resolution 2574 (commonly referred to as the *Moratorium Resolution*) calling for a ban on deep seabed mining in the Area, pending establishment of an international legal regime to regulate such activities.[61]

Despite vigorous Western opposition to this moratorium, a move towards consensus came in December 1970, with the General Assembly's unanimous adoption of the Declaration of Principles Governing the Sea-Bed and the Ocean Floor, and the Subsoil Thereof, Beyond the Limits of National Jurisdiction (*1970 Seabed Declaration*).[62] Adopted by a majority of 108 votes in favour and none against, with fourteen abstentions, the 1970 Seabed Declaration was, to some extent, 'a concretisation of Dr Pardo's proposal'.[63] The instrument included key common heritage elements that would later find expression within UNCLOS.[64]

Crucially, the 1970 Seabed Declaration affirmed that the deep seabed and its resources constitute the common heritage of mankind (para 1), to be used only

[56] Seabed Committee, 'Report of the Committee on Peaceful Uses of the Sea-bed and the Ocean Floor beyond the limits of National Jurisdiction' (1969) A/7622, 14, para 20 <https://digitallibrary.un.org/record/718410?ln=en>; see also Virginia Commentary 96.

[57] Seabed Committee (n 56) 14, para 21.

[58] Seabed Committee (n 56) 14–15, paras 25–26.

[59] Seabed Committee (n 56) 31, para 96.

[60] Churchill and Lowe (n 5) 226. This division is evident, e.g. in Legal Sub-committee deliberations: Seabed Committee (n 56) at 14–15, paras 23–25 and 27.

[61] UNGA Res 2574 (XXIV) (15 December 1969) (passed with 62 votes in favour, 28 votes against, 28 abstentions).

[62] UNGA Res 2749 (XXV) (17 December 1970).

[63] Garrison (n 31) 23; see also Baslar (n 1) 82.

[64] Chapter 4 will consider this in more detail, when assessing the extent to which UNCLOS operationalises key components of the common heritage ideal.

for peaceful purposes (para 5). Giving content to the common heritage principle, the instrument affirmed that all deep seabed mining activities would be 'governed by the international regime to be established' (para 4). The instrument proscribed states from exercising sovereignty over the deep seabed, and states and other actors from appropriating it (para 2). Equally, it prohibited states and other actors from 'exercis[ing] or acquir[ing] rights with respect to the area or its resources incompatible with the international regime to be established and the principles of this Declaration' (para 3). Other key features of the common heritage, as embodied in the 1970 Seabed Declaration, included that 'exploration of the area and the exploitation of its resources shall be carried out for the benefit of mankind as a whole, irrespective of the geographical location of States, whether land-locked or coastal, and taking into particular consideration the interests and needs of the developing countries' (para 7, and see also para 9). It also required implementation of marine environmental protections (para 11).

However, although the 1970 Seabed Declaration was significant in cementing broad political will behind the common heritage concept across the international community as a whole, '[t]he main reason for its acceptability was its delphic construction'.[65] Securing 'acceptability at the cost of certainty', the instrument 'admitted a wide range of interpretations'.[66] This allowed Western states to maintain that free use of deep seabed resources was permitted in accordance with freedom of the high seas, pending establishment of an international legal regime, while developing states adopted an opposing stance, claiming that the moratorium on deep seabed exploitation remained in place until the achievement of an international regime for deep seabed resources.[67] In a further discrepancy of views, while developing states regarded the 1970 Seabed Declaration as evidence of customary law, industrialised states viewed it as a mere expression of political intent.[68]

Despite significant disagreement as to the precise scope of the common heritage concept, the international community was, nonetheless, united in its desire for a supranational framework for deep seabed mining.[69] Irrespective of its legal status, the 1970 Seabed Declaration paved the way for the adoption of a treaty regime to govern the deep seabed, setting the scene for the UNCLOS III negotiations.[70] These

[65] Churchill and Lowe (n 5) 227.

[66] Churchill and Lowe (n 5) 228.

[67] Churchill and Lowe (n 5) 228.

[68] Churchill and Lowe (n 5) 228; Garrison (n 31) 23; Egede (2011) (n 12) 57, 66; see also analysis by Goldie (n 30). This book will consider issues of customary law in relation to deep seabed mining in Chapter 5.

[69] Koskenniemi and Lehto (n 5) 536, 538, 552–553.

[70] 1970 Seabed Declaration (n 62) para 9. See also UNGA Res 2750 (XXV) (17 December 1970) (on the Reservation Exclusively for Peaceful Purposes of the Sea-bed and the Ocean Floor, and the Subsoil thereof, Underlying the High Seas beyond the Limits of Present National Jurisdiction and Use of their Resources in the Interests of Mankind, and Convening of a Conference on the Law of the Sea); see, further, the similarly titled UNGA Res 3029 (XXVII) (18 December 1972) and UNGA Res 3067 (XXVIII) (16 November 1973).

negotiations commenced in 1973 and lasted until the Convention was adopted in 1982, as the following section will consider.

3.1.4 The Difficult Road to the UNCLOS Deep Seabed Mining Regime

The deep seabed mining regime contained within UNCLOS has an arduous negotiating history.[71] Almost all states agreed on the principle that the deep seabed constituted the common heritage of mankind. Similarly, they sought supranational control of deep seabed mining. However, the precise content of any such international regime was hotly disputed. UNCLOS III became a struggle to unite two conceptions of deep seabed control: on the one hand, a vision of liberal, individualistic, commercial autonomy (championed by industrialised states); and, on the other hand, an opposing view prioritising communal, communitarian, collectivist values (advocated by developing states). At its lowest common denominator, '[t]he disagreement which underlay the debate concerned the capacity of market liberalism v. socialism to produce the general good. This was, of course, a disagreement which the Conference could not discuss in the open'.[72]

This underlying division concerning deep seabed mining was symptomatic of the broader tension within the Convention between 'communal and individualistic demands'.[73] Indeed, critics argue that this opposition between community and individuality underpins the liberal legal paradigm more generally,[74] and that this can be read across to the international law context.[75]

For developing states, the desired communitarian outcome for deep seabed resource management became aligned, in many respects, to the broader demands of the movement for a New International Economic Order (*NIEO*). For these states, 'the fate of seabed resources had always been linked to an attempt

[71] For a detailed account, see Virginia Commentary 35–68; see also 224–229. See, further, Koskenniemi and Lehto (n 5) 536–552; Alan Boyle and Christine Chinkin, 'UNCLOS III and the Process of International Law-making' in Tafsir Malick Ndiaye and Rüdiger Wolfrum (eds), *Law of the Sea, Environmental Law and Settlement of Disputes* (Martinus Nijhoff Publishers 2007), 376–381; Tommy Koh, 'Negotiating the UN Convention on the Law of the Sea: A Practitioner's Reflection' in Simon Chesterman, David M Malone and Santiago Villalpando (eds), *The Oxford Handbook of United Nations Treaties* (OUP 2019); Isabel Feichtner, 'Sharing the Riches of the Sea: The Redistributive and Fiscal Dimension of Deep Seabed Exploitation' (2019) 30 EJIL 601, 605–611, 614–617.

[72] Koskenniemi and Lehto (n 5) 553; see also Baslar (n 1) 80.

[73] Martti Koskenniemi, *From Apology to Utopia: The Structure of International Legal Argument* (CUP 2005) 488 (see also 489–497 for detailed analysis, and examples of ways in which UNCLOS aims to safeguard both communitarian and individual values by constructing a 'formal-procedural framework for the conduct of inter-sovereign relations' (489), seeking to 'secure a balance and provide each State with what it needs' (491). See also Cassese (1986) (n 7) 392).

[74] See, e.g. Duncan Kennedy, 'The Structure of Blackstone's Commentaries' (1979) 28 Buff L Rev 205, 211ff.

[75] See, e.g. Koskenniemi (2005) (n 73) 475ff.

at a transformation of the structures of world economy'.[76] The NIEO movement emerged in the early years of UNCLOS III.[77] Many of the goals that developing states sought to achieve at UNCLOS III (such as transfer of technology, benefit sharing, production policies and favourable treatment for developing states) were consistent with NIEO premises.[78] For developing states, achievement of an appropriate deep seabed regime became all the more vital, as a template for other supranational regimes for resource management.[79]

As Boyle and Chinkin explain, fundamental to the success of the UNCLOS III conference negotiations was 'the innovative and largely unprecedented negotiating methods and procedures employed'.[80] In order to try and achieve a solution acceptable to all, the Convention negotiations changed approach radically from the previous two UN conferences on the law of the sea. Both UNCLOS I (in 1958) and II (in 1960) had relied upon the ILC to produce initial draft treaty articles for conference participants to discuss. In contrast, UNCLOS III was an avowedly political process, aiming to produce a consensus text 'within the Conference itself' that would command broad support across the international community.[81] To this end, UNCLOS III adopted a consensus approach that was conducted in the shadow of the vote.[82] Throughout the protracted nine-year period of negotiations, this 'active' consensus approach was instrumental in allowing the conference to proceed

[76] Koskenniemi and Lehto (n 5) 554; see also Baslar (n 1) 210–211.

[77] On 1 May 1974, the GA passed two important NIEO resolutions: UNGA Res 3201 (S-VI) (1 May 1974) (Declaration on the Establishment of a New International Economic Order) and UNGA Res 3202 (S-VI) (1 May 1974) (Programme of Action on the Establishment of a New International Economic Order). See also Robert L Friedheim and William J Durch, 'The International Seabed Resources Agency Negotiations and the New International Economic Order' (1977) 31 Int'l Org 343; Elisabeth Mann Borgese, 'The New International Economic Order and the Law of the Sea' (1977) 14 San Diego L Rev 584; Francisco Orrego Vicuña, 'The Regime for the Exploitation of the Seabed Mineral Resources and the Quest for a New International Economic Order of the Oceans: A Latin-American View' (1978) 10 Law Amer 774; Lawrence Juda, 'UNCLOS III and the New International Economic Order' (1979) 7 OD Int'l L 221; Roderick C Ogley, 'The Law of the Sea Draft Convention and the New International Economic Order' (1981) 5 Marine Pol'y 240; Richard J Payne and Jamal R Nassar, 'The New International Economic Order at Sea' (1982) 17 J Developing Areas 31.

[78] Koskenniemi and Lehto (n 5) 540; Noyes (2012) (n 1) 459. Indeed, as Koskenniemi notes, citing UNCLOS, '[t]he communitarian strand of the NIEO rhetoric is best exemplified by the idea of the "common heritage of mankind"': Koskenniemi (2005) (n 73) 485, fn 34. For the suggestion that developing states may have been deliberately misinformed about the lucrative prospects of seabed mining, perhaps so that concessions by developing states regarding deep seabed mining could be 'traded off against other NIEO demands', see Surabhi Ranganathan, 'Ocean Floor Grab: International Law and the Making of an Extractive Imaginary' (2019) 30 EJIL 573, 594–595; see also Feichtner (n 71) 611.

[79] See, e.g. Koskenniemi and Lehto (n 5) 540–541; see also Lee Kimball, 'Implications of the Arrangement Made for Deep Seabed Mining for Other Joint Exploitations' (1980) 15 Colum J World Bus 52.

[80] Boyle and Chinkin (n 71) 376; see also Louis B Sohn, 'Voting Procedures in United Nations Conferences for the Codification of International Law' (1975) 69 AJIL 310; Philip Allot, 'Power Sharing in the Law of the Sea' 77 AJIL (1983) 1.

[81] Boyle and Chinkin (n 71) 377; see also Jens Evensen, 'Working Methods and Procedures in the Third United Nations Conference on the Law of the Sea' (1986) 199 RdC 425.

[82] Boyle and Chinkin (n 71) 378, fn 29 (as Boyle and Chinkin note therein, '[t]he Conference Rules of Procedure in fact provided for adoption of articles by two-thirds majority vote, but a "Gentleman's Agreement" incorporated consensus decision-making into the working procedure of the conference').

towards a universal text.[83] By preserving the possibility of taking contentious matters to a vote, this motivated the negotiating parties to avoid deadlock.[84] The other key feature of the UNCLOS III negotiations was the notion of the draft Convention as a 'package deal'.[85] States compromised in order to eventually arrive at a text on which, in theory, all participants could agree.

By 1980, the negotiating parties had reached a 'fragile compromise' on key elements of the deep seabed regime.[86] The conference had agreed to include, within the Convention, the key elements of Pardo's common heritage ideal, as embodied in the 1970 Seabed Declaration, such as common management of deep seabed mining through international machinery, a prohibition on unilateral mining activities and an emphasis on benefits for humanity and marine environmental protection. Significantly, industrialised states had achieved institutionalisation of a 'parallel system', pursuant to which commercial actors would be entitled to mine the deep seabed directly, subject to the Authority's control. This US-led approach overcame opposing views of the G77 and industrialised states on the 'fundamental nature of the system of access to seabed resources and whether exploitation of the Area should be carried out by the Authority directly or by States and other entities under the fiscal and administrative supervision of the Authority'.[87] This US innovation cemented the role of private actors as direct participants within deep seabed mining. Meanwhile, developing states secured, within the Convention text, a powerful Authority and various benefit-sharing elements.[88]

However, underlying operationalisation of key common heritage aspects within the Convention text was intensifying tension between individualistic and communitarian preferences. For industrialised states, particularly contentious features included the expansive role envisaged for the ISA's intended mining arm the Enterprise, and the planned subsidisation of the Enterprise by States Parties.[89] They also had concerns about the balance of power within the Authority, and the extent of the Authority's mandate to review and update the Convention regime by means of a review conference. The other main focus of their discontent related to aspects of the planned equal participation and benefit-sharing arrangements, such

[83] Barry Buzan, 'Negotiating by Consensus: Developments in Technique at the UN Conference on the Law of the Sea' (1981) 75 AJIL 324, 329, 334–335.

[84] Boyle and Chinkin (n 71) 378.

[85] Hugo Caminos and Michael R Molitor, 'Progressive Development of International Law and the Package-deal' (1985) 79 AJIL 871, 873–878; Evensen (n 81) 485; Koskenniemi and Lehto (n 5) 540; Boyle and Chinkin (n 71) 378–379.

[86] Koskenniemi and Lehto (n 5) 541.

[87] Virginia Commentary 297; see also 305ff. See, further, Wolfrum (1983) (n 31) 324; Jule Siegfried, 'Article 153' in Proelss Commentary 1082–1083.

[88] See, e.g. overview by Baslar (n 1) 211–213.

[89] Indeed, as Koskenniemi and Lehto note, the true reason underlying the clash between developed and industrialised states was 'the acceptability of the new concept of an "international industry", the role of the Enterprise as an operative arm of the ISA': Koskenniemi and Lehto (n 5) 543.

as requirements for mandatory transfer of technology, planned production limitations, the intended compensation fund and financial terms of mining contracts.[90]

This tension crystallised in early 1981, when – following a change in administration – the US abstained from substantive discussions at UNCLOS III, while undertaking a comprehensive policy review of its position towards the conference.[91] This change in US position was met with 'disbelief and consternation' by the chairman of the G77.[92] During 1982, US objections to the deep seabed regime prompted a collapse of consensus and plunged UNCLOS III into crisis.[93] Against this backdrop, the conference held a majority vote on the final draft text of the Convention. Participants voted overwhelmingly to adopt UNCLOS, with only four voting against (including the US). However, several industrialised states abstained from the vote as, like the US, they viewed the underlying balance within the Convention's common heritage regime as having swung too far in favour of developing states.[94]

Throughout the 1980s, a stalemate endured, as many industrialised states refused to ratify UNCLOS due to its approach to deep seabed mining, thereby stymieing the Convention's entry into force.[95] During this period, industrialised states developed an interim 'reciprocating states regime', designed to allow deep seabed mining to commence, pending international agreement. This alternative 'regime' took the form of national legislation, and intergovernmental agreements between industrialised states.[96] This was designed to implement an interim parallel regime, pending entry into force of the Convention, and to allow states to

[90] DH Anderson, 'Further Efforts to Ensure Universal Participation in the United Nations Convention on the Law of the Sea' (1994) 43 ICLQ 886, 886; W Scott Burke and Frank S Brokaw, 'Ideology and the Law of the Sea' in Bernard H Oxman, David D Caron and Charles LO Buderi (eds), *Law of the Sea: US Policy Dilemma* (Institute for Contemporary Studies Press 1983); see also Koskenniemi and Lehto (n 5) 542; Natalie Klein, *Dispute Settlement in the UN Convention on the Law of the Sea* (CUP 2005) 330–334.

[91] Bernard H Oxman, 'The Third United Nations Conference on the Law of the Sea: The Tenth Session (1981)' (1982) 76 AJIL 1, 2–13; Koskenniemi and Lehto (n 5) 541–542.

[92] 'Statement by Chairman of the G77' (10 August 1981) as quoted in Oxman (1982) (n 91) 3.

[93] Koskenniemi and Lehto (n 5) 542; Boyle and Chinkin (n 71) 379. See, generally, James L Malone, 'The United States and the Law of the Sea After UNCLOS III' (1983) 46(2) Law and Contemporary Problems 29; Bernard H Oxman, David D Caron and Charles LO Buderi (eds), *Law of the Sea: US Policy Dilemma* (Institute for Contemporary Studies Press 1983); Markus G Schmidt, *Common Heritage or Common Burden? The United States Position on the Development of a Regime for Deep Sea-bed Mining in the Law of the Sea Convention* (Clarendon 1989). For overviews of the inclusion of special rules for so-called 'pioneer investors', as a last minute compromise designed to appease industrialised states by affording a system for protection of existing investments in deep seabed mining, see Churchill and Lowe (n 5) 230–231; Lodge (2002) (n 18) 276–277, 279. These modifications now have only historical relevance, and so engagement with them is beyond the scope of this study.

[94] Churchill and Lowe (n 5) 231; Tuerk (n 5) 282.

[95] In numerical terms, there were enough developing states to bring the Convention into force acting alone (only sixty state ratifications were necessary to achieve this, as per UNCLOS, art 308). However, in practice, the Convention system could not operate successfully without political and financial support from industrialised states. See Robert Jennings and Arthur Watts, *Oppenheim's International Law: Vol 1, Peace, pts 2–4* (9th edn, Longman 1996) 814; see also Koskenniemi and Lehto (n 5) 534–535, 542–544; Churchill and Lowe (n 5) 230–231; Lodge (2002) (n 18) 272.

[96] For a helpful overview of, and citations to, relevant legislation/agreements, see Klein (n 90) 339–344; see also Baslar (n 1) 214–215.

undertake deep seabed mining activities in accordance with the freedom of the high seas principle.[97]

Predictably, this putative 'regime' provoked a furore amongst proponents of UNCLOS, such as the G77 and Eastern European states.[98] The Preparatory Commission for the Convention condemned the approach of reciprocating states, stating unequivocally that UNCLOS established 'the only regime for exploration and exploitation of the Area and its resources', and that any claim outside of the UNCLOS framework would be 'wholly illegal' and would 'not be recognised'.[99] However, declining metal prices and lack of commercial feasibility of deep seabed mining diverted a 'head-on clash' between reciprocating states, and supporters of UNCLOS.[100]

Eventually, in 1994, opposing state factions managed to reach a compromise. Hailed as a 'masterpiece of diplomatic ingenuity',[101] the solution took the form of the Agreement on the Implementation of Part XI of UNCLOS (*1994 Agreement*).[102] While retaining the tenor of the deep seabed regime as originally envisaged by UNCLOS, the 1994 Agreement made significant modifications to its operation, eliminating some of its more controversial aspects.[103]

[97] For detailed analysis of the reciprocating states regime, see Brown (2001) (n 5) ch 7; see also Koskenniemi and Lehto (n 5) 544–546; Baslar (n 1) 89, 214–215; Churchill and Lowe (n 5) 232–235; Klein (n 90) 336–346; Jaeckel (2017) (n 42) 82–84. As deep seabed mining stalled for economic and technological reasons, exploitation activities under this contrary 'regime' never came to fruition.

[98] See, e.g. 'Statement by Chairman of the G77 on 13 August 1984' (16 August 1984) Document No LOS/PCN/48 denouncing the reciprocating states regime as 'contrary to the letter and spirit of the Law of the Sea Convention and hav[ing] no legal validity'.

[99] 'Declaration adopted by Preparatory Commission on 30 August 1985' (2 September 1985) Document No LOS/PCN/72, paras 1–2. See Churchill and Lowe (n 5) 234–235 for analysis of the extent to which unilateral mining activities at that time may have contravened customary law, concluding (at 234) that '[t]hat view had some force'. However, while recognising that '[t]here seems to be no good reason for denying that a series of resolutions, inside and outside the United Nations, which purported to declare the unlawfulness of unilateral legislation could have this effect [of generating customary law]', reciprocating states 'could not have been bound by any such rule' due to their status as persistent objectors (at 235). See also Klein (n 90) 338 (concluding that 'the status of [relevant GA] resolutions as reflecting or creating custom was questionable, however, in light of the inconsistent practice of States with capacity to mine and because of the nebulous concepts included in the resolutions' (citations omitted)). On the extent to which the current UNCLOS regime has customary status, and consideration of the persistent objector doctrine, see Chapter 5, Section 5.2.

[100] Churchill and Lowe (n 5) 237; see also Koskenniemi and Lehto (n 5) 546–547.

[101] Koskenniemi and Lehto (n 5) 549.

[102] The 1994 Agreement has 150 States Parties (all of which are also parties to UNCLOS): DOALOS, 'Chronological List of Ratifications of, Accessions and Successions to the Convention and the Related Agreements' (9 March 2020) <www.un.org/Depts/los/reference_files/chronological_lists_of_ratifications.htm>. See also UNGA Res 47/65 (11 December 1992) UN Doc A/RES/47/65 (on Law of the Sea) (*1992 Resolution*), which precipitated negotiation of the 1994 Agreement.

[103] On the fundamental changes introduced by the 1994 Agreement, see Anderson (n 90); Bernard H Oxman, 'The 1994 Agreement and the Convention' (1994) 88 AJIL 687; Louis B Sohn, 'International Law Implications of the 1994 Agreement' (1994) 88 AJIL 696; ED Brown, 'The 1994 Agreement on the Implementation of Part XI of the UN Convention on the Law of the Sea: Breakthrough to Universality?' (1995) 19 Marine Pol'y 5; LDM Nelson, 'The New Deep Sea-bed Mining Regime' (1995) 10 Int'l J Marine Coastal L 189; Koskenniemi and Lehto (n 5) 535, 549–551; RP Anand, 'Common Heritage of Mankind: Mutilation of an Idea' (1997) 37 Indian J Int'l L 1; Churchill and Lowe (n 5) 238, 248–251; Virginia Commentary 4, 67; Lodge (2002) (n 18) 272.

The 1994 Agreement shifted the common heritage concept within the deep seabed regime to take more account of 'market-oriented approaches'.[104] Notably, this rebalancing of the common heritage regime for deep seabed mining had greatest impact upon its benefit-sharing aspects.[105] For example, the 1994 Agreement significantly inhibited the role of the Enterprise and its subsidisation, as well as curtailing mandatory transfer of technology, production limitations, the planned compensation fund and the financial terms of mining contracts. It also revised other aspects of the regime, mentioned above, that posed obstacles to industrialised states' ratification of UNCLOS, including provisions relating to the Authority's decision-making process and its powers to conduct a review conference of the Convention regime.[106]

In light of the 1994 Agreement's modification of the deep seabed regime, UNCLOS entered into force on 16 November 1994. Some critics have argued that the 1994 Agreement eviscerated the regime's common heritage aspects.[107] Yet, the issue is 'not so straightforward'.[108] The 1994 Agreement reaffirms the common heritage principle while realigning the Convention regime's closely fought communitarian–individualism balance, such as to render it more palatable to industrialised states. It does so by tipping the balance of the regime towards commercial autonomy. But, notwithstanding the 1994 Agreement's qualification of the implementation of certain common heritage goals (such as benefit-sharing aspects), many commentators argue that the 1994 Agreement modified the regime 'without ... sacrificing the core of the principle'.[109]

This rebalancing of the common heritage within the 1994 Agreement emphasises, above all, the importance of market principles for the common heritage's ultimate realisation. As Baslar recognised (writing in 1998), this recalibration 'affected ultimately the spirit of the [common heritage] concept' by 'reformulat[ing] the application of the common heritage in the light

[104] 1994 Agreement, preamble. This rebalancing was foreshadowed in 1992 Resolution (n 102) para 5 (which recognised 'that political and economic changes, including particularly a growing reliance on market principles, underscore the need to re-evaluate, in the light of the issues of concern to some States, matters in the regime to be applied to the Area and its resources, and that a productive dialogue on such issues involving all interested parties would facilitate the prospect of universal participation in the Convention, for the benefit of mankind as a whole').

[105] See, e.g. Jaeckel (2017) (n 42) 86 (noting that, by virtue of the 1994 Agreement's amendments, 'the meaning of the common heritage principle in the seabed mining context has been reinterpreted to substantially reduce the benefit sharing elements').

[106] For analysis of these aspects, see Chapter 4.

[107] See, e.g. Anand (n 103). See also Koskenniemi and Lehto (n 5) 551 (noting the argument that the 1994 Agreement constituted an 'unmitigated victory for the ideology of the market and a final blow to efforts to establish a new international economic order, based on regulatory policies and the creation of an international industry for the attainment of distributionary goals').

[108] Koskenniemi and Lehto (n 5) 551.

[109] Wolfrum (2009) (n 31) para 1. See also Jaeckel (2017) (n 42) 86 (affirming that, despite the 1994 Agreement's amendments, the common heritage principle as embodied within UNCLOS 'continues to be a revolutionary concept and the basic principle underlying the ISA regime').

of recent political, economic and technological changes'.[110] By virtue of the 1994 Agreement, '"[m]arket principles" and "universality" (accommodating industrialized States) were now linked with the idea of the common heritage, illustrating the transformed economic and political atmosphere'.[111] Therefore, the finely tuned balance between market principles and benefit of mankind considerations is inherent within the common heritage itself. To realise the common heritage successfully, deep seabed mining activities must satisfy both communitarian and market-oriented goals.

In light of the preceding analysis, the following section will now set out the common heritage's key modern-day components (while Chapter 4 will subsequently assess the extent to which they are operationalised within UNCLOS).

3.2 Key Features Underpinning the Modern Common Heritage Concept Applicable to Deep Seabed Mining

To some extent, the common heritage principle is 'rather nebulous'.[112] As noted above, the international community could achieve broad consensus behind inclusion of the common heritage concept within the 1970 Seabed Declaration only because its drafting was sufficiently ambiguous to appease all sides.[113] Due to underlying ideological divisions between developing and industrialised states, Guntrip argues that varying interpretations of the common heritage concept have been adopted, and that '[t]hese interpretations have not been reconciled and there has been no juridical consideration of the common heritage of mankind principle to clarify them'.[114] Nevertheless, as Wolfrum describes, although '[n]o fully agreed definition' of the common heritage concept exists, 'it is possible to identify several common features, or, rather, a hard core of that principle'.[115] Despite acknowledging a degree of blurring at the edges of the common heritage concept,

[110] Baslar (n 1) 215–216 (see, further, his analysis at 216 of the 'political metamorphosis' that occurred between the 1970s and the 1990s, 'culminat[ing] in a new atmosphere wherein the decline of socialism and centrally planned economies [were] being replaced with free market economies and liberalism').

[111] Koskenniemi and Lehto (n 5) 549, citing the 1992 Resolution (n 102) preamble and para 5. See also Fritz (n 5) 457; Jaeckel (2017) (n 42) 114. See, further, Feichtner (n 71) 621 (arguing that the 1994 Agreement 'reformulates the regime's objectives and presents its "market orientation" as a win-win situation. According to this reformulation, greater market orientation will ensure that effective exploitation takes place').

[112] Egede (2017) (n 31) 1; similarly, see also Baslar (n 1) 79; Holmila (n 5) 195; Egede (2011) (n 12) 60; Lodge (2012) (n 30) 734; Noyes (2012) (n 1) 454.

[113] Churchill and Lowe (n 5) 227.

[114] Guntrip (2003) (n 14) 377 (citations omitted); see also 404 (on the common heritage principle as an 'inchoate concept').

[115] Wolfrum (2009) (n 31) para 3. This echoes Hart's concept of the 'core of certainty', as contrasted to the 'penumbra of doubt', in application of general rules to specific circumstances, as discussed in Chapter 1, n 49; see also HLA Hart, *The Concept of Law* (3rd edn, OUP 2012) 123.

this section will confirm the concept's central components within the present-day deep seabed mining context.

Irrespective of ideological tensions at its roots, key features of the common heritage concept are evident from its historical development (as portrayed in Section 3.1). From the outset, building upon Pardo's initial portrayal, the common heritage concept in the deep seabed mining context began to coagulate around certain central elements. The General Assembly's deliberations further developed these elements, particularly within the text of the 1970 Seabed Declaration.[116] In his detailed survey of key literature concerning the common heritage concept generally, Egede notes that commentators have tended to classify the concrete core of the common heritage concept as comprising around four or five main elements,[117] echoing Pardo's original vision.[118] Commonly cited elements include the principles of: (1) common management of the deep seabed; (2) non-appropriation or alienation of the deep seabed or its resources; (3) sharing of deep seabed benefits; (4) protection of the marine environment (which, as will be discussed, is sometimes tied to the ideas of sustainable development and preservation of the deep seabed for future generations); and, potentially, (5) usage of the deep seabed for peaceful purposes only.[119]

The following analysis will sketch the components underpinning the common heritage concept in general terms (while subsequent chapters will go on to assess the extent to which these elements are captured within specific provisions and processes of the UNCLOS deep seabed mining regime).

3.2.1 Component 1 – The Common Management Principle

Firstly, to realise the common heritage of mankind, there must be common management of the Area through an institutional regime. Within the deep seabed mining context, inclusion of a form of common management was evident from the outset.[120] The common heritage includes the need for an 'international management regime' involving 'institutional machinery' to govern deep seabed mining.[121] This 'procedural element' of the common heritage principle can be styled as 'requiring that exploration and exploitation of resources must be managed under

[116] 1970 Seabed Declaration (n 62).

[117] Egede (2017) (n 31) 3; see also Baslar (n 1) 82–84.

[118] See Section 3.1.1 above, at text to nn 28–30.

[119] See, generally, White (n 30) 535; Joyner (1986) (n 31) 191–192; Heim (n 31) 827; Frakes (n 31) 411–413; Guntrip (2003) (n 14) 377, 387–393; Holmila (n 5) 195–202; Shackelford (n 12) 111, 117–118; Wolfrum (2009) (n 31) para 26; Noyes (2012) (n 1) 450–454; Tuerk (n 5) 280; Fritz (n 5) 460.

[120] See, e.g. Pardo (1967a) (n 4) para 15 (and this chapter's earlier analysis in Section 3.1.1, text to nn 23–24); 1970 Seabed Declaration (n 62) para 4. See, further, Koskenniemi and Lehto (n 5) 536, 538, 552–553; Baslar (n 1) 92.

[121] Wolfrum (1983) (n 31) 324 and Guntrip (2003) (n 14) 392–393, respectively. See also White (n 30) 536–537; Joyner (1986) (n 31) 191–192; Holmila (n 5) 198–199; Noyes (2012) (n 1) 451, 453.

treaty-based mechanisms'.[122] Common management of the Area through an institutional regime comports with the broader development of governance principles for areas beyond national jurisdiction more generally, including in relation to the deep seabed.[123]

3.2.2 Component 2 – The Prohibition of Unilateral Mining Activities

As Section 3.1 has demonstrated, when considering the historical evolution of the common heritage's application to deep seabed mining, one of the most contested elements was the extent to which the common heritage principle prohibited unilateral mining activities. Pardo's vision mandated that the deep seabed should not be 'subject to national appropriation in any manner whatsoever'.[124] The 1970 Seabed Declaration developed this further, prohibiting states from exercising sovereignty over the deep seabed, and proscribing states and other actors from unilaterally appropriating the deep seabed or 'exercis[ing] or acquir[ing] rights with respect to the area or its resources incompatible with the international regime to be established and the principles of this Declaration'.[125] Underlying this component is the notion that the deep seabed and its resources are the common heritage of mankind, and that, on this basis, rights in relation to the deep seabed are vested in mankind as a whole.[126]

There is a close connection between the first two components of the common heritage concept (common management and the prohibition of unilateral activities). As Wolfrum notes, '[t]here exists a logical link between the status of the Area and its resources and the utilization regime'.[127] Deep seabed mining activities are to be collectively regulated by an institutional (global) regime and, as a corollary to this, all unilateral mining activities outside of the regime are proscribed.[128] Only if both elements are realised will the deep seabed mining regime have attained a sufficient institutional framework to achieve its common heritage goals on a global level.

Taken together, the common heritage's first two components are perhaps most significant for their procedural implications. Providing a framework for common management, and prohibiting unilateral activities outside of this framework,

122 Noyes (2012) (n 1) 453; see also Baslar (n 1) 94.

123 See previous discussion in Section 3.1.2, text to nn 50–51.

124 Pardo (1967a) (n 4) para 10(a).

125 1970 Seabed Declaration (n 62) paras 2–3.

126 See discussion by Noyes (2012) (n 1) 451–452; cf Joyner (1986) (n 31) 192–193.

127 Wolfrum (1983) (n 31) 317. See also Baslar (n 1) 85–91. See, generally, GJH van Hoof, 'Legal Status of the Concept of the Common Heritage of Mankind' (1986) 7 Grotiana 49, 67–71; Holmila (n 5) 195–198.

128 For related analysis, see Egede (2011) (n 12) 57; Baslar (n 1) 92.

creates a legal process within which deep seabed mining activities can be regulated and conducted.[129] Indeed, the Convention's pursuit of this goal comports with its broader aim 'to solve the tension between [communal and individualistic] values by creating a formal-procedural framework for the conduct of inter-sovereign relations'.[130] As such, UNCLOS creates an 'architecture' – a procedural structure – in which states can pursue certain policies,[131] such as permitting certain actors to engage in deep seabed mining.

Therefore, for the purposes of this book's analysis, the ramifications of the first two components of the common heritage concept are most manifest in procedural terms, as they are inexorably bound up with the creation of legal processes and an appropriate institutional mechanism. In contrast, as the following analysis will reveal, the third and fourth common heritage components (benefit sharing and marine environmental protection, respectively) go to the substantive heart of the common heritage, given their significant material implications.[132]

3.2.3 Component 3 – The Benefit-sharing Principle

Underlying the common heritage nature of the deep seabed is Pardo's notion that deep seabed mining should be undertaken 'for the exclusive benefit of mankind as a whole', with the needs of developing countries to be afforded 'preferential consideration'.[133] The scope and precise elements of this benefit-sharing principle are

[129] Noyes describes this as 'a procedural element of the [common heritage] principle, requiring that exploration and exploitation of resources must be managed under treaty-based mechanisms': Noyes (2012) (n 1) 453.

[130] Koskenniemi (2005) (n 73) 489.

[131] See, e.g. Koskenniemi (2005) (n 73) 489, citing Kennedy's analysis of 'the Convention as a procedural "architecture" – a system of deferral of material solution beyond the Convention text': David Kennedy, *International Legal Structures* (Nomos Verlagsgesellschaft 1987) 201–245.

[132] This book uses the terms 'process' and 'substance' in general terms to capture, on the one hand, the rules that define the procedural scope of an institutional regime, in terms of the actors entitled to act within the regime and the extent of the regime's processes, regulatory procedures and reach, versus, on the other hand, the material, substantive content of the rules within the regime imposing duties or creating rights for actors within it. Broadly speaking, 'we may say that the substantive law defines the remedy and the right, while the law of procedure defines the modes and conditions of the application of the one to the other': John William Salmond and Glanville Llewelyn Williams, *Jurisprudence* (10th edn, Sweet and Maxwell 1947) 476. However, as Kennedy cautions (in identifying and applying three types of discourse within international law: sources, process and substance), the categories of process and substance cannot always be easily distinguished, and there may be overlap between the two. For example, 'a "process" rule about jurisdictional limits of sovereign powers may not seem far from a "substance" rule about the prohibited acts of sovereign power': Kennedy (1987) (n 131) 110. See also critique by Claire EM Jervis, '*Jurisdictional Immunities* Revisited: An Analysis of the Procedure Substance Distinction in International Law' (2019) 30 EJIL 105 (warning against adoption of a procedural/substantive distinction in too categorical a manner, particularly in relation to the rules of state immunity). Therefore, this book's distinction between process and substance will be applied with a degree of caution, recognising that while it can be helpful to assess common heritage aspects from a procedural or substantive perspective, this is not a rigid distinction, and there are elements of overlap between these two categories.

[133] Pardo (1967a) (n 4) para 13; see also para 10(d). See, further, 1970 Seabed Declaration (n 62) paras 7, 9.

contentious. However, evidently, this component includes sharing of both financial and other benefits related to deep seabed mining. For example, Pardo described that this component 'implied an active sharing of benefits, not only financial but also benefits derived from shared management and transfer of technology'.[134]

This 'substantive requirement of some sort of sharing of benefits' is underpinned by varying justifications.[135] It is rationalised, alternately, as a form of preferential treatment for developing states or, conversely, as an element tied to equal participation in deep seabed mining.[136] The former approach has met with controversy because, as Wolfrum emphasises, the preferential treatment aspect may more appropriately be classified as having 'its roots in the development aid philosophy', in contrast to the common heritage's equal participation conception, which aims to achieve '*de facto* equality among States' by 'placing all States with respect to the use of the sea-bed on the same footing'.[137]

In its equal participation guise, benefit sharing may serve as a form of compensation for those states lacking the means to become active in deep seabed mining (thereby, 'the receipt of revenues form[s] the equivalent of direct participation in deep sea-bed activities').[138] Moreover, benefit sharing could foster equal participation of developing states, both in negative terms by 'limit[ing] the activities of industrialized countries so as to create room for all countries to participate in deep sea-bed mining activities' (for example, through anti-monopolisation provisions); and by positively creating 'equal opportunities' for all countries to participate in deep seabed mining (for example, through transfer of technology requirements, together with other methods, such as the use of reserved areas and the role of the Enterprise in mining).[139]

Therefore, benefit sharing comprises not only the sharing of financial and other economic benefits derived from deep seabed mining, but also some notion of equal participation in activities in the Area. Accordingly, Wolfrum styles the benefit-sharing component as having a broad 'distributive effect'.[140] As Noyes emphasises,

[134] Pardo (1979) (n 29) 139. See also Baslar (n 1) 98; Noyes (2012) (n 1) 451.

[135] Noyes (2012) (n 1) 453. See also Barnes (n 51) 285, categorising the governance principle of sustainable and equitable use beyond national jurisdiction (which overlaps, to some extent, with the common heritage benefit-sharing principle) as 'advanc[ing] a substantive goal rather than a procedural approach'.

[136] Wolfrum (1983) (n 31) 321–323.

[137] Wolfrum (1983) (n 31) 323. See also Joyner (1986) (n 31) 192–193 and Noyes (2012) (n 1) 452–453.

[138] Wolfrum (1983) (n 31) 321.

[139] Wolfrum (1983) (n 31) 323.

[140] Wolfrum (2009) (n 31) para 18. On application of the common heritage's benefit-sharing principle within the deep seabed mining context as an exercise in distributive justice, see Edwin Egede, *Politics of International Law and International Justice* (Edinburgh UP 2013) 307, 310, 336–337; Tomilola Akanle Eni-Ibukun, *International Environmental Law and Distributive Justice* (Routledge 2014) 30–32. See, generally, Peri Roberts and Peter Sutch, 'The Global Commons and International Distributive Justice' in Camilla Boisen and Matthew C Murray (eds), *Distributive Justice Debates in Political and Social Thought: Perspectives on Finding a Fair Share* (Routledge 2016).

this benefit-sharing component implies elements of 'distributive justice', leading it to be 'the most novel and controversial feature of the [common heritage] principle'.[141] Broader movements for governance principles over areas beyond national jurisdiction also argue for the inclusion of substantive elements related to the benefit-sharing principle, such as requirements for sustainable and equitable use.[142]

Notwithstanding that the elements of equal participation and sharing of financial and other benefits are inherent within the common heritage's benefit-sharing component, there is a degree of fluidity in the threshold to satisfy these elements. For example, Joyner indicates that the common heritage exists on a spectrum, with the 'extremist', 'NIEO variety' of benefit sharing situated at the 'radical' end.[143] However, arguments have been made for more moderate versions of the benefit-sharing component.[144] For example (as this book will consider in Chapter 4), by adjusting the balance within the common heritage (between liberalism and communitarianism), the 1994 Agreement tempered the Convention's benefit-sharing aspects, retaining the principle but significantly diluting its operation.[145]

3.2.4 Component 4 – The Principle of Marine Environmental Protection

From the inception of the common heritage approach to deep seabed mining, the inclusion of some form of marine environmental protection has been a key element.[146] However, this component of the common heritage is, perhaps, the one that has increased most significantly in importance in the intervening decades since Pardo's speech, in light of the development of international environmental law,[147] including principles such as the precautionary approach.[148]

141 Noyes (2012) (n 1) 451; see also Wolfrum (2009) (n 31) para 19; Marie Bourrel, Torsten Thiele and Duncan Currie, 'The Common Heritage of Mankind as a Means to Assess and Advance Equity in Deep Sea Mining' (2016) Marine Pol'y 1, 2. See, generally, Baslar (n 1) 96–99.

142 See, e.g. Oude Elferink (2012a) (n 51) 233–236 (considering issues of 'equitable use', 'access to resources' and 'benefit sharing' as intrinsic within this governance principle (at 236)). See also Barnes (n 51) 285; Freestone (2012) (n 51) 200–201.

143 Joyner (1986) (n 31) 192–193.

144 On this, see, e.g. Wolfrum (1983) (n 31) 322–323.

145 See also earlier analysis in Section 3.1.4, text to nn 105–106.

146 See, e.g. Pardo (1967a) (n 4) para 10(e); 1970 Seabed Declaration (n 62) para 11. See also Wolfrum (1983) (n 31) 320; Baslar (n 1) 235; Karin Mickelson, 'Common Heritage of Mankind as a Limit to Exploitation of the Global Commons' (2019) 30 EJIL 635, 637–641, 659. cf analysis by Noyes (2012) (n 1) 452.

147 For example, the preamble to the 1994 Agreement recognises the growing importance of international environmental law ('[m]indful of the importance of the Convention for the protection and preservation of the marine environment and of the growing concern for the global environment'). On the relationship between the common heritage and international environmental law more generally, see Baslar (n 1) ch 8.

148 See, generally, Jaeckel (2017) (n 42).

It may be the component ripest for reconceptualisation in the modern era.[149]

The principle of marine environmental protection shares its roots with the benefit-sharing principle. Commentators acknowledge that marine environmental protection is part of the broader idea of the common heritage as the 'benefit of mankind'.[150] Conceptually, there is overlap between the two components: the marine environmental protection component is intertwined with the principle that the benefits of the deep seabed must also be shared with future generations.[151] Reservation for future generations necessarily implies marine environmental protection. Wolfrum describes this as the 'intertemporal dimension' of the common heritage of mankind.[152] Therefore, as with the benefit-sharing principle, the principle of marine environmental protection also has important substantive implications.[153]

There is tension between the principle of marine environmental protection and what Feichtner terms the 'exploitation bias' inherent within the deep seabed regime.[154] Some commentators argue against the underlying assumption that deep seabed mining will advance the benefit of mankind, on the basis that this 'forestalls the question as to whether the seabed should be mined at all'.[155] For example, Kim criticises the 'prevailing view' that 'it would benefit no one if the Area is left undeveloped' and argues that '[i]t is time to question the assumption that commercializing the Area will benefit all humankind', given its potential detrimental impact on the marine environment.[156] While it is true that, in the deep seabed regime, the 'CHM [common heritage of mankind] is linked to economic exploitation',[157]

149 Baslar (n 1) 99.

150 See, e.g. Lodge (2012) (n 30) 738–740 (using the umbrella term 'benefit of mankind' to categorise 'a number of closely related' common heritage elements, including 'equal participation, rational use of resources, environmental stewardship and equitable sharing of financial and economic benefits').

151 Pardo (1979) (n 29) 139; Tuerk (n 5) 280.

152 Wolfrum (2009) (n 31) para 22. See also Joyner (1986) (n 31) 195.

153 See, e.g. Barnes (n 51), classifying the governance principle of protection and preservation of the marine environment (which overlaps with the fourth common heritage component under consideration here) as a 'substantive goal' (at 264), and noting that this element is primarily 'a principle of substance rather than process' (at 276). See also Wolfrum (1983) (n 31) 318–319 (recognising the substantive import of the common heritage's marine protection component). As discussed in the present chapter at n 132, this book employs the term 'substance' or 'substantive' in a general manner to classify rules that have material, substantive content in imposing duties or creating rights for actors within the deep seabed mining regime. However, one should note that, within international environmental law, the process/substance distinction is often applied in more specific ways: namely, to distinguish between substantive environmental obligations setting standards to be met and procedural obligations concerning 'duties to notify, warn, inform, or consult', and to undertake environmental impact assessments: Jutta Brunnée, 'Procedure and Substance in International Environmental Law: Confused at a Higher Level?' (2016) 5(6) ESIL Reflections <http://esil-sedi.eu/?p=1344>.

154 Feichtner (n 71) 603.

155 Ranganathan (2019) (n 78) 597; see also Mickelson (n 146) 659–660 (noting that the common heritage concept, as captured in the UNCLOS regime 'largely sidesteps one question: rather than pursuing "better" exploitation, should we be exploiting at all?').

156 Rakhyun E Kim, 'Should Deep Seabed Mining Be Allowed?' (2017) 82 Marine Pol'y 134, 134–135.

157 Feichtner (n 71) 603 (citation omitted) (cf Ranganathan describing the regime as 'turn[ing] the seabed over to the extractive interests of states and corporations': Ranganathan (2019) (n 78) 596). See

such commercial activity will only be consistent with the common heritage to the extent that it realises equitable sharing of benefits and is conducted in accordance with marine environmental safeguards. The challenge for the common heritage concept will be to realise these interconnected components (as the present analysis will address in the following chapters).

Recognising the link between benefit sharing and environmental protection, Baslar categorises the latter as a form of 'burden-sharing', given that 'the protection of the global environment requires the sharing of burdens and sacrifices rather than benefits'.[158] Like other commentators, Baslar also notes that elements of environmental protection are premised upon ideas of sustainable development and sustainable management (and associated principles of equity and distributive justice).[159] More generally, the marine environmental protection component of the common heritage concept lends weight to the broader call for governance principles beyond national jurisdiction, which include various environmentally-focused principles (such as protection and preservation of the marine environment, the precautionary approach, and sustainable and equitable use).[160]

3.2.5 Is Reservation for Peaceful Purposes a Component of the Common Heritage Concept?

The reservation of the Area for peaceful purposes is sometimes cited as forming part of the common heritage concept.[161] Against the backdrop of the Cold War, the demilitarisation of the deep seabed was a key concern during initial discussions of the deep seabed as common heritage.[162] However, before UNCLOS III commenced, this matter had waned in significance, and was transferred to the disarmament context,[163] where it became the subject of a separate treaty.[164] Therefore,

also Lakshman Guruswamy, 'International Environmental Law: Boundaries, Landmarks, and Realities' (1995) 10 Nat Res & Env 43, 48 (arguing that the common heritage concept 'is directed to maximizing resource exploitation and economic returns' and that, accordingly, 'its thrust remains redistribution not conservation'). See, further, Mickelson (n 146) 643–646 (for nuanced discussion of 'competing views as to whether resource exploitation was the primary objective of the deep seabed regime' (643) and attempts to reconcile this with principles of marine conservation).

[158] Baslar (n 1) 99–100 (citations omitted).

[159] Baslar (n 1) 100–101, 103–105; Bourrel, Thiele and Currie (n 141) 3–4. See also Wolfrum (2009) (n 31) para 22 (recognising sustainable development as '[a]n important part of the intertemporal dimension of the common heritage principle') and para 23. See, further, Noyes (2012) (n 1) 466, fn 90.

[160] See, e.g. Oude Elferink (2012a) (n 51) 215–217, 225–228, 233–236, 245. See also Barnes (n 51) 276–277, 282, 285; Freestone (2012) (n 51) 201.

[161] See, e.g. Wolfrum (1983) (n 31) 319–320; Guntrip (2003) (n 14) 389–392; Holmila (n 5) 200–201; Wolfrum (2009) (n 31) para 24.

[162] Baslar (n 1) 105.

[163] Koskenniemi and Lehto (n 5) 537–538; Lodge (2012) (n 30) 736.

[164] Treaty on the Prohibition of the Emplacement of Nuclear Weapons and Other Weapons of Mass Destruction on the Sea-bed and the Ocean Floor and in the Subsoil Thereof (adopted 11 February 1971, entered into force 18 May 1972) 955 UNTS 115.

'[o]ne may argue ... that this element constitutes a principle of its own, unrelated to the common heritage'.[165] Thus, although the reservation of the Area for peaceful purposes is an important international legal norm, it constitutes a self-standing principle, separate from the common heritage principle. On this basis, this study will exclude consideration of the norm of peaceful seabed usage from its assessment of the common heritage of mankind.

3.2.6 Additional Components of the Common Heritage Concept?

There has been 'much debate' as to the precise elements that comprise the common heritage concept.[166] Nevertheless, as the preceding analysis has demonstrated, the common heritage concept can be distilled into four central components, within the present-day deep seabed mining context: common management, no unilateral mining activities, benefit sharing and marine environmental protection. Although there is broad agreement on these four key components, some commentators have lobbied for the inclusion of other elements within the ambit of the common heritage.[167] For example, Joyner maintains that the common heritage concept encompasses the 'conduct of scientific research in the region', which should be 'freely and openly permissible'.[168] However, beyond recognising this as a potential element of benefit sharing, most commentators do not classify scientific research as a self-standing element of the common heritage concept.[169]

Similarly, other elements, such as calls for transparency in decision-making, and open sharing of information,[170] could be treated as being inherent within the common management and benefit-sharing aspects of the common heritage concept, respectively. Equally, many aspects of the common heritage championed by NIEO proponents, such as technology transfer and production limitations, are included (to the extent that they have been retained) within the benefit-sharing principle. Another notable aspect is the extent to which the common heritage concept designates 'mankind' as a new class of beneficiary, raising issues of democratic entitlement and self-determination.[171]

[165] Wolfrum (2009) (n 31) para 24; see also Baslar (n 1) 106–107; Noyes (2012) (n 1) 452.
[166] Noyes (2012) (n 1) 451.
[167] See overview by Baslar (n 1) 84–85.
[168] Joyner (1986) (n 31) 192.
[169] See, e.g. analysis by Noyes (2012) (n 1) 454.
[170] For such calls in the global governance context, see, e.g. Barnes (n 51) 285–287; Oude Elferink (2012a) (n 51) 236–241.
[171] Wolfrum (1983) (n 31) 318–391 (concluding, however (at 319), that 'participants with respect to the utilization of the common heritage are States and not "mankind" as an independent subject of international law'); see, further, Baslar (n 1) 70ff (for analysis of 'mankind' as a new legal personality). See also Noyes (2012) (n 1) 454 (querying the extent to which the common heritage principle 'embodies a type of human right').

The present study will not examine these issues, which sit on the periphery of the common heritage concept, and will instead focus on the four key components as set out above. Moreover, underlying these four components is the balance between community and autonomy, which the following section will briefly note.

3.2.7 The Common Heritage's Underlying Community/Autonomy Equilibrium

As this study has demonstrated,[172] the common heritage principle is premised on a balance between communitarian interests (such as realisation of a benefit for humanity) and more individualistic, capitalist concerns ('market-oriented approaches' that permit commercial actors to participate directly within the system on competitive terms[173]). The common heritage concept, within today's deep seabed regime, is a product of this closely defined balance between 'the benefit of mankind as a whole' and 'market principles';[174] or, in other words, between 'community and autonomy'.[175] These opposing strands are incorporated within the concept itself, and the common heritage can only be realised successfully to the extent that it provides a balance between them.[176]

***

In summation, as the preceding analysis has illustrated, irrespective of potential indeterminacies around the edges of the common heritage concept, the concept contains four central components in the deep seabed mining context. Determining the extent to which UNCLOS has operationalised these components, and establishing whether they can be attained while maintaining a balance between humanity's interests and commercial market principles, will be the acid tests for the deep seabed regime.

3.3 Conclusion: Devising an Analytical Framework to Evaluate Achievement of the Common Heritage Concept in Relation to Deep Seabed Mining Activities by Corporate Entities

This book aims to determine the compatibility between corporate deep seabed mining activities and realisation of the common heritage of mankind within the

172 See previous analysis in Section 3.1.4 at text to nn 72–75 and 104–111.
173 1994 Agreement, preamble.
174 1992 Resolution (n 102) para 5.
175 Koskenniemi (2005) (n 73) 476, and see 488–493.
176 In this regard, as Koskenniemi acknowledges, '[n]either community nor autonomy can be exclusive goals', as that risks a collapse into utopia or apology, respectively: Koskenniemi (2005) (n 73) 476.

UNCLOS regime. As Section 3.2 has demonstrated, in the modern-day deep seabed mining context, the common heritage concept comprises four central components: (1) the common management principle; (2) the prohibition of unilateral mining activities; (3) the benefit-sharing principle; and (4) the principle of marine environmental protection. This study must assess the extent to which these components are operationalised within UNCLOS, and the means by which they apply to corporate actors.

Moreover, deep seabed mining must foster benefits for humanity while being conducted in accordance with market principles. This underlying tension between humanity's interest in the common heritage and commercial actors' interest in conducting deep seabed mining activities in a commercially viable manner is at the heart of the UNCLOS regime. The regime must deliver both to fulfil the common heritage, on the regime's own terms. This balance is particularly significant in relation to corporate activity. As the introduction to this book explained, the success or otherwise of private-sector involvement may have an impact on the commercial viability of the deep seabed mining industry.[177] Given the considerable technological challenges and risks posed by extracting minerals from the deep ocean floor, mining activities require an outlay of substantial capital. For the deep seabed mining industry to flourish, investment by private actors could be a significant factor.[178] In practical terms, this makes the regime's realisation of a market-oriented, commercially friendly approach all the more vital for its longer-term success.

In order to evaluate the impact of corporate mining activities on the operation of the deep seabed mining regime, this study must address the way in which the balance within the common heritage may play out, in practice. Given that the UNCLOS regulatory regime is still under construction, this study necessarily offers only an interim assessment. However, this interim assessment will perform a much-needed 'health check' on the extent to which the regime is developing in a manner that may realise benefits for humankind while facilitating corporate mining activity.

In light of all of these factors, this study will employ the following framework of analysis, in order to determine whether corporate mining activities will be consistent with the realisation of the common heritage. It comprises four sequential steps, as set out in the Table 3.1 below.

[177] See analysis of the increasing role of private actors in deep seabed mining activities and the significance of this role for development of the industry, as set out in the introduction to this book, at text to nn 31–36.

[178] See Fritz (n 5) 461–462; Japan, 'Comments on the Draft Regulations on Exploitation of Mineral Resources in the Area (ISBA/25/C/WP1)' (October 2019) 1 <https://isa.org.jm/files/files/documents/201910%20Japan%27s%20comments%20on%20draft%20regulations.pdf>. See, generally, Catherine Danley, 'Diving to New Depths: How Green Energy Markets can Push Mining Companies into the Deep Sea, and why Nations must Balance Mineral Exploitation with Marine Conservation' (2019–20) 44 Wm & Mary Env L & Pol'y Rev 219.

Table 3.1 This Study's Framework of Analysis

Step 1:	Firstly, does the UNCLOS deep seabed mining regime provide a procedural framework for common management of the deep seabed (***common heritage component 1***)? And by what means does this framework apply to participants within the regime, including corporate actors?
Step 2:	Secondly, and decisively for the global reach of the UNCLOS procedural framework, to what extent does the prohibition of unilateral deep seabed mining activities (***common heritage component 2***) prevent external actors, including corporate actors, from acting incompatibly with the UNCLOS regime?
Step 3:	Thirdly, if these procedural steps are satisfied, and one deep seabed mining system is in place for internal and external actors, is the substantive content of the existing regime sufficient to prevent corporate actors from undermining the common heritage's key material components (namely, the intertwined elements of benefit sharing (***common heritage component 3***) and marine environmental protection (***common heritage component 4***))?
Step 4:	Finally, to the extent that these substantive goals are secured within the regime, and the regime is, therefore, on course to realise benefits to humanity, does the regime also sufficiently enshrine market principles? In particular, does it strike an appropriate regulatory balance between 'benefit of humanity' concerns and investment protection rights for deep seabed miners (***the community/autonomy equilibrium***)?*

*As Chapter 7 will address in more detail, investment protection rights are, in practice, likely to be a key factor in securing corporate investment in the Area and, therefore, constitute an important barometer of the extent to which the regime is sufficiently 'market-oriented' (in the words of the preamble to the 1994 Agreement).

To address each of these steps, the remainder of this book will be divided into two parts. Part II will focus on determining the extent to which the UNCLOS deep seabed mining regime creates a procedural framework, operationalising the common heritage, which is binding on actors both inside and outside of the regime (thereby addressing Steps 1 and 2). Broadly speaking, Part II's focus is on securing the common heritage as a matter of 'process'.[179] To that end, as Chapter 4 will demonstrate, UNCLOS creates a procedural architecture for the pursuit of deep seabed mining activities which, prima facie, enshrines within it the four key common heritage components. As Chapter 5 will establish, this procedural framework has global reach, as it prohibits external actors from conducting unilateral mining activities outside of the Convention regime.

However, by establishing a formal legal process for deep seabed mining activities, the Convention takes us only part of the way towards realising the common

[179] For a note on this book's intended usage of the terms 'process' and 'substance', see Section 3.2.2 at n 132.

heritage. What of attainment of the common heritage objectives of benefit sharing and marine environmental protection? Arguably, UNCLOS enshrines these material goals in a 'formal-procedural way' but engages in a 'strategy of referral', postponing their ultimate realisation to further institutional procedures.[180] The Convention does not contain, within itself, the detailed mechanisms for benefit sharing and marine environmental protection. Rather, the substance of these matters is deferred, to be resolved by ISA regulation. In this manner, UNCLOS refers the material, substantive solution 'away from itself'.[181] For example, 'the provisions on the deep seabed, instead of creating material compensatory duties, establish a massive procedure (the [ISA]) within which, under a complicated decision-making system, compensatory measures would be adopted in the future'.[182]

Therefore, in order to determine the extent to which increasing commercial deep seabed mining activities will impact upon the common heritage's material goals, this study must step beyond the Convention's formal procedural framework. It must assess the extent to which the ISA's developing regulatory framework (and accompanying implementation and enforcement powers) may foster benefit sharing and marine environmental protection. Part III will turn to addressing this task. In so doing, the focus of Part III will necessarily be on the more substantive, material aspects of the Convention's deep seabed mining regime: common heritage as 'substance'.[183]

Within Part III, Chapter 6 will address Step 3 of this study's framework of analysis by determining whether the ISA's regulatory regime is developing in a manner which may support benefit sharing and marine environmental protection in the face of commercial mining activities. Given that the specifics of the ISA's regulatory regime are still evolving, Chapter 6 will confine itself to affording a flavour of the regime's current status, while situating it within its broader context in terms of matters of implementation, responsibility and enforcement. Thereafter, Chapter 7 will address Step 4 by evaluating the extent to which the UNCLOS regime strikes an appropriate regulatory balance between 'benefit of

[180] Koskenniemi (2005) (n 73) 492–493. See also Allot (n 80) 10 (noting that UNCLOS, in general, is 'a massive structure of powers', 'without parallel or precedent in the scale of its delegation of power') and 16 (remarking that the Convention's 'deep seabed governmental system (legislative, executive, judicial) waits upon its implementation by countless subordinate decisions taken within the framework of the Convention structure').

[181] Koskenniemi (2005) (n 73) 493; and see, generally, Kennedy (1987) (n 131) 201–245.

[182] Koskenniemi (2005) (n 73) 492 (citing UNCLOS, arts 150–187); see also 493–494 (explaining that the Convention's 'strategy of referral' is such that various material elements, such as benefit-sharing aspects like production policies, are deferred to ISA consideration, to be decided by the agreement of 'all interested parties').

[183] On the intended meaning of 'substance' within this book, see this chapter's previous discussion at n 132. However, as noted therein, there is a degree of overlap between the terms 'process' and 'substance'. Therefore, there will necessarily be some related procedural implications to Part III's assessment.

humanity' concerns and market-focused investment protection rights for deep seabed miners.

In light of this analysis, this book will reach conclusions on the extent to which the UNCLOS deep seabed mining regime should be sufficient to facilitate commercial mining activities by corporate actors while realising overall benefits for humankind.

PART II

THE COMMON HERITAGE AS PROCESS – ANCHORING THE DEEP SEABED MINING REGIME APPLICABLE TO CORPORATE ACTORS WITHIN ITS INSTITUTIONAL CONTEXT

Roll on, thou deep and dark blue Ocean, roll!
Ten thousand fleets sweep over thee in vain;
Man marks the earth with ruin; his control
Stops with the shore

(Lord Byron, *Childe Harold's Pilgrimage: Canto IV*, 1818)

Introduction to Part II

This part will focus upon determining the extent to which the Convention creates a procedural framework for deep seabed mining that operationalises the common heritage's key components and is binding on actors both inside and outside the regime, including corporate actors. Firstly, Chapter 4 will assess the Convention's common management system for deep seabed mining and the means by which it applies to participants within the regime, including corporate actors. By doing so, Chapter 4 will address Step 1 of this study's framework of analysis (set out in Section 3.3).

Thereafter, Chapter 5 will tackle Step 2 by considering the global reach of the UNCLOS procedural framework. It will do so by determining whether the prohibition of unilateral deep seabed mining activities prevents external actors, including corporations, from pursuing such activities outside of UNCLOS.

4
Common Management through Institutional Architecture – What is the Scope of the UNCLOS Deep Seabed Mining Regime and the Role of the ISA within it?

The UNCLOS regime aims to secure common management of deep seabed resources by two parallel means. Firstly, it endeavours to implement common management via a system of common rules for the Area. Section 4.1 will address this by assessing key aspects of the Convention's deep seabed mining regime. Secondly, and more radically, UNCLOS seeks to implement a dynamic, evolving system of common management through a unique and unprecedented form of institutional power: the ISA. Section 4.2 will deconstruct the pivotal role of the ISA as custodian, developer and regulator of the deep seabed mining regime. Once this chapter has evaluated the extent to which the Convention regime achieves a system of common management for deep seabed mining, it will turn, in Section 4.3, to determine the means by which this filters down to apply to private corporate actors operating within the regime.

4.1 Common Management through Common Rules: Overarching Principles of the UNCLOS Deep Seabed Mining Regime

The deep seabed mining regime is spread across various instruments. Its main body is contained within Part XI of UNCLOS, together with Annex III to UNCLOS (which sets out the application process and conditions for deep seabed mining). The original Convention regime was modified substantially by the 1994 Agreement.[1] The provisions of Part XI of UNCLOS, and the 1994 Agreement, are

[1] The 1994 Agreement eliminated certain controversial aspects of the original UNCLOS scheme for deep seabed mining, to overcome long-running opposition by industrialised states. See Chapter 3, text to nn 103–111.

International Law and Corporate Actors in Deep Seabed Mining. Joanna Dingwall, Oxford University Press. © Joanna Dingwall 2021. DOI: 10.1093/oso/9780192898265.003.0005

to be interpreted and applied together as a single instrument. In the event of a discrepancy between them, the provisions of the 1994 Agreement are decisive.[2] In an echo of the 'package deal' approach of UNCLOS III,[3] the Convention (including the deep seabed regime within it) must be ratified by States Parties in full, without reservations.[4] The following analysis will address the main contours of the regime, to assess the extent to which the components underpinning the common heritage of mankind (as set out in Chapter 3, Section 3.2) appear on the face of the regime.

4.1.1 Key Components of the Common Heritage Concept Captured by the UNCLOS Deep Seabed Mining Regime

The principle that '[t]he Area and its resources are the common heritage of mankind' is contained within Article 136 of UNCLOS. This principle constitutes the apex of the UNCLOS deep seabed mining regime.[5] The regime insulates the common heritage principle from amendment.[6] Nevertheless, the drafters stopped short of imbuing the common heritage with *jus cogens* status[7] during UNCLOS III.[8]

[2] 1994 Agreement, art 2(1). cf Robin R Churchill and A Vaughan Lowe, *The Law of the Sea* (3rd edn, Manchester UP 1999) 238, fn 45 (noting that 'the [1994] Agreement gives rise to many complex questions of treaty law, modifying as it does the effect of [UNCLOS] in a manner clearly not envisaged by [UNCLOS] arts 310–14, and purporting to prevail over [UNCLOS]').

[3] On which, see Chapter 3, text to n 85.

[4] UNCLOS, art 309. cf art 310 (allowing certain state declarations and statements). See alsoLDM Nelson, 'Declarations, Statements and Disguised Reservations with Respect to the Convention on the Law of the Sea' (2001) 50 ICLQ 767.

[5] To some extent, the common heritage concept could almost be viewed, within the deep seabed mining regime, as akin to a Kelsenian *Grundnorm* (i.e. the basic norm that serves as the source of validity of all other norms within the system). See, generally, Hans Kelsen, *Pure Theory of Law* (Max Knight tr, 7th edn, University of California Press 1967).

[6] UNCLOS, art 311(6) specifies that 'there shall be no amendments to the basic principle relating to the common heritage of mankind ... and that [States Parties] shall not be party to any agreement in derogation thereof'. See also UNCLOS, art 155(2) (allowing a review conference of the Convention regime to 'ensure the maintenance of the principle of the common heritage of mankind' and various concomitant elements, including the ISA's role as custodian of the deep seabed, non-appropriation requirements, equal participation and sharing of benefits and marine environmental protection). Despite the 1994 Agreement's significant curtailment of the review conference, the 1994 Agreement (Annex, s 4) reinforces that, although amendments to Part XI of UNCLOS and the 1994 Agreement are permissible in accordance with the UNCLOS amendment process, the principles contained in Article 155(2) of UNCLOS 'shall be maintained'.

[7] VCLT, art 53 codifies the concept of *jus cogens*, providing that 'a peremptory norm of general international law is a norm accepted and recognized by the international community of States as a whole as a norm from which no derogation is permitted'.

[8] Myron H Nordquist and others (eds), *United Nations Convention on the Law of the Sea 1982: A Commentary*, vol V (Martinus Nijhoff Publishers 1989) 241–243 (the original Chilean proposal for Article 311(6) was to designate the common heritage as a *jus cogens* norm: due to opposition to this approach, Article 311(6) was redrafted into its current form). See also James Harrison, *Making the Law of the Sea* (CUP 2011) 133–134; Nele Matz-Lück, 'Article 311' in Proelss Commentary 2018. Notably, as per UNCLOS, arts 312–316 (amendment of the Convention), UNCLOS, art 311(6) is itself not immune from amendment (although, in practice, an amendment attempt would prompt outrage).

Even although the common heritage principle contained within Article 136 is 'the underlying principle upon which the regime for seabed mining ... rests',[9] the Convention does not attempt to define it. Rather, as Baslar describes, 'Article 136 ... gives us an eleven-word-puzzle'.[10] To interpret the meaning of the 'common heritage' within Article 136, one must apply the rules of treaty interpretation.[11] Together with its ordinary meaning, other key factors include the provision's context, interpreted in light of its object and purpose.[12] Also relevant, as a supplementary means of interpretation, are the *travaux préparatoires*.[13]

Viewing Article 136 in context requires taking account of the Convention's deep seabed mining regime as a whole. As Noyes recognises, the terms of UNCLOS and the 1994 Agreement serve to 'limit the indeterminacy of the [common heritage] principle as developed in that treaty regime'.[14] Although the common heritage concept is 'undefined', 'its meaning for the purposes of the Convention can be derived from the other provisions of Part XI'.[15] The Virginia Commentary recognises the role of the common heritage's historical development (as recounted in Chapter 3, Section 3.1) in determining the concept's content within the Convention.[16] In particular, the UNCLOS regime incorporates the four components assessed in Chapter 3, Section 3.2, as constituting key aspects of the common heritage concept.

The first of these (the principle of common management) is the focus of this chapter's examination more generally. The second common heritage component, prohibiting unilateral deep seabed mining activities, is expressed in Article 137 of UNCLOS. This provision addresses two separate issues: 'the legal status of the Area (paragraph 1) and the legal status of its resources (paragraphs 1, 2 and 3)'.[17] As regards the *legal status of the Area*, paragraph 1 proscribes states from exerting sovereignty over the Area, and it also prohibits states and any other actors from appropriating any part of it. Paragraph 1 proscribes recognition of any such claims. In relation to the *legal status of deep seabed resources*, paragraph 1 also prohibits states

[9] Virginia Commentary 95–96.

[10] Kemal Baslar, *The Concept of the Common Heritage of Mankind in International Law* (Martin Nijhoff Publishers 1998) 206.

[11] See overview of these rules in Chapter 1, at text to nn 16–19. See also Baslar (n 10) 207–210.

[12] VCLT, art 31(1).

[13] VCLT, art 32.

[14] John E Noyes, 'The Common Heritage of Mankind: Past, Present, and Future' (2012) 40 Denv J Int'l L & P 447, 454; see also Silja Vöneky and Anja Höfelmeier, 'Article 136' in Proelss Commentary 955 (noting that, 'while Art. 136 proclaims the employment of the [common heritage] principle, the subsequent articles install the different aspects').

[15] Virginia Commentary 99 (as the present study noted in Chapter 3, at n 18, the Virginia Commentary has a status almost akin to the Convention's *travaux préparatoires*); see, further, Michael W Lodge, 'The Common Heritage of Mankind' (2012) 27 Int'l J Marine Coastal L 733, 734.

[16] See, e.g. Virginia Commentary 96 (on UNCLOS, art 136 as 'reaffirmation' of the 1970 Seabed Declaration, UNGA Res 2749 (XXV) (17 December 1970)). See also Lodge (2012) (n 15) 734, fn 4.

[17] Virginia Commentary 103 (see also 103–111 on drafting history of this provision).

and other actors from appropriating any part of the Area's resources, and prevents the recognition of such appropriation.

Building upon this, paragraph 2 affirms that all rights over deep seabed resources 'are vested in mankind as a whole' and deputises the Authority to act on mankind's behalf. Pursuant to paragraph 2, deep seabed resources cannot be alienated. However, this paragraph recognises that deep seabed minerals (i.e. extracted resources) can be alienated in accordance with the UNCLOS regime. In doing so, this provision incorporates a 'negative dimension': '[t]he prohibition of all unilateral mining or appropriation of minerals'.[18] Actors only become eligible to conduct deep seabed mining activities (and ultimately alienate deep seabed minerals by extracting them from the Area) by contracting with the ISA and agreeing to ISA oversight.[19] In practice, an ISA contractor will only gain title to deep seabed minerals upon their 'recovery' from the Area,[20] 'implying that prior to recovery of the minerals, the contractor has no title'.[21]

Finally, but of no less importance, paragraph 3 of Article 137 addresses the *legal status of deep seabed minerals* (i.e. resources after their extraction from the Area). By providing that all states and other actors can 'claim, acquire or exercise rights' over deep seabed minerals only through the UNCLOS regime, and that any rights attained outside the system are not to be recognised, paragraph 3 prohibits illicit trade in deep seabed minerals extracted in contravention of the UNCLOS regime. For example, if a private actor mined the deep seabed unilaterally (in violation of Article 137(2)) and extracted deep seabed minerals, states could prevent that actor from selling those minerals on their territory (in accordance with Article 137(3)).

Taken as a whole, Article 137's prohibition of unilateral activities underpins the common management principle. For the regime to achieve a true and universal system of common management, all actors outside of the regime must be prohibited from engaging in deep seabed mining activities unilaterally.[22] Chapter 5 will consider this further when determining the reach of the prohibition on unilateral activities, and the extent to which external actors (including private corporate actors) are prohibited, under international law, from undertaking deep seabed mining activities outside of UNCLOS.

The third common heritage component (the benefit-sharing principle) is enshrined in the Convention as a key goal of the regime. Deep seabed mining in the

18 Silja Vöneky and Anja Höfelmeier, 'Article 137' in Proelss Commentary 963.

19 UNCLOS, arts 153 and 157(1); 1994 Agreement, Annex, s 1(1).

20 UNCLOS, Annex III, art 1.

21 Virginia Commentary 110.

22 UNCLOS, art 138 is also important in this regard, as it provides that 'general conduct of States in relation to the Area' must be in accordance with the UNCLOS deep seabed mining regime and other rules of international law: therefore, it 'may be seen as a reinforcement of the fact that a freedom of exploitation does not exist; instead, exploitation is subject to express consent and control by the Authority': Silja Vöneky and Anja Höfelmeier, 'Article 138' in Proelss Commentary 967 (citation omitted).

Area must be carried out only 'for the benefit of mankind as a whole'.[23] The regime captures the benefit-sharing principle's twin goals of equal participation in deep seabed mining and equitable sharing of benefits derived from such activities.[24] For example, as regards equal participation, the regime must take into account the interests of developing states and promote their effective participation.[25] Many aspects designed to foster equal participation are contained within the ISA's licensing process, so they are built into the regime's underlying procedural framework. These elements include anti-monopolisation provisions, a system for reservation of areas and the potential role of the ISA's mining arm, the Enterprise (as Section 4.2.3 will address).

As regards equitable sharing of benefits, a key feature that proved contentious at UNCLOS III, but was nevertheless preserved by the 1994 Agreement, concerns redistribution of the profits that deep seabed mining may yield. Article 140(2) of UNCLOS empowers the ISA to provide for equitable sharing of 'financial and other economic benefits' derived from activities in the Area.[26] These benefits are to be shared equitably, on a non-discriminatory basis, through a mechanism which the ISA has still to devise.[27] Although the ISA has yet to develop such rules, the ISA must, in formulating them, take the interests and needs of developing states into 'particular consideration'.[28] The ISA's role will, therefore, be pivotal in developing a workable regime for equitable sharing of benefits (as Section 4.2.2 will demonstrate).[29]

Finally, the Convention regime incorporates the fourth common heritage component: the principle of marine environmental protection. This principle operates within the broader context of the Convention's general regime for protection and preservation of the environment (UNCLOS, Part XII).[30] Moreover, in relation to deep seabed mining, states and the ISA must conduct their activities in a manner consistent with general international law, including customary international law: this encompasses various international environmental law principles, such as

[23] UNCLOS, art 140(1); see also arts 153, 157(1) and Annex III.

[24] See, e.g. analysis by Silja Vöneky and Anja Höfelmeier, 'Article 140' in Proelss Commentary 980.

[25] UNCLOS, arts 148, 150, 152(2). cf analysis in Chapter 3, at text to nn 136–137.

[26] See also UNCLOS, arts 160(2)(f)(i), 160(2)(g), 162(2)(o)(i), 165(2)(f), 173(2)(a); 1994 Agreement, Annex, s 9(7)(f).

[27] UNCLOS, art 140(2).

[28] UNCLOS, arts 160(2)(f)(i) and 162(2)(o)(i).

[29] Chapter 6 will also consider the substantive content of the benefit-sharing component, in assessing ISA development of this component through regulatory processes.

[30] On the Convention's approach to marine environmental protection, see, generally, Jonathan I Charney, 'The Marine Environment and the 1982 United Nations Convention on the Law of the Sea' (1994) 28 Int'l Law 879; Catherine Redgwell, 'From Permission to Prohibition: The 1982 Convention on the Law of the Sea and Protection of the Marine Environment' in David Freestone, Richard Barnes and David Ong (eds), *Law of the Sea – Progress and Prospects* (OUP 2006); David M Ong, 'The 1982 UN Convention on the Law of the Sea and Marine Environmental Protection' in Malgosia Fitzmaurice, David M Ong and Panos Merkouris (eds), *Research Handbook on International Environmental Law* (Edward Elgar Publishing 2010).

the duty to apply the precautionary approach.[31] As Jaeckel notes, the ISA's mandate is infused with the Convention's 'broad and all-encompassing aim to protect and preserve the marine environment'.[32]

The protection of the marine environment forms a significant element of the UNCLOS deep seabed regime.[33] The Seabed Disputes Chamber (*Chamber*) of ITLOS has gone so far as to recognise obligations of marine preservation in the Area (and the high seas) as having an '*erga omnes* character'.[34] Described as 'the core of the regime',[35] protection of the marine environment is addressed within Article 145 of UNCLOS, which requires 'necessary measures' to be taken 'with respect to activities in the Area to ensure effective protection for the marine environment from harmful effects which may arise from such activities'.[36] Seeking to strike a balance between allowing deep seabed mining activities while preserving the marine environment, this provision authorises the ISA to adopt rules, regulations and procedures in order to prevent, reduce and control pollution and other marine environmental hazards in relation to activities in the Area.[37]

The 1994 Agreement further reinforces protection of the Area's marine environment. Recognising 'the importance of the Convention for the protection and preservation of the marine environment and of the growing concern for the global environment',[38] the 1994 Agreement designates the adoption of a regulatory regime for marine environmental protection as one of the priorities upon which the ISA must focus between the entry into force of the Convention and the commencement of exploitation activities.[39]

As Chapter 6 will evaluate further, the regulatory regime which the ISA has adopted to date 'spell[s] out in considerable detail the obligations of contractors,

[31] See, e.g. ITLOS AO, paras 122, 125ff. See, generally, Aline L Jaeckel, *The International Seabed Authority and the Precautionary Principle – Balancing Deep Seabed Mineral Mining and Marine Environmental Protection* (Brill 2017) 122.

[32] Jaeckel (2017) (n 31) 122.

[33] For analysis of issues concerning environmental protection in deep seabed mining, see, e.g. Kristina M Gjerde, 'Challenges to Protecting the Marine Environment beyond National Jurisdiction' (2012) 27 Int'l J Marine Coastal L 839; Alex G Oude Elferink, 'Environmental Impact Assessment in Areas beyond National Jurisdiction' (2012) 27 Int'l J Marine Coastal L 449; Rüdiger Wolfrum, 'The Contribution of the Regulations of the International Seabed Authority to the Progressive Development of International Environmental Law' in Michael W Lodge and Myron H Nordquist (eds), *Peaceful Order in the World's Oceans* (Brill 2014); Tullio Scovazzi, 'The Exploitation of Resources of the Deep Seabed and the Protection of the Environment' (2014) 57 GYIL 181; Aline Jaeckel, 'An Environmental Management Strategy for the International Seabed Authority? The Legal Basis' (2015) 30 Int'l J Marine Coastal L 93; Jaeckel (2017) (n 31) 121–131.

[34] ITLOS AO, para 180. Obligations *erga omnes* are those owed to the international community as a whole, in which all states 'have a legal interest in their protection': *Barcelona Traction, Light and Power Company, Limited* (Judgment) [1970] ICJ Rep 3, para 33.

[35] Churchill and Lowe (n 2) 239.

[36] See also UNCLOS, art 147 (accommodation of activities in the Area and in the marine environment).

[37] See also UNCLOS, Annex III, art 17(1)(b)(xii), (2)(f). See, further, UNCLOS, art 162(2)(w) and (x) and analysis in Virginia Commentary 196.

[38] 1994 Agreement, preamble.

[39] 1994 Agreement, Annex, s1(5)(g); see also Virginia Commentary 197–198.

sponsoring States, and the Authority with respect to the protection and preservation of the marine environment'.[40] Nevertheless, as with the rules applicable to equitable sharing of economic benefits derived from deep seabed mining, the rules for environmental protection in the Area remain a work in progress, and their ultimate effectiveness will depend on the Authority's powers to develop them further (as Section 4.2 will evaluate).

4.1.2 Other Common Management Rules within the UNCLOS Deep Seabed Mining Regime

In addition to the features set out above, the regime also includes some further notable aspects. Pursuant to Article 141, the Area is 'open to use exclusively for peaceful purposes'.[41] The regime puts in place principles to resolve issues concerning resources straddling the boundary between the Area and coastal state jurisdiction.[42] Another important feature, in which the ISA has a key role, is promotion of marine scientific research in the Area.[43] Importantly, this also has benefit-sharing implications, as such research must be carried out 'for the benefit of mankind as a whole'.[44] To that end, the ISA established, in 2006, an endowment fund for marine scientific research in the Area, aiming to promote and encourage the conduct of such research for the benefit of humanity.[45] The regime also aims to safeguard human life in the Area. Article 146 requires 'necessary measures' to be taken to 'ensure effective protection of human life' and empowers the ISA to adopt an appropriate regulatory regime to 'supplement existing international law'.[46] By

[40] Virginia Commentary 192.

[41] For further information on the drafting history and scope of this provision, see Virginia Commentary 145–150; and see this book's analysis in Chapter 3, Section 3.2.5. See also UNCLOS, art 138 (requiring state conduct in relation to the Area to be in accordance, inter alia, with the principles of the UN Charter 'and other rules of international law in the interests of maintaining peace and security and promoting international co-operation and mutual understanding').

[42] UNCLOS, art 142. On the development of this provision, see Virginia Commentary 151–159.

[43] UNCLOS, art 143; see also UNCLOS, Part XIII (Marine Scientific Research), more generally, on the conduct of promotion of marine scientific research throughout the oceans, including within the Area (on which, see UNCLOS, art 256 (marine scientific research in the Area)). On the drafting history and scope of UNCLOS, art 143, and its interaction with Part XIII, see Virginia Commentary 160–172.

[44] UNCLOS, art 143(1). On this aspect, see also Silja Vöneky and Felix Beck, 'Article 143' in Proelss Commentary 997.

[45] ISA Assembly, 'Resolution Establishing an Endowment Fund for Marine Scientific Research in the Area' (16 August 2006) ISBA/12/A/11.

[46] UNCLOS, art 146. See, generally, Virginia Commentary 200–205. As it notes (at 201), such necessary measures to protect human life 'may encompass elements of a variety of topics, including the safety of navigation, safety of life at sea, operational safeguards and maintenance requirements for activities in the Area, and labor regulations governing activities in the Area'. In light of the array of existing international instruments that govern these areas, the Virginia Commentary (at 204) considers it 'unlikely' that the Authority would need to adopt additional regulations, rules or procedures 'to supplement existing international law' in terms of Article 146. On the extent of protection of life at sea, including within the Area, see Irini Papanicolopulu, *International Law and the Protection of People at Sea* (OUP 2018).

virtue of Article 149, the regime also provides safeguarding measures in relation to archaeological or historical objects found in the Area.[47]

Crucially, as part of its international legal normative framework for deep seabed mining, the Convention implements sophisticated systems of responsibility and dispute settlement in respect of deep seabed mining activities. This book will defer consideration of these aspects to Part III (in the context of assessing the material consequences of the regime for corporate actors). However, it is sufficient to note for present purposes that the international responsibility of deep seabed mining contractors for their wrongful conduct is a key element of the regime. A deep seabed mining contractor 'shall have responsibility or liability for any damage arising out of wrongful acts in the conduct of its operations'.[48] The Convention's dispute resolution system for deep seabed mining disputes also provides a direct role for deep seabed mining contractors, endowing them with standing to instigate, or defend against, such disputes.[49]

4.1.3 The UNCLOS Deep Seabed Mining Regime Implements a System of Common Management through Common Rules

The Convention's regime for deep seabed mining creates a system of common management by implementing a framework of common rules. The Convention provides rules for common management of deep seabed resources in Part XI and Annex III, as modified by the 1994 Agreement. These rules include the overarching components of the common heritage concept set out in Chapter 3, Section 3.2: there is to be common management of the regime through the ISA; there must be no unilateral deep seabed mining activities outside of the regime; deep seabed mining must be undertaken in a way that encourages equal participation and allows for equitable sharing of benefits; and deep seabed mining activities must be conducted in a manner that is compatible with the preservation of the marine environment. Thus, prima facie, the regime secures the key common heritage components within its procedural framework.

Nevertheless, despite the far-reaching, ambitious architecture afforded by UNCLOS, many of its precise workings are preserved for ISA development. The Convention's framework for deep seabed mining deliberately retains a 'substantive emptiness'.[50] By virtue of the compromise achieved in the 1994 Agreement, the

[47] UNCLOS, art 149 (providing, inter alia, that such objects 'shall be preserved or disposed of for the benefit of mankind as a whole'). See also Virginia Commentary 226–232.

[48] UNCLOS, Annex III, art 22.

[49] UNCLOS, art 187 and Annex VI, art 37.

[50] Martti Koskenniemi and Marja Lehto, 'The Privilege of Universality: International Law, Economic Ideology and Seabed Resources' (1996) 65 Nordic J Int'l L 533, 555 (this 'substantive emptiness' was the only means by which disputing factions could reach agreement on the Convention's provisions on deep seabed mining).

Convention's deep seabed regime was watered down and rendered more anodyne.[51] This dilution postponed certain key elements of the regime for the Authority's ultimate development. Therefore, achievement of a successful common management regime for deep seabed mining depends heavily on the ISA's powers to develop and implement the regime. Section 4.2 will now assess whether the underlying regime provides the ISA with the requisite powers to develop a regulatory regime sufficient to achieve common management through institutional power, thereby giving 'concrete institutional form' to the common heritage principle.[52]

4.2 Common Management through Institutional Power: The Role of the ISA

In practice, much of the regime requires further development by the institutional authority in charge of its operation: the ISA. This section will deconstruct the ISA's varying roles as custodian, developer and regulator of the deep seabed mining regime. It will do so by evaluating the following three features: the ISA's governance structure and balance of power (Section 4.2.1); the ISA's role in the evolution of the regime, particularly through its progressive development of the Mining Code (Section 4.2.2); and, perhaps most importantly of all, in terms of the operationalisation of the regime, the functioning of the ISA's licensing process and the role of corporate participants within it (Section 4.2.3).

4.2.1 The ISA's Structure and Balance of Power

The Authority is an intergovernmental body sitting in Kingston, Jamaica. It has 168 members, comprising all States Parties to UNCLOS. The ISA also has some thirty states participating in its activities as observers, including the US, together with various observer international organisations and NGOs.[53]

As an international organisation, the ISA has international legal personality, entitling it to the full range of rights and duties of an international person.[54] As the following analysis will reveal, the ISA is a unique and unusual body with far-reaching institutional powers of a kind which are, arguably, unparalleled within

[51] This is evident, in particular, as regards various benefit-sharing aspects of the ISA's licensing process, as will be discussed in Section 4.2.3.2.

[52] Jan-Stefan Fritz, 'Deep Sea Anarchy: Mining at the Frontiers of International Law' (2015) 30 Int'l J Marine Coastal L 445, 463.

[53] UNCLOS, art 156(3); see also ISA, 'Observers' <www.isa.org.jm/observers> for the current list of ISA observers; see, further, Harrison (2011) (n 8) 128 on the role of these observers.

[54] UNCLOS, art 176. See also *Reparation for Injuries Suffered in the Service of the United Nations* (Advisory Opinion) [1949] ICJ Rep 174, 179; Markos Karavias, *Corporate Obligations under International Law* (OUP 2013) 121.

the international legal system.[55] The ISA plays the crucial role of custodian of the deep seabed: a role that is enshrined in both UNCLOS and the 1994 Agreement.[56] The ISA's mandate is expressed most clearly in Article 157(1) of UNCLOS: '[t]he Authority is the Organization through which States Parties shall, in accordance with [Part XI], organize and control activities in the Area, particularly with a view to administering the resources of the Area'. The ISA is entrusted with the role of organising, implementing and controlling activities in the Area 'on behalf of mankind as a whole'.[57]

The 1994 Agreement sought to streamline and adapt the Authority's operation to render it more consistent with 'market-oriented approaches'.[58] To that end, the 1994 Agreement applies an 'evolutionary approach' to the Authority's functions, postponing the operationalisation of certain organs and reducing operating costs.[59] Notwithstanding these modifications, the ISA remains the world's 'only organisation specifically required to give effect to the common heritage principle'.[60] The ISA possesses a unique opportunity to operationalise the content of the principle and 'furnish ... it with practical meaning'.[61]

As Wolfrum describes, the Authority's powers include both prescriptive and executive functions.[62] The Authority prescribes the regulatory regime for deep seabed mining,[63] and also exercises supervisory authority to ensure that participants adhere to the regime.[64] In so doing, the Authority boasts 'surprisingly extensive enforcement powers'.[65] Notably, the Authority also possesses the competence

[55] See analysis by Rüdiger Wolfrum, 'Legitimacy of International Law and the Exercise of Administrative Functions: The Example of the International Seabed Authority, the International Maritime Organization (IMO) and International Fisheries Organizations' in Armin von Bogdandy and others (eds), *The Exercise of Public Authority by International Institutions – Advancing International Institutional Law* (Springer 2010) 917 (citing the ISA as a 'rare' example of an international entity 'exercising functions equivalent to those of States', on the basis that it exercises executive and legislative functions and has jurisdiction to enforce its rules directly, via a binding dispute resolution system. Therefore, the ISA is 'without question, a prime example of what may be referred to as an international administration' (at 934). On the concept of international administration, see, generally, JHH Weiler, 'The Geology of International Law – Governance, Democracy and Legitimacy' (2004) 64 ZaöRV 547). See also Jaeckel (2017) (n 31) 146–148.

[56] UNCLOS, art 137(2); see also arts 153 and 157(1), and 1994 Agreement, Annex, s 1(1).

[57] UNCLOS, art 153(1); see also art 137(2).

[58] 1994 Agreement, preamble.

[59] 1994 Agreement, Annex, s 1(3)–(4). On the 1994 Agreement's aim of 'cost-effectiveness', see, further, Harrison (2011) (n 8) 116–117. For useful analysis of ISA financial arrangements, see Jaeckel (2017) (n 31) 110–111.

[60] Jaeckel (2017) (n 31) 87.

[61] Jaeckel (2017) (n 31) 88.

[62] Wolfrum (2010) (n 55) 931–933.

[63] Significantly, the Authority's regulatory regime becomes binding upon States Parties without them having to ratify it: see, further, Wolfrum (2010) (n 55) 932; see also Harrison (2011) (n 8) 123.

[64] As Wolfrum notes, although ISA supervisory functions are shared with States Parties, the ISA has ultimate controlling responsibility to ensure State Party compliance (see UNCLOS, art 153(4)). Importantly, '[t]his control function on the part of the Authority is independent from the affirmative consent of the States Parties or the companies engaged in the deep seabed mining activities': Wolfrum (2010) (n 55) 932.

[65] Jaeckel (2017) (n 31) 114.

to become a participant in deep seabed mining activities through its mining organ, the Enterprise (once operational).[66]

At present, the ISA's powers are most evident in relation to two functions: progressive development of the regulatory regime governing deep seabed mining, and implementation and control of the deep seabed licensing regime. The ISA's practical operation of its functions in these two respects will be considered in Sections 4.2.2 and 4.2.3, respectively. To set the scene for this forthcoming analysis, the remainder of the present section will focus, more generally, upon the ISA's structure and balance of power.

The ISA comprises three principal organs: the Assembly, a plenary body in which all States Parties are represented; the thirty-six-member Council elected by the Assembly, which constitutes the ISA's executive organ; and the Secretariat, which is responsible for the ISA's administration, and is led by the Secretary-General.[67] Importantly, from a legal perspective, the ISA is assisted by its Legal and Technical Commission (*LTC*), which is an organ of the Council.[68] The Convention also provided for the Council to be supported by an Economic Planning Commission, but in keeping with the 1994 Agreement's drive for institutional efficiency, the Council has not yet established this body.[69] Similarly, the Authority's mining arm, the Enterprise, is not yet operational.[70] As well as streamlining certain aspects of the Authority, the 1994 Agreement also provided it with one further organ: the Finance Committee, a subsidiary organ of the Assembly, composed of representatives of the Council.[71]

The finely tuned balance of the ISA's power was a contentious negotiating issue.[72] The Assembly and the Council play leading roles within the ISA. The Assembly is styled as the 'supreme organ of the Authority';[73] however, the 1994 Agreement scaled back its powers significantly, in favour of the Council.[74] Prior to the adoption of the 1994 Agreement, the Convention was drafted to endow the Assembly

[66] UNCLOS, arts 153(2)(a), 158(2) and 170; 1994 Agreement, Annex, s 2. For analysis of the Enterprise, see Section 4.2.3.2. See also Wolfrum (2010) (n 55) 933–934.

[67] See, in particular, UNCLOS, arts 158(1), 159–162, 166; 1994 Agreement, Annex, ss 1 and 3.

[68] UNCLOS, arts 163(1)(b), 165. The Council elects LTC members for five-year terms, based on qualifications relevant to deep seabed mining, including legal/technical expertise. Currently, the LTC has thirty members, including economists, lawyers, mining engineers, environmental experts and oceanographers.

[69] UNCLOS, arts 163(1)(a), 164; cf 1994 Agreement, Annex, s 1(4) (providing that the LTC is to perform functions of the Economic Planning Commission 'until such a time as the Council decides otherwise or until the approval of the first plan of work for exploitation').

[70] UNCLOS, arts 158(2) and 170; 1994 Agreement, Annex, s 2.

[71] 1994 Agreement, Annex, s 9; see also s 3(4), (7); for analysis of the role of the Finance Committee and the drafting history of its inception, see Virginia Commentary 407–408.

[72] On the divisive drafting history of Article 160 of UNCLOS (which defines the Assembly's powers) and the battle between industrialised/developing states as to the ISA's power structure, see Virginia Commentary 391–403; see also analysis of the Authority's decision-making processes at 404–408. See, further, Churchill and Lowe (n 2) 228, 244–247; Harrison (2011) (n 8) 124; Fritz (n 52) 451–452.

[73] UNCLOS, art 160(1).

[74] See, e.g. Churchill and Lowe (n 2) 240; see also Wolfrum (2010) (n 55) 929.

with broad competences to establish ISA policies.[75] The 1994 Agreement fettered the Assembly's powers by requiring that 'general policies of the Authority shall be established by the Assembly *in collaboration with the Council*'.[76] Indeed, as regards matters that are in the sphere of competence of the Assembly and the Council, the 1994 Agreement mandates that '[i]f the Assembly does not accept the recommendation of the Council on any matter, it shall return the matter to the Council for further consideration'.[77] In such circumstances, the Council must then reconsider the matter in light of the Assembly's views.[78] However, this process effectively provides the Council with the last word, and the 'pivotal role' in forming ISA policies.[79]

The reduction of the Assembly's powers was part of the effort to appease industrialised states by constraining G77 influence, thereby tempering the ISA's power to push through majority decisions on contentious issues (such as equitable distribution rules and other financial terms of mining contracts). To that end, the 1994 Agreement also modified both the decision-making processes in the Authority and the composition of the Council.[80] As regards the latter, the 1994 Agreement implemented a complex formula designed to ensure equitable representation of countries from various groups, including states engaged in seabed mineral exploration and states that are land-based producers of seabed minerals, through a chamber-based system.[81] As a result of this, '[b]roadly speaking, the more important a decision is for sea-bed mining interests the more it is insulated from simple majority decision-making within the Authority'.[82]

To some extent, the changes which the 1994 Agreement wrought upon the institutional regime have rendered the Authority 'a much more "normal" organisation in comparison with the Authority described in the Convention'.[83] Nevertheless, the Authority retains a broad and comprehensive mandate concerning deep seabed mining activities, with a robust range of prescriptive and executive functions, together with extensive enforcement powers. For example, one of the Assembly's key competencies is to consider and approve the regulatory regime for deep seabed mining, including rules on exploration, exploitation and equitable sharing of financial and other economic benefits; this regime constitutes the Authority's Mining

[75] UNCLOS, art 160(1).
[76] 1994 Agreement, Annex, s 3(1) (emphasis added); see also Churchill and Lowe (n 2) 245.
[77] 1994 Agreement, Annex, s 3(4).
[78] 1994 Agreement, Annex, s 3(4).
[79] Churchill and Lowe (n 2) 245 ('[t]he Assembly can do no more than refuse to confirm decisions on these matters taken by other organs; and ... the procedure is designed so that this power cannot be used to frustrate certain key stages of the approval of sea-bed mining operations'). See also Jaeckel (2017) (n 31) 93 (concluding that the Council 'can be regarded as the main decision-making organ' in the ISA); Valentin J Schatz, 'Article 160' in Proelss Commentary 1135–1137 (noting, at 1135, that 'it is in fact the Council which enjoys true supremacy').
[80] 1994 Agreement, Annex, s 3. See also Churchill and Lowe (n 2) 244–247; Virginia Commentary 406–407; Wolfrum (2010) (n 55) 927–929; Jaeckel (2017) (n 31) 100–106.
[81] 1994 Agreement, Annex, s 3(9)–(10), (15)–(16).
[82] See Churchill and Lowe (n 2) 244–245.
[83] Tullio Treves, 'The Law of the Sea "System" of Institutions' (1998) 2 Max Planck YB UN L 325, 335.

Code.[84] The Council, in turn, has the responsibility for provisionally adopting, and recommending to the Assembly, the rules, regulations and procedures of the Mining Code.[85] The Council does so on the basis of drafts prepared by the LTC.[86]

In tandem with its responsibilities concerning the regulatory regime, the Council plays a central role in approving plans of work for activities in the Area,[87] again acting upon LTC recommendation.[88] The LTC, in addition to its roles in drafting the Authority's regulatory regime and reviewing applications for mining contracts, has wide powers to prepare assessments of the environmental impact of deep seabed activities, and to make recommendations to the Council concerning marine environmental protection.[89]

Accompanying these functions, the ISA has the authority to oversee performance of deep seabed mining contracts through a wide arsenal of monitoring, inspection and enforcement powers.[90] The Council, in particular, exercises key competencies in this regard, assisted by the LTC. The Council has ultimate authority to 'exercise such control over activities in the Area as is necessary for the purpose of securing compliance' in accordance with Article 153(4) of UNCLOS, and the Authority's Mining Code, and to commence proceedings on behalf of the Authority at the Chamber of ITLOS in cases of non-compliance.[91] On this basis, the Council may exercise a broad range of supervisory powers.[92] The LTC assists the Council in the exercise of these functions in various respects.[93]

In conclusion, taking all of its far-reaching powers into account, the Authority is in a unique position to develop and operationalise common heritage content in the

[84] UNCLOS, art 160(2)(f)(i)–(ii); on development of the Mining Code, see Section 4.2.2.

[85] UNCLOS, art 162(2)(o)(i)–(ii).

[86] UNCLOS, art 165(2)(f).

[87] 1994 Agreement, Annex, s 3(11)(a); on the ISA's licensing process for deep seabed mining activities, see Section 4.2.3.

[88] UNCLOS, art 165(2)(b).

[89] UNCLOS, art 165(2)(d)–(e).

[90] Chapter 6 will address these aspects in more detail. However, by way of example, see UNCLOS, art 153(4)–(5) (ISA to exercise control over activities to ensure compliance, including by taking measures to induce compliance, and by inspecting installations) and 157 (general and incidental powers); Annex III, art 18 (ISA penalties upon contractors); 1994 Agreement, Annex, s 1(1).

[91] UNCLOS, art 162(2)(l) and 162(2)(u), respectively. Part III of this book will discuss, in more detail, the role of ITLOS, and the Chamber specifically, within deep seabed mining disputes.

[92] For example, the Council's mandate includes the following powers: to supervise and coordinate implementation of Part XI of UNCLOS and to invite the Assembly to consider instances of non-compliance (art 162(2)(a)); to issue emergency orders, including for suspension/adjustment of mining activities to prevent serious harm to the marine environment (art 162(2)(w)); and to disapprove areas for exploitation due to serious risk of environmental harm (art 162(2)(x)). Moreover, the Council can establish mechanisms to direct and supervise a staff of inspectors to monitor and inspect mining activities (art 162(2)(z)).

[93] For example, upon Council request, the LTC may supervise activities in the Area (art 165(2)(c)). The LTC may also make recommendations to the Council concerning: establishment of a programme to monitor aspects of activities in the Area (art 165(2)(h)); commencement of proceedings at the Chamber by the Authority (art 165(2)(i)); issuance of emergency orders, or disapproval of areas for exploitation, to prevent serious harm to the marine environment (art 165(2)(k)–(l)); and direction and supervision of the staff of inspectors monitoring mining activities (art 165(2)(m)).

deep seabed mining context. To this end, Jaeckel is correct to describe the ISA as a 'testing ground for the practical scope and implications of this philosophical notion [the common heritage] that remains both controversial and holds potential'.[94] Notwithstanding the shift in the internal balance of the ISA's decision-making process effected by the 1994 Agreement, the ISA retains significant powers to develop the Mining Code, and to oversee, implement and control the licensing process for deep seabed mining, as the following analysis will now address.[95]

4.2.2 The ISA's Development of the Deep Seabed Mining Regime

The ISA possesses broad powers to adopt any rules, regulations and procedures necessary for the conduct of mining activities in the Area.[96] These rules include regulations to govern exploration and exploitation activities, protection of the marine environment and equitable sharing of financial and other economic benefits from deep seabed mining activities.[97] In this respect, as Harrison notes, one can distinguish the ISA from the majority of other international organisations, whose powers to progressively develop underlying treaty regimes usually require further authorisation by states: '[i]n contrast, rules and regulations validly adopted by the Authority are binding, regardless of individual state consent'.[98] As explored above, the Council, in practice, plays a leading role in adoption of these rules, on the basis of LTC drafts.[99] The Council's decision-making process for approval of the Mining Code is, therefore, hugely significant, and its importance explains why the Council's decision-making procedures were 'one of the most intractable issues' of UNCLOS III.[100]

The UNCLOS regime insulates Council decisions on the Mining Code from simple majority vote. The Council must take such decisions by consensus,[101] which means 'the absence of any formal objection'.[102] As the regime prescribes no other

[94] Jaeckel (2017) (n 31) 87.

[95] See, e.g. Jaeckel (2017) (n 31) 187 (arguing that, despite the 1994 Agreement's amendments, 'the powers of the ISA to shape the seabed mining regime and to set general environmental standards for deep seabed mining remain substantial').

[96] UNCLOS, arts 140(2), 145, 160(2)(f), 162(2)(o), 165(2)(f), and Annex III, art 17; 1994 Agreement, Annex, s 1(1), (5)(f)–(g), (15).

[97] Rules in relation to all of these areas form part of the Mining Code: ISA, 'The Mining Code' <www.isa.org.jm/mining-code>.

[98] Harrison (2011) (n 8) 123, citing Philippe Sands and Pierre Klein, *Bowett's Law of International Institutions* (6th edn, Sweet & Maxwell 2009) 267 and UNCLOS, arts 208–209. See also Jaeckel (2017) (n 31) 93, 145–147.

[99] The LTC is tasked with drafting rules, regulations and procedures and submitting them to the Council (UNCLOS, art 165(2)(f)). The LTC adopts draft regulations by consensus, if possible, or, failing that, by majority vote: 1994 Agreement, Annex, s 3(2), (13).

[100] Virginia Commentary 404. As Section 4.2.1 demonstrated, the 1994 Agreement revised Council decision-making processes significantly, in order to gain industrialised states' support for UNCLOS.

[101] UNCLOS, art 161(8)(d).

[102] UNCLOS, art 161(8)(e).

voting method in the event of Council failure to reach consensus, in practice this means that veto by one Council member may lead to deadlock in the adoption of parts of the Mining Code. In that sense, one could describe this decision-making process to be more akin to a form of unanimity[103] rather than the typical process of consensus that the Convention employs elsewhere, and which allows the option of a vote, if necessary, to resolve an impasse.[104] In the event that any State Party with a seat on the Council chooses to exercise its veto power, this can effectively stall the adoption of rules, regulations or procedures being considered by the Council. However, to mitigate the risk of a blocked Council, the Convention has a conciliation procedure and other procedural mechanisms to facilitate Council decision-making.[105]

Once the Council has agreed on draft regulations, it recommends them for Assembly approval. The Assembly may approve them by consensus or, if necessary, via two-thirds majority vote.[106] If the Assembly cannot agree to approve the regulations, it must resubmit the draft to the Council for further consideration.[107] Notably, as regards draft regulations concerning mineral exploration or exploitation activities, the Council is entitled to adopt, and provisionally apply, such draft regulations, pending Assembly approval.[108] Accordingly, even if the Assembly rejects these draft regulations and returns them to the Council for re-evaluation, the draft regulations would continue to apply provisionally. In this scenario, such draft regulations 'may remain provisionally valid for an indefinite period of time', as there is no time limit within which the Council must finish its reconsideration of draft regulations rejected by the Assembly.[109] Overall, the Council plays the instrumental role in the adoption of the Mining Code (as the LTC does in its drafting), with the Assembly assuming an ancillary role.[110]

The Authority may also amend the Mining Code, using the same procedures. To that end, the LTC is authorised to keep the Mining Code under review, and to periodically recommend any necessary amendments to the Council.[111] This is in addition to the Authority's overarching powers to conduct periodic reviews of the deep seabed regime more generally. In accordance with Article 154 of

[103] Harrison (2011) (n 8) 125–126.
[104] See, e.g. 1994 Agreement, Annex, s 3(3), (5).
[105] UNCLOS, art 161(8)(e) (conciliation procedure); see also Churchill and Lowe (n 2) 246–247 on the regime's additional procedural mechanisms to ease Council decision-making. See, further, Harrison (2011) (n 8) 125.
[106] 1994 Agreement, Annex, s 3(2)–(3).
[107] 1994 Agreement, Annex, s 3(4).
[108] UNCLOS, art 162(2)(o)(ii). In contrast, as regards rules on equitable sharing of financial and other economic benefits, the Council may merely recommend these rules to the Assembly and await Assembly approval before applying them: UNCLOS, art 162(2)(o)(i).
[109] Harrison (2011) (n 8) 126; see also Jaeckel (2017) (n 31) 102.
[110] Harrison (2011) (n 8) 126–127; Jaeckel (2017) (n 31) 103. The Finance Committee also plays a role in giving recommendations on the content of financial rules and regulations, and concerning equitable sharing of financial and other economic benefits: 1994 Agreement, Annex, s 9(7)(a), (f).
[111] UNCLOS, art 165(2)(g).

UNCLOS, the Assembly has the power to 'undertake a general and systematic review of the manner in which the international regime of the Area established in this Convention has operated in practice'. On the basis of this review, the Assembly may adopt or recommend measures to improve the functioning of the regime.[112]

Originally, the Convention also contained a process that would have allowed the Assembly to convene a formal review conference fifteen years after the start of commercial production in the Area.[113] This would have permitted the Assembly to review the entire operation of Part XI of UNCLOS, together with relevant annexes, in order to amend the system in response to any failure to achieve common heritage goals.[114] However, the 1994 Agreement modified the Article 155 process for the review conference significantly, disapplying most of it.[115] Now, only upon Council recommendation may the Assembly conduct a review of the matters indicated in Article 155(1) of UNCLOS, and any amendments are to be adopted pursuant to the Convention's regular process for amendments relating to activities in the Area (as contained in Articles 314 to 316).[116]

The Mining Code adds another layer to the regime, and constitutes secondary law by the ISA, which forms part of international law.[117] Thus far, the ISA has adopted three sets of regulations, concerning prospecting and exploration activities for three types of minerals (polymetallic nodules, polymetallic sulphides and cobalt-rich crusts[118]), together with environmental

[112] The Authority's first review began in 2016: see ISA Assembly, 'Letter Dated 3 February 2017 from the Chair of the Committee Established by the Assembly to Carry out a Periodic Review of the International Regime of the Area Pursuant to Article 154 of UNCLOS to the Secretary-General of the ISA' (attaching Final Report of Review Committee) (8 February 2017) ISBA/23/A/3.

[113] UNCLOS, art 155. The Convention's review conference procedure under Article 155 is wholly distinct from its Article 154 procedure for periodic review: Virginia Commentary 314.

[114] See UNCLOS, art 155(1), (3)–(4) (these provisions were disapplied by 1994 Agreement, Annex, s 4).

[115] 1994 Agreement, Annex, s 4. As noted in Chapter 3, the Convention's original process for the review conference was one of the aspects to which industrialised states objected. Provoking particular controversy was the intended procedure for amendments, which were to be adopted by a three-quarters majority of States Parties (UNCLOS, art 155(4)); see, further, Jule Siegfried, 'Article 155' in Proelss Commentary 1094–1097.

[116] See UNCLOS, art 155, read with 1994 Agreement, Annex, s 4. In terms of the Convention's amendment process, to make an amendment 'relating exclusively to activities in the Area', both the Council and the Assembly must approve it (art 314(1)) and, to bring it into force, three-quarters of States Parties must ratify it (art 316(5)). As Siegfried notes, this ensures '[t]he mining States' option to veto an amendment' in the Council: Jule Siegfried, 'Article 155' in Proelss Commentary 1097.

[117] Karavias (n 54) 121–122; see also Gwenaëlle Le Gurun, 'Annex III' in Proelss Commentary 2245.

[118] ISA, 'Regulations on Prospecting and Exploration for Polymetallic Nodules in the Area' (adopted 13 July 2000) ISBA/6/A/18, (updated 22 July 2013) ISBA/19/C/17 (as amended by ISBA/19/A/12 (25 July 2013) and ISBA/20/A/9 (24 July 2014)) (*Nodules Regulations*); ISA, 'Regulations on Prospecting and Exploration for Polymetallic Sulphides in the Area' (adopted 7 May 2010) ISBA/16/A/12/Rev1 (as amended by ISBA/19/A/12 (25 July 2013) and ISBA/20/A/10 (24 July 2014)) (*Sulphides Regulations*); ISA, 'Regulations on Prospecting and Exploration for Cobalt-Rich Ferromanganese Crusts in the Area' (adopted 27 July 2012) ISBA/18/A/11 (as amended by ISBA/19/A/12 (25 July 2013)) (*Cobalt Regulations*).

recommendations and other recommendations of a technical or administrative nature.[119]

Recognising that activities on the seabed are beginning to outstrip legal developments, the ISA is working to regulate the forthcoming exploitation phase. To date, the ISA has issued various iterations of draft regulations addressing the exploitation phase of mining activities. The ISA provided initial draft regulations concerning exploitation in July 2016.[120] In light of consultations with stakeholders, and various other interactive workshops and collaborative activities,[121] the ISA released updated versions of the draft exploitation regulations in August 2017,[122] April 2018[123] and July 2018.[124] Following this, in March 2019, the LTC issued the current version of the draft exploitation regulations and standard contract terms (*DERs*).[125] On the basis of stakeholder comments, the Secretariat prepared an overview of various issues requiring resolution within the draft text, together with a collation of Council members' comments, annotated as detailed edits to the DERs.[126] Accordingly, the ISA's development of the Mining Code to regulate all aspects of the forthcoming exploitation phase remains a work in progress.

The ISA had set itself the ambitious goal of finalising the DERs during 2020.[127] To facilitate this, the Council established, in February 2020, informal working groups to advance discussions on key elements of the draft text (namely, marine environmental protection, compliance matters and institutional aspects).[128] However, the

[119] See, e.g. ISA LTC, 'Recommendations for the Guidance of Contractors for the Assessment of the Possible Environmental Impacts Arising from Exploration for Marine Minerals in the Area' (30 March 2020) ISBA/25/LTC/6/Rev1.

[120] ISA LTC, 'Report – Developing a Regulatory Framework for Mineral Exploitation in the Area' (July 2016) <www.isa.org.jm/files/documents/EN/Regs/DraftExpl/Draft_ExplReg_SCT.pdf>.

[121] For a helpful overview of this process, see ISA, 'Draft Exploitation Regulations' <www.isa.org.jm/index.php/mining-code/ongoing-development-regulations-exploitation-mineral-resources-area>.

[122] ISA Secretariat, 'Draft Regulations on Exploitation of Mineral Resources in the Area' (8 August 2017) ISBA/23/LTC/CRP.3*.

[123] ISA LTC, 'Draft Regulations on Exploitation of Mineral Resources in the Area' (30 April 2018) ISBA/24/LTC/WP.1.

[124] ISA LTC, 'Draft Regulations on Exploitation of Mineral Resources in the Area' (9 July 2018) ISBA/24/LTC/WP.1/Rev1.

[125] ISA LTC, 'Draft Regulations on Exploitation of Mineral Resources in the Area' (22 March 2019) ISBA/25/C/WP.1. See also LTC note accompanying this release: ISA LTC, 'Draft Regulations on Exploitation of Mineral Resources in the Area – Note by the Legal and Technical Commission' (27 March 2019) ISBA/25/C/18.

[126] ISA Secretariat, 'Comments on the Draft Regulations on the Exploitation of Mineral Resources in the Area' (4 December 2019) ISBA/26/C/2; ISA Secretariat, 'Draft Regulations on Exploitation of Mineral Resources in the Area – Collation of Specific Drafting Suggestions by Members of the Council' (17 December 2019) ISBA/26/C/CRP.1.

[127] ISA LTC, 'Report of the Chair of the Legal and Technical Commission on the Work of the Commission at its Session in 2017' (9 August 2017) ISBA/23/C/13, Annex.

[128] ISA Council, 'Decision of the Council concerning Working Methods to Advance Discussions on the Draft Regulations for Exploitation of Mineral Resources in the Area' (21 February 2020) ISBA/26/C/11.

impact of the COVID-19 pandemic has further delayed the ISA's progress in this regard,[129] and 'the exact duration of the delay is difficult to assess'.[130]

These ongoing delays have drawn attention to a controversial, previously unused mechanism within the 1994 Agreement, whereby the Council could (in theory) approve a plan of work for exploitation 'provisionally', in the absence of finalised rules on exploitation.[131] This process allows a state, where it has a national who intends to submit an exploitation application, to request the Council to elaborate and adopt exploitation regulations.[132] The clock is then set running for the Council to adopt such rules 'within two years of the request'.[133] If the Council has not managed to finalise exploitation regulations within this two-year period but has a pending application for a plan of work for exploitation, the Council should 'consider and provisionally approve' such a plan on the basis of the existing Convention regime and any provisionally adopted rules.[134] Canadian mining company DeepGreen (which has interests in three ISA contracts) has indicated that it would consider trying to rely on this 'so-called two-year rule'.[135]

Opponents of deep seabed mining have argued that this potential 'nuclear option' evidences 'fundamental bias towards exploitation at the heart of the ISA', at the expense of environmental protection.[136] However, in practice, there are numerous obstacles to reliance on the two-year rule. For example, in the case of a corporate contractor, the contractor would need to convince its sponsoring state to make a request for the exploitation regulations to be expedited, and the underlying application would need to secure Council approval on a provisional basis.[137] It remains to be seen whether any state would be willing to invoke the two-year rule, or whether this provision is more of a historical anomaly, intended to reassure industrialised states that progress towards exploitation could not be blocked indefinitely in the event of deadlock between States Parties on the terms of exploitation

[129] For example, due to the pandemic, the ISA had to postpone the second part of its twenty-sixth session; ISA, 'Twenty-Sixth Session of the ISA (Part II) Further Postponed to Late 2020' (2 September 2020) <www.isa.org.jm/news/twenty-sixth-session-international-seabed-authority-part-ii-further-postponed-late-2020>.

[130] Klaas Willaert, 'Deep Sea Mining in the Area: Clouded in Plumes of Uncertainty' (2020) 26 JIML 291, 292.

[131] 1994 Agreement, Annex, s 1(15).

[132] 1994 Agreement, Annex, s 1(15)(b).

[133] 1994 Agreement, Annex, s 1(15)(b).

[134] 1994 Agreement, Annex, s 1(15)(c).

[135] As reported in Todd Woody, 'Covid-19 Throws Seabed Mining Negotiations off Track' (*China Dialogue Ocean*, 7 May 2020) <https://chinadialogueocean.net/13685-covid-19-could-throw-seabed-mining-negotiations-off-track/> (quoting DeepGreen CEO and chairman, Gerard Barron, as saying in relation to triggering the two-year rule that 'it's not off the table, that's for sure').

[136] Greenpeace, 'In Deep Water: The Emerging Threat of Deep Sea Mining' (2019) at 22 <www.greenpeace.org/international/publication/22578/deep-sea-mining-in-deep-water/>.

[137] For discussion of likely difficulties in securing approval of an exploitation application in these circumstances, see Willaert (2020a) (n 130) 295 (also querying whether a contractor would actually pursue provisional approval, given the significant investments underpinning exploitation activities, and the need for regulatory certainty).

activities. This would be similar, in some respects, to the Council's ability to adopt and provisionally apply draft regulations, pending Assembly approval, as discussed earlier in this section.[138]

Overall, as this section has demonstrated, the Authority has significant power to develop the deep seabed regime progressively, both through its drafting and amendment of the Mining Code and by virtue of its review powers over the operation of the entire regime. In keeping with this far-reaching regulatory role, one of the ISA's main competencies is to issue contracts for exploration and exploitation of the deep seabed in accordance with the Mining Code. The following section will address this licensing process.

4.2.3 The ISA's Licensing Process for Deep Seabed Mining Activities and Corporate Participation Therein

4.2.3.1 Introduction to the Licensing Process

The Convention contains a contract-based licensing system for entities wishing to explore for, or exploit, deep seabed minerals, in which the ISA acts as licensing authority.[139] This section will introduce the mechanics of this licensing process, while Section 4.2.3.2 will provide a flavour of its key benefit-sharing aspects. Against that backdrop, Section 4.2.3.3 will assess corporate participation within the licensing process.

Article 153 of UNCLOS is at the heart of the licensing system.[140] Activities in the Area may be carried out by the Enterprise, once operational (art 153(2)(a)), or by States Parties to UNCLOS or 'state enterprises or natural or juridical persons which possess the nationality of States Parties or are effectively controlled by them or their nationals, when sponsored by such States' (art 153(2)(b)).[141] Prospective

[138] See text to nn 108–109.

[139] On the terms 'exploration' and 'exploitation', see Nodules, Sulphides and Cobalt Regulations, reg 1(3). Exploration entails 'searching ... with exclusive rights, the analysis of such deposits, the use and testing of recovery systems and equipment, processing facilities and transportation systems and the carrying out of studies of the environmental, technical, economic, commercial and other appropriate factors that must be taken into account in exploitation' (ibid). Exploitation is 'recovery for commercial purposes of [resources] in the Area and the extraction of minerals therefrom, including the construction and operation of mining, processing and transportation systems, for the production and marketing of metals' (ibid). See ITLOS AO, paras 82–97 for further analysis. The DERs define 'exploration' and 'exploitation' in similar terms, but also include 'decommissioning and closure of mining operations' within the definition of exploitation (see DERs, sch). Prospecting activities are subject to notification requirements, but are otherwise outside of the ISA's licensing regime and beyond the scope of this book's analysis (see introduction, n 23).

[140] Virginia Commentary 297, 308.

[141] See also UNCLOS, Annex III, art 4(1), (3). States Parties do not require to demonstrate state sponsorship, by virtue of their sovereign status: see UNCLOS, Annex III, art 4(5) (providing that the procedure for assessing qualifications of State Party applicants 'shall take into account their character as States'); this interpretation is confirmed by ITLOS AO, para 79. cf state enterprises, to whom sponsorship requirements do apply: reg 11(1) of the Nodules, Sulphides and Cobalt Regulations; see also ITLOS AO, para 74.

contractors may seek ISA approval of a formal written plan of work.[142] To apply for approval of a plan of work for exploration for nodules, sulphides or cobalt crusts, the application fee is US$500,000.[143]

UNCLOS provides for a 'strict and carefully designed decision-making process' for dealing with licensing applications.[144] Much of the underlying process, including basic conditions for mining activities, is contained in Annex III of the Convention, as modified by the 1994 Agreement and supplemented by the ISA's regulations.[145] Applicants must satisfy certain financial and technical requirements, taking into account performance under previous ISA contracts, and they must also provide certain undertakings.[146] For example, the 1994 Agreement established a monetary threshold for the satisfaction of these elements.[147] Ensuring that the applicant satisfies these requirements is critical, given the tremendous costs and technical acumen involved in deep seabed mining activities. Each application must contain 'specific and sufficient information to enable the Council to determine whether the applicant is financially and technically capable of carrying out the proposed plan of work for exploration and of fulfilling its financial obligations to the Authority'.[148]

The Mining Code requires corporate entities to include copies of various financial documents, including audited financial statements for the last three years.[149] If the applicant is a 'subsidiary of another entity', the application must include financial statements from that entity, together with a statement by that entity confirming

[142] UNCLOS, art 153(3) and Annex III, art 3.

[143] Nodules Regulations, reg 19; Sulphides and Cobalt Regulations, reg 21 (cf UNCLOS, Annex III, art 13(2) and 1994 Agreement, Annex, s 8(3)); see discussion of this fee's evolution by Gwenaëlle Le Gurun, 'Annex III' in Proelss Commentary 2208). The level of the application fee in respect of exploitation activities has not yet been set: DERs, reg 86 and Appendix II.

[144] James Harrison, 'The Sustainable Development of Mineral Resources in the International Seabed Area: The Role of the Authority in Balancing Economic Development and Environmental Protection' (2014) University of Edinburgh School of Law Working Paper No 2014/50, 24 <www.scil.ed.ac.uk/__data/assets/pdf_file/0009/166545/James_Harrison_SCIL_Working_Paper_No_3.pdf>.

[145] For a comprehensive analysis of Annex III, as augmented by the 1994 Agreement and the Mining Code, see Gwenaëlle Le Gurun, 'Annex III' in Proelss Commentary 2113–2274.

[146] UNCLOS, Annex III, art 4(2), (6). See, further, regs 12–14 of the Nodules Regulations and regs 13–15 of the Sulphides and Cobalt Regulations (containing requirements concerning financial and technical capabilities, previous ISA contracts and undertakings to be assumed by applicants). The DERs incorporate equivalent requirements within Part II and Annex I.

[147] 1994 Agreement, Annex, s 1(6)(a)(i) (deeming an applicant to have 'met the financial and technical qualifications necessary for approval of a plan of work' if it is certified by its sponsoring state (or states) that it has 'expended an amount equivalent to at least US$30 million in research and exploration activities and has expended no less than 10 per cent of that amount in the location, survey and evaluation of the area referred to in the plan of work'). These terms are reproduced in Nodules Regulations, reg 12(2), including the US$30 million threshold.

[148] Nodules Regulations, reg 12(1); Sulphides Regulations, reg 13(1); Cobalt Regulations, reg 13(1). Similar requirements are contained in DERs, Annex I, paras 18 and 21 (Annex I provides a sample application form for approval of a plan of work).

[149] Nodules Regulations, reg 12(5); Sulphides Regulations, reg 13(4); Cobalt Regulations, reg 13(4) (subject to Nodules Regulations, reg 12(6); Sulphides Regulations, reg 13(4)(a); Cobalt Regulations, reg 13(5), as regards newly organised entities that do not possess all the relevant documents). Similarly, see DERs, Annex I, para 21(c).

that 'the applicant will have the financial resources to carry out the plan of work'.[150] If the applicant intends to finance its plan of work by borrowing, it must detail this within the application.[151]

An applicant must describe its capabilities, including 'previous experience, knowledge, skills, technical qualifications and [relevant] expertise', information concerning equipment and methods expected to be used in conducting exploratory activities, and details of the applicant's 'financial and technical capability to respond to any incident or activity which causes serious harm to the marine environment'.[152] As the stakes will be higher during exploitation, an applicant for a plan of work for exploitation must include various additional plans, detailing its financial and technical capabilities and ability to respond to emergencies.[153]

The Council is responsible for approving applications, and may do so upon LTC recommendation.[154] While the exploration regulations and the DERs both require the LTC to apply ISA rules and procedures in a 'uniform and non-discriminatory manner', and to have regard to 'principles, policies and objectives relating to activities in the Area' as provided within the UNCLOS regime,[155] the DERs also enjoin the LTC to have regard to 'the manner in which the proposed Plan of Work contributes to realizing benefits for mankind as a whole'.[156] This would imply that, in deciding whether to recommend approval of exploitation applications, the LTC should be assessing the extent to which an individual plan of work for exploitation may contribute to the realisation of benefits for humanity.

If the plan of work complies with the UNCLOS regime, the Annex III process admits of only three limited grounds on which the Authority may disapprove it. Firstly, a plan can be disapproved if it includes an area that has already been approved in another plan of work (or is included in another plan that the Authority is considering already).[157] Secondly, there are grounds for disapproval if a plan relates to an area that the Council disapproves as an area for exploitation due to substantial evidence

150 Nodules Regulations, reg 12(7); Sulphides Regulations, reg 13(4)(b); Cobalt Regulations, reg 13(6); DERs, Annex I, para 21(c)(ii).

151 Nodules Regulations, reg 12(9); Sulphides Regulations, reg 13(5); Cobalt Regulations, reg 13(8); DERs, Annex I, para 22.

152 Nodules Regulations, reg 12(10); Sulphides Regulations, reg 13(6); Cobalt Regulations, reg 13(9).

153 See DERs, reg 7(3) and, e.g. Annexes II (mining workplan), III (financing plan), IV (environmental impact statement, including, at part 10, measures to be taken to respond to accidental events and natural hazards), V (emergency response and contingency plan) and VII (environmental management and monitoring plan).

154 UNCLOS, arts 153(3), 165(2)(b) and Annex III, art 6; 1994 Agreement, Annex, ss 1(6), 3(11). For analysis of this process, as developed by ISA regulations, see Gwenaëlle Le Gurun, 'Annex III' in Proelss Commentary 2156–2161. See also Nodules Regulations, regs 21–22; Sulphides Regulations, regs 23–24; Cobalt Regulations, regs 23–24; DERs, regs 10–16.

155 Nodules Regulations, reg 21(10), (12); Sulphides Regulations, reg 23(10), (12); Cobalt Regulations, reg 23(10), (12); DERs, reg 12(3).

156 DERs, reg 12(3).

157 UNCLOS, Annex III, art 6(3)(a). See, further, Nodules Regulations, reg 21(6)(a)–(b); Sulphides Regulations, reg 23(6)(a)–(b); Cobalt Regulations, reg 23(6)(a)–(b); DERs, reg 15(2)(a)–(b).

indicating the risk of serious harm to the marine environment.[158] Thirdly, a plan can be disapproved for falling foul of monopolisation restrictions.[159] In practice, there is a fourth ground for disapproval: the LTC cannot recommend approval of a plan of work if all or part of the area covered by it is located in a reserved area (unless the applicant is eligible to apply in respect of such an area).[160]

On the basis of the LTC's report, the Council will decide whether to approve an application.[161] The 1994 Agreement curtailed the Council's ability to disapprove an application, by requiring that it can only vote against an LTC recommendation for approval of a plan of work if it does so by 'a two-thirds majority of its members present and voting, including a majority of members present and voting in each of the chambers of the Council'.[162] Pursuant to this decision-making process, it is 'very difficult' for the Council to overturn the LTC's recommendations for approval of a plan of work.[163]

Once an application is approved and signed, it takes the form of a contract between the ISA and the contractor, bestowing the contractor with exclusive rights to explore for (or exploit) minerals in the area covered by the contract for a fifteen-year term.[164] Throughout the duration of deep seabed mining operations, the ISA possesses broad powers to oversee contractual performance, including by monitoring performance, inspecting installations and enforcing compliance with contractual terms (as will be considered further in Chapter 6).[165]

[158] UNCLOS, Annex III, art 6(3)(b), read with UNCLOS, art 162(2)(x). See also Nodules Regulations, reg 21(6)(c); Sulphides Regulations, reg 23(6)(c); Cobalt Regulations, reg 23(6)(c); DERs, reg 15(2)(c).

[159] UNCLOS, Annex III, art 6(3)(c), (4). See also Nodules Regulations, reg 21(6)(d), (7); Sulphides Regulations, reg 23(7); Cobalt Regulations, reg 23(7); DERs, reg 15(3). For further consideration of the rules restricting monopolies, see Section 4.2.3.2 below.

[160] Nodules Regulations, reg 21(8); Sulphides Regulations, reg 23(8); Cobalt Regulations, reg 23(8); DERs, reg 15(2)(d). Section 4.2.3.2 below will address the concept of reserved areas in more detail.

[161] 1994 Agreement, Annex, ss 1(6), 3(11)(a).

[162] 1994 Agreement, Annex, s 3(11)(a).

[163] Harrison (2014) (n 144) 24. There is also a prescribed time period within which the Council must make its decision, at the expiry of which the Council will be deemed to have approved the LTC's recommendation (1994 Agreement, Annex, s 3(11)(a)). As Harrison notes, '[b]oth of these innovations in the decision-making procedure are intended to remove the politics from what are perceived to be decisions of a purely technical nature' (Harrison, ibid). See also Virginia Commentary 690 (noting that these procedures 'import a large degree of automaticity into the process of approval of plans of work and, to some extent, override the provisions on Annex III, articles 6 and 7'). See, further, Jaeckel (2017) (n 31) 104–105, 240.

[164] UNCLOS, art 153(3), (6) and Annex III, arts 3 and 16; see also 1994 Agreement, Annex, s1(6)(a)(i), (9).

[165] UNCLOS, arts 153(4)–(5), 157, 160, 162, 165 and Annex III, art 18; 1994 Agreement, Annex, s 1(1). See also analysis in Section 4.2.1 at text to nn 90–93. The ISA's wide regulatory and enforcement powers are reflected in the Mining Code (e.g. standard clauses to mining contracts, contained in fourth annex of Nodules, Sulphides and Cobalt Regulations, at ss 10 (annual reports by contractor to ISA), 14 (ISA inspection of contractor's vessels and installations to monitor compliance), 21 (ISA suspension or termination of contract and applicable penalties)). The DERs develop and build upon ISA supervisory powers, integrating annual reporting requirements (reg 38) and ISA powers to audit and inspect contractor records (reg 75), together with broad ISA powers to inspect contractor vessels/installations (regs 96–100); the draft standard contractual clauses in Annex X contain the ISA's powers to suspend or terminate the contract (see s 12).

4.2.3.2 Key Benefit-sharing Aspects within the Licensing Process

The Convention's licensing process aims to foster benefit-sharing goals of equal participation in deep seabed mining and equitable sharing of benefits derived from such activities.[166] As this section will consider, three particular aspects of the licensing process aim to encourage participation by developing states, and to prevent dominance of developed states: the anti-monopolisation rules, the proposed role of the Enterprise and the operation of the system of reserved areas.[167]

As regards monopolisation, the Authority's ability to approve an application for a plan of work is subject to certain constraints, aimed to prevent any one entity from gaining a dominant position in the Area.[168] In respect of nodules, size limitations apply to the cumulative areas covered by plans of work.[169] In relation to nodules, sulphides and cobalt crusts, the LTC is not permitted to recommend approval of a plan of work if doing so would lead to creation of a monopoly.[170] In practice, determination of what constitutes a monopoly remains elusive, and the ISA has noted that application of anti-monopolisation safeguards continues to be 'problematic'.[171] Given these shortcomings, the issues of monopolisation and abuse of a dominant position remain on the Authority's agenda for development.[172]

The role of the Enterprise and the system of reservation of areas both stem from the vision of the UNCLOS regime as a 'parallel' system.[173] States and state-sponsored entities were to be permitted to explore for, and exploit, seabed resources in tandem with the Enterprise.[174] To facilitate this, the Convention incorporates a system of 'site banking'.[175] Pursuant to this approach, a contractor (other than the Enterprise or any entity applying to explore a reserved area) must, in its plan of work, identify a total area for exploration or exploitation that is 'sufficiently large and of sufficient estimated commercial value to allow two mining operations' and 'indicate the coordinates dividing the area into two parts of equal estimated

[166] See Section 4.1.1, at text to nn 23–29.

[167] Consideration of the financial side of the benefit-sharing principle will be reserved for Chapter 6, as the regime defers this aspect to development through the Mining Code.

[168] UNCLOS, Annex III, art 6(3)(c), (4); Nodules Regulations, reg 21(6)(d), (7); Sulphides Regulations, reg 23(7); Cobalt Regulations, reg 23(7); DERs, reg 15(3). See also Gwenaëlle Le Gurun, 'Annex III' in Proelss Commentary 2160.

[169] UNCLOS, Annex III, art 6(3)(c), (4); Nodules Regulations, reg 21(6)(d).

[170] Nodules Regulations, reg 21(7); Sulphides Regulations, reg 23(7); Cobalt Regulations, reg 23(7); DERs, reg 15(3).

[171] ISA Secretariat, 'Monopolization of Activities in the Area' (6 June 2014) ISBA/20/LTC/11, para 9; see also para 15. See, further, ISA Secretariat, 'Issues Related to the Sponsorship of Contracts for Exploration in the Area, Monopolisation, Effective Control and Related Matters' (21 June 2016) ISBA/22/LTC/13, para 8.

[172] ISA LTC, 'Agenda of the Legal and Technical Commission' (24 February 2020) ISBA/26/LTC/1, para 14.

[173] Virginia Commentary 297 and 301 (and see 297–312, generally, on development and negotiation of the parallel system in the context of the drafting of UNCLOS, art 153).

[174] UNCLOS, art 153(2); see also Annex IV (Statute of the Enterprise), much of which was modified de facto by the 1994 Agreement.

[175] Virginia Commentary 297.

commercial value'.[176] The ISA must then designate one part of the submitted area as a 'reserved area'.[177] Given the expense and technical skill involved in surveying for mining sites and estimating their value, the contribution of reserved areas by developed states (or their sponsored entities) 'represents their contribution to the Enterprise and developing States to enable their participation in the development of mineral resources in the Area'.[178]

As originally constructed, the parallel system anticipated that mining activities in reserved areas would be conducted 'solely' by 'the Authority through the Enterprise or in association with developing States'.[179] Pursuant to Article 9 of Annex III of UNCLOS, the original intention was for the Enterprise to be entitled to undertake activities in reserved areas, acting alone or in a joint venture with States Parties or other eligible entities (provided that it offered the 'opportunity of effective participation' to developing States Parties or their nationals).[180] If the Enterprise did not elect to undertake activities within a particular reserved area, Article 9(4) empowered the Authority to consider applications in respect of reserved areas by developing States Parties (or persons sponsored and 'effectively controlled' by such states).[181]

However, in an effort to resolve one of the most contentious issues preventing sufficiently widespread support for UNCLOS across the international community,[182] the 1994 Agreement suspended the role of the Enterprise indefinitely, providing for the Secretariat to perform its functions in the interim.[183] This constitutes part of the 1994 Agreement's 'evolutionary approach' to the ISA's functioning.[184] Once operational, the Enterprise is restricted to conducting initial operations 'through joint ventures'.[185] The Enterprise's operationalisation will

[176] UNCLOS, Annex III, art 8.

[177] See UNCLOS, Annex III, arts 8 and 9, and 1994 Agreement, Annex, s 1(10).

[178] Gwenaëlle Le Gurun, 'Annex III' in Proelss Commentary 2168. The benefits of applying to explore a reserved area are twofold: firstly, it allows an applicant access to an area that has already been surveyed as having value (a costly, complex and time-consuming exercise); moreover, when applying to explore a reserved area, an eligible applicant is not required to submit a reserved area as part of its application (which, again, saves on costs, expertise and time); see John Gibson, 'Deep Seabed Mining and Marine Environmental Protection: Advisory Opinion of the International Tribunal for the Law of the Sea on the Responsibilities and Obligations of States Sponsoring Activities in the Area' (2011) 21 Water Law 189, 193.

[179] UNCLOS, Annex III, art 8.

[180] UNCLOS, Annex III, art 9(1)–(2). In practice, as addressed below, the operation of this provision has been revised by the 1994 Agreement, Annex, s 2 (2), (5).

[181] UNCLOS, Annex III, art 9(4).

[182] See Chapter 3, Section 3.1.4; see also Koskenniemi and Lehto (n 50) 543.

[183] 1994 Agreement, Annex, s 2(1). Another heavily disputed aspect of the Enterprise's role was the extent to which States Parties would subsidise it (as per UNCLOS, arts 170(4), 171, 173(2)(b) and Annex IV, art 11). The 1994 Agreement scaled back subsidisation requirements: 1994 Agreement, Annex, s 2(3). On curtailment of transfer of technology requirements, see this section's subsequent discussion at text to n 210.

[184] 1994 Agreement, Annex, s 1(3). Under the evolutionary approach, 'the Authority begins life as a small, cost-effective and relatively simple organisation but may develop in response to changing circumstances' (Churchill and Lowe (n 2) 238, citations omitted).

[185] 1994 Agreement, Annex, s 2(2).

occur, at the earliest, upon approval of the first plan of work for exploitation, or upon the Council's receipt of an application for a joint venture operation with the Enterprise.[186]

In recent years, the Enterprise's role has been subject to renewed attention. The ISA received two proposals to enter negotiations to form a joint venture with the Enterprise. The first of these came from Canadian company Nautilus in 2013,[187] and the second from Poland in 2018.[188] The Secretary-General appointed a special representative to the Enterprise, on a temporary basis, to consider and report on Poland's joint venture proposal.[189] Following negotiations, the special representative provided the ISA with a draft proposal for a joint venture between the Enterprise and Poland.[190] In 2019, the special representative issued a further report studying issues related to the Enterprise's operation, focusing on legal, technical and financial implications.[191] The operation of the Enterprise continues to be on the ISA's agenda, and the LTC has recommended appointment of an interim Director-General of the Enterprise.[192]

Given that the Enterprise is not yet operational, by what means are activities conducted in reserved areas at present? In accordance with modifications enacted by the 1994 Agreement, the state or entity that contributes a particular area to the ISA, as a reserved area, has the right of first refusal to enter into a joint venture agreement with the Enterprise for exploration and exploitation of that reserved area.[193] However, if the Enterprise elects not to undertake activities in a reserved

[186] 1994 Agreement, Annex, s 2(2); cf UNCLOS, art 153(2)–(3).

[187] ISA Council, 'Proposal for a Joint Venture Operation with the Enterprise' (20 March 2013) ISBA/19/C/4; ISA Council, 'Considerations Relating to a Proposal by Nautilus Minerals Inc for a Joint Venture Operation with the Enterprise – Report by the Secretary-General' (4 April 2013) ISBA/19/C/6. On Council rejection of that proposal as 'premature', see ISA Council, 'Statement of the President of the Council of the ISA on the Work of the Council During the Nineteenth Session' (24 July 2013) ISBA/19/C/18, para 16.

[188] ISA Council, 'Report by the Secretary-General – Considerations Relating to a Proposal by the Government of Poland for a Possible Joint-venture Operation with the Enterprise' (25 May 2018) ISBA/24/C/12.

[189] ISA Council, 'Letter dated 17 December 2018 from the Special Representative of the Secretary-General of the ISA for the Enterprise addressed to the Secretary-General of the ISA' (3 January 2019) ISBA/25/C/7, Annex, para 3.

[190] This draft proposal is contained in the special representative's report, as enclosure II; see ISBA/25/C/7. For Council consideration of this report, see ISA Council, 'Decision of the Council of the ISA Relating to the Special Representative of the Secretary-General of the ISA for the Enterprise' (1 March 2019) ISBA/25/C/16.

[191] ISA Council, 'Issues Relating to the Operation of the Enterprise, in particular the Legal, Technical and Financial Implications for the ISA and for States Parties to UNCLOS' (12 June 2019) ISBA/25/C/26. See also ISA Council, 'Decision of the Council of the ISA Relating to the Special Representative of the Secretary-General of the ISA for the Enterprise' (22 July 2019) ISBA/25/C/36.

[192] ISA LTC, 'Report of the Chair of the Legal and Technical Commission on the Work of the Commission at the First Part of its Twenty-sixth Session' (9 March 2020) ISBA/26/C/12, para 41. Since 2013, there has been no interim director-general of the Enterprise, after the previous postholder retired.

[193] 1994 Agreement, Annex, s 2(5) (cf UNCLOS, Annex III, arts 8 and 9). This is reflected, also, in Nodules Regulations, reg 17(4); Sulphides Regulations, reg 18(4); and Cobalt Regulations, reg 18(4). In addition, in the event that the Enterprise, a developing State Party or its sponsored entity does not submit an application to explore a reserved area within fifteen years of either the area being reserved by the Authority or the Enterprise becoming operational (whichever is later), the 1994 Agreement allows

area (and, for the time being, it cannot do so[194]), then developing states and entities sponsored by and 'effectively controlled' by them, including private actors, may be eligible to undertake activities in that reserved area, in accordance with Article 9(4) of Annex III of UNCLOS.[195]

In practice, developing states, or entities sponsored and effectively controlled by them, have been relying upon Annex III, Article 9(4) as a means to apply to explore reserved areas. Currently, this is the 'primary way' by which a reserved area can be explored, given that the Enterprise is not yet functioning.[196] As the Chamber of ITLOS has acknowledged, Annex III, Article 9(4) furthers the equal participation aspect of benefit sharing, in offering a means of 'enabling the developing States to participate in deep seabed mining on an equal footing with developed States', thereby contributing towards the Convention's goal of realising 'a just and equitable international economic order which takes into account the interests and needs of mankind as a whole and, in particular, the special interests and needs of developing countries'.[197]

Presently, seven ISA contracts (all concerning nodules exploration) are being conducted within reserved areas in the CCZ. Of the seven contractors that are active in reserved areas, four are private corporations based in developing states (sponsored by Jamaica, Nauru, Singapore and Tonga, respectively), while the remaining three contractors are state enterprises (sponsored by China, the Cook Islands and Kiribati, respectively, with the latter two subject to partnership arrangements with private corporate actors).[198] Consequently, over the last decade, 'the participation of developing countries in the development of reserved areas has become a reality giving effect to the parallel system'.[199] Nevertheless, as the following section will evaluate, increasing corporate participation in reserved areas and forms of collaboration between private actors and developing states may have implications for the realisation of the common heritage.

Notably, the system for reservation of areas has been further adapted in relation to sulphides and cobalt crusts exploration. The ISA modified the site-banking

the original contractor who contributed a reserved area to apply to explore it (provided that they offer to include the Enterprise as a joint venture partner): 1994 Agreement, Annex, s 2(5); Nodules Regulations, reg 17(3); Sulphides Regulations, reg 18(3); Cobalt Regulations, reg 18(3). For analysis of this 'consequence and further development of the parallel system', see Gwenaëlle Le Gurun, 'Annex III' in Proelss Commentary 2189.

[194] As described above, the 1994 Agreement renders it 'practically impossible' for the Enterprise to undertake such activities, pending operationalisation: Gwenaëlle Le Gurun, 'Annex III' in Proelss Commentary 2181.

[195] See also Nodules Regulations, reg 17(1)–(2); Sulphides Regulations, reg 18(1)–(2); Cobalt Regulations, reg 18(1)–(2). This 'effective control' test will be considered, in detail, in the following section, when assessing its application to corporate actors.

[196] Gwenaëlle Le Gurun, 'Annex III' in Proelss Commentary 2181.

[197] ITLOS AO, para 163, quoting UNCLOS, preamble, para 5.

[198] For further details of these contracts in reserved areas, see Appendix 2.

[199] Gwenaëlle Le Gurun, 'Annex III' in Proelss Commentary 2176; see also 2183–2185.

system to take account of the differing characteristics of those resources as compared to nodules.[200] Under this revised approach, an applicant seeking permission to explore for sulphides or cobalt crusts may offer an equity interest in a joint venture arrangement to the Enterprise instead of submitting a reserved area.[201] In practice, this approach has proved popular. All applicants for sulphides and cobalt crusts exploration, bar one,[202] have elected to offer an equity interest instead of a reserved area. These arrangements will take effect when these contractors enter into contracts for exploitation, and the Enterprise may hold an equity interest of between 20 and 50% in each.[203]

This modification also raises potential issues for the common heritage's realisation. This adaptation was 'not expressly foreseen in the Convention, which ... was premised upon the parallel system'.[204] Arguably, this evidences the potential of the regulatory regime to evolve to meet new types of challenges or commercial demands. To some extent, this evolution could be construed as capturing the balance between the regime's communitarian and market-oriented goals. As Le Gurun describes, it 'was proposed as an alternative system being consistent both with the market-oriented approach contained in the 1994 Implementation Agreement and with the parallel system which is pivotal in the regime of the common heritage of mankind'.[205]

However, some commentators have critiqued this movement away from the parallel system as posing 'implications for the operationalisation of the common heritage principle', on the basis that it erodes the reserved area system, which is a significant mechanism in assisting the participation of developing states in the Area.[206] This joint venture approach 'only considers an equity interest as a tangible outcome', not active participation of developing states through provision of reserved areas (which 'lowers the threshold' for active participation by affording 'commercially viable mining sites').[207] Notwithstanding this, the LTC is

[200] See Gwenaëlle Le Gurun, 'Annex III' in Proelss Commentary, 2172–2173 (noting, in respect of sulphides and cobalt crusts, that 'identification, if possible, of two sites of equal estimated commercial value would require substantial and onerous survey work', rendering the site-banking system difficult to achieve).

[201] Sulphides Regulations, regs 16 and 19; Cobalt Regulations, regs 16 and 19.

[202] Russia, in respect of cobalt crusts exploration: see ISA LTC, 'Report and Recommendations of the Legal and Technical Commission to the Council of the ISA Relating to an Application for the Approval of a Plan of Work for Exploration for Cobalt-rich Ferromanganese Crusts by the Ministry of Natural Resources and Environment of the Russian Federation' (25 February 2014) ISBA/20/C/4.

[203] Sulphides Regulations, reg 19(2)(a)–(b); Cobalt Regulations, reg 19(2)(a)–(b).

[204] Harrison (2011) (n 8) 145; see also Harrison (2014) (n 144) 26–27. See, further, ISBA/22/LTC/13, para 9 (for ISA Secretariat acknowledgement that 'increased adoption of the joint venture option could result in a considerable decrease in the amount of reserved areas available for future generations, thus having direct implications on the parallel system').

[205] Gwenaëlle Le Gurun, 'Annex III' in Proelss Commentary 2173.

[206] Aline Jaeckel, Jeff A Ardron and Kristina M Gjerde, 'Sharing Benefits of the Common Heritage of Mankind – is the Deep Seabed Mining Regime Ready?' (2016) 70 Marine Pol'y 198, 201.

[207] Jaeckel, Ardron and Gjerde (2016) (n 206) 201 (acknowledging that the position is not clear-cut, as the equity interest/joint venture approach could 'offer a more secure revenue stream to the Enterprise' in the longer term, with benefits for developing states).

considering whether to amend the Nodules Regulations to align them with this approach, by permitting contractors to offer the Enterprise an equity interest in a joint venture instead of a reserved area.[208]

Another benefit-sharing aspect of the Convention's original licensing regime for deep seabed mining activities which has been modified concerns transfer of technology. Like the parallel system for deep seabed mining, the transfer of technology requirements were intended to facilitate developing state participation. However, to appease industrialised states, 'which considered them an unacceptable undermining of the principles of intellectual property ownership',[209] the 1994 Agreement streamlined the transfer of technology requirements to render them consistent with protection of intellectual property rights.[210] The 1994 Agreement also altered attempts to insulate developing states that were reliant on land-based mining from adverse economic impacts of deep seabed mining upon their domestic economies. Instead, it based the development of resources in the Area upon 'sound commercial principles', subjecting such activities to the General Agreement on Tariffs and Trade and its successor agreements[211] and abolishing most subsidies for mining activities.[212]

On the whole, despite modification by the 1994 Agreement, the ISA's licensing process continues to enshrine various benefit-sharing aspects of the common heritage, intended to foster equal participation in deep seabed mining. The most

[208] ISA LTC, 'Report of the Chair of the Legal and Technical Commission on the Work of the Commission at the First Part of its Twenty-Fourth Session' (26 April 2018) ISBA/24/C/9, para 18; see also the ISA Secretariat's detailed background report on this matter: ISA Secretariat, 'Issues Related to the Possible Alignment of the Authority's Regulations on Prospecting and Exploration concerning the Offer of an Equity Interest in a Joint Venture Arrangement' (6 February 2018) ISBA/24/LTC/4.

[209] Churchill and Lowe (n 2) 249; see also Natalie Klein, *Dispute Settlement in the UN Convention on the Law of the Sea* (CUP 2005) 330–331.

[210] Mandatory transfer of technology requirements, originally detailed in UNCLOS, art 144 and Annex III, art 5, were modified by the 1994 Agreement, Annex, s 5 (adapting operation of UNCLOS, art 144 and disapplying Annex III, art 5). In practice, in furtherance of UNCLOS, art 144 and Annex III, art 15, contractors provide training opportunities for the Authority/developing states as part of their exploration contracts; see Nodules Regulations, reg 27; Sulphides Regulations, reg 29; Cobalt Regulations, reg 29; and standard clauses to mining contracts, s 8, fourth annex of Nodules, Sulphides and Cobalt Regulations (similarly, see DERs, regs 7(3)(g), 37 and Annex X, s 3.2(d) (requiring various training commitments, including submission of training plans with plans of work)). See also UNCLOS, Part XIV (Development and Transfer of Marine Technology), especially arts 273 (providing that 'States shall cooperate actively with competent international organizations and the Authority to encourage and facilitate the transfer to developing States, their nationals and the Enterprise of skills and marine technology with regard to activities in the Area') and 274 (Objectives of the Authority). See, further, DERs, reg 3 (duty to cooperate and exchange information).

[211] See, e.g. General Agreement on Tariffs and Trade (adopted 15 April 1994, entered into force 1 January 1995) 1867 UNTS 187.

[212] 1994 Agreement, Annex, s 6(1)(a)–(c). cf Article 151 of UNCLOS, which set out detailed production policies, including production ceilings, intended to insulate developing states that were reliant on land-based mining from adverse economic impacts as a result of a potential deep seabed mining boom. Most of the detailed provisions in Article 151 were removed by the 1994 Agreement (Annex, s 6(7)). However, the 1994 Agreement retains the economic assistance fund for developing states, to be developed in accordance with UNCLOS, art 151(10) (see 1994 Agreement, Annex, s 7). See, generally, Klein (n 209) 331–334; Jaeckel (2017) (n 31) 86.

striking of these are the elements addressed in this section: the anti-monopolisation rules, the planned role for the Enterprise and the system of reservation of areas. For now, the role of the Enterprise is deferred to the further operation of the regime. In the meantime, as addressed above, other elements for equal participation (such as the system of reserved areas and the anti-monopolisation provisions) are already operating, arguably to the advantage of private corporate participants. In order to understand the manner in which the licensing regime has facilitated this 'new way of doing business',[213] the following section will consider the ISA's licensing application process from the perspective of a private corporate actor.

4.2.3.3 Corporate Participation within the Licensing Process

As the preceding analysis demonstrated, the Convention regime establishes a sophisticated licensing process for deep seabed mining activities, enshrining the role of corporate actors as participants. This section will consider the extent of corporate participation and the new forms of collaboration that have emerged between developing states and private corporate actors. As this section will address, the ISA's regulatory approach to the regime's requirement of 'effective control' is a key factor facilitating such conduct, and the consequences of this upon the realisation of the common heritage remain to be seen.

Over the last decade, private corporations have cemented their role as participants in deep seabed mining. Of the ISA's thirty-one mining contracts, seven are held with private corporate actors.[214] These seven contracts allow for exploration for polymetallic nodules within specified areas of the CCZ.[215] The first of these contractors is Nauru Ocean Resources Inc (*NORI*), a Nauruan national.[216] At the time of its initial application, NORI was a wholly owned subsidiary of Canadian mining company Nautilus.[217] By the time of its renewed application in 2011, NORI had ended its relationship with Nautilus and was owned by two state-controlled foundations (Nauru Education and Training Foundation and Nauru Health and Environment Foundation).[218] However, NORI is now a private corporate

[213] ISBA/22/LTC/13, para 1.

[214] Appendix 1 includes an overview of each of these contractors.

[215] Appendix 2 includes details of each of these contracts. On the CCZ, see Chapter 2, at text following n 55.

[216] ISA Council, 'Decision of the Council Relating to a Request for Approval of a Plan of Work for Exploration for Polymetallic Nodules submitted by Nauru Ocean Resources Inc' (19 July 2011) ISBA/17/C/14; ISA LTC, 'Report and Recommendations to the Council of the ISA Relating to an Application for the Approval of a Plan of Work for Exploration by Nauru Ocean Resources Inc' (11 July 2011) ISBA/17/C/9.

[217] ISA LTC, 'Nauru Resources Inc – Application for Approval of a Plan of Work for Exploration' (21 April 2008) ISBA/14/LTC/L.2, paras 2 and 10. See also ISBA/17/C/9, para 17.

[218] ISA LTC, 'Application for Approval of a Plan of Work for Exploration for Polymetallic Nodules in the Area by Nauru Ocean Resources Incorporated' (21 June 2011) ISBA/17/LTC/L.4, paras 3–5 (as described at para 4, at the time of this application, NORI was controlled by a board of directors comprising Nauru's minister for commerce, industry and environment, and minister for foreign affairs, plus Nautilus founder (and subsequent creator of DeepGreen), David Heydon). See also ISBA/17/C/9, paras 15–17.

actor: presently, it is a wholly owned subsidiary of Canadian mining company DeepGreen.[219]

The second private corporate contractor, Tonga Offshore Mining Limited (*TOML*), is now also owned by DeepGreen. Tongan national TOML entered an ISA contract at the start of 2012.[220] TOML was previously owned by Nautilus[221] but, following the latter's financial collapse, it was acquired by DeepGreen.[222] In 2013, the ISA entered contracts with two further private corporate actors: Belgian corporation Global Sea Mineral Resources NV (*GSR*), which is the deep sea exploratory division of the Belgian corporate group DEME,[223] and UK Seabed Resources Ltd (*UKSRL*), a UK national that is a wholly owned subsidiary of US defence company Lockheed Martin Corporation.[224]

In 2015, the ISA entered into a contract with a Singaporean company: Ocean Mineral Singapore Pte Ltd (*OMS*), which is majority-owned by Keppel Corporation (also Singaporean and one of the world's largest offshore and marine groups), with

[219] DeepGreen Metals Inc, 'Copper, Nickel, Cobalt & Manganese Derived from Polymetallic Nodules' (DeepGreen Press Release, April 2020) <https://deep.green/deepgreen-derives-metal-from-polymetallic-nodules/>. DeepGreen holds NORI indirectly through its wholly owned Singaporean subsidiary, DeepGreen Engineering Pte Ltd, as illustrated in the DeepGreen corporate chart within Sustainable Opportunities Acquisition Corp, 'Form S–4, Registration Statement' (US Securities and Exchange Commission, 8 April 2021) ('Form S–4') at 134 <https://sec.report/Document/0001213900-21-020731/fs42021_sustainableoppacq.htm> (as this document also explains (at 8ff), DeepGreen is in the process of merging to become a publicly listed company, and it plans to trade as The Metals Company; for further details, see Appendix 1 to this book).

[220] ISA Council, 'Decision of the Council Relating to a Request for Approval of a Plan of Work for Exploration for Polymetallic Nodules submitted by Tonga Offshore Mining Limited' (19 July 2011) ISBA/17/C/15; ISA LTC, 'Report and Recommendations to the Council of the ISA Relating to an Application for the Approval of a Plan of Work for Exploration for Polymetallic Nodules by Tonga Offshore Mining Limited' (8 July 2011) ISBA/17/C/10. Technically, when TOML entered its ISA contract in January 2012, it was the first private corporate contractor to enter a contractual relationship with the ISA, given that NORI was a state-controlled corporation at that time (see citations at n 218).

[221] ISBA/17/C/10, para 15.

[222] On Nautilus's collapse, see Chapter 2, n 47; on DeepGreen's acquisition of TOML, which occurred in March 2020, see DeepGreen Metals Inc, 'DeepGreen Acquires Third Seabed Contract Area, with the Potential to Solve the Supply Bottleneck of Critical Battery Metals' (DeepGreen Press Release, April 2020) <https://deep.green/deepgreen-acquires-third-seabed-contract-area-to-explore-for-polymetallic-nodules/>. For a corporate chart of TOML's holding structure, see Form S–4 (n 219) 134.

[223] On GSR's application, which was made through G-TEC Sea Mineral Resources NV (subsequently acquired by DEME and renamed as GSR), see ISA Council, 'Decision of the Council of the ISA Relating to a Request for Approval of a Plan of Work for Exploration for Polymetallic Nodules submitted by G-TEC Sea Mineral Resources NV' (26 July 2012) ISBA/18/C/28; ISA LTC, 'Report and Recommendations of the Legal and Technical Commission to the Council of the ISA Relating to an Application for the Approval of a Plan of Work for Exploration for Polymetallic Nodules by G-TEC Sea Mineral Resources NV' (20 July 2012) ISBA/18/C/19. For further information on GSR, see DEME's website <www.deme-gsr.com/>.

[224] UKSRL is a wholly owned subsidiary of Lockheed Martin UK Holdings Ltd, the UK-based component of Lockheed Martin Corporation. On UKSRL's application, see ISA Council, 'Decision of the Council of the ISA Relating to a Request for Approval of a Plan of Work for Exploration for Polymetallic Nodules submitted by UK Seabed Resources Ltd' (26 July 2012) ISBA/18/C/27; ISA LTC, 'Report and Recommendations of the Legal and Technical Commission to the Council of the ISA Relating to an Application for the Approval of a Plan of Work for Exploration for Polymetallic Nodules by UK Seabed Resources Ltd' (18 July 2012) ISBA/18/C/17.

UKSRL holding a minority shareholding in OMS.[225] Thereafter, in 2016, UKSRL entered into its second contract with the ISA.[226] Finally, in 2021, the ISA entered into its seventh contract with a private corporate actor: Blue Minerals Jamaica Limited (*BMJ*), a Jamaican corporation.[227]

In addition to these seven private corporate contracts, two of the ISA's contracts with state enterprises (the Cook Islands Investment Corporation (*CIIC*) and Kiribati's Marawa Research and Exploration Ltd (*Marawa*)) are, in fact, being conducted through partnership arrangements with private corporate entities (GSR[228] and a subsidiary of DeepGreen,[229] respectively). Although these partnership arrangements are private agreements, certain details have been publicly disclosed. CIIC describes that its arrangement with GSR affords it 'access to the technical resources and capabilities of [GSR]', including through 'joint exploration cruises', allowing CIIC to 'reduce mobilization costs and optimize results'.[230] As regards Marawa, DeepGreen's subsidiary entered into an option agreement with Marawa and Kiribati (allowing DeepGreen to purchase exploration rights over nodules sites in the CCZ granted to Marawa by the ISA) and a services agreement (granting DeepGreen exclusive rights to recover nodules from Marawa's contract area, after

[225] ISA Council, 'Decision of the Council Relating to an Application for the Approval of a Plan of Work for Exploration for Polymetallic Nodules submitted by Ocean Mineral Singapore Pte Ltd' (21 July 2014) ISBA/20/C/27; ISA LTC, 'Report and Recommendations to the Council of the ISA Relating to an Application for the Approval of a Plan of Work for Exploration by Ocean Mineral Singapore Pte Ltd' (25 February 2014) ISBA/20/C/7, para 10. See also Keppel Corporation, 'Joint Venture Agreement with UK Seabed Resources Ltd and Lion City Capital Partners Pte Ltd' (Press Release, April 2013) <www.kepcorp.com/en/download.ashx?id=4877>.

[226] ISA Council, 'Decision of the Council Relating to an Application for the Approval of a Plan of Work for Exploration for Polymetallic Nodules submitted by UK Seabed Resources Ltd' (21 July 2014) ISBA/20/C/25; ISA LTC, 'Report and Recommendations of the Legal and Technical Commission to the Council of the ISA Relating to an Application for the Approval of a Plan of Work for Exploration for Polymetallic Nodules by UK Seabed Resources Ltd' (26 February 2014) ISBA/20/C/5.

[227] ISBA/26/C/27/Rev1; see also ISA LTC, 'Report and Recommendations of the Legal and Technical Commission to the Council of the ISA Relating to an Application for Approval of a Plan of Work for Exploration for Polymetallic Nodules by Blue Minerals Jamaica Ltd' (6 August 2020) ISBA/26/C/22.

[228] On CIIC's joint venture with GSR, see ISA LTC, 'Report and Recommendations of the Legal and Technical Commission to the Council of the ISA Relating to an Application for the Approval of a Plan of Work for Exploration for Polymetallic Nodules by the Cook Islands Investment Corporation' (9 July 2014) ISBA/20/C/18, para 19; Michael Henry, 'International Seabed Authority Contract Signing' (*Cook Islands Investment Corporations Online News*, July 2016) <http://ciiconline.com/latestnews/international-seabed-authority-contract-signing/>.

[229] On Marawa's partnership arrangement, see DeepGreen's website <https://deep.green/sponsoring-states/>; see also DeepGreen Resources Inc, 'DeepGreen Resources Inc Announces Partnership with Maersk Supply Service A/S in Deepsea Metals Industry' (22 March 2017) <www.newswire.ca/news-releases/deepgreen-resources-inc-announces-partnership-with-maersk-supply-service-as-in-deepsea-metals-industry-616799114.html> (describing that DeepGreen is conducting activities in what, at that time, was its second contract area (i.e. Marawa's allocated area) through its wholly owned Singaporean subsidiary, DeepGreen Engineering Pte Ltd). For further details, see Form S-4 (n 219) 131, 167–168.

[230] ISBA/20/C/18, para 19.

paying all relevant ISA fees and royalties, and in return for royalty payments to Kiribati at an undisclosed rate).[231]

Accordingly, the last decade has been marked by the accelerating involvement of private corporate actors in activities in the Area. A notable feature of this trend is the prevalence of private corporate actor participation within reserved areas. Indeed, over half of the ISA's seven existing contracts with private corporate actors are concerned with nodules exploration of reserved areas.[232] In addition, the contracts of CIIC and Marawa are in respect of exploration activities in reserved areas.[233] Thus, over 85% of all deep seabed mining activities in reserved areas are being conducted by private corporate actors (which, in turn, are owned primarily by corporations based in *developed* states). Perhaps even more strikingly, almost half of the contracts held in reserved areas on behalf of developing state enterprises are being performed by subsidiaries of just one private corporate actor: the Canadian mining company DeepGreen (notwithstanding the fact that DeepGreen was not the original applicant in respect of any of these ISA contracts).

In another interesting dynamic, observed by the LTC, in some instances a 'model of collaboration' has emerged 'in the execution of the plan of work between the contractor that contributed to the reserved area and the contractor, sponsored by a developing State, that is granted that reserved area'.[234] For example, the reserved area that CIIC is exploring (through joint venture agreement with GSR) is the site that GSR previously contributed as a reserved area.[235] GSR has partnered with CIIC in order to explore this reserved area.[236] Similarly, OMS is exploring a reserved area (in conjunction with minority shareholder UKSRL) that was originally contributed by UKSRL.[237] In order to do so 'in an efficient and cost-effective manner', OMS is collaborating with UKSRL in the execution of the plan of work for this reserved area.[238]

Are these forms of collaboration between developing states and private corporate actors consistent with UNCLOS? What are their implications for achievement of the common heritage? As the remainder of this section will demonstrate,

[231] Form S-4 (n 219) 168 (the services agreement presupposes that Marawa will be granted an exploitation contract by the ISA, in relation to which DeepGreen has agreed to pay the application fee and annual administrative costs).

[232] NORI, TOML, OMS and BMJ have contracts with the ISA for exploration of reserved areas; see ISBA/17/C/9, paras 1, 25; ISBA/17/C/10, paras 1, 20; ISBA/20/C/7, paras 1, 15; and ISBA/26/C/22, paras 1 and 15, respectively; see also Appendix 2.

[233] See ISBA/20/C/18, paras 1, 13; ISA LTC, 'Report and Recommendations of the Legal and Technical Commission to the Council of the ISA Relating to an Application for the Approval of a Plan of Work for Exploration for Polymetallic Nodules by Marawa Research and Exploration Ltd' (18 July 2012) ISBA/18/C/18, paras 1, 15.

[234] ISBA/22/C/17, para 55.

[235] ISBA/20/C/18, para 13.

[236] ISBA/20/C/18, para 19.

[237] ISBA/20/C/7, para 15.

[238] ISA LTC, 'Application for Approval of a Plan of Work for Exploration for Polymetallic Nodules by Ocean Mineral Singapore Pte Ltd' (25 May 2013) ISBA/19/LTC/11, para 8.

although the precise consequences of such conduct have yet to be determined, such behaviour is permitted by the regime through the conduit of the requirements of nationality or effective control.

Nationality and effective control are the bases for corporate participation within deep seabed mining. In accordance with Article 153(2)(b) of the Convention, corporate eligibility to participate within the regime requires state sponsorship, which is premised upon nationality or effective control. Article 4(3) of Annex III makes clear that if a corporate entity wishes to secure a contract to explore for deep seabed resources, it must obtain sponsorship from all states of which it is a national. If the entity is a consortium with various nationalities, it must be sponsored by each of those states, and if 'the applicant is effectively controlled by another State Party or its nationals', the sponsorship of that state is also required.[239] These requirements are reflected in the Mining Code.[240]

As noted in the preceding section, the requirement of effective control also features in allocation of reserved areas. Article 9(4) of Annex III allows entities sponsored and 'effectively controlled' by developing states to apply to explore such areas.[241] Notably, Article 9(4) requires an entity that is seeking to conduct activities in a reserved area to be both sponsored *and* effectively controlled by a developing state or states that are States Parties to the Convention. This dual requirement is intended to foster equal participation by developing states, ensuring that only entities which are effectively controlled by developing states are eligible to obtain access to reserved areas pursuant to Article 9(4).

Given their significance, what constitutes 'nationality' or 'effective control' for the purposes of corporate participation in deep seabed mining? As examined in Chapter 1, establishing corporate nationality and associated matters of control for the purposes of international law are often vexed questions. Rules vary by context.[242] To some extent, the Convention's approach remains 'ambiguous'.[243] The regime does not define 'nationality' or 'effective control'.[244] The concept of effective control, in particular, is susceptible to varying interpretations.[245] It could simply mean regulatory control, or else it could require a form of economic control.

[239] UNCLOS, Annex III, art 4(3); see also ITLOS AO, para 77.

[240] See regs 9(b) and 11(1)–(2) of the Nodules, Sulphides and Cobalt Regulations; DERs, regs 5(1)(b), 6(1)–(2).

[241] As Section 4.2.3.2 addressed, this is the sole means by which entities are active, presently, within reserved areas.

[242] See Chapter 1, Section 1.2.2 (particularly text to nn 124–125).

[243] Andrés Sebastián Rojas and Freedom-Kai Phillips, Centre for International Governance Innovation, 'Effective Control and Deep Seabed Mining: Toward a Definition' (February 2019) Liability Issues for Deep Seabed Mining Series, paper no 7 at 1 <www.cigionline.org/sites/default/files/documents/Deep%20Seabed%20Paper%20No.7_0.pdf>.

[244] See ISBA/20/LTC/10, para 10 (noting the scant drafting history in this regard, citing the Virginia Commentary); see also Rojas and Phillips (n 243) 6.

[245] For analysis of this term, see Rojas and Phillips (n 243); see also ISA Secretariat examination in ISBA/20/LTC/10, as considered by the LTC in ISA LTC, 'Summary Report of the Chair of the Legal and Technical Commission on the Work of the Commission during the Twentieth Session of the ISA'

In practice, the ISA has endorsed a regulatory approach to effective control, leaving it to the discretion of sponsoring states to determine eligibility for sponsorship as a matter of domestic law.[246] This regulatory approach to effective control is evident within the operation of the licensing regime. For example, certain corporations (such as Canada's DeepGreen and the US's Lockheed Martin) are conducting deep seabed mining activities through wholly owned subsidiaries in host states (NORI in Nauru, TOML in Tonga and UK-based UKSRL). For DeepGreen, an advantage to this approach has been in allowing it – a company incorporated in a developed state – to explore reserved areas through subsidiaries based in developing states.[247] For Lockheed Martin, a US corporation which cannot obtain sponsorship from its home state (given that the US is not a party to UNCLOS), establishing a subsidiary in the UK has afforded it a means of participation.[248] These types of arrangement also have implications in terms of attribution of liability.[249]

Two of these subsidiaries (TOML and UKSRL) obtained ISA contracts based on host state sponsorship alone, irrespective of substantial underlying relationships with parent corporations.[250] TOML's application, in particular, brought the issue of effective control sharply into focus. TOML is a private company incorporated in Tonga and, at the time of its application, was a wholly owned subsidiary of Canadian mining company Nautilus.[251] Notwithstanding Nautilus's ultimate ownership of '100 per cent of the shares of TOML',[252] the LTC was satisfied that effective control of TOML resided in Tonga and not in Canada.[253] This prompted significant

(16 July 2014) ISBA/20/C/20, paras 25–29. See, further, Gwenaëlle Le Gurun, 'Annex III' in Proelss Commentary 2139–2140, 2187–2188.

[246] See, e.g. ISBA/20/C/20, paras 27–28; see also ISBA/20/LTC/10, paras 7, 12, 21; ISA Secretariat, 'Issues Related to the Sponsorship by States of Contracts for Exploration in the Area and Related Matters' (9 June 2015) ISBA/21/LTC/12, para 5.

[247] See also discussion in Section 4.2.3.2, at text to nn 195–198.

[248] Chapter 5 will consider the position of actors situated outwith UNCLOS, such as non-States Parties and their nationals.

[249] Tara Davenport, Centre for International Governance Innovation, 'Responsibility and Liability for Damage Arising out of Activities in the Area: Attribution of Liability' (January 2019) Liability Issues for Deep Seabed Mining Series, paper no 4 <www.cigionline.org/sites/default/files/documents/deep%20seabed%20mining%20paper%20no%204_2.pdf> (noting, at 15, that the Convention regime does 'not contemplate [the] possibility' that a parent company or its home state 'should be held liable for the wrongful acts of its subsidiary that result in damage').

[250] See LTC consideration of applications by TOML (ISBA/17/C/10, paras 19, 32) and UKSRL (ISBA/18/C/17, para 30 and ISBA/20/C/5, para 30), accepting that these applicants had demonstrated nationality/effective control, on the basis solely of host state sponsorship. cf NORI, which was a state-controlled entity at the time the ISA approved its application: ISBA/17/C/9, paras 15–17.

[251] ISBA/17/C/10, para 15 (Nautilus held TOML through another wholly owned subsidiary, Canadian company United Nickel Ltd).

[252] ISBA/17/C/10, para 15.

[253] See ISBA/17/C/10, para 32 (accepting 'that the applicant is a qualified applicant'). In its deliberations, the LTC did not elaborate the grounds on which Tonga could be said to exercise effective control over TOML, other than to acknowledge that Tonga had provided a certificate of sponsorship 'in due and proper form', pursuant to which 'Tonga stated that the applicant is under [its] effective control': ibid, para 19.

Council debate, with some consternation as to whether TOML's Tongan sponsorship was sufficient to satisfy the effective control requirement.[254] Ultimately, the Council approved TOML's application, following LTC emphasis on the fact that Tonga's sponsorship certificate was 'in due and proper form', coupled with Tongan interjection that such applications serve as a route for 'meaningful participation' by developing states in activities in the Area.[255]

This interpretation of effective control as requiring regulatory control 'strictly complies with the wording of the [Convention]'.[256] Indeed, the Chamber of ITLOS endorsed implicitly the permissibility of such an approach when addressing 'the need to prevent commercial enterprises based in developed States from setting up companies in developing States, acquiring their nationality and obtaining their sponsorship in the hope of being subjected to less burdensome regulations and controls'.[257] The Chamber warned against applying differentiated responsibilities between developing and developed states, as it could lead to '[t]he spread of sponsoring States "of convenience"', thereby jeopardising the uniform application of marine environmental protection standards, other safety standards and the protection of the common heritage of mankind.[258] In doing so, the Chamber acknowledged tacitly that the regime poses no barrier to Western companies routing operations through developing states (with regulatory control but no substantive, economic control) and participating pursuant to developing state sponsorship.[259]

Adopting a regulatory approach to effective control is consistent with the rules of treaty interpretation. Articles 31 to 33 of the VCLT contain these default rules.[260] Pursuant to the general rule of interpretation, the Convention's eligibility tests of nationality or effective control must be 'interpreted in good faith in accordance with the ordinary meaning to be given to the terms of the treaty in their context and in the light of its object and purpose'.[261] Context takes account of the text of the Convention, including its preamble and annexes.[262] Other factors that can be

[254] See ISA Press Release, 'Seabed Council Approves Four Applications for Exploratory Contracts with Authority in Deep Seabed Area' (19 July 2011) SB/17/11, 3 (with, e.g. Brazil claiming that 'effective control [of TOML] appeared to reside in Canada').

[255] SB/17/11, 3; see also ISBA/17/C/15, para 2.

[256] See, e.g. Gibson (n 178) 193; Harrison (2014) (n 144) 23; cf Rojas and Phillips (n 243) 10 (expressing concerns about '[t]his narrow reading of effective control', and cautioning that the 'economic reality of new business models ... whereby a contractor is registered in a developing jurisdiction yet remains a wholly owned subsidiary of an experienced mining company in a developed jurisdiction' should also be taken into account for the purposes of effective control).

[257] ITLOS AO, para 159.

[258] ITLOS AO, para 159.

[259] See also Gibson (n 178) 195 (noting that the Chamber 'did not question the other advantages that such companies may gain through access to reserved areas'). For analysis of this phenomenon of 'forum shopping' within the deep seabed mining context, see Klaas Willaert, 'Forum Shopping within the Context of Deep Sea Mining: Towards Sponsoring States of Convenience?' (2019) 52 RBDI 116.

[260] See Chapter 1, text to nn 13–19, noting the customary status of these rules, and their application to the Convention regime, as acknowledged by ITLOS AO, para 58 (and see para 60, confirming VCLT interpretation rules 'may, by analogy, provide guidance' on interpretation of the Mining Code).

[261] VCLT, art 31(1).

[262] VCLT, art 31(2).

considered, together with context, are the Mining Code[263] and subsequent state practice with regard to the practical application of the Convention's sponsorship regime.[264] As a supplementary means of interpretation, the Convention's *travaux préparatoires* are also relevant.[265]

The broader context indicates that effective control for the purposes of Article 153(2)(b) (and relevant Annex III provisions, such as Article 4(3) and Article 9(4)) can be satisfied by regulatory control alone. This interpretation is evident from the wording of other provisions within UNCLOS. For example, the nexus between sponsorship and regulatory control is clear from the operation of Article 139 of UNCLOS. Article 139(1) replicates Article 153(2)(b), in pertinent part, requiring States Parties to ensure that activities in the Area conducted by them, their state enterprises or by entities 'which possess the nationality of States Parties or are effectively controlled by them or their nationals' are compliant with UNCLOS. Article 139(2) further requires States Parties to secure effective compliance by state-sponsored entities, by taking 'all necessary and appropriate measures', as a matter of domestic law.[266]

The extent of a state sponsor's obligations in this regard was a key focus of the Chamber when delivering its advisory opinion in 2011.[267] As the Chamber affirmed, sponsorship aims to ensure that 'obligations set out in the Convention, a treaty under international law which binds only States Parties thereto, are complied with by entities that are subjects of domestic legal systems'.[268] Accordingly, there is a logical link between Article 153(2)(b) (requiring nationality/effective

[263] VCLT, art 31(3)(a) includes, as a relevant factor for interpretation, 'any subsequent agreement between the parties regarding the interpretation of the treaty or the application of its provisions'. Arguably, the Mining Code (adopted by States Parties in relation to application of the Convention regime) can be construed as broadly analogous to a subsequent agreement for the purposes of VCLT, art 31(3)(a): Rojas and Phillips (n 243) 5. See also ITLOS AO, para 60 (recognising that ISA regulations are 'binding texts negotiated by States and adopted through a procedure similar to that used in multilateral conferences', rendering the VCLT relevant to their interpretation, and also noting 'the close connection between these texts and the Convention').

[264] VCLT, art 31(3)(b) allows subsequent practice to be taken into account if it is 'in the application of the treaty which establishes the agreement of the parties regarding its interpretation'. Arguably, practical application of the Convention's sponsorship regime, both by States Parties individually (acting to sponsor entities), and acting collectively through the ISA (e.g. as Council members approving applications), are relevant factors for interpretation, in terms of VCLT, art 31(3)(b).

[265] VCLT, art 32 (allowing reliance on supplementary means of interpretation, such as preparatory works, to 'confirm' a meaning that is 'ambiguous or obscure' or leads to a result that is 'manifestly absurd or unreasonable'). However, as noted in the present section (at n 244), the drafting history of UNCLOS does not shed light on operation of the nationality/effective control standard.

[266] See UNCLOS, art 139(2), read with art 153(4) and Annex III, art 4(4) (providing that state sponsors have 'responsibility to ensure, within their legal systems' that sponsored entities comply with the UNCLOS regime).

[267] See ITLOS AO, paras 108, 110, 118–120, 227ff. Distribution of responsibility for deep seabed mining activities will be discussed further in Chapter 6, Section 6.4.2.

[268] ITLOS AO, para 75; as the Chamber acknowledged, this is achieved, also, by ISA regulations, which apply to all contractors. As Section 4.3 will consider, ISA contracts are also instrumental in this respect. Due to the contractual relationship, contractors become directly bound to adhere to the UNCLOS regime.

control for state sponsorship) and Article 139 (requiring States Parties to ensure compliance by entities subject to their domestic legal systems). The Convention places emphasis on nationality or effective control of non-state entities as preconditions for their participation in deep seabed mining, to ensure that sponsoring states have direct routes of regulatory control in respect of sponsored entities.[269]

This approach is influenced by the fact that a state's decision to sponsor an entity is a matter for that state's discretion. The sponsorship decision is 'a specific act emanating from the will of the State or States of nationality and of effective control'.[270] As the ISA has noted, 'this implies that the onus is on the sponsoring State to ensure that those criteria [of nationality/effective control] are satisfied before taking the decision to sponsor an entity'.[271] By the same token, the sponsoring state is entitled to define the conditions for effective control within its domestic legal system: 'if a sponsoring State finds it useful to elaborate on the conditions to grant its sponsorship, it has the competence to address this question within its domestic legal framework'.[272]

The terms of the Mining Code confirm this interpretation. Regulation 10(3) of the Nodules, Sulphides and Cobalt Regulations provides '[s]ome guidance' on the meaning of effective control by specifying the application material that a corporate applicant must include.[273] A corporate applicant must specify its principal place of business or domicile and, if applicable, its place of registration.[274] In accordance with Regulation 11, the applicant must also provide a certificate of sponsorship issued by its state(s) of nationality or effective control.[275] In this certificate, the sponsoring state pledges whether the applicant is '(i) [a] national of the sponsoring State; or (ii) [s]ubject to the effective control of the sponsoring State or its nationals'.[276] Taken together, all of this information forms the basis for LTC determination of whether an applicant meets the sponsorship requirements.[277]

269 See Jule Siegfried, 'Article 153' in Proelss Commentary 1084 ('[t]hese prerequisites [of nationality or effective control] aim at guaranteeing the State party's potential to actually control the respective entity' (citation omitted)). See also ISBA/20/LTC/10, para 12 (recognising that '[t]he nature and scope of the obligations and liability of sponsoring States provide essential insights as to the context and purpose of the effective control test').

270 ITLOS AO, para 78.

271 ISBA/20/LTC/10, para 7.

272 ISBA/20/LTC/10, para 12; see also para 21. The LTC has affirmed this position: ISBA/20/C/20, paras 27–28. This echoes ITLOS AO, para 234 (finding that '[t]he sponsoring State may find it necessary, depending upon its legal system, to include in its domestic law provisions that are necessary for implementing its obligations under the Convention', and that these provisions may include 'conditions for issuing a certificate of sponsorship'). On risks of incoherence and 'legal variability' in leaving each state to determine what constitutes effective control, see Rojas and Phillips (n 243) 9 (arguing that '[a]n internationally negotiated solution under the ISA would be preferred and could confer the legal certainty required by the Secretariat, the states parties and stakeholders').

273 As noted in ISBA/20/LTC/10, para 11.

274 Reg 10(3)(b) of the Nodules, Sulphides and Cobalt Regulations; also reproduced in DERs, reg 5(3)(b). The applicant's certificate of registration should be attached to its application: Annex II of the Nodules, Sulphides and Cobalt Regulations; DERs, Annex I.

275 Reg 11(1)–(2) of the Nodules, Sulphides and Cobalt Regulations; DERs, reg 6(1)–(2).

276 Reg 11(3)(c) of the Nodules, Sulphides and Cobalt Regulations; DERs, reg 6(3)(c).

277 ISBA/20/LTC/10, para 11; ISBA/20/C/20, para 28.

These regulatory requirements focus on the formal relationship between corporate applicant and state sponsor. To establish state sponsorship, an entity does not need to demonstrate a real or substantial connection with its sponsoring state. The Mining Code does not require the ISA to investigate the origins of a corporate applicant's capital or the economic reality of a deep seabed mining venture, in terms of the nationality of the venture's ultimate controllers and beneficiaries, for the purposes of determining effective control.[278] Instead, 'the fact of incorporation/registration and the grant of nationality (i.e. regulatory control) [is] the critical, or dominant, factor, notwithstanding the practical realities as to control over policy, capital, finance and management'.[279]

Therefore, the sponsorship requirement may be satisfied if a corporate entity can demonstrate that it is incorporated in a given state (for the purposes of Regulation 10(3)), and that state is willing and able to provide a certificate of sponsorship attesting that the corporation is its national, and is under its effective control (in terms of Regulation 11(3)(c)).[280] Accordingly, although 'nationality and effective control appear as two distinct concepts' within the terms of the deep seabed regime,[281] in practice the ISA has been content to discern both elements from the same evidence.[282]

In adopting this approach, the ISA has taken account of other applications of the control test within international law. For example, the LTC has noted that 'the Part XI regime, as well as other legal contexts, used the same critical criteria of incorporation, registration and granting of nationality (i.e. regulatory control) to determine effective control'.[283] In particular, the Secretariat has considered the rules concerning nationality of flag state vessels and matters of civil aviation, finding that the adoption of a regulatory approach to issues such as nationality and control was a common factor across these contexts.[284] The Secretariat also distinguished the approach to corporate nationality in diplomatic protection, which may require some 'close and permanent connection' between the state exercising diplomatic

[278] This stands in contrast to the Mining Code's approach to an applicant's financial capabilities, where a parent company's financial resources can be taken into account to determine the applicant's financial position: see Nodules Regulations, reg 12(7); Sulphides Regulations, reg 13(4)(b); Cobalt Regulations, reg 13(6); DERs, Annex I, para 21(c)(ii).

[279] ISBA/20/LTC/10, para 21.

[280] See regs 10(3) and 11(3)(c) of the Nodules, Sulphides and Cobalt Regulations. See also ISBA/20/LTC/10, para 22.

[281] Rojas and Phillips (n 243) 4.

[282] See, e.g. ISBA/20/C/20, para 28. See also Harrison (2014) (n 144) 23; Rojas and Phillips (n 243) 7.

[283] ISBA/20/C/20, para 27.

[284] ISBA/20/LTC/10, paras 14, 19–20, 21 (in the context of civil aviation, cf Rojas and Phillips (n 243) 8). On similarities between the Convention approach to nationality/control for corporate participation within the Area and operation of the Convention's system of flag state nationality of ships, see Chapter 1, text to nn 119–125. Another area of international law that features an effective control test is the law of state responsibility (requiring effective control before private entity actions are attributable to a state). However, given the differing context and scope of the effective control test for the purposes of state responsibility, it is not instructive in the present context.

protection and the corporation,[285] on the basis that applying this approach in the deep seabed mining context would not necessarily ensure that the sponsoring state exercises regulatory control over the sponsored corporation.[286]

However, perhaps the most apposite comparison in this regard is between the ISA's approach and the typical investment treaty approach to corporate nationality and control.[287] An overriding feature of the latter context is the refusal by investment tribunals to read restrictions into the definition of protected investors if such restrictions are not present in the treaty text.[288] For example, in interpreting the definition of 'investor' within the Ukraine–Lithuania BIT (pursuant to VCLT rules of treaty interpretation), the *Tokios* tribunal declined to restrict the definition's scope on the basis of a control test found elsewhere in the BIT.[289] In reaching this conclusion, the arbitral tribunal applied the 'well established presumption' *expressio unius est exclusio alterius* (express mention of one thing excludes all others),[290] finding that the absence of a control test in the relevant provision was a 'deliberate choice of the Contracting Parties' and not for the tribunal to second-guess.[291]

Equally, within the deep seabed mining context, if States Parties had intended the effective control requirement to include an element of economic control, they could have inserted such a restriction within the Convention text, or included it within the Mining Code. This argument is all the more compelling when one takes account of the wording of certain other provisions of the regime that are predicated on the substantive relationship between a prospective contractor and its parent corporation.[292] Therefore, the absence of a substantive test for effective control within Article 153(2)(b) of UNCLOS (or in Annex III, Articles 4(3) and 9(4)) can be construed as a deliberate omission on the part of the drafters.

285 As per *Barcelona Traction* (n 34), para 71. For analysis of the approach to corporate nationality within diplomatic protection, see Chapter 1, text to nn 82–94.

286 ISBA/20/LTC/10, para 17.

287 On the prevailing investment treaty approach to nationality/control, see Chapter 1, text to nn 99–101, 106–107.

288 See Chapter 1, nn 99–101 and citations therein.

289 *Tokios Tokelės v Ukraine* (Decision on Jurisdiction) ICSID Case No ARB/02/18 (29 April 2004).

290 *Tokios* (n 289), para 30.

291 *Tokios* (n 289), para 36; see also para 39.

292 For example, in relation to the financial requirements for corporate participation, the Mining Code requires the financial position of parent companies to be taken into account: Nodules Regulations, reg 12(7); Sulphides Regulations, reg 13(4)(b); Cobalt Regulations, reg 13(6); DERs, Annex I, para 21(c)(ii). Further, as regards transfer of technology, UNCLOS, Annex III, art 5(3)(c) (now disapplied by 1994 Agreement, Annex, s 5(2)) acknowledged the 'closeness of the relationship and the degree of control or influence' between a contractor and a corporation with which it has a 'substantial corporate relationship' (i.e. a parent company), to determine whether the contractor had made reasonable endeavours to obtain, from its parent company, the legal right to transfer technology to the Enterprise. Rojas and Phillips note that UNCLOS, Annex III, art 5(3)(c) 'makes the most direct reference to the economic reality of the relationship', arguing that this 'sheds additional light on the intended formulation of effective control' within the sponsorship regime: Rojas/Phillips (n 243) 5. However, applying the presumption *expressio unius est exclusio alterius*, the fact that UNCLOS, art 153(2)(b) is not premised on the substance of the relationship between an applicant and its parent company, for the purposes of determining where effective control truly lies, implies that additional qualifications cannot be read into the text.

In summation, a corporation may establish a shell company in a developing state, obtain sponsorship from that state and enter a mining contract with the ISA through this subsidiary to explore reserved areas (provided that other eligibility requirements are satisfied).[293] In these circumstances, the ISA has not required the state of nationality of the parent company to provide an additional certificate of sponsorship as a prerequisite of the subsidiary's participation within the regime, 'as long as formal separation between the two entities is maintained'.[294]

In practice, what does this mean for the achievement of the common heritage? Does the licensing system operate to advance market-oriented goals at the expense of communitarian, benefit-of-mankind concerns? Or does it attain a balance between the two? This remains to be seen. Gibson criticises 'the opportunistic creation of companies in countries of convenience', and queries whether it is 'desirable' that private corporate actors from developed states should be permitted to 'take advantage of the flexibility of international corporate structures in order to gain access to mineral resources in reserved areas'.[295] Willaert also notes that this may be a 'risky development' that could 'drastically undermine' the common heritage principle.[296] By condoning such behaviour, the ISA runs the risk that corporate actors will continue to route their investments through subsidiaries in developing states, to gain access to reserved areas, until the bank of reserved areas is depleted entirely.[297] Moreover, these new arrangements could result in monopolistic behaviour, as they may 'inadvertently lead to the dominance of the interests of developed States in seabed activities in reserved areas, a predicament which the parallel system and annex III, article 9, were deliberately designed to discourage'.[298]

Yet, despite these concerns, it is difficult to avoid concluding that joining forces with private actors may afford developing states with one of the only viable means

[293] As discussed, the ISA's contract with Tonga-sponsored TOML is a key example of this.

[294] ISBA/20/LTC/10, para 22; as regards the need for 'formal separation' identified by the ISA Secretariat, investment arbitral tribunals have noted that, rather than being 'a mere formality', this formal separation between entities in corporate structures constitutes 'the fundamental building block of the global economy': *Autopista Concesionada de Venezuela CA v Bolivarian Republic of Venezuela* (Decision on Jurisdiction) ICSID Case No ARB/00/5 (27 September 2001), para 67; affirmed in *Aguas del Tunari SA v Republic of Bolivia* (Decision on Jurisdiction) ICSID Case No ARB/02/3 (21 October 2005), para 245 at fn 218.

[295] Gibson (n 178) 193.

[296] Willaert (2019a) (n 259) 137.

[297] Gibson (n 178) 193, 197.

[298] ISBA/22/LTC/13, para 8. See also Elie Jarmache, 'Vingt Ans Après: Les Fonds Marins' in Stéphane Doumbé-Billé and Jean-Marc Thouvenin (eds), *Ombres et Lumières du Droit International: Mélanges en L'honneur du Professeur Habib Slim* (A Pedone 2016) 186–187 (warning of the danger that certain forms of collaborations between private corporations and developing states could lead to disguised monopolies). See further critique in Greenpeace, 'Deep Trouble: The Murky World of the Deep Sea Mining Industry' (December 2020) <www.greenpeace.org/static/planet4-international-stateless/c86ff110-pto-deep-trouble-report-final-1.pdf> (especially at 9, arguing that 'development of the deep sea mining industry has become increasingly concentrated in the hands of a small number of private corporations based in wealthy nations, with strong links to extractive and polluting industries, operating through complex and opaque structures of sub-contractors, partnerships or subsidiaries').

of participation within the system.[299] For example, in its application for a plan of work, CIIC stated that its combined approach with GSR would enable it to 'enhance all relevant synergies in scientific, ecological and economical research and studies to the absolute maximum'.[300] Equally, OMS hailed the 'significant advantages' to be realised by collaboration with UKSRL, in terms of ability to 'share data, equipment and resources'.[301] Nauru, the developing state sponsor to private corporate actor NORI, has emphasised that, for effective participation in activities in the Area by developing states, 'these States must engage entities in the global private sector (in much the same way as some developing countries require foreign direct investment)'.[302] Also, during Council consideration of TOML's application for a plan of work (sponsored by Tonga), Tonga reminded the Council of its status as a developing state, and stressed that TOML's application represented 'one way such States could realize meaningful participation in operations in the Area'.[303] Therefore, to some extent, as Lodge has argued, 'the spirit of the parallel system has been maintained by making it possible for developing States to participate in the Area'.[304] As Lodge has remarked, in relation to forms of developing state and private actor collaboration:

> [T]he best conclusion may be that it is too early to say whether this type of arrangement provides a viable precedent for the future participation of developing countries in deep seabed mining. Much will depend on whether these ventures are successful in producing long-term economic benefits for the sponsoring States and for the Authority.[305]

Nevertheless, this matter may be subject to future development. For example, in 2019, the African Group's recommendations on legal liability in relation to deep seabed mining argued for greater ISA scrutiny of 'effective control' at the application stage, including 'consideration of where the contractor's assets and management

[299] Helmut Tuerk, 'The International Seabed Area' in Malgosia Fitzmaurice and Norman A Martinez Gutierrez (eds), *The IMLI Manual on International Maritime Law*, vol I (OUP 2014) 301. See also Gibson (n 178) 193 (acknowledging that developing states may 'stand to benefit financially and in other ways' from such collaborations).

[300] ISA LTC, 'Application for Approval of a Plan of Work for Exploration for Polymetallic Nodules by the Cook Islands Investment Corporation' (8 November 2013) ISBA/20/LTC/3 para 13.

[301] ISBA/19/LTC/11, para 8.

[302] Remarks by Nauru in ISBA/16/C/6, para 1.

[303] SB/17/11, 4.

[304] Michael Lodge, 'The Deep Seabed' in Donald R Rothwell and others (eds), *The Oxford Handbook on the Law of the Sea* (OUP 2015) 245. Similarly, see Gwenaëlle Le Gurun, 'Annex III' in Proelss Commentary 2184. cf Isabel Feichtner, 'Sharing the Riches of the Sea: The Redistributive and Fiscal Dimension of Deep Seabed Exploitation' (2019) 30 EJIL 601, 631 (arguing that financial prospects from sponsoring deep seabed mining activities for developing states, such as Nauru, are 'bleak').

[305] Michael W Lodge, 'Satya Nandan's Legacy for the Common Heritage of Mankind' in Michael W Lodge and Myron H Nordquist (eds), *Peaceful Order in the World's Oceans* (Brill 2014) 293–294.

are located'.[306] Moreover, stakeholder comments on the DERs have raised the need to clarify the concept of effective control, in the exploitation context.[307] The matter of effective control also remains on the ISA's agenda, particularly in relation to its interaction with the benefit-sharing aspects of the licensing regime.[308]

On the basis of the above analysis, what we can conclude, for now, is that the ISA's licensing process operates to create a common management framework, but defers realisation of several key common heritage benefit-sharing elements to the ISA's further development of the regime.[309] As noted in Section 4.2.3.2, some of the benefit-sharing elements, such as the system of reserved areas and the anti-monopolisation provisions, are already operating in practice, although they continue to be subject to further development (including, for example, through establishment of the joint venture/equity interest option as regards sulphides and cobalt crusts). Meanwhile, the regime has deferred other benefit-sharing features entirely to further institutional development (such as operationalisation of the Enterprise and establishment of payment mechanisms for exploitation contracts). To the extent that the regime's 'participation objective has given way to a focus on market supply and revenue generation'[310] – evidenced, perhaps, by the Enterprise's postponement, indirect Western participation in reserved areas and the inclusion of a joint venture/equity interest option for sulphides and cobalt crusts – this places even greater weight on the regime's financial mechanisms to secure and deliver benefit-sharing aspects (as will be considered in Chapter 6).

4.2.4 The UNCLOS Deep Seabed Mining Regime Implements a System of Common Management through Institutional Power

As the preceding analysis has demonstrated, UNCLOS establishes a system of common management for deep seabed mining that has as its foundation

[306] ISA Council, 'Recommendations on Legal Liability – Submitted by the African Group' (5 June 2019) ISBA/25/C/25, para 5(c). The African Group is one of the Assembly's blocs of States Parties (alongside the Asia-Pacific Group, the Eastern European Group, the Latin American and Caribbean States Group and the Western European and Other States Group): ISA, 'Regional Groups' <www.isa.org.jm/regional-groups>.

[307] ISBA/26/C/2, Annex, para 5. Notably, the statement of risks in relation to DeepGreen's planned merger acknowledges that some critics call 'for the use of a beneficial ownership test for state sponsorship' and that there are 'no guarantees' that the current approach to effective control 'will be universally accepted in the future': Form S-4 (n 219) 46.

[308] See, e.g. ISBA/26/LTC/1, para 14.

[309] On this 'strategy of referral' at work within UNCLOS, see Chapter 3 discussion at text to nn 180–182.

[310] As argued by Feichtner (n 304) 603. See also Jarmache (n 298) 187 (noting that present forms of collaboration concerning reserved areas may jeopardise the ability of developing states to become fully involved as participants in the deep seabed, in terms of acquiring scientific and technological knowledge).

the ISA's unique institutional system. The ISA is the driving force within the regime, performing significant roles as custodian, developer, regulator and enforcer (and, potentially, as future participant in mining activities, through the Enterprise). In accordance with its carefully defined balance of power and decision-making processes, the ISA is progressively developing the regulatory regime, through creation of a comprehensive Mining Code. The ISA also shapes the overall direction of deep seabed mining activities and determines the extent of participation within these, given its role in the licensing process. As Chapter 6 will explore further, the ISA may perform a significant implementation and enforcement role in relation to contractor activities, including by monitoring performance, inspecting installations and enforcing compliance with contractual terms.

The 1994 Agreement adjusted the balance of power within the Authority, strengthening the less representative Council at the expense of the all-party Assembly. Nevertheless, despite this move away from a truly majoritarian system, the ISA remains a significant and unique body. As the African Group emphasised in 2017, the Authority 'is the only functioning international organization that directly regulates and manages natural resources that no state can appropriate for itself'.[311] Indeed, the ISA is a prime example of the way in which international law and international institutions can provide a 'shared surface' on which to allow political opponents to participate in a collective discourse about deep seabed mining, on the basis of common rules and institutions.[312]

By virtue of its power to develop the regime, the ISA is playing a key role in imbuing the 'substantive emptiness'[313] of the underlying regime with tangible content. As this chapter has explored, the underlying Convention regime provides the ISA with requisite powers to shape and develop a regulatory regime that should be sufficient to achieve common management through institutional power. Accordingly, the ISA's pre-eminent role within the Convention's deep seabed regime, of which its far-reaching regulatory and supervisory powers are a prominent feature, provides the means by which the regime can secure its common heritage goals, as a matter of process.

[311] IISD Reporting Services, 'Summary of the Twenty-third Annual Session of the ISA: 8–18 August 2017' (21 August 2017) 25:151 Earth Negotiations Bulletin 16 <http://enb.iisd.org/download/pdf/enb25151e.pdf>.

[312] cf Martti Koskenniemi, 'What is International Law for?' in Malcolm D Evans (ed), *International Law* (5th edn, OUP 2018) 46.

[313] Koskenniemi and Lehto (n 50) 555.

4.3 The Nature of Obligations for Corporate Actors Operating within the UNCLOS Deep Seabed Mining Regime

By what means does the Convention's system of common management filter down to apply to non-state actors active within the regime, such as private corporate entities participating as ISA contractors?[314] As Chapter 1, Section 1.2.4 illustrated, when assessing the appropriate methodological approach to corporate obligations at international law, Karavias's three essential tests for the presence of such obligations are instructive in the present context.[315] Firstly, one must be able to point to an international law rule directly binding upon corporations. Secondly, there must be corporate responsibility under international law. Finally, enforcement at international law constitutes good 'evidence' of the presence of a corporate obligation under international law.[316]

As Karavias himself concludes when assessing whether ISA mining contracts create direct, binding obligations for a contracting corporation under international law, such contracts satisfy these three elements.[317] These contracts 'are subject to international law and the obligations these contracts produce for contracting parties are of an international law nature'; they attract corporate responsibility under international law in the event of violation; and they are subject to international law enforcement mechanisms.[318] Karavias's three conclusions in this regard are correct on the bases outlined below.

Firstly, ISA mining contracts create international law rules directly binding upon corporations.[319] Upon signing an ISA contract, a private contractor becomes directly bound to adhere to various international legal obligations concerning deep seabed mining. This happens as a result of the operation of the contractual framework.

Taking the example of the Nodules Regulations, these regulations contain, as annexes, a template of the exploration contract (Annex III), and standard clauses to the contract (Annex IV). These annexes form the basis of any nodules exploration contract. The transposition of the Convention's deep seabed mining regime

[314] This section is focused solely upon the means by which the UNCLOS deep seabed mining regime becomes binding upon corporate actors that are nationals of States Parties to UNCLOS. However, Chapter 5, in the course of determining the reach of the common heritage's prohibition on unilateral mining activities, will consider the extent to which the Convention's deep seabed mining regime may impose obligations on external actors outside of that regime (i.e. non-States Parties and their nationals).

[315] See, further, Karavias (n 54) 10–16.

[316] Karavias (n 54) 156; see also the present book's discussion in Chapter 1, Section 1.2.4 at text to nn 181–186, demonstrating that, while Karavias's final test (enforcement of corporate responsibility via international law) is strong evidence of the international character of the underlying corporate obligation, lack of enforcement mechanisms is not determinative.

[317] See, generally, Karavias's detailed, rigorous assessment throughout Chapter IV (in which he also considers the status of private loan agreements concluded between private investors and the International Bank for Reconstruction and Development): Karavias (n 54).

[318] Karavias (n 54) 161; see also 162.

[319] See the conclusions reached by Karavias (n 54) to this effect at 138, 140, 142–143, 161.

to the legal framework of the nodules exploration contract is evident from the operation of certain provisions. Firstly, the nodules exploration contract incorporates the standard clauses into the contract (as per Annex III, clause 1). The terms of both the standard clauses and the Nodules Regulations themselves are subject to the Convention's deep seabed mining regime (see Regulation 1 and Annex IV, section 1). In addition, the standard clauses require that the contractor must accept and comply with the Convention deep seabed mining regime (section 13), and that this regime and international law is the applicable law to the contract (section 27.1). Hence, as Karavias explains:

> The Standard Clauses, in turn, transpose the content of the [UNCLOS] provisions regarding activities in the Area and of the Regulations into the contractual arrangement, thus providing a nexus between [UNCLOS] and the secondary law enacted by the ISA and the contract for exploration.[320]

An equivalent result is achieved as regards sulphides and cobalt crusts exploration by virtue of corresponding provisions within the Sulphides and Cobalt Regulations. The DERs also contain provisions that would achieve the same end in relation to exploitation contracts.[321] Consequently, by virtue of entry into an ISA contract, a private corporate entity is bound directly by international law rules, satisfying Karavias's first test.[322]

Contracts between the ISA and private actors constitute one of the rare examples within the international legal system of obligations being directly binding on a corporation under international law, due to the status of these contracts as 'internationalised functional contracts'.[323] Such contracts are 'contracts made by an international organisation in direct implementation of its functions', where the internationalisation 'proceeds from the need of the organization to safeguard the execution of its core functions'.[324] Contracts between the ISA and private corporate actors are internationalised in this manner because they satisfy two key tests, namely that the ISA's contractual terms form part of the ISA's 'external secondary

[320] Karavias (n 54) 124; see also ITLOS AO, para 75.

[321] The DERs impose direct obligations upon contractors to adhere to the UNCLOS regime by combined operation of the following provisions: Annex IX, clause A (incorporating standard clauses into exploitation contracts); reg 1 and Annex X, ss 1–2 (rendering the terms of both the standard clauses and the DERs subject to the UNCLOS regime); Annex X, s 3.3 (requiring the contractor to accept and comply with this regime); and Annex X, s 17.1 (providing that this regime, and international law, are the applicable laws governing the contract).

[322] Karavias (n 54) 161–162. On the extent to which corporate actors are also bound directly by the UNCLOS regime, by operation of treaty law or customary law, see Chapter 5, Section 5.3, which considers this issue when assessing the regime's impact on external actors (i.e. non-States Parties to UNCLOS and their nationals).

[323] Karavias (n 54) 117–126, 141–143; see also Harrison (2011) (n 8) 123.

[324] Karavias (n 54) 117 and 118, respectively. See, generally, AA Fatouros, 'International Law and the Internationalized Contract' (1980) 74 AJIL 137.

law',[325] and that international law is the express choice of law governing the ISA contract.[326] The 'exceptional' nature of ISA contracts as internationalised contracts has its roots in the decision of UNCLOS States Parties 'to grant corporations the requisite capacity to enter into agreements with international organizations governed by international law'.[327] The creation of direct obligations binding on private corporate contractors under ISA contracts is premised on consent of states to this unique arrangement.

Turning now to the second and third elements of Karavias's tests for corporate obligations under international law, as noted above (and as Chapter 6 will consider further), private corporate actors may be subject to international responsibility, and may participate in international enforcement mechanisms in relation to their activities in the Area, under an ISA contract. By virtue of their status as ISA contractors, private corporate actors are directly responsible, as a matter of international law, in respect of any wrongful acts that they commit in the Area while conducting deep seabed mining activities.[328] Similarly, private corporate entities which are ISA contractors (or prospective contractors) have standing to participate in certain categories of seabed mining disputes before the Chamber at ITLOS.[329]

As such, the Convention creates direct obligations upon non-state actors that are active within the deep seabed mining regime through the medium of ISA contracts. In addition to this direct method of imposition of corporate obligations, corporations operating within the legal system of a State Party to UNCLOS are also, notably, subject to the UNCLOS deep seabed mining regime by virtue of the operation of domestic law,[330] but this 'indirect' application of UNCLOS is beyond the scope of the present analysis.[331]

[325] Karavias (n 54) 122 (as Karavias notes, this provides a 'preliminary indication of the international law nature of the obligations [ISA contracts] may impose'); see also 118.

[326] See Karavias (n 54) 136–138.

[327] Karavias (n 54) 140–141; see also 142–143.

[328] UNCLOS, Annex III, art 22; see also art 4(4) of that Annex. See also Karavias (n 54) 145, 147, 155, 161.

[329] UNCLOS, art 187(c)–(e); see also Annex VI, art 37; see, further, Karavias (n 54) 156–157, 161.

[330] As noted previously in this chapter, States Parties must implement the UNCLOS deep seabed mining regime within their domestic legal systems, to ensure that any activities that they (or their sponsored entities) conduct in the Area are performed consistently with Part XI of UNCLOS: see UNCLOS, arts 139(2), 153(4) and Annex III, art 4(4). Therefore, a corporate actor would be obliged, by domestic law, to adhere to the Convention's deep seabed mining regime: see ITLOS AO, paras 74, 75, 108 and 224. A corporate actor may also be bound by the Convention's regime by the terms of any sponsorship agreement between it and its sponsoring state. As noted by the Chamber (ibid, para 225), a sponsorship agreement is a private agreement concluded between the sponsoring state and the (prospective) contractor, in accordance with the sponsoring state's domestic law regime.

[331] On the distinction between 'direct' and 'indirect' corporate obligations under international law, see Chapter 1, Section 1.2.4, especially text to nn 162–164.

4.4 Conclusion

As this chapter has demonstrated, the Convention's deep seabed mining regime creates a common management system. This system applies to non-state actors, such as corporate entities, as a matter of international law. Accordingly, Step 1 of this study's framework analysis (as per Chapter 3, Section 3.3) is satisfied as regards corporate actors participating within the UNCLOS deep seabed mining regime: the regime is binding upon them. The following chapter will now consider this issue from the perspective of actors positioned outside the regime. To what extent is the regime capable of constraining external actors? Specifically, are nationals of non-States Parties to UNCLOS bound by the prohibition of unilateral deep seabed mining activities? This will be the focus of Chapter 5.

5
Preventing Unilateral Deep Seabed Mining Activities – To What Extent Does the UNCLOS Regime Constrain External Actors?

The terms of the Convention are clear that only internal actors can undertake deep seabed mining activities *within* the UNCLOS system. As the preceding chapter has demonstrated, in order for an actor to participate within the Convention's deep seabed mining regime, that actor must either be a State Party to UNCLOS or an entity sponsored by a State Party.[1] Accordingly, a private actor seeking to participate within the UNCLOS regime must obtain sponsorship from all states of which it is a national, and '[i]f another State or its nationals exercises effective control, the sponsorship of that State is also necessary'.[2] Under UNCLOS, only 'States Parties' are entitled to grant sponsorship for the purposes of participation in the regime.[3] Only upon receiving appropriate sponsorship will a private actor then be entitled to submit an application to the ISA to conduct exploration or exploitation activities.[4]

However, this begs the following question: what is the position of actors operating *outside of the regime*? These external actors could be states that are not parties to UNCLOS, or nationals of such states. For example, non-States Parties to UNCLOS (*NSPs*) include Colombia, Iran, Israel, North Korea, Peru, Turkey, the US and Venezuela. What would be the legal consequences if a US national, or a national of another NSP, attempted to explore for resources in the Area? Similarly, in the event that an existing State Party to UNCLOS decided to withdraw from the

[1] UNCLOS, art 153(2)(b) (see also art 153(2)(a), providing for participation of the Enterprise, once operational). On corporate participation, see analysis in Chapter 4, Section 4.2.3.3.

[2] ITLOS AO, para 77. See UNCLOS, Annex III, art 4(3); reg 11(1)–(2) of the Nodules, Sulphides and Cobalt Regulations; DERs, reg 6(1)–(2).

[3] UNCLOS, art 153(2)(b); see also 1994 Agreement, Annex, s 1(6)(a)(i), which specifies that a state sponsor must be a State Party or – historically – a state applying the 1994 Agreement 'provisionally', pending its entry into force (1994 Agreement, art 7; this provision is now dormant following the Agreement's entry into force).

[4] See Jan-Stefan Fritz, 'Deep Sea Anarchy: Mining at the Frontiers of International Law' (2015) 30 Int'l J Marine Coastal L 445, 464 (noting that 'States have clearly accepted that only States can seek the right to mine minerals in the Area. With this shift it is no longer possible for a private-sector company to enter the Area and exploit marine minerals without State sponsorship.').

International Law and Corporate Actors in Deep Seabed Mining. Joanna Dingwall, Oxford University Press. © Joanna Dingwall 2021. DOI: 10.1093/oso/9780192898265.003.0006

Convention, what would be the legal status of any ongoing mining activities by that state, or its nationals, in the Area?[5]

Currently, there are no definitive answers to these queries. To address them, this chapter will assess the procedural reach of UNCLOS's prohibition on unilateral mining activities, and the extent to which external actors are permitted, under international law, to participate in deep seabed mining activities outside of UNCLOS (thereby completing Step 2 of this study's framework of analysis).

Thus far, there are two means by which corporate entities have participated in deep seabed mining activities under UNCLOS. Most commonly this has occurred by corporate actors entering into mining contracts with the ISA directly. However, as noted previously, there is also an indirect route for corporate participation in the Area. A corporate entity may achieve this by entering into a joint venture with a state or state actor holding an ISA contract.[6] Therefore, in order to truly ascertain whether the prohibition of unilateral mining activities is realised vis-à-vis corporate actors outside of the regime, this chapter must determine whether the procedural reach of the UNCLOS deep seabed mining regime extends to include both NSPs and nationals of NSPs. It will do so by considering, firstly, the reach of the regime as a matter of treaty law (Section 5.1). Thereafter, Section 5.2 will assess the status of the regime under customary law. Finally, Section 5.3 will offer conclusions on the extent to which the regime imposes direct obligations upon external corporate actors.

5.1 The Reach of the UNCLOS Deep Seabed Mining Regime as Treaty Law

5.1.1 Assessing the Extent of Third State Obligations within the UNCLOS Deep Seabed Mining Regime

Many provisions of the Convention's deep seabed mining regime appear to be directed towards all states, as opposed to States Parties only. For example, certain provisions include 'States' as their addressees, in contrast to other provisions which address 'States Parties' only.[7] A key provision in this regard is Article 137 of UNCLOS, which prohibits unilateral mining activities outside of the regime. In

[5] For example, in 2016 there were indications that China – the most active state, to date, in terms of ISA contracts granted – was considering withdrawing from UNCLOS to protest against the Permanent Court of Arbitration's decision concerning the South China Sea (*In the Matter of the South China Sea Arbitration (Philippines v China)* (Award, 12 July 2016) PCA Case No 2013-19). See, e.g. 'Beijing Indicates it may Exit UN Sea Convention if South China Sea Ruling Disappoints' *Japan Times* (Tokyo, 21 June 2016) <www.japantimes.co.jp/news/2016/06/21/national/politics-diplomacy/beijing-indicates-may-exit-u-n-sea-convention-south-china-sea-ruling-disappoints/#.V865iE32byp>.

[6] For examples of this practice, see discussion in Chapter 4, at text to nn 228–229.

[7] See Lee's tabular overview of UNCLOS provisions which have all 'States' as their addressees, as compared to those addressed to 'States Parties' only, including in relation to deep seabed mining: Luke T Lee, 'The Law of the Sea Convention and Third States' (1983) 77 AJIL 541, 550. See also Stephen

wording which appears to go beyond an injunction to States Parties alone, Article 137(1) prohibits every 'State' from claiming sovereignty over any part of the Area or its resources. It further proscribes all states and private actors from alienating deep seabed resources unilaterally.[8]

One can contrast Article 137 to certain other provisions of the Convention's deep seabed regime, which expressly apply only to 'States *Parties*'.[9] Arguably, in accordance with the rules of treaty interpretation, this difference in wording between such provisions must have been intended to have some effect.[10] In this regard, one can draw a comparison with the PCIJ's finding that the use of the general term 'women' within Article 3 of the Convention on Night Work of Women 1919 had to be interpreted in accordance with its natural meaning and, as such, its application was not restricted to women who were manual workers.[11] Consequently, on the basis of the natural meaning of certain provisions of UNCLOS, including Article 137, it would appear that they may seek to address NSPs (and other actors). However, as a matter of treaty law, could the injunctions within Article 137 of UNCLOS apply to NSPs, prohibiting them from undertaking unilateral mining activities in the Area?

The law of treaties is underpinned by the principle of state consent. This is reflected in Article 26 of the VCLT, which provides that '[e]very treaty in force is binding upon the parties to it' (reflecting the principle of *pacta sunt servanda*). The rule that treaties create rights and obligations only for parties to the treaty 'remains one of the fundamental principles of the international community'.[12] As a corollary to this key principle, generally a treaty will apply, as a matter of treaty law, only to its parties and not to third states (where a third state is 'a State not a party to the treaty').[13] For third states that are not party to a treaty, that treaty is *res inter alios acta* (i.e. things done between others do not create rights or duties for non-parties).[14]

This general rule against third state application is codified in Article 34 of the VCLT: '[a] treaty does not create either obligations or rights for a third State without its consent'. Underpinning this norm are the principles of sovereign

Vasciannie, 'Part XI of the Law of the Sea Convention and Third States: Some General Observations' (1989) 48 CLJ 85, 91.

[8] UNCLOS, art 137(2); see also art 137(3) (extending similar prohibitions to deep seabed mineral recovery). See more detailed analysis of Article 137's operation in Chapter 4, at text to nn 17–22.

[9] For example, cf Article 139(1), providing for responsibility of 'States Parties' to ensure compliance in the Area. More generally, see Lee (n 7) 550.

[10] On the rules of treaty interpretation, see Chapter 1, text to nn 13–19.

[11] *Interpretation of Convention of 1919 Concerning Employment of Women During Night* (Advisory Opinion) [1932] PCIJ Rep Series A/B No 50, paras 29–67.

[12] Budislav Vukas, 'Treaties, Third Party Effect' in Rüdiger Wolfrum (ed), *The Max Planck Encyclopedia of Public International Law* (OUP 2011) para 19.

[13] VCLT, art 2(1)(h).

[14] Malgosia Fitzmaurice, 'Third Parties and the Law of Treaties' (2002) 6 Max Planck YB UN L 37, 38; David J Bederman, 'Third Party Rights and Obligations in Treaties' in Duncan B Hollis (ed), *The Oxford Guide to Treaties* (OUP 2012) 328–330, 337.

independence and equality of states,[15] together with the maxim *pacta tertiis nec nocent nec prosunt* (pursuant to which a treaty binds only its parties and not third states).[16] As Fitzmaurice describes, the *pacta tertiis* principle 'has been recognised in states' practice as fundamental, and its existence has never been questioned'.[17]

However, notwithstanding the pedigree and import of this general rule against third state application, in certain limited situations a treaty may confer rights or obligations upon a third state. The VCLT recognises this. Following its general Article 34 rule in favour of third state consent, the VCLT's subsequent provisions set out the ways in which a third state may consent to imposition of obligations (art 35), conferral of rights (art 36) and revocation or modification of rights or obligations (art 37) as a matter of treaty law. Thereafter, Article 38 acknowledges another key exception to the general rule: the possibility that a treaty provision may form customary law, and bind a third state via that medium.[18]

So, for example, for a treaty to create obligations which apply to third states, Article 35 of the VCLT specifies that it must satisfy two tests. Specifically, in accordance with VCLT, Article 35, an obligation will arise for a third state from a treaty provision, 'if the parties to the treaty intend the provision to be the means of establishing the obligation' and, crucially, if 'the third State expressly accepts that obligation in writing'.

Therefore, in order to establish that UNCLOS, Article 137 creates binding obligations upon NSPs, one would need to demonstrate two factors: first, that States Parties to UNCLOS intended the prohibition in Article 137 to be binding upon third states; and, second, that the third state in question 'expressly accepts that obligation in writing'. Thus, firstly, one must appraise the drafters' intentions as to the universal nature of the Article 137 prohibition. The Virginia Commentary to Article 137 notes that this provision was worded with 'deliberate obscurity', in an echo of the 1970 Seabed Declaration, which was itself an attempt to reconcile the rift between developing and industrialised states on the status of the deep seabed.[19] This rift notwithstanding, in many respects UNCLOS III did evidence broad consensus behind inclusion of robust rules prohibiting unilateral mining activities in

[15] Fitzmaurice (n 14) 46 and discussion at fn 16 and references therein. See also Robert Jennings and Arthur Watts, *Oppenheim's International Law: Vol 1, Peace, pts 2–4* (9th edn, Longman 1996) 1260, including citations at fn 3.

[16] Fitzmaurice (n 14) 38, 136; Vukas (n 12) para 2 (arguing that *pacta tertiis* is a general principle of law, in terms of Article 38(1)(c) of the ICJ Statute, as confirmed in decisions of international tribunals and writings of jurists).

[17] Fitzmaurice (n 14) 38 (citations omitted) and 136, respectively. See also Vasciannie (n 7) 87. For analysis and critique of *pacta tertiis,* cf Francesco Salerno, 'Treaties Establishing Objective Regimes' in Enzo Cannizzaro (ed), *The Law of Treaties beyond the Vienna Convention* (OUP 2011) 229–230; see also James Harrison, *Making the Law of the Sea* (CUP 2011) 5–9.

[18] Notably, in the scenario envisaged by VCLT, art 38, a third state is bound by the medium of customary law rather than by application of the treaty itself: Jennings and Watts (n 15) 1261, fn 8.

[19] Virginia Commentary 109; see also 1970 Seabed Declaration, UNGA Res 2749 (XXV) (17 December 1970), especially paras 2 and 3.

the Area.[20] Therefore, there is some basis to argue that the drafters intended Article 137 to bind the international community as a whole.

However, in order to satisfy Article 35 of the VCLT, one would also need to undertake a case-by-case analysis of consent in respect of any NSPs against whom one sought to apply Article 137 of UNCLOS. Pursuant to this approach, only if the NSP in question had consented to the imposition of Article 137 of UNCLOS 'in writing' could it be applied against that state.[21] Article 35's high threshold of written consent for imposition of obligations stands in contrast to other provisions of the VCLT which permit tacit consent. For example, Article 36 of the VCLT allows tacit consent in order for a treaty to confer rights upon third states.[22]

Some commentators have argued that existing in tandem with Article 35 of the VCLT is a parallel customary rule on imposition of treaty obligations on third states.[23] Under this analysis, this parallel rule has similarities in content to VCLT, Article 36 (conferral of rights), in that 'tacit or presumed assent may also be considered sufficient' for the imposition of obligations.[24] On this basis, taking the example of the US as an NSP, one could try to argue that by certain of its actions in support of, and in accordance with, the UNCLOS deep seabed regime,[25] the US could be construed as having consented to the Article 137 UNCLOS obligation in terms of Article 35 of the VCLT, read alongside customary law. However, this would be a difficult position to sustain, given the emphasis on written consent in Article 35 of the VCLT itself.

Overall, given the sanctity of the *pacta tertiis* principle, there is a significant threshold to discharge before evidencing that a provision such as Article 137 of UNCLOS creates obligations on third states, as a matter of treaty law.[26] Notwithstanding the apparent general intention that Article 137 should prohibit unilateral mining activities across the international community as a whole, at present no NSPs have consented to the imposition of this obligation in a manner which would satisfy Article 35 of the VCLT, and create obligations on these third states, as a matter of treaty law. Nevertheless, might certain aspects of the Convention's deep seabed mining provisions bind third states, as a matter of treaty law, by virtue of their status as an objective regime? The following section will address this query.

[20] Section 5.2 will consider this point further when assessing the customary status of this provision. See generally Virginia Commentary 103–111 on drafting history of UNCLOS, art 137.

[21] VCLT, art 35.

[22] VCLT, art 36(1) ('assent shall be presumed so long as the contrary is not indicated').

[23] Salerno (n 17) 234. cf Jennings and Watts (n 15) 1262, fn 12; Bederman (2012) (n 14) 337.

[24] Salerno (n 17) 234; see, generally, 233–234.

[25] On which, see Section 5.2.3.3 (evaluating US practice in relation to the UNCLOS deep seabed regime, including the parallel US domestic law on deep seabed mining).

[26] See, e.g. Silja Vöneky and Anja Höfelmeier, 'Article 137' in Proelss Commentary 963 (noting that the *pacta tertiis* principle 'impedes any effect on third parties' by UNCLOS, art 137).

5.1.2 Assessing the Extent to which the UNCLOS Deep Seabed Mining Regime Constitutes an Objective Regime

Another potential route for application of the Convention's deep seabed mining regime to NSPs is pursuant to the concept of the objective regime. In a 'possible variation' to the VCLT system, some commentary, and instances of practice, supports the assessment that certain treaties constitute objective regimes, creating rights and obligations for third states.[27] Such treaties 'are international agreements setting up "objective rules" whose effects spread *erga omnes*, even if the number of states parties is limited'.[28] As this section will address, both the scope and status of the concept of objective regimes are contested and controversial in international law.[29]

For clarity, it can be helpful to distinguish between two related strands of the objective regimes doctrine.[30] Firstly, there is the more classic conception of the objective regime as a treaty concerning a location or territory which, under strict conditions, may create rights and obligations for third states.[31] As Tams explains, '[c]ontrary to normal treaty law, these treaties are said to give rise to objective law, binding on treaty members as well as third parties'.[32]

Special Rapporteur Waldock encapsulated this classic conception when he introduced his definition of objective regimes to the ILC in 1964.[33] Key elements of the concept include, firstly, that 'the intention of the parties is to create in the general interest general obligations and rights'.[34] Secondly, the concept of objective regimes applies only to particular types of treaties, namely those 'relating to a particular region, State, territory, locality, river, waterway, or to a particular area of sea, sea-bed, or air-space'.[35] Thirdly, in order for the treaty to constitute an objective regime, either the parties to the treaty must include 'any State having territorial competence with reference to the subject-matter of the treaty' or any such state must

[27] Fitzmaurice (n 14) 66; see also Salerno (n 17) 327 (describing the objective regimes doctrine as an 'evolutionary interpretation' of the VCLT regime of third states rights). On the related/overlapping concept of 'status treaties', see Christian J Tams, *Enforcing Obligations Erga Omnes in International Law* (CUP 2005) 80; see also Fitzmaurice (n 14) 71.

[28] See Salerno (n 17) 225; see also Fitzmaurice (n 14) 44, 66–83; Carlos Fernández de Casadevante Romani, 'Objective Regime' in Rüdiger Wolfrum (ed), *The Max Planck Encyclopedia of Public International Law* (OUP 2010); Harrison (2011) (n 17) 8–11. On the concept of obligations *erga omnes* (those owed to the international community as a whole, in which all states 'have a legal interest in their protection'), see *Barcelona Traction, Light and Power Company, Limited* (Judgment) [1970] ICJ Rep 3, para 33; on their enforcement in international law, see, generally, Tams (n 27).

[29] For a useful overview and analysis of the theory and practice behind the concept of objective regimes, see Fitzmaurice (n 14), especially 66–83; see also Romani (n 28) paras 1, 17 and, generally, Bederman (2012) (n 14).

[30] Vasciannie (n 7) 89; Bederman (2012) (n 14) 342.

[31] Vasciannie (n 7) 89; Bederman (2012) (n 14) 342.

[32] Tams (n 27) 81.

[33] ILC, 'Third Report on the Law of Treaties by Sir Humphrey Waldock, Special Rapporteur' (1964) UN Doc A/CN.4/167, 26; see analysis in Fitzmaurice (n 14) 74; Salerno (n 17) 226–227.

[34] Waldock (n 33) 26.

[35] Waldock (n 33) 26; see also discussion of this element at Fitzmaurice (n 14) 66.

have consented to the relevant provisions.[36] Moreover, for an objective regime to be opposable against a third state, that state must have consented to it (either expressly or impliedly, including through acquiescence).[37]

State practice underpinning the doctrine is predominantly rooted in nineteenth-century treaties and territorial issues.[38] Key examples include treaties concerning navigation and canals (as considered in the *Wimbledon* case concerning free navigation of the Kiel Canal),[39] and territorial issues such as cessation and boundaries, internationalisation of territories, international settlements and neutralisation of territories (such as the demilitarisation of the Åland Islands).[40] Other potential support for the doctrine includes the ICJ's approach to the international status of South West Africa,[41] together with the legal regime for the Antarctic.[42]

The second strand of the objective regimes doctrine is a variant on the first, but focused on institution-building rather than location or territory. It concerns the 'idea that a substantial number of States may create obligations for third States by establishing entities or organisations with legal personality and an objective character'.[43] The ICJ captured this strand in its *Reparation* Advisory Opinion, when considering whether the UN had capacity to bring an international claim for reparations against a third state, holding that:

> [F]ifty States, representing the vast majority of members of the international community, had the power, in conformity with international law, to bring into being an entity possessing objective international personality, and not merely personality recognized by them alone, together with capacity to bring international claims.[44]

36 Waldock (n 33) 26.

37 Waldock (n 33) 26–27. To some extent, there is overlap between the regime for third states contained in the VCLT, and the objective regimes doctrine, insofar as both require third state consent or participation to a certain degree before a treaty provision will be binding upon that state.

38 Romani (n 28) para 6.

39 *SS Wimbledon Case* [1923] PCIJ Rep Series A No 1, 10; see also Fitzmaurice (n 14) 84–87 (including analysis of objective status of legal regimes for the Suez and Panama canals, at 100–109).

40 See Fitzmaurice (n 14) 96–100. More generally, see Lee (n 7) 565; Tams (n 27) 82; Romani (n 28) paras 6–7; Salerno (n 17) 226–227.

41 *International Status of South West Africa* (Advisory Opinion) [1950] ICJ Rep 128, 132–133; see also Fitzmaurice (n 14) 93–96.

42 Fitzmaurice (n 14) 121–130; Bederman (2012) (n 14) 344.

43 Vasciannie (n 7) 89. See also Bederman (2012) (n 14) 342. See further Tams (n 27) 104–105.

44 *Reparation for Injuries Suffered in the Service of the United Nations* (Advisory Opinion) [1949] ICJ Rep 174, 185. See also Vasciannie (n 7) 90; Fitzmaurice (n 14) 91–93; Bederman (2012) (n 14) 335. In his separate opinion in the *South West Africa Case,* Lord McNair reinforced this second strand of the objective regimes doctrine, opining that, '[f]rom time to time it happens that a group of great Powers, or a large number of States both great and small, assume a power to create by a multipartite treaty some new international régime or status, which soon acquires a degree of acceptance and durability extending beyond the limits of the actual contracting parties, and giving it an objective existence. This power is used when some public interest is involved, and its exercise often occurs in the course of the peace settlement at the end of a great war': Separate Opinion of Lord McNair in *South West Africa Case* (n 41) 153. For a critique of this approach, see Fitzmaurice (n 14) 94–96.

As Bederman notes, the effect of this pronouncement was that 'the ambit of objective regimes was augmented to include the organic or constituent instruments of vitally significant, global international institutions'.[45] As Akande describes, pursuant to this approach, 'the personality of international organizations is in fact objective, which means that it is opposable to non-members and that non-members are bound to accept that organization as a separate legal person'.[46] Hence, certain international organisations (such as the ISA) 'with a membership consisting of the vast majority of the international community possess objective international personality'.[47]

State practice, judicial and scholarly support notwithstanding, the overall category of objective regimes has an uncertain status within international law. As Fitzmaurice has remarked, 'certain important issues concerning objective *régimes* (including their very existence) remain still unresolved'.[48] Ultimately, the ILC excluded the category of objective regimes from the VCLT, due to fears that the major powers would exploit the concept for their own ends.[49] However, as Harrison explains, '[d]espite its absence from the [VCLT], it does not follow that the doctrine of objective regimes no longer has any validity in international law'.[50] Despite the ILC's rejection of the doctrine, it 'has had remarkable staying power'.[51] Given the tenacity of the doctrine, it would be remiss to discount it entirely when considering the impact of the UNCLOS deep seabed regime on NSPs, as a matter of treaty law. Assuming *arguendo* that its role is accepted, does the Convention's regime for deep seabed mining constitute an objective regime, constraining the behaviour of external actors?

Turning to consider the first strand of the objective regimes doctrine, some commentators argue that the UNCLOS deep seabed regime 'easily fits into the original model of objective regimes'.[52] In his classic definition of objective regimes, Waldock does indeed mention treaties dealing with the seabed as one of the classes of agreements which may constitute an objective regime.[53] However, as noted by

[45] Bederman (2012) (n 14) 342.

[46] Dapo Akande, 'International Organizations' in Malcolm D Evans (ed), *International Law* (5th edn, OUP 2018) 233 (citation omitted); see also Kirsten Schmalenbach, 'International Organizations or Institutions, General Aspects' in Rüdiger Wolfrum (ed), *The Max Planck Encyclopedia of Public International Law* (OUP 2014) paras 25–26.

[47] Akande (2018) (n 46) 233. On the overwhelming participation of the international community within the ISA (both as member and observer states), see analysis in Section 5.2.3.2 at text to nn 142–143.

[48] Fitzmaurice (n 14) 82, 111, 136; similarly, see Romani (n 28) paras 6–8, 15–17.

[49] Fitzmaurice (n 14) 74–75; Salerno (n 17) 227; Harrison (2011) (n 17) 9; Romani (n 28) para 11 (discussing ILC concerns that the concept would allow 'treaties made by the Great Powers [to be] used (as had happened in the past) to impose certain conditions on other States').

[50] Harrison (2011) (n 17) 9; see also 10.

[51] Bederman (2012) (n 14) 341. For similar assessment, see Tams (n 27) 83.

[52] Salerno (n 17) 228, citing H Mosler, 'The International Society as a Legal Community' (1974) 140 RdC 234, 252; see also Helmut Tuerk, 'The International Seabed Area' in Malgosia Fitzmaurice and Norman A Martinez Gutierrez (eds), *The IMLI Manual on International Maritime Law*, vol I (OUP 2014) 285.

[53] Waldock (n 33) 26.

Fitzmaurice, 'the legal character of the deep seabed' does not conform to 'the conceptual approach of *Waldock* as to what in his view constituted an objective *régime*', because Waldock's conception applies only to classes of treaties applicable to territories or areas over which at least one of the parties has competence.[54] Manifestly, the deep seabed is an Area beyond the competence of all states.[55] Therefore, a priori, the deep seabed regime cannot constitute an objective regime, in terms of the first strand of the doctrine.

Arguably, the deep seabed regime would more readily fit into the second strand of the doctrine. To paraphrase the *Reparation* advisory opinion, as regards deep seabed mining, the 'vast majority of members of the international community' brought into being 'an entity possessing objective international personality', the ISA, to govern deep seabed mining.[56] As this chapter will address in more detail, there is overwhelming global participation in the ISA by the international community, including by NSPs as observer states.[57] On that basis, it is incontrovertible that the ISA has international legal personality and that its existence is opposable against external actors, such as NSPs.

However, despite the objective personality of the ISA, it does not necessarily follow that individual rules of the deep seabed regime are binding upon NSPs, as an objective regime, without some further basis for this in international law (whether that basis is in the VCLT rules of third state application (which Section 5.1.1 has rejected) or customary law (to be considered in Section 5.2)). Vasciannie reaches a similar conclusion. Writing in 1989, before the creation of the Authority, he finds that 'even if the Authority acquires objective legal personality, it will not have regulatory competence over the activities of [NSPs]' as 'there is no legal precedent to support the view that organisations with objective character have the power to create obligations which are binding *erga omnes*'.[58]

[54] Fitzmaurice (n 14) 111, citing Vasciannie (n 7) 90. See also Rüdiger Wolfrum, 'The Principle of the Common Heritage of Mankind' (1983) 43 Heidelberg J Int'l L 312, 337 (concluding that UNCLOS 'cannot be regarded as a so-called objective régime which, concluded by a group of States, imposes upon third States the obligation to acquiesce to it'); Harrison (2011) (n 17) 10.

[55] UNCLOS, art 1(1)(1).

[56] cf *Reparation* Advisory Opinion (n 44) 185. On the ISA's international legal personality, see also UNCLOS, art 176; Markos Karavias, *Corporate Obligations under International Law* (OUP 2013) 121.

[57] See Section 5.2.3.2, at text to nn 142–143.

[58] Vasciannie (n 7) 92. See also Lee (n 7) 568 (arguing that to 'uphold the universally binding force of those provisions of [UNCLOS] which are endowed with "public law character" as part of a constitutive or semi-legislative treaty … the source of that binding force would remain custom'). See, further, Fitzmaurice (n 14) 111–112, 115 (concluding that the UNCLOS deep seabed regime does not constitute an objective regime, either before or after the 1994 Agreement); ED Brown, *Sea-bed Energy and Minerals: The International Legal Regime*, vol 2 (Martin Nijhoff Publishers 2001) 59 (considering the UNCLOS deep seabed regime generally, from the perspective of third states, and concluding 'that there would seem to be no reason to depart from the normal rule that *pacta tertiis nec nocent nec prosunt*'). cf Tuerk (n 52) 285 (concluding that the obligation in Article 137 of UNCLOS establishes an 'objective legal regime', binding on all states with 'a legal status similar to that of *jus cogens*'); in a similar vein, see also Rüdiger Wolfrum, 'Common Heritage of Mankind' in Rüdiger Wolfrum (ed), *The Max Planck Encyclopedia of Public International Law* (OUP 2009) para 13 ('the prohibition of occupation and appropriation [in Article 137] has been given a legal status the effect of which is similar to that of *ius cogens*').

Consequently, the 'objective regimes' approach to the Convention's deep seabed regime only takes us part of the way towards realising a regime with global reach. The ISA has objective legal personality as against NSPs, and its existence is opposable against them. However, that does not necessarily render the individual rules of the deep seabed regime (such as the prohibition on unilateral mining activities) applicable against NSPs, as an objective regime. The only remaining, unconsidered medium to achieve that result would be customary law, which the following section will now address.

5.2 The Reach of the UNCLOS Deep Seabed Mining Regime as Customary Law

Do elements of the Convention's deep seabed mining regime, such as the prohibition of unilateral mining activities, constitute customary law?[59] To resolve this question, the following analysis must, firstly, provide a brief methodological note on the formation of customary law (Section 5.2.1), together with an assessment of the extent to which the common heritage principle has customary status within the deep seabed mining context (Section 5.2.2). Thereafter, the main body of this analysis will turn to assess the customary status of the Convention's deep seabed mining regime itself (Section 5.2.3).

5.2.1 Methodological Note on the Formation of Customary Law

Custom is 'evidence of a general practice accepted as law'.[60] In order to establish the existence of a customary rule, two elements must be present. The first element is the objective component: the existence of practice by states. Second, and more difficult to quantify, there is the 'subjective element': *opinio juris*.[61] *Opinio juris* is the belief, by states, that certain behaviour is legally obligatory, permitted or prohibited.[62]

In determining the process for custom formation, ICJ jurisprudence is instructive. As the ICJ held in the *North Sea Continental Shelf Cases*, state practice must be undertaken in such a manner 'as to be evidence of a belief that this

[59] Aspects of this section are also addressed in Joanna Dingwall, 'Commercial Mining Activities in the Deep Seabed Beyond National Jurisdiction: The International Legal Framework' in Catherine Banet (ed), *The Law of the Seabed: Access, Uses, and Protection of Seabed Resources* (Brill 2020).

[60] ICJ Statute, art 38(1)(b). To similar effect, see ILC, 'Identification of Customary International Law – Text of the Draft Conclusions as Adopted by the Drafting Committee on Second Reading' (17 May 2018) UN Doc A/CN.4/L.908 (*ILC CIL Conclusions*), conclusion 2. The GA endorsed these conclusions in UNGA Res 73/203 (20 December 2018) UN Doc A/RES/73/203.

[61] *North Sea Continental Shelf Cases* [1969] ICJ Rep 3, para 77.

[62] See analysis in Michael Akehurst, 'Custom as a Source of International Law' (1974–75) 47 BYIL 53, 37–38, 53.

practice is rendered obligatory by the existence of a rule of law requiring it'.[63] Accordingly, '[t]he States concerned must therefore feel that they are conforming to what amounts to a legal obligation'.[64] If a state abstains from a particular course of action, this may be evidence of state practice counting towards custom, but only to the extent that it is 'based on their being conscious of having a duty to abstain would it be possible to speak of an international custom'.[65] Equally, in certain circumstances, inaction may count as a form of *opinio juris*, evidencing a state's acquiescence in the formation of a customary rule.[66] To contribute to custom formation, state practice must be general, meaning that it 'must be sufficiently widespread and representative'.[67] Consistency of state practice is another key factor: 'the conduct of States should, in general, be consistent with such [customary] rules'.[68] The need for consistency does not require state practice to be in 'absolutely rigorous conformity' with the potential rule.[69] However, state practice must exhibit a degree of continuity if it is to influence the creation of customary law. There must be evidence of a 'settled practice'.[70] The requisite level of repetition and consistency required for custom formation will largely depend on the particular circumstances:

> [T]his test cannot be, nor is it, one endowed with any absolute character: it is of its very nature relative. Criteria of frequency, continuity and uniformity are involved. However, not all rules are susceptible to verification by all these criteria.[71]

Duration and generality of the practice may be secondary to the relative importance of the states engendering formation of the customary rule. As the ICJ has

[63] *North Sea Continental Shelf* (n 61), para 77.

[64] *North Sea Continental Shelf* (n 61), para 77.

[65] *SS Lotus Case (France v Turkey)* [1927] PCIJ Rep Series A No 10, 28. See also ILC CIL Conclusions (n 60), conclusion 6(1) (confirming that 'under certain circumstances', state practice for custom formation may include inaction). See, further, ILC draft commentaries to this conclusion: ILC, 'Identification of Customary International Law – Text of the Draft Conclusions and Commentaries Thereto' in 'Report of the International Law Commission of the Work of its 70th Session' (30 April to 1 June and 2 July to 10 August 2018) UN Doc A/73/10 (*ILC CIL Commentaries*) 133.

[66] See ILC CIL Conclusions (n 60), conclusion 10(3) ('[f]ailure to react over time to a practice may serve as evidence of acceptance as law (*opinio juris*), provided that States were in a position to react and the circumstances called for some reaction'.); for analysis with references to sources, see ILC CIL Commentaries (n 65) 141–142.

[67] ILC CIL Conclusions (n 60), conclusion 8(1).

[68] *Military and Paramilitary Activities in and against Nicaragua (Nicaragua v United States of America)* (Merits) [1986] ICJ Rep 14, para 186.

[69] *Nicaragua* (n 68), para 186; see also *Anglo-Norwegian Fisheries* [1951] ICJ Rep 116, 128 and 138 ('too much importance need not be attached to [a] few uncertainties or contradictions [in State practice], real or apparent'); Dissenting Opinion of Judge Lachs in *North Sea Continental Shelf* (n 61) 229 ('to become binding, a rule or principle of international law need not pass the test of universal acceptance').

[70] *North Sea Continental Shelf* (n 61), para 77.

[71] Dissenting Opinion of Judge Lachs in *North Sea Continental Shelf* (n 61) 229.

acknowledged, when considering state practice for custom formation, the practice of specially affected states is of particular relevance.[72]

For the most part, general customary law binds all members of the international community.[73] There are two main exceptions to this. The first exception concerns rules of international law that have the status of *jus dispositivum* rather than *jus cogens*. The former category comprises rules of general international law which states can modify *inter se*. In contrast, the latter are those norms from which states are not allowed to derogate.[74] *Jus cogens* norms aside, states are free to depart from general customary law by making alternative rules (either by treaty or by 'particular' customary law).[75] Secondly, as will be considered further below, a customary rule may not be opposable against a specific state if that state has persistently objected to the rule while it was in the process of formation, provided that the state consistently maintains its objection (the persistent objector doctrine).[76]

5.2.2 The Customary Law Status of the Common Heritage of Mankind Concept

The Convention's deep seabed mining regime is premised on the concept of the common heritage of mankind. Therefore, the customary status of this underlying concept has implications for the customary status of aspects of the Convention regime. As recounted in Chapter 3, in the period following Pardo's 1967 proposal that the deep seabed should constitute a global common, the common heritage concept quickly caught the international community's imagination. Higgins acknowledges that, 'in a short space of time, this [common heritage] notion was widely perceived as having a normative quality'.[77] Despite significant disagreement as to the precise scope of the common heritage concept, the international community was, nonetheless, united in its desire for a supranational framework for deep seabed mining.[78]

[72] See, e.g. *North Sea Continental Shelf* (n 61), para 73 (emphasising the importance of participation in custom formation by 'States whose interests were specially affected', and discounting landlocked states, in an evaluation of rules on continental shelf delimitation); see also para 74.

[73] *North Sea Continental Shelf* (n 61), para 63 ('general or customary law rules and obligations ... by their very nature, must have equal force for all members of the international community, and cannot therefore be the subject of any right of unilateral exclusion exercisable at will by any one of them in its own favour'.); see also ILC CIL Commentaries (n 65) 152. Notably, customary rules can coexist with treaty rules 'even where the two have the same content and even among parties to the treaty'; see ILC CIL Commentaries (n 65) 122, fn 663, citing, inter alia, *Nicaragua* (n 68) paras 174–179.

[74] VCLT, art 53.

[75] On the operation of particular customary law, see ILC CIL Conclusions (n 60), conclusion 16; ILC CIL Commentaries (n 65) 154–156.

[76] ILC CIL Conclusions (n 60), conclusion 15. See analysis in Section 5.2.3.4.

[77] Rosalyn Higgins, *Problems & Process – International Law and How we Use It* (Clarendon Press 1994) 131.

[78] Martti Koskenniemi and Marja Lehto, 'The Privilege of Universality: International Law, Economic Ideology and Seabed Resources' (1996) 65 Nordic J Int'l L 533, 536, 538, 552–553.

Accordingly, within the international community, there was wide-ranging acceptance that the common heritage concept formed part of general international law, although its exact content was contested. As Jennings and Watts have remarked, '[t]here can be no serious doubt that this principle is one of general law; its precise meaning and its practical implications are another matter'.[79]

In the deep seabed mining context, states have evidenced varying views as to the precise content of the common heritage concept. Chapter 3 has already examined the historical division in the international community's approach to the common heritage. For example, the US, while accepting the principle of the common heritage of mankind, adopted an interpretation diametrically opposed to the developing states' approach, by imbuing the principle with an 'open access interpretation'.[80] Pursuant to this US interpretation, while all states would be free to participate within the Area, no one state could exert exclusive control over it.[81] Writing in 1983, while the future of the UNCLOS deep seabed mining regime hung in the balance, Wolfrum concluded that:

> [T]he content of the common heritage principle has been accepted as part of customary international law only in its general aspects; no agreement, however, exists with respect to the specific obligations of potential deep sea-bed miners.[82]

Nevertheless, as already demonstrated (in Chapter 3, Section 3.2), the common heritage concept is sufficiently determinate to be categorised into a number of key components in the deep seabed mining context. As Chapter 4 then assessed, UNCLOS operationalises these components and enshrines them within the deep seabed mining regime. But what status does that regime have at customary law? The following section will address this query.

5.2.3 The Customary Law Status of the UNCLOS Deep Seabed Mining Regime

Many aspects of the Convention are recognised as constituting customs binding on all states, irrespective of whether or not they are parties to the Convention.[83] Yet, the extent to which the UNCLOS deep seabed mining regime is customary in

[79] Jennings and Watts (n 15) 813, fn 5; similarly, see Wolfrum (1983) (n 54) 335, 336; John E Noyes, 'The Common Heritage of Mankind: Past, Present, and Future' (2012) 40 Denv J Int'l L & P 447, 455, 456. See, further, International Law Association, 'Declaration on the Progressive Development of Principles of Public International Law Relating to a New International Economic Order' (ILA, Report of the Sixty-second Conference, 1987).

[80] LFE Goldie, 'A Note on Some Diverse Meanings of "The Common Heritage of Mankind"' (1983) 10 Syracuse J Int'l L & Com 69, 80.

[81] See Goldie (n 80) 80–81; Noyes (2012) (n 79) 451–452.

[82] Wolfrum (1983) (n 54) 335, 336.

[83] See, e.g. Robin R Churchill and A Vaughan Lowe, *The Law of the Sea* (3rd edn, Manchester UP 1999) 24; Alan Boyle and Christine Chinkin, 'UNCLOS III and the Process of International

nature is unresolved. Commentary evidences conflicting views as to the regime's customary status. Various commentators have found that the deep seabed mining regime under UNCLOS has not yet attained the level of customary law.[84] In contrast, other commentators take the view that elements of the Convention's deep seabed mining regime now form part of general international law. For example, Koskenniemi and Lehto categorise the UNCLOS deep seabed regime as 'having become part of the normative reality', and maintain that '[u]nilateral mining outside the Convention will be illegal'.[85]

Determining whether the regime has become customary in nature involves assessing the relationship between treaty and customary law. Treaty regimes and customary law can interact in various ways,[86] and there are three main means by which treaties may contribute to the identification of customary law.

Firstly, a treaty may codify an existing custom; or, secondly, it may crystallise an incipient customary rule as it forms.[87] In the instant case, the Convention's inclusion of the deep seabed mining regime did not represent codification or crystallisation of customary law. Despite the international community's general support for the common heritage concept's application to deep seabed mining in the Area, consensus in General Assembly resolutions such as the 1970 Seabed Declaration and broad agreement on the need for international regulation, the international community was divided, for many years, as to the precise form that the deep seabed regime should take.[88] This division endured during the negotiation of relevant General Assembly Resolutions, throughout UNCLOS III and in the period from the adoption of UNCLOS in 1982 until the conclusion of the 1994 Agreement.[89]

On that basis, when assessing the status of the deep seabed mining regime in 2002, Fitzmaurice concluded that the regime did not constitute customary law,

Law-making' in Tafsir Malick Ndiaye and Rüdiger Wolfrum (eds), *Law of the Sea, Environmental Law and Settlement of Disputes* (Martinus Nijhoff Publishers 2007) 376, 380; Harrison (2011) (n 17) 52–56.

[84] See, e.g. Fitzmaurice (n 14) 111, 115; Christopher C Joyner, *International Law in the 21st Century* (Rowman & Littlefield 2005) 220; Harrison (2011) (n 17) 57–59.

[85] Koskenniemi and Lehto (n 78) 551–552. Similarly, see Erkki Holmila, 'Common Heritage of Mankind in the Law of the Sea' (2005) 1 Acta Societatis Martensis 187, 202–205; Edwin Egede, *Africa and the Deep Seabed Regime: Politics and International Law of the Common Heritage of Mankind* (Springer 2011) 66–69; Noyes (2012) (n 79) 465; Michael W Lodge, 'Satya Nandan's Legacy for the Common Heritage of Mankind' in Michael W Lodge and Myron H Nordquist (eds), *Peaceful Order in the World's Oceans* (Brill 2014) 282–298; Silja Vöneky and Anja Höfelmeier, 'Article 137' in Proelss Commentary 964.

[86] For enumeration of ways in which treaties may intersect with custom, see RR Baxter, 'Multilateral Treaties as Evidence of Customary International Law' (1965–66) 41 BYIL 275, 298–300; see also Yoram Dinstein, 'The Interaction between Customary International Law and Treaties' (2006) 322 RdC 243. See, further, ILC CIL Conclusions (n 60), conclusion 11; ILC CIL Commentaries (n 65) 143–146; ILC, 'Third Report on Identification of Customary Law by Michael Wood, Special Rapporteur' (27 March 2015) UN Doc A/CN.4/682, 19–41.

[87] This is reflected in ILC CIL Conclusions (n 60), conclusion 11(1)(a)–(b).

[88] See Chapter 3, Section 3.1.

[89] On the drafting history of the UNCLOS deep seabed mining regime, see, generally, Virginia Commentary.

either before or after the 1994 Agreement, due to lack of state practice.[90] One would, indeed, struggle to attribute customary status to the original UNCLOS regime adopted in 1982, given the division between state positions, and in light of the interim 'reciprocating states' regime that ran parallel to it.[91] As the ICJ held in its *Nuclear Weapons* advisory opinion, in circumstances where there is significant division in legal consensus amongst states, it may be impossible to infer a sufficiently unified *opinio juris* to engender formation of general customary law.[92]

As regards the status of the regime immediately following the adoption of the 1994 Agreement, Fitzmaurice is correct in her conjecture that '[i]t seems doubtful that the *régime* is already a part of customary law, certainly not the new *régime* under the [1994] Agreement'.[93] The 1994 Agreement ushered in new rules that did not have an existing basis in state practice. Consequently, the UNCLOS deep seabed mining regime, either as originally drafted in 1982 or as amended in 1994, did not constitute codification or crystallisation of customary law.

The third means by which the Convention's deep seabed mining regime, or aspects of it, could, nevertheless, attain the status of custom is if its provisions have generated new customary law.[94] In the *North Sea Continental Shelf Cases*, the ICJ recognised that it is 'perfectly possible' for treaty provisions to pass into general international law in this way, while cautioning that 'this result is not lightly to be regarded as having been attained'.[95]

In order for this process to occur, the treaty provisions in question must have a 'fundamentally norm-creating character such as could be regarded as the basis for a general rule of law'.[96] Moreover, the ICJ held that, in order for treaty provisions to create new customary rules, 'even without the passage of any considerable period of time, a very widespread and representative participation in the convention might suffice of itself, provided it included that of States whose interests were specially affected'.[97] In circumstances involving the 'passage of only a short period of time', the ICJ held that an 'indispensable requirement' for a treaty provision to form a new customary rule would be that:

> State practice, including that of States whose interests are specially affected, should have been both extensive and virtually uniform in the sense of the

90 Fitzmaurice (n 14) 110–111, 115.

91 On this, see also previous discussion in Chapter 3, at text to n 99. See also Vasciannie (n 7) 87–88 (writing in 1989, and concluding that the Convention's deep seabed mining regime did not constitute customary law on those grounds).

92 *Legality of the Threat or Use of Nuclear Weapons* (Advisory Opinion) [1996] ICJ Rep 226, para 67.

93 Fitzmaurice (n 14) 115.

94 ILC CIL Conclusions (n 60), conclusion 11(1)(c); VCLT, art 38.

95 *North Sea Continental Shelf* (n 61), para 71 (the ICJ recognised that this 'constitutes indeed one of the recognised methods by which new rules of customary international law may be formed'). On this process of custom formation, see also Wood (2015) (n 86) 24–29 (including wealth of citations therein).

96 *North Sea Continental Shelf* (n 61), para 72.

97 *North Sea Continental Shelf* (n 61), para 73.

> provision invoked; and should moreover have occurred in such a way as to show a general recognition that a rule of law or legal obligation is involved.[98]

The following sections will apply these elements in order to assess whether aspects of the deep seabed mining regime may have become customary law pursuant to this process.

5.2.3.1 Assessing Norm-creating Aspects of the UNCLOS Deep Seabed Mining Regime

For a treaty provision to give rise to a new rule of customary law, the provision must have a 'fundamentally norm-creating character'.[99] This requirement contains an element of circularity. For example, Kolb argues that '[i]t is not because a rule is fundamentally law-creating that it may become customary; it is because it will have become customary through the practice of states that it may be termed, if this is desired, fundamentally law-creating'.[100] Therefore, the extent to which a treaty provision is framed in sufficiently broad terms to create a general rule may be a useful indicator of its capacity to generate custom rather than a *sine qua non*.[101]

Nevertheless, the extent to which specific treaty provisions of the Convention's deep seabed mining regime are of a suitably norm-creating character is a relevant factor in determining their propensity to generate customary law. For example, at one end of the spectrum, the operation of customary law would be exceedingly unlikely to render the minutiae of the ISA's institutional mechanisms binding upon the Convention's NSPs.[102] As Wood, the ILC's Special Rapporteur on the identification of customary international law, indicates when considering this issue more generally, 'provisions [of a fundamentally norm-creating character] are unlikely to include those providing a role for particular institutions established by [a] treaty'.[103]

However, detailed institutional mechanisms aside, several aspects of the Convention's deep seabed regime could have the capacity to generate customary

[98] *North Sea Continental Shelf* (n 61), para 74.

[99] *North Sea Continental Shelf* (n 61), para 72; for analysis of this requirement, see Wood (2015) (n 86) 25–26.

[100] Robert Kolb, 'Selected Problems in the Theory of Customary International Law' (2003) 50 NILR 119, 148.

[101] See Kolb (n 100) 148 ('in interpreting a provision with a view to establishing its customary nature, it may be reasonable to presume that an excessively narrow or specific norm does not easily qualify as general international law').

[102] See Jonathan I Charney, 'The United States and the Law of the Sea After UNCLOS III – The Impact of General International Law' (1983) 46(2) Law and Contemporary Problems 37, 49 ('[a]n obligation to create or join an international organisation [such as the ISA] would not be likely to find its way into a rule of general international law'). See also Harrison (2011) (n 17) 58, citing Tullio Treves, 'UNCLOS as a Non-universally Ratified Instrument' in Albert W Koers and Bernard H Oxman (eds), *The 1982 Convention on the Law of the Sea* (Law of the Sea Institute 1983) 685 and R Jennings, 'The Discipline of International Law' (ILA, Report of the Fifty-seventh Conference, 1976) 620, 626. See, further, Egede (2011) (n 85) 67.

[103] Wood (2015) (n 86) 25–26, and see citations at fn 93 therein.

law, in that they are 'articulated in general terms, so as to potentially be universally binding'.[104] For example, Noyes argues that '[t]oday, the view that many, if not all, non-institutional provisions of the Convention reflect customary international law cannot be lightly dismissed'.[105] Similarly, Treves argues in favour of 'a [rebuttable] presumption that the provisions of the Convention correspond to customary law' (while acknowledging that the Convention's institutional and dispute resolution provisions apply only on a treaty basis).[106]

As regards deep seabed mining in particular, the UNCLOS regime boasts various key provisions that could generate customary law rules. Key contenders for custom formation would include the general rule that the common heritage and its resources constitute the common heritage of mankind (UNCLOS, art 136), the prohibition on unilateral deep seabed mining activities (art 137), the injunction that general state conduct in the Area must be in accordance with international law (art 138) and the requirement that deep seabed mining activities must be carried out for the benefit of mankind (art 140).[107] For example, D'Amato maintains that, at a minimum, the UNCLOS principles (contained in arts 136 and 140, respectively) that 'deep seabed minerals are the common heritage of mankind, and that proceeds from their exploitation should be shared by all nations', constitute norms of customary law.[108]

It is beyond the scope of the present analysis to undertake detailed provision-by-provision assessment of each article of the UNCLOS deep seabed regime to ascertain the extent to which each reflects customary law. However, in order to analyse the reach of the regime as customary law, the pivotal provision to assess is Article 137, which addresses the legal status of the Area and its resources, and prohibits unilateral deep seabed mining activities by all actors.[109] For example, as Charney notes, the obligation not to exploit deep seabed resources outside of a general international agreement may well form the basis of international law on the subject.[110] Indeed, Article 137 would constitute a key basis in this regard, because it is by virtue of the exclusionary rules in Article 137 that all states and other

[104] This is Verdier and Voeten's interpretation of the requirement that treaty provisions be of a norm-creating character: Pierre-Hugues Verdier and Erik Voeten, 'Precedent, Compliance and Change in Customary International Law: An Explanatory Theory' (2014) 108 AJIL 389, 426.

[105] John E Noyes, 'The Law of the Sea Convention and the United States of America' (2014) 47 RBDI 15, 32.

[106] Tullio Treves, 'UNCLOS at Thirty: Open Challenges' (2013) 27 Ocean YB 49, 51.

[107] Notably, the latter three provisions have 'States' as their addressees, in contrast to certain other UNCLOS provisions which address 'States Parties' only (e.g., cf UNCLOS, arts 139 and 153, regulating the conduct of 'States Parties' in the Area). See also previous analysis in Section 5.1.1, at n 7.

[108] Anthony D'Amato, 'An Alternative to the Law of the Sea Convention' (1983) 77 AJIL 281, 282–283. See also Egede (2011) (n 85) 68.

[109] By contrast, UNCLOS art 138, although significant in requiring 'general conduct of States in relation to the Area' to be in accordance with the UNCLOS deep seabed mining regime and other rules of international law, confines its focus to state actors.

[110] Charney (1983b) (n 102) 49 (references omitted); see also Silja Vöneky and Anja Höfelmeier, 'Article 136' in Proelss Commentary 956.

actors are proscribed from undertaking deep seabed mining activities in the Area, outside of the UNCLOS regime.

Taken as a whole, this provision serves to impose a 'prohibition on sovereign claims' in respect of the Area, a 'principle of non-appropriation' prohibiting unilateral mining activities, and a 'duty of non-recognition'.[111] Article 137(1) prohibits all states from exerting sovereignty over the Area, and all states and other actors from appropriating any part of the Area or its resources. Building upon this, Article 137(2) affirms that all rights over deep seabed resources 'are vested in mankind as a whole' and deputises the Authority to act on mankind's behalf. Pursuant to paragraph 2 of this provision, deep seabed resources cannot be alienated. However, paragraph 2 recognises that deep seabed minerals (i.e. extracted resources) can be alienated in accordance with the UNCLOS regime. Finally, Article 137(3) addresses the legal status of deep seabed minerals and provides that all states and other actors can 'claim, acquire or exercise rights' over such minerals only through the UNCLOS regime. Consequently, any rights attained outside the system are not to be recognised.

As discussed previously, states and other actors become eligible, pursuant to UNCLOS, to conduct deep seabed mining activities only by contracting with the ISA and agreeing to ISA oversight.[112] Excepting the Enterprise, only States Parties or entities with State Party sponsorship are entitled to participate within the UNCLOS deep seabed mining regime.[113] Accordingly, if Article 137 has customary status, it would effectively proscribe all external actors (be they NSPs or their nationals) from undertaking unilateral deep seabed mining activities and, ultimately, from trading in any minerals recovered unilaterally from the deep seabed. The following sections will assess the extent to which this obligation not to undertake unilateral deep seabed mining activities has attained the status of customary law.

5.2.3.2 Assessing State Participation and Conduct in Relation to the UNCLOS Deep Seabed Mining Regime

As the ICJ recognised in the *North Sea Continental Shelf Cases*, one means by which treaty provisions with a sufficiently norm-creating nature may generate customary law is if there is 'very widespread and representative participation in the convention', especially amongst specially affected states.[114] What form may such participation take? Case law and commentary makes clear that for a treaty provision to pass into customary law, one must be able to point to sufficient state practice and *opinio juris* for this custom formation.[115] Therefore, in determining the extent to which

[111] Silja Vöneky and Anja Höfelmeier, 'Article 137' in Proelss Commentary 960–963.
[112] UNCLOS, arts 153 and 157(1); 1994 Agreement, Annex, s 1(1).
[113] UNCLOS, arts 153(2)(b).
[114] *North Sea Continental Shelf* (n 61), para 73.
[115] ILC CIL Conclusions (n 60), conclusion 11(1)(c); ILC CIL Commentaries (n 65) 146. See, further, Wood (2015) (n 86) 26–27 at fn 94, and citations therein (summarising commentary to the effect that participation in a multilateral treaty, in and of itself, is unlikely to give rise to custom

the Convention's prohibition of unilateral deep seabed mining activities has customary status, ultimately there are no real shortcuts to satisfying these usual tests for custom formation.

However, in the context of a law-creating treaty, in what manner may state practice and *opinio juris* manifest itself? As noted above, the ICJ held, in the *North Sea Continental Shelf Cases*, that, notwithstanding the passage of only a short period of time, a treaty may nevertheless generate new customary rules, provided that 'State practice, including that of States whose interests are specially affected, should have been both extensive and virtually uniform in the sense of the provision invoked'.[116] In seeking to determine whether treaty law had become customary in that case, Baxter submits that the ICJ 'quite properly looked *exclusively* at the conduct of non-parties'.[117] Such an approach poses difficulties in the context of examination of UNCLOS, as so few states are non-parties to the regime. At first assessment, there would appear to be little practice outside of the regime upon which to rely. Baxter extrapolates that such circumstances render it 'virtually impossible to determine whether the treaty has indeed passed into customary law'.[118] Pursuant to this so-called 'Baxter paradox', 'as the number of parties to a treaty increases it becomes more difficult to demonstrate what is the state of customary international law *dehors* the treaty'.[119]

However, one should not overstate the significance of the Baxter paradox. As the ILC and various commentators have recognised, the conduct of non-parties to a treaty, although important, remains just one of several factors that one must consider in seeking to identify whether a treaty provision has generated customary law. For example, the ILC notes that, in addition to non-party practice, the practice of state parties to a treaty in their relations with non-parties will also have 'particular value'.[120] Moreover, conduct by states in the period before they became parties to a given treaty may be indicative of the extent to which those states evidenced *opinio juris* in favour of a customary rule underpinning the treaty in question

formation). See also *North Sea Continental Shelf* (n 61), para 74 and *Nicaragua* (n 68), para 184 (where the ICJ held that, in order to determine whether a treaty rule has attained customary status, '[t]he Court must satisfy itself that the existence of the rule in the *opinio juris* of States is confirmed by practice').

[116] *North Sea Continental Shelf* (n 61), para 74.

[117] RR Baxter, 'Treaties and Custom' (1970) 129 RdC 27, 64 (emphasis added).

[118] Baxter (1970) (n 117) 96.

[119] Baxter (1970) (n 117) 64; see also ILC CIL Commentaries (n 65) 139, fn 726; Wood (2015) (n 86) 28. For discussion of the Baxter paradox in the context of international humanitarian law and the Geneva Conventions of 1949, see Theodor Meron, 'The Geneva Conventions as Customary Law' (1987) 81 AJIL 361, 365.

[120] ILC CIL Commentaries (n 65) 146; see also 139. See, further, Wood (2015) (n 86) 28–29; Hugh Thirlway, 'Professor Baxter's Legacy: Still Paradoxical?' (2017) 6(3) ESIL Reflections 1, 4 <http://esil-sedi.eu/?p=1713>.

(even if such conduct was insufficient to generate custom at the time of the treaty's inception).[121]

Conduct by state parties to a treaty as amongst themselves, although 'generally less helpful' as it is 'likely to be chiefly motivated by the conventional obligation',[122] may nevertheless have some significance in assessing a treaty's customary status. Baxter himself acknowledges that state party conduct retains some relevance for custom formation.[123] Various commentators have also argued that continued practice by state parties to a treaty is a relevant factor for custom formation.[124] For example, Crawford notes the normative weight of widespread treaty participation in 'generat[ing] a presumption of *opinio juris*'.[125] As the ILC has recognised when addressing this issue, '[t]he number of parties to a treaty may be an important factor in determining whether particular rules set forth therein reflect customary international law', and 'treaties that have obtained near-universal acceptance may be seen as particularly indicative in this respect'.[126]

Applying these factors cumulatively in the UNCLOS context supports the conclusion that unilateral mining outside of the regime is prohibited by customary law. State conduct during the period before the regime's entry into force is one such factor lending weight to this conclusion. Although the international community's *opinio juris* was divided during this period, the fact remains that many states believed that nascent rules within the regime, such as the prohibition of unilateral deep seabed mining, were customary in nature.[127] For example, many states attributed customary status to General Assembly resolutions addressing the common heritage of mankind and precipitating the development of the UNCLOS regime.[128]

As the ICJ has recognised, General Assembly resolutions can feed into the process of custom formation, including by providing evidence of 'the emergence of an *opinio juris*'.[129] Moreover, 'a series of resolutions may show the gradual evolution of the *opinio juris* required for the establishment of a new rule'.[130] During the mid 1980s, in the period following the Convention's adoption, numerous states

[121] See analysis by Thirlway (n 120) 3–4 (noting (at 3) that discounting such conduct as immaterial for custom formation, on the basis that the state at issue subsequently became a party to the treaty, is 'being wise after the event').

[122] Wood (2015) (n 86) 28.

[123] Baxter (1970) (n 117) 52.

[124] See, e.g. Fausto Pocar, 'Protocol I Additional to the Geneva Conventions and Customary International Law' in Yoram Dinstein and Fania Domb (eds), *The Progression of International Law* (Brill 2011) 199; James Crawford, 'Chance, Order, Change: The Course of International Law' (2013) 365 RdC 109, para 168. See also analysis of this position in Thirlway (n 120) 5–6.

[125] Crawford (2013) (n 124) at para 167.

[126] ILC CIL Commentaries (n 65) 143–144 (citing, inter alia, *Partial Award: Prisoners of War, Ethiopia's Claim 4* (Eritrea–Ethiopia Claims Commission, Decision of 1 July 2003) 26 RIAA 73, 86–87, para 31).

[127] See citations in Chapter 3, at n 68. See, further, 'Letter by the G77 Chairman to the President of UNCLOS III' (29 August 1980) Document A/CONF.62/106.

[128] Churchill and Lowe (n 83) 234–235.

[129] *Nuclear Weapons* (Advisory Opinion) (n 92), para 70.

[130] *Nuclear Weapons* (Advisory Opinion) (n 92), para 70.

invoked the Convention's customary status in protesting against the actions of the reciprocating states.[131] Notwithstanding the fact that this supportive state conduct was insufficient to generate custom around the time of the regime's inception (due to the underlying division of opinion within the international community), this early practice and *opinio juris* by states in favour of the customary status of the Convention's deep seabed mining rules feeds into the process of custom formation, nevertheless.

Moreover, one should not discount the normative weight of the UNCLOS III process itself. Even although the Convention's deep seabed mining regime did not codify or crystallise customary law, the Convention's status as a 'consensus package-deal treaty' lends it a 'powerful law-making effect'.[132] Taken together, the practice of the drafting states in negotiating a consensus approach to deep seabed mining, together with '[s]ome measure of implementation and acquiescence ... to test the reality of what has been agreed' can contribute towards custom formation.[133] For example, as the drafting history of Article 137 evidences, in many respects the negotiating states evidenced broad consensus behind the inclusion of firm rules concerning non-appropriation of the deep seabed.[134]

In this regard, the conduct of the reciprocating states is notable. Although apparently incompatible with the Convention's planned prohibition of unilateral mining activities, the activities of reciprocating states during the period after the Convention's adoption evidences their awareness that they owed some form of duty towards the fledgling UNCLOS regime. The reciprocating states did not denounce the movement towards an international deep seabed regime and assert unfettered rights to mine the deep seabed on a unilateral basis. Rather, they recognised the emerging international regime but proclaimed their right to mine, pending its establishment. Reciprocating states' domestic legislation, including the Deep Seabed Hard Mineral Resources Act, in the US, 'were formulated in an interim manner so as to remain formally compatible with the Convention and did not assert sovereignty or sovereign rights over the deep seabed'.[135] In this vein, as Higgins notes when assessing domestic laws enacted by reciprocating states:

> It is an interesting illustration of the gradual fashioning of practice, and perhaps *opinio juris*, that some of these measures made provision for the putting-on-one-side of sums for contribution, in due course, to an international institutional

[131] See, e.g. Churchill and Lowe (n 83) 234–235; see also Chapter 3 of this book, text to nn 98–99.
[132] Boyle and Chinkin (n 83) 387.
[133] Boyle and Chinkin (n 83) 387, see also 388.
[134] See, generally, Virginia Commentary 103–111 on drafting history of this provision.
[135] Koskenniemi and Lehto (n 78) 544–545; see also Natalie Klein, *Dispute Settlement in the UN Convention on the Law of the Sea* (CUP 2005) 337, 339; Kemal Baslar, *The Concept of the Common Heritage of Mankind in International Law* (Martin Nijhoff Publishers 1998) 214. See also discussion in Section 5.2.3.3, at text to nn 157–159.

fund that might be required if the UNCLOS proposals for the deep sea-bed succeeded.[136]

Therefore, by acknowledging the interim nature of the reciprocating states regime and appealing to its temporary nature as a means to justify its compatibility with the movement towards an international deep seabed regime, the reciprocating states' conduct during this period displayed kernels of *opinio juris* and state practice which also feed into the custom-formation process.[137] Consequently, taken as a whole, state conduct in the period leading up to the Convention's adoption and entry into force did provide some support for the regime as customary law, albeit of an insufficient level for the regime to attain customary status at that time.

However, during the intervening decades since the UNCLOS deep seabed regime entered into force, overwhelming state participation has seen the regime gain 'nearly universal acceptance'.[138] Firstly, the continued and unified adherence of States Parties to the regime evidences 'their attitude towards customary international law, to be weighed together with all other consistent and inconsistent evidence of the state of customary international law'.[139] In this regard, Lodge points to 'near-universal acceptance of the Convention regime', emphasising that '[a]ll pre-existing claims [to deep seabed mining sites] have been brought within the single regime created by the Convention and the 1994 Agreement'.[140] Similarly, Wood notes that '[e]ven those opposed to Part XI do not suggest that deep sea mining would be viable, in practical terms let alone legally, outside the Convention'.[141] Given that state conduct within the regime has been overwhelmingly consistent, this gives credence to the argument that elements of the UNCLOS deep seabed regime (such as the prohibition on unilateral mining activities) now have customary status.

Secondly, the widespread acceptance and recognition of the regime within the broader international community also supports the conclusion that there is a

[136] Higgins (1994) (n 77) 132; see also 133.

[137] See *Nicaragua* (n 68), para 186 (where the ICJ acknowledged that, in relation to customary law, '[i]f a State acts in a way *prima facie* incompatible with a recognized rule, but defends its conduct by appealing to exceptions or justifications contained within the rule itself, then whether or not the State's conduct is in fact justifiable on that basis, the significance of that attitude is to confirm rather than to weaken the rule').

[138] This was the standard applied by the Eritrea–Ethiopia Claims Commission in recognising the customary status of the four Geneva Conventions of 1949: *Ethiopia's Claim* (n 126), para 31; it was also endorsed in ILC CIL Commentaries (n 65) 143–144.

[139] Baxter (1970) (n 117) 52.

[140] Michael W Lodge, 'The Common Heritage of Mankind' (2012) 27 Int'l J Marine Coastal L 733, 738; see also 737.

[141] Michael C Wood, 'The International Seabed Authority: Fifth to Twelfth Sessions (1999–2006)' (2007) 11 Max Planck YB UN L 47, 55. See also Wood's earlier assessment (in 1999) that, due to 'wide acceptance' of UNCLOS and the 1994 Agreement, it is 'harder to maintain that customary international law permits unilateral deep seabed mining': Michael C Wood, 'International Seabed Authority: The First Four Years' (1999) 3 Max Planck YB UN L 173, 188–189.

customary prohibition on mining in the Area outside of the regime. The UNCLOS deep seabed regime now enjoys overwhelming participation within the international community, including participation by NSPs (as set out in Table 5.1, overleaf). With the exception of one landlocked state (Kosovo), every state in the world is now either a party to UNCLOS (167 states plus the EU), a party to the 1994 Agreement (149 states plus the EU),[142] or an observer state at the ISA (thirty States).[143] As regards the latter category, states participating in the ISA as observers evidently recognise the role of the ISA, and they can play a role in the ISA's work, including by contributing towards the ongoing stakeholder process for development of the Mining Code. Moreover, as Table 5.1 describes, several observer states have engaged in the regime in additional ways, historically. For example, of the thirty observer states, fourteen have signed but not ratified UNCLOS and one (the US) has signed but not ratified the 1994 Agreement.[144]

Notably, eleven observer states participated previously in the ISA as provisional members before transitioning to become observer states. Article 7(1) of the 1994 Agreement provided for the agreement's provisional application from 16 November 1994 for certain categories of actors, including states that had consented to its adoption in the UN General Assembly (absent notification in writing to the contrary) and signatories to the 1994 Agreement (again, absent contrary notification).[145] The US, by virtue of its signature of the 1994 Agreement on 29 July 1994, began to provisionally apply the agreement from 16 November 1994.[146] A further ten NSPs became provisional members of the ISA on 16 November 1994, due to their previous consent to adoption of the 1994 Agreement in the General Assembly.[147]

[142] All 150 parties to the 1994 Agreement have also ratified, or acceded to, UNCLOS.

[143] The list of ISA observers is available here: <www.isa.org.jm/observers>. As Table 5.1 notes, of the thirty ISA observer states, sixteen are landlocked. For a striking image of the global reach of the deep seabed mining regime, see the world map in ISA, 'Secretary-General Annual Report' (2020) at 14 <https://isa.org.jm/files/files/documents/ISA_Annual_Report_2020_ENG.pdf>.

[144] See UN Treaty Collection (*UNTC*) record on status of UNCLOS (21 September 2020) <https://treaties.un.org/Pages/ViewDetailsIII.aspx?src=TREATY&mtdsg_no=XXI-6&chapter=21&Temp=mtdsg3&clang=_en> and UNTC record on status of the 1994 Agreement (21 September 2020) <https://treaties.un.org/Pages/ViewDetails.aspx?src=TREATY&mtdsg_no=XXI-6-a&chapter=21&clang=_en>.

[145] 1994 Agreement, art 7(1)(a)–(b) (see also art 7(1)(c)–(d), providing for provisional application through consent or accession).

[146] See UNTC on status of 1994 Agreement (n 144). The US became a provisional member on the basis of its signature, in accordance with 1994 Agreement, art 7(1)(b): see US statement in this regard in UNGA '99th Meeting' (48th Session) (27 July 1994) UN Doc A/48/PV.99 at 7.

[147] The GA adopted the 1994 Agreement in UNGA Res 48/263 (28 July 1994) UN Doc A/RES/48/263 by an overwhelming 121 votes to none, with seven abstentions: UNGA '101st Meeting' (48th Session) (28 July 1994) UN Doc A/48/PV.101. Twelve NSPs consented to adoption of the 1994 Agreement in the GA: Afghanistan, Andorra, Bhutan, Burundi, Cambodia, Eritrea, Ethiopia, Iran, Libya, Liechtenstein, the UAE and the US. Of these states, only Iran provided notification that it did not intend to provisionally apply the 1994 Agreement. Leaving Iran and the US aside, the remaining ten NSPs were subject to the provisional application of the 1994 Agreement via art 7(1)(a). See, generally, UNTC on status of 1994 Agreement (n 144).

Table 5.1 Extent of Participation by Non-States Parties within the UNCLOS Deep Seabed Mining Regime

Non-State Party to UNCLOS*	ISA Observer State	UNCLOS Signatory**	Signatory to the 1994 Agreement***	Provisional Application of the 1994 Agreement****	Landlocked*****
Afghanistan	✓	✓(18 Mar 1983)	✗	✓	✓
Andorra	✓	✗	✗	✓	✓
Bhutan	✓	✓(10 Dec 1982)	✗	✓	✓
Burundi	✓	✓(10 Dec 1982)	✗	✓	✓
Cambodia	✓	✓(1 Jul 1983)	✗	✓	✗
Central African Republic	✓	✓(4 Dec 1984)	✗	✗	✓
Colombia	✓	✓(10 Dec 1982)	✗	✗	✗
El Salvador	✓	✓(5 Dec 1984)	✗	✗	✗
Eritrea	✓	✗	✗	✓	✗
Ethiopia	✓	✓(10 Dec 1982)	✗	✓	✓
Holy See	✓	✗	✗	✗	✓
Iran	✓	✓(10 Dec 1982)	✗	✗	✗
Israel	✓	✗	✗	✗	✗
Kazakhstan	✓	✗	✗	✗	✓
Kosovo	✗	✗	✗	✗	✓
Kyrgyzstan	✓	✗	✗	✗	✓
Libya	✓	✓(3 Dec 1984)	✗	✓	✗
Liechtenstein	✓	✓(30 Nov 1984)	✗	✓	✓
North Korea	✓	✓(10 Dec 1982)	✗	✗	✗
Peru	✓	✗	✗	✗	✗
Rwanda	✓	✓(10 Dec 1982)	✗	✗	✓

Continued

Table 5.1 *Continued*

Non-State Party to UNCLOS[*]	ISA Observer State	UNCLOS Signatory[**]	Signatory to the 1994 Agreement[***]	Provisional Application of the 1994 Agreement[****]	Landlocked[*****]
San Marino	✓	✗	✗	✗	✓
South Sudan	✓	✗	✗	✗	✓
Syria	✓	✗	✗	✗	✗
Tajikistan	✓	✗	✗	✗	✓
Turkey	✓	✗	✗	✗	✗
Turkmenistan	✓	✗	✗	✗	✓
United Arab Emirates	✓	✓(10 Dec 1982)	✗	✓	✗
United States	✓	✗	✓(29 Jul 1994)	✓	✗
Uzbekistan	✓	✗	✗	✗	✓
Venezuela	✓	✗	✗	✗	✗

[*]This list includes states within the international community that are not States Parties to UNCLOS or the 1994 Agreement.

[**]See UNTC on status of UNCLOS (n 144).

[***]See UNTC on status of 1994 Agreement (n 144).

[****]See UNTC on status of 1994 Agreement (n 144).

[*****]This analysis classifies Kazakhstan and Turkmenistan as landlocked states, due to the special status of the Caspian Sea, which is an inland lake subject to a bespoke legal regime agreed by the littoral states: Convention on the Legal Status of the Caspian Sea (signed 12 August 2018) <http://en.kremlin.ru/supplement/5328>.

When the 1994 Agreement entered into force definitively on 28 July 1996, it allowed provisional membership to continue until 16 November 1996 upon notification by a provisional member (with the possibility of extension).[148] Provisional members Cambodia, the UAE and the US requested to continue to participate in the ISA on a provisional basis.[149] Thereafter, both the UAE and the US obtained extensions allowing provisional membership to continue until 16 November 1998.[150] Although this participation is within the terms of the treaty regime (rather on the

[148] 1994 Agreement, Annex, s 1(12)(a).

[149] See UNTC on status of 1994 Agreement (n 144).

[150] See ISA Council, 'Decision of the Council of the ISA Relating to the Extension of Membership on a Provisional Basis' (18 March 1997) ISBA/3/C/3 (UAE extension approval); ISA Council, 'Decision of the Council of the ISA Relating to the Extension of Membership on a Provisional Basis' (29 August 1996) ISBA/C/9 (US extension approval).

basis of customary law), it does evidence some degree of acceptance of, and acquiescence in, the deep seabed mining regime amongst NSPs, irrespective of their non-treaty party status.

This widespread participation within, and recognition of, the ISA system across all states in the international community, together with the lack of contrary deep seabed mining practice outside of the UNCLOS regime, augments the claim that a state or other actor undertaking unilateral deep seabed mining activities would violate customary law. Furthermore, as the following section will reveal, specific assessment of US conduct towards the regime (as perhaps the most active NSP in relation to the deep seabed) strengthens this conclusion.

5.2.3.3 Assessing US Conduct in Relation to the UNCLOS Deep Seabed Mining Regime

As addressed above, conduct of non-parties to treaties remains a vital element in determining whether treaty provisions have become customary law.[151] Of the NSPs to the Convention considered in the preceding section, the US's practice in relation to deep seabed mining is the most substantial. Therefore, this section will provide specific analysis of US practice in this regard, as a significant barometer as to the customary status of aspects of the Convention's deep seabed mining regime.

Despite the US's NSP status, US activity has, in many respects, not been in conflict with the UNCLOS deep seabed mining regime. Indeed, the US State Department has previously indicated its belief that 'the [1994] Agreement, by restructuring the seabed mining regime along free market lines, endorses the consistent view of the United States that the common heritage principle fully comports with private economic activity in accordance with market principles'.[152] On that basis, the US signed the 1994 Agreement on 29 July 1994, and initially participated in the ISA as a provisional member, as described in the previous section.[153]

American ratification of, or accession to, a treaty requires two-thirds of the US Senate to consent, together with presidential approval.[154] Former president

151 See, e.g. ILC CIL Commentaries (n 65) 146; see also Wood (2015) (n 86) 28–29.

152 President Clinton, 'Message from the President of the United States Transmitting United Nations Convention on the Law of the Sea with Annexes and the Agreement Relating to the Implementation of Part XI of the United Nations Convention on the Law of the Sea with Annex' (1994) 61 <www.foreign.senate.gov/imo/media/doc/treaty_103-39.pdf>; see also Marjorie Ann Browne, 'The Law of the Sea Convention and US Policy' (Foreign Affairs, Defense, and Trade Division, Congressional Research Service, CRS Issue Brief for Congress, Updated 16 June 2006) CRS-12 <www.gc.noaa.gov/documents/gcil_crs_2006_report.pdf>.

153 Upon signature of the 1994 Agreement, the US announced that '[p]rovisional application by the United States will allow us to advance our seabed mining interests by participating in the [ISA] from the outset to ensure that the implementation of the regime is consistent with those interests' (quote reproduced in Browne (n 152) CRS-9). Similarly, on 29 July 1996, when requesting extension of its provisional membership, the US pledged to 'continue to make good faith efforts to become a party to the Agreement and the Convention': ISA Council, 'Requests for Extension of Provisional Membership' (13 August 1996) ISBA/C/4, 3. See, further, Jonathan I Charney, 'US Provisional Application of the 1994 Deep Seabed Agreement' (1994) 88 AJIL 705.

154 US Constitution, art II § 2.

Trump aside, every US administration since the inception of the 1994 Agreement has endeavoured to pass the ratification of UNCLOS through the senate, without success.[155] Due to its failure to ratify the UNCLOS regime, the US's provisional membership of the ISA ended on 16 November 1998, and it lost its seats in the ISA's institutions. Since then, the US has actively participated in the ISA as an observer state.[156]

The US maintains a domestic regime for the exploration and exploitation of mineral resources in the Area. The US enacted its Deep Seabed Hard Mineral Resources Act (the *US Act*) in 1980.[157] This unilateral legislation was part of the interim reciprocating states regime which industrialised states pursued during the deadlock preventing their participation in the Convention as originally drafted. As considered above, the US legislation was intended as a temporary measure, and various aspects of the US Act envisaged the establishment of an international regime. For example, the US Act provided for a 'Deep Seabed Revenue Sharing Trust Fund', with the intention of sharing deep seabed mining profits with other states pursuant to an international treaty regime.[158] As Garrison acknowledges, by inclusion of features such as trust funds, unilateral legislation such as the US Act could be viewed as strengthening the assertion that the US (and other reciprocating states) 'felt they were obliged to reflect a degree of benefit-sharing as a consequence of observing the [common heritage] principle'.[159]

[155] On US attempts to ratify UNCLOS, see US Department of State, 'Law of the Sea Convention – Timeline' (7 March 2019) www.state.gov/law-of-the-sea-convention/ . See also J Ashley Roach and Robert W Smith, *Excessive Maritime Claims* (3rd edn, Martinus Nijhoff Publishers 2012) 636. For an overview of the process, see Browne (n 152) and Noyes (2014) (n 105) 16–19. See also John A Duff, 'A Note on the United States and the Law of the Sea: Looking Back and Moving Forward' (2004) 35 OD Int'l L 195; John A Duff, 'The United States and the Law of the Sea Convention: Sliding Back from Accession and Ratification' (2005–2006) 11 Ocean Coastal LJ 1. President Biden's approach remains to be seen, but he has previously aided attempts towards US ratification of UNCLOS. See, e.g. then-Senator Biden's 2007 statement (as chair of the Senate Committee on Foreign Relations) in support of UNCLOS: Senator Joseph R Biden Jr, 'Prepared Statement' (The United Nations Convention on the Law of the Sea (Treaty Doc 103-39), Hearings before the Senate Committee on Foreign Relations, 27 September and 4 October 2007) 47 <www.govinfo.gov/content/pkg/CHRG-110shrg45282/pdf/CHRG-110shrg45282.pdf>.

[156] For example, in 2019, the US submitted stakeholder comments on the DERs, demonstrating clear engagement with the regime: US, 'Draft Regulations on Exploitation of Mineral Resources in the Area – United States Comments, October 2019' (October 2019) <https://isa.org.jm/files/files/documents/USA%20Comments%20on%20ISBA%2025-C-WP1%20Oct%202019.pdf>. See also Harrison (2011) (n 17) 128 noting that the US, although not an ISA member, has 'at times taken an active part in [ISA] discussions'.

[157] Deep Seabed Hard Mineral Resources Act 30 USC §§ 1401–1473 (2002) (enacted 28 June 1980) (USA); see also NOAA, Deep Seabed Mining Regulations for Exploration Licenses 15 Code of Federal Regulations § 970.100 2016.

[158] US Act §1472.

[159] Christopher Garrison, 'Beneath the Surface: The Common Heritage of Mankind' (2007) 1 KEStudies at 65 <www.kestudies.org/wp-content/uploads/2019/06/chrisg_21-144-3-PB.pdf>; see also D'Amato (n 108) 283. See further Koskenniemi and Lehto (n 78) 544–545; Klein (n 135) 337, 339. See also previous discussion in Section 5.2.3.2, text to nn 135–137.

The US National Oceanic and Atmospheric Administration (*NOAA*) administers the US Act. Although NOAA's website states that '[f]or the United States, the Deep Seabed Hard Mineral Resources Act, administered by NOAA, governs the deep seabed mining activities of US entities',[160] no deep seabed mining operations have ever commenced under the US Act. In 1984, NOAA issued four licences to US entities for exploration activities in the CCZ.[161] Namely, NOAA granted licence USA-1 to Ocean Minerals Company (*OMCO*) (a consortium 50% owned by subsidiaries of what is now Lockheed Martin Corporation), USA-2 to Ocean Management Inc (*OMI*), USA-3 to Ocean Mining Associates (*OMA*) and USA-4 to Kennecott Consortium (*Kennecott*). Only two of these licences remain active (USA-1 and USA-4),[162] and Lockheed Martin holds both of them.[163] Lockheed Martin has made clear that it cannot participate in the Area unless the US ratifies UNCLOS:

> Lockheed Martin has maintained US-licensed deep seabed claims since the 1980s. These are currently the only active US-based claims.... However, the multi-million dollar investments needed to establish an ocean-based resource development business must be predicated upon clear legal rights established and protected under the treaty-based framework of the [UNCLOS] Convention, including the [ISA].[164]

[160] NOAA website <www.gc.noaa.gov/gcil_seabed_management.html>: notably, on this page, NOAA acknowledges the role of the UNCLOS deep seabed mining regime, explaining that, '[u]nder customary international law, and as reflected in [UNCLOS], different legal regimes manage seabed activities', and noting that UNCLOS 'provides the legal framework for the regimes governing seabed activities such as mineral development and the laying of cables and pipelines', while the ISA 'facilitates international cooperation in the management of mineral development in the Area'.

[161] US Department of Commerce, NOAA, 'Deep Seabed Mining – Report to Congress' (December 1987) 5–6 <www.gc.noaa.gov/documents/gcil_dsm_87_20110607084359.pdf>.

[162] In August 1997, OMA relinquished its licence to explore (USA-3). Subsequently, in March 1999, OMI surrendered its licence to explore (USA-2): US Department of Commerce, NOAA, 'Deep Seabed Mining; Lapse of Exploration License' (1 July 1999) Vol 64, Issue 126 FR 35631. Part of the licence site that was covered by USA-3 is now included within GSR's contract with the ISA for nodules exploration: ISBA/18/C/19, para 14.

[163] In 1993, Kennecott surrendered its licence to USA-4, and it was acquired by OMCO (50% owned by Lockheed Martin). As of 1995, Lockheed Martin had acquired full ownership of licences to USA-1 and USA-4: see US Department of Commerce, NOAA, 'Deep Seabed Mining – Report to Congress' (December 1995), i <www.gc.noaa.gov/documents/gcil_dsm_1995_report.pdf>.

[164] Letter from Robert J Stephens, chairman and CEO of Lockheed Martin Corporation to John Kerry, chairman of Senate Committee on Foreign Relations (17 May 2012) (The United Nations Convention on the Law of the Sea (Treaty Doc 103-39), Hearings before the Senate Committee on Foreign Relations, 23 May and 14, 28 June 2012) 74 <www.foreign.senate.gov/imo/media/doc/052312_061412_062812_Transcript_The%20Law%20of%20the%20Sea%20Convention%20Treaty%20Doc%20103%2039.pdf>. Similarly, see Secretary Hillary Rodham Clinton, 'Prepared Statement' (ibid at 15: '[f]or companies to obtain security of tenure to deep seabed mining sites, they must be sponsored by a party to the Convention. And without such security of tenure, industry has told us that it will not risk the significant investment needed to extract these valuable resources. I want to be clear that there is no means for the United States to support its domestic deep seabed mining industry as a non-party.')

Accordingly, when applying to extend licences USA-1 and USA-4 in 2011, and when doing so again in 2017, Lockheed Martin stated, on both occasions, that before it could conduct at-sea exploratory activities pursuant to these licences, it would require international security of tenure.[165] As both NOAA and the US Department of State have recognised, in order for Lockheed Martin's US licence claims to be afforded 'international recognition' and security of tenure, the US would need to accede to UNCLOS.[166] Indeed, the US Department of State opined that if Lockheed Martin proceeded with exploration activities absent international recognition, this would violate the terms of its licences over USA-1 and USA-4.[167]

In September 2017 (when renewing Lockheed Martin's licences over USA-1 and USA-4), NOAA provided its clearest expression to date of the interaction of these US licences with the UNCLOS regime. Firstly, NOAA acknowledged that the US Act's 'express purpose' is to establish an interim deep seabed mining regime, pending US ratification of UNCLOS.[168] As NOAA explained, a licence under the US Act 'gives the holder the exclusive right to explore a specific area, but only as against other US entities'.[169] On this basis, '[a]ny rights a US company may have domestically are not secured internationally because US companies are not able to go through the internationally recognized process at the [ISA] established for Parties to [UNCLOS]'.[170]

Therefore, in practice, Lockheed Martin's US licences are caught in a seemingly irreconcilable paradox. Mining cannot proceed under the USA-1 and USA-4 licences without US accession to UNCLOS. However, if the US accedes to UNCLOS, Lockheed Martin 'would have to abandon its US licence[s] and proceed under the UNCLOS system'.[171] In a remark reflecting this contradiction, during a court case

[165] US Department of Commerce, NOAA, 'Deep Seabed Mining: Request for Extension of Exploration Licenses' (29 February 2012) Vol 77, Issue 40 FR 12245; US Department of Commerce, NOAA, 'Deep Seabed Mining: Request for Extension of Exploration Licenses' (20 April 2017) Vol 82, Issue 75 FR 18613.

[166] US Department of Commerce, NOAA, 'Extension of Deep Seabed Exploration Licenses: Response to Comments' (30 December 2015) Vol 80, Issue 250 FR 81529, 81530.

[167] 80 FR 81529 (n 166) 81530. To similar effect, see 77 FR 12245 (n 165) 12246; US Department of Commerce, NOAA, 'Coastal Programs Division' (10 July 2012) Vol 77, Issue 132 FR 40586.

[168] US Department of Commerce, NOAA, 'Deep Seabed Mining: Approval of Exploration License Extensions' (7 September 2017) Vol 82, Issue 172 FR 42327, 42328.

[169] 82 FR 42327 (n 168) 42328.

[170] 82 FR 42327 (n 168) 42328. As per Churchill and Lowe (n 83) 234, arguably the fatal flaw in the reciprocating states system (of which the US Act formed part) was its inability to create sufficiently secure title for deep seabed miners: 'while the Reciprocating States would claim that sea-bed miners were entitled to "reasonable regard" from other users of the high seas … so that there should be no wilful interference with mining vessels, their laws did not – and, in so far as they were based on the freedom of the high seas, could not – create exclusive rights over sea-bed sites enforceable against other States outside of the Reciprocating States Regime. There was nothing to stop any other State, or the Authority, issuing licences overlapping with those issued by the Reciprocating States; nor could nationals of other States be prevented from exploiting parts of licensed sites, as long as they did not "unreasonably" interfere with mining by the licensee or any other operators.'

[171] Noyes (2014) (n 105) 17.

concerning Lockheed Martin's licence extension,[172] NOAA reportedly admitted that '[n]o deep seabed mining will take place under these licences, or ever has'.[173]

Consequently, viewed in its entirety, much of the US's activity (and inactivity) in relation to deep seabed mining has either recognised the UNCLOS regime, or at least avoided overt inconsistency with it. As preceding analysis has explored, no US mining activities have occurred in the deep seabed, not even pursuant to the US Act's 'interim' deep seabed mining regime; nor will they commence without US accession to UNCLOS. Notably, in practice, US entities have chosen to route deep seabed mining activities through subsidiaries based in the jurisdiction of UNCLOS States Parties, in order to gain the international recognition and security of tenure that they require to finance and engage in expensive, technically challenging exploration activities in the Area. For example, as discussed in Chapter 4, US corporation Lockheed Martin holds two ISA contracts through its UK subsidiary (UKSRL), thereby circumventing the US's status as an NSP, and its resultant ineligibility to provide sponsorship, under the Convention.[174]

***

As the analysis above has demonstrated, various factors support the conclusion that to undertake deep seabed mining activities outside of UNCLOS would be contrary to customary law. In practice, the UNCLOS deep seabed mining regime is now 'the only game in town', and any competing regime would 'surely be condemned as inconsistent with international law'.[175] Deep seabed mining activities are being conducted under the auspices of the ISA, and '[f]ears that activities in the Area can take place outside of the regime set out in the Convention have not materialized'.[176] The UNCLOS deep seabed mining regime is adhered to, or recognised, by

[172] Following NOAA's extension of Lockheed Martin's licences over USA-1 and USA-4 in June 2012, the Center for Biological Diversity filed a civil action against NOAA, citing violation of domestic law due to failure to conduct environmental review in extending the licences: *Center for Biological Diversity v Penny Pritzker and NOAA*, US District Court for the District of Columbia, Complaint for Declaratory Relief (13 May 2015). In November 2016, NOAA settled this lawsuit, agreeing to conduct environmental analysis if and when NOAA authorises Lockheed Martin to move to the next phase of at-sea exploration: *Center for Biological Diversity v Penny Pritzker and NOAA*, US District Court for the District of Columbia, Joint Motion to Dismiss and Proposed Order (30 November 2016). See also Center for Biological Diversity, 'Settlement: Trump Administration must Study Environmental Risks before Approving Deep-sea Mining' (Press Release, 30 November 2016) <www.biologicaldiversity.org/news/press_releases/2016/deep-sea-mining-11-30-2016.html>.

[173] As quoted in Juan Carlos Rodriguez, 'NOAA Says Deep-sea Mining Suit must be Tossed' (*Law 360*, 20 October 2015) www.law360.com/articles/716660/noaa-says-deep-sea-mining-suit-must-be-tossed (reporting NOAA's indication that, without further review and analysis, not even exploration activities would take place under US licences; see also 80 FR 81529 (n 166) 81530. NOAA reiterated this position when extending the licences in 2017: 82 FR 42327 (n 168) 42328–42329).

[174] See Chapter 4, at text to nn 224, 226, 248–250 and references therein.

[175] Noyes (2012) (n 79) 465.

[176] Gwenaëlle Le Gurun, 'Annex III' in Proelss Commentary 2130–2131. Similarly, see Lodge (2014a) (n 85) 291. As Wood noted in 1999, 'it is increasingly unlikely that commercial deep seabed mining would be contemplated outside the international regime. The risks, including legal risks, are simply too great': Wood (1999) (n 141) 189.

the international community as a whole. This nearly universal acceptance of the regime, coupled with the lack of contrary deep seabed mining practice outside of the regime (including by key NSPs, such as the US), renders it difficult to refute the claim that a state or other actor undertaking unilateral deep seabed mining activities would violate customary law.[177] Egede reaches a similar conclusion upon assessment of state practice, concluding that the UNCLOS deep seabed regime is 'binding on all states (both states parties and nonstates parties) and consequently no state, not even non-parties, may unilaterally embark on mining activities in the Area'.[178]

Nevertheless, notwithstanding the customary status of the Convention's prohibition on unilateral mining activities, is this prohibition binding on the entire international community? Or, alternatively, could an NSP avail itself of the persistent objector doctrine to argue that customary elements of the UNCLOS deep seabed mining regime are not opposable against it? The following section will consider this issue.

5.2.3.4 Assessing the Role of the Persistent Objector Doctrine in Relation to the UNCLOS Deep Seabed Mining Regime

Pursuant to the doctrine of persistent objection, a state opposing the creation of a general customary rule may be able to opt out of its application, in the event that the state makes its opposition clear while the rule is in the process of formation, and maintains its stance persistently thereafter. As Akehurst describes, '[a] State is not bound by a customary rule if it has consistently opposed that rule from its inception'.[179]

The scope of the persistent objector doctrine has been controversial. For example, Charney argues that any role played by the persistent objector doctrine is confined to the process of custom formation, and is 'of temporary or strategic value in the evolution of rules of international law'.[180] Nevertheless, ICJ case law

[177] See, e.g. LDM Nelson, 'The New Deep Sea-bed Mining Regime' (1995) 10 Int'l J Marine Coastal L 189, 202; Koskenniemi and Lehto (n 78) 551–552; Wood (1999) (n 141) 188–189; Holmila (n 85) 205; Egede (2011) (n 85) 66–69; Noyes (2012) (n 79) 465; Lodge (2014a) (n 85) 282–298; Silja Vöneky and Anja Höfelmeier, 'Article 137' in Proelss Commentary 964; Klaas Willaert, 'Deep Sea Mining and the United States: Unbound Powerhouse or Odd Man Out?' (2020) 124 Marine Pol'y 1, 5, 8.

[178] Egede (2011) (n 85) 69. See also David Anderson, '"Constitutionalization" and the Law of the Sea' in Centre for International Governance, 'Annual Report' (University of Leeds, 2007) <www.yumpu.com/en/document/read/31752146/annual-report-2007-school-of-law-university-of-leeds> (finding, at 37–38, that '[t]he [UNCLOS] regime is applicable on a global basis and any attempt to conduct mining operations on a unilateral basis would meet with the sternest opposition. Any right to do so that, in the past, may have existed as a matter of customary law on the freedom of the seas must now have withered away as a result of the express terms of the adjusted Convention and the practice of States, including both Parties and non-Parties, in regard to the ISA.')

[179] Akehurst (n 62) 53, 24; see also Gerald Fitzmaurice, 'The Law and Procedure of the International Court of Justice, 1951–54: General Principles and Sources of Law' (1953) 30 BYIL 1, 24–26; Ted L Stein, 'The Approach of the Different Drummer: The Principle of the Persistent Objector in International Law' (1985) 26 Harv Int'l LJ 457. cf Jonathan I Charney, 'The Persistent Objector Rule and the Development of Customary International Law' (1985) 56 BYIL 1.

[180] Charney (1985) (n 179) 24.

has afforded the doctrine a degree of support. In the *Anglo-Norwegian Fisheries Case*, the ICJ held that a particular rule of delimitation, which the UK was seeking to apply against Norway, did not constitute customary law.[181] After reaching this conclusion, the ICJ noted that '[i]n any event the ten-mile rule would appear to be inapplicable as against Norway inasmuch as she has always opposed any attempt to apply it to the Norwegian coast'.[182] Following comprehensive review of the status of the persistent objector doctrine, the ILC elected to include it within its Draft Conclusions on Identification of Customary International Law.[183]

In the deep seabed mining context, could an NSP seek to style itself as a persistent objector, arguing that the customary prohibition of unilateral deep seabed mining is not opposable against it? The US would appear to be the most probable candidate to avail itself of this approach, given that US opposition to the original UNCLOS deep seabed regime was a key factor in US non-ratification of the Convention.

However, any attempt by the US to rely on the persistent objector doctrine in relation to the deep seabed regime would be wholly unconvincing: put simply, the US has not persistently and consistently objected to the Convention's deep seabed regime since its inception. As the ILC explains, the application of the persistent objector doctrine 'is subject to stringent requirements'.[184] Objection must be 'unambiguous' and 'maintained persistently ... both before and after the rule of customary law has emerged'.[185] Additionally, 'repeated objections must be consistent overall, that is, without significant contradictions'.[186] The conduct of the US in relation to the deep seabed regime does not satisfy these requirements.

Far from being a persistent objector to the existing UNCLOS deep seabed regime, the US was an active participant in its renegotiation. Moreover, that renegotiation, by way of the 1994 Agreement, satisfied US policy objectives.[187] As a result of this, the US signed the 1994 Agreement and acted as a provisional member of the

[181] *Anglo-Norwegian Fisheries* (n 69) 131.

[182] *Anglo-Norwegian Fisheries* (n 69) 131. Similarly, see *Asylum Case* [1950] ICJ Rep 266, 277–78 (addressing formation of local or regional custom and finding that 'even if it could be supposed that ... a custom of [diplomatic asylum] existed between certain Latin-American States only, it could not be invoked against Peru which, far from having by its attitude adhered to it, has, on the contrary, repudiated it'). See also Dissenting Opinion of Judge Lachs in *North Sea Continental Shelf* (n 61) 229 (in addressing what he describes as a 'permitted derogation' from custom, Judge Lachs held that '[n]or can a general rule which is not of the nature of *jus cogens* prevent some States from adopting an attitude apart. They may have opposed the rule from its inception and may, unilaterally, or in agreement with others, decide upon different solutions of the problem involved.'); see also *Fisheries Jurisdiction Case (UK v Iceland)* (Merits) [1974] ICJ Rep 3, 29–30 (and analysis of this decision in Charney (1985) (n 179) 10–11).

[183] ILC CIL Conclusions (n 60), conclusion 15; see also ILC CIL Commentaries (n 65) 152–154; Wood (2015) (n 86) 59–67.

[184] ILC CIL Commentaries (n 65) 152.

[185] ILC CIL Commentaries (n 65) 153 (remarking also that 'there is no such thing as a subsequent objector rule').

[186] ILC CIL Commentaries (n 65) 154.

[187] See overview in Bernard H Oxman, 'The 1994 Agreement and the Convention' (1994) 88 AJIL 687. See also previous discussion in Section 5.2.3.3 at text to n 152.

ISA between November 1994 and November 1998. Since then, the US has participated within the ISA's system as an observer state. Further, as the preceding section has addressed, the US's domestic conduct in relation to deep seabed mining has either recognised the UNCLOS regime, or at least avoided overt inconsistency with it.[188]

In addition, as a signatory to the 1994 Agreement, the US is under an ongoing obligation not to defeat the object and purpose of that Agreement. Article 18 of the VCLT obliges a state that has signed, but not ratified, a treaty 'to refrain from acts which would defeat the object and purpose of a treaty' in the interim period between that state's signature and ratification of the treaty.[189] The US is not a party to the VCLT; however, Article 18 is recognised as having customary status,[190] including by the US.[191] As a signatory to the 1994 Agreement, the US is under an obligation not to defeat its 'object and purpose'. The precise scope of this obligation is contentious, but it would likely require the US to act in good faith to avoid undermining the ISA regime for deep seabed mining (including, for example, by abstention from unilateral mining). Accordingly, it would be untenable for the US to rely on a persistent objector approach to the UNCLOS deep seabed regime while it is simultaneously under an Article 18 VCLT obligation not to undermine the 1994 Agreement implementing that regime.

Therefore, on the basis of the US's previous participation within, and continued recognition of, the UNCLOS deep seabed regime, the US cannot convincingly style itself as a persistent objector against any customary elements of that regime, such as the prohibition on unilateral mining activities.[192] Notably, even if the US could have relied on the persistent objector doctrine to avoid the application of the regime, this route would not be available to any other states unless they could demonstrate that they had opposed the regime consistently since its inception. In particular, any states withdrawing from UNCLOS would not be able to argue that they were persistent objectors to the deep seabed mining provisions.

[188] See Section 5.2.3.3.

[189] For analysis, see David S Jonas and Thomas N Saunders, 'The Object and Purpose of a Treaty: Three Interpretative Methods' (2010) 43 Vand J Transnat'l L 565, 595 ('Article 18 is known as the "interim obligation" because it governs state conduct in the period between a state signalling its intention to join a treaty (i.e. signature) and the moment the state either becomes bound to the treaty (i.e. ratification) or makes clear its intention not to become a party to the treaty.')

[190] Paolo Palchetti, 'Article 18 of the 1969 Vienna Convention: A Vague and Ineffective Obligation or a Useful Means for Strengthening Legal Cooperation?' in Enzo Cannizzaro (ed), *The Law of Treaties beyond the Vienna Convention* (OUP 2011) 25.

[191] See overview of US practice in this regard in Curtis A Bradley, 'Unratified Treaties, Domestic Politics, and the US Constitution' (2007) 48 Harv Int'l LJ 307, fn 35–36 and accompanying text. Indeed, the US has recognised that signing UNCLOS would trigger application of the Article 18 VCLT obligation: see fn 36 in Bradley on acknowledgement by US ambassador Elliot Richardson that signature of UNCLOS 'imposes no obligation other than refraining from acts which would defeat the object and purpose of the treaty', and that '[t]he Vienna Convention provisions, including Article 18, are for the most part codifications of customary international law': US Department of State, 'The Law of Treaties and other International Agreements' (1979) Dig US Pr Int'l L 1 at 692.

[192] See also Willaert (2020b) (n 177) 5–6 (reaching the same conclusion on similar grounds).

Despite withdrawal from the Convention, they would continue to be bound by any elements that constitute customary law, such as the prohibition on unilateral deep seabed mining activities.

5.3 The Extent of Obligations Imposed by the UNCLOS Deep Seabed Mining Regime upon External Corporate Actors

Drawing on preceding analysis, this section will consider whether the UNCLOS deep seabed regime binds corporations directly as a matter of treaty law (Section 5.3.1) or customary law (Section 5.3.2).[193] As Chapter 4, Section 4.3 has already demonstrated, the UNCLOS deep seabed mining regime directly binds corporate actors participating within it, as a matter of international law. This is by virtue of the status of ISA mining contracts as internationalised functional contracts subject to international responsibility and enforcement.[194] However, if the regime also creates direct obligations for corporate actors via the text of the Convention itself, or by virtue of the regime's customary status, this would be a means by which external corporate actors could also be bound by the regime.[195]

5.3.1 Obligations upon External Corporate Actors as a Matter of Treaty Law

Do any elements of the UNCLOS deep seabed mining regime have direct preclusive effect upon corporate actors, as a matter of treaty law alone?[196] As Chapter 1 established, international law may impose obligations directly upon non-state actors, such as corporate entities, in certain closely defined circumstances.[197] One means by which states may implement direct obligations upon corporations is through treaty law.[198] However, although imposition of direct corporate obligations is 'theoretically conceivable',[199] it is rarely evident in practice. Instead, it is more common

[193] On the distinction between 'direct' and 'indirect' corporate obligations under international law, see Chapter 1, Section 1.2.4, especially text to nn 162–164.

[194] On this, see Chapter 4 at text to nn 323–329.

[195] Moreover, treaty and customary law could constitute a further means by which internal corporate participants are bound by the UNCLOS deep seabed mining regime (in addition to the medium of ISA contracts).

[196] That is, without reliance on domestic law incorporation of UNCLOS, and irrespective of the role of ISA contracts in incorporating the UNCLOS deep seabed mining regime for participants.

[197] See analysis in Chapter 1, Section 1.2.4. See also, e.g. Karavias (n 56) 6; Carlos M Vázquez, 'Direct vs Indirect Obligations of Corporations under International Law' (2004–05) 43 Colum J Transnat'l L 927, 930–932; Steven R Ratner, 'Corporations and Human Rights: A Theory of Legal Responsibility' (2001) 111 Yale LJ 443, 488.

[198] See generally Karavias (n 56) ch II ('Corporate Obligations under Treaty Law').

[199] Karavias (n 56) 6.

for a treaty that addresses corporate conduct to do so indirectly, requiring state parties to the treaty to take steps, within their domestic law, to regulate corporate conduct.[200]

For example, after surveying the body of international human rights and criminal treaties, including treaties concerning transnational financial crime, Karavias concludes that they 'fall short of directly regulating corporate conduct', as they instead oblige state parties to regulate corporate conduct at the domestic level.[201] This 'indirect' approach is exemplified by recent endeavours towards enactment of a treaty regulating business and human rights by the UN Human Rights Council's open-ended intergovernmental working group on transnational corporations and other business enterprises, with respect to human rights (*OEIGWG*). The current draft treaty, as released by OEIGWG in August 2020, provides for state party obligations to regulate corporations at the domestic level, but stops short of establishing direct corporate obligations, as a matter of international law.[202] Therefore, as a general rule, '[i]nternational law rules cannot be lightly presumed to regulate corporations directly'.[203]

Irrespective of the rarity of direct corporate obligations within international law, the fact remains that 'corporations may become bearers of obligations under international law, albeit exceptionally and in accordance with State consent'.[204] While recognising that, as a general rule, '[t]he binding force of a treaty and its effects concern in principle the contracting states only, and not their nationals', Jennings and Watts emphasise that:

[200] See Vázquez (n 197) 932–936 (providing examples and analysis of indirect obligations on corporations); see also Ratner (n 197) 488 (detailing indirect obligations which international law has imposed on corporate conduct 'by prescribing international labor law, environmental law, anti-corruption law, and economic sanctions').

[201] Karavias (n 56) 67 (and ch II generally).

[202] OEIGWG Chairmanship, 'Legally Binding Instrument to Regulate, in International Human Rights Law, the Activities of Transnational Corporations and Other Business Enterprises' (Second Revised Draft, 6 August 2020) <www.ohchr.org/Documents/HRBodies/HRCouncil/WGTransCorp/Session6/OEIGWG_Chair-Rapporteur_second_revised_draft_LBI_on_TNCs_and_OBEs_with_respect_to_Human_Rights.pdf>. For analysis of OEIGWG endeavours (including earlier attempts to include direct corporate obligations), see Markus Krajewski, 'A Nightmare or a Noble Dream? Establishing Investor Obligations through Treaty-making and Treaty-application' (2020) 5 BHRJ 105, 110–112. For an interesting parallel, see Nadia Bernaz and Irene Pietropaoli, 'Developing a Business and Human Rights Treaty: Lessons from the Deep Seabed Mining Regime under the United Nations Convention on the Law of the Sea' [2020] BHRJ 1 (arguing that OEIGWG should draw on the UNCLOS deep seabed regime by incorporating direct human rights obligations on corporate actors and creating an appropriate system for shared responsibility/liability).

[203] Karavias (n 56) 13. Similarly, see Marko Milanovic, 'Is the Rome Statute Binding on Individuals? (And Why We Should Care)' (2011) 9 JICJ 25, 46 ('it is still very rare for international law generally, and treaties particularly, to directly impose obligations on individuals and non-state actors').

[204] Karavias (n 56) 9 (citations omitted). Notably, in contrast to the position as regards third states (addressed in Section 5.1.1), the *pacta tertiis* principle 'does not prevent states from binding non-state actors': Milanovic (2011a) (n 203) 46, fn 89 (see also 27, 38, 45). Similarly, see Anne Peters, *Beyond Human Rights – The Legal Status of the Individual in International Law* (CUP 2016) 72–73 (concluding, at 73, that 'it is not appropriate to apply the *pacta tertiis* principle to non-State actors', such as corporate actors).

> This rule can, as has been said by the [PCIJ], be altered by the express or implied terms of the treaty, when its provisions become self-executory (even, occasionally, as regards persons who are not nationals of the contracting state concerned).[205]

By way of example, Jennings and Watts cite the PCIJ's advisory opinion in the *Jurisdiction of the Courts of Danzig* that the intention of the treaty parties may evidence the 'adoption by the Parties of some definite rules creating individual rights and obligations and enforceable by the national courts'.[206]

Moreover, in *LaGrand* the ICJ recognised the direct effect of treaties on individuals, holding that Article 36(1)(b) of the Vienna Convention on Diplomatic Relations (*VCDR*) 'creates individual rights'.[207] As Portmann notes, in this case, the ICJ 'focused exclusively on the interpretation of the treaty norm in question'.[208] The ICJ's main concern was to interpret Article 36(1) of the VCDR in accordance with the rules of treaty interpretation.[209] On this basis, the ICJ concluded that the provisions in question had direct effect on individuals, '[b]ased on the text of these provisions'.[210] As Peters acknowledges, when determining the conditions under which 'a treaty norm impose[s] direct international obligations on individuals ... The starting point for answering this question must in all cases be the wording of the treaty itself'.[211]

Although rarely evident in practice, it is possible for international investment treaties to impose direct obligations on corporations. The purpose of international investment agreements, such as BITs, is to promote and protect foreign investments. Therefore, the prevailing tendency is for such agreements to confer rights on investors and obligations on host states, without providing for corresponding legal duties on investors, as a matter of international law.[212] This is one of the factors

[205] Jennings and Watts (n 15) 1253 (citations omitted), noting, inter alia, that within the EU *acquis communautaire*, many 'provisions of the treaties establishing the European Communities have direct effects for individuals in the member states'. On direct effect of EU law, see Case 26-62 *Van Gend en Loos v Nederlandse Administratie der Belastingen* [1963] ECR 1. On potential for direct effect of international treaties on individuals, see, generally, Roland Portmann, *Legal Personality in International Law* (CUP 2010) 19–22, 277–278 and citations therein; Milanovic (2011a) (n 203) 38ff; Peters (n 204) 87ff; see also Waldock (n 33) 45–46 (providing commentary on previous draft Article 66 of VCLT (omitted in final draft), which recognised applicability of certain treaties to individuals).

[206] *Jurisdiction of the Courts of Danzig* (Advisory Opinion) [1928] PCIJ Rep Series B No 15, para 37; Jennings and Watts (n 15) 1253. On conflicting interpretations of this opinion, see Portmann (n 205) 68ff; Karavias (n 56) 8–10; and, generally, Peters (n 204).

[207] *LaGrand Case (Germany v United States of America)* (Judgment) [2001] ICJ Rep 466, para 77 (reaffirmed in *Avena and Other Mexican Nationals (Mexico v United States of America)* (Judgment) [2004] ICJ Rep 12, para 40). See also citation in Chapter 1, at n 154.

[208] Portmann (n 205) 197; see also 200–202, 278.

[209] See overview of these rules in Chapter 1, at text to nn 16–19.

[210] *LaGrand* (n 207), para 77.

[211] Peters (n 204) 87; see also 88–89 (although Peters focuses on legal status of the individual in international law, her definition of the term 'individual' extends to include other legal persons, such as corporate actors, where appropriate to her analysis: (ibid 9–10)).

[212] See Karsten Nowrot, 'Obligations of Investors' in Marc Bungenberg and others (eds), *International Investment Law: A Handbook* (Nomos/Hart 2015) 1154–1155.

which has provoked a perceived crisis of legitimacy for the international investment law system.[213] Nevertheless, despite the 'still clearly visible reluctance of most countries to stipulate direct obligations of investors in international agreements',[214] there is no conceptual barrier to the inclusion of investor obligations within such treaties. This is evidenced by certain investment treaty texts, particularly various model investment treaties, that include direct investor obligations.[215] The key example, in this regard, is Article 18 of the Morocco–Nigeria BIT (signed, but not yet in force), which provides for direct human rights obligations for investors, together with environmental and labour standards.[216] This demonstrates that there are 'no systematic objections to an incorporation of private entities like foreign investors in the international legal order as addressees of obligations enshrined in investment treaties'.[217]

As this study has already explained, the key obligation to consider, in order to determine the global reach of the UNCLOS deep seabed mining regime, is the Article 137 prohibition on unilateral mining activities.[218] If Article 137 is binding upon external corporate actors, it would prohibit them from participating in deep seabed mining outside of UNCLOS, as a matter of international law. On its face, Article 137 appears to have broad application: it attempts to constrain '*any* State or natural or juridical person' from unilaterally undertaking deep seabed mining activities.[219] The wording of the provision appears to address all states and all persons, regardless of nationality. While a literal reading of the provision may support

[213] See analysis and citations in Kevin Crow, 'International Law and Corporate Participation in Times of Armed Conflict' (2019) 37 Berkley J Int'l L 64, 66–67; Krajewski (n 202) 106; Nowrot (n 212) 1160. On recent attempts at reform, see Anthea Roberts, 'Incremental, Systemic, and Paradigmatic Reform of Investor–State Arbitration' (2018) 112 AJIL 410.

[214] Nowrot (n 212) 1164.

[215] See examples cited by Nowrot (n 212) 1161–1163 (including model BITs of Ghana and Botswana); see further examples and analysis in Krajewski (n 202) 114–116 and Lorenzo Cotula, 'Raising the Bar on Responsible Investment: What Role for Investment Treaties?' (International Institute for Environment and Development Briefing, March 2018) at 3 <https://pubs.iied.org/sites/default/files/pdfs/migrate/17454IIED.pdf>.

[216] Reciprocal Investment Promotion and Protection Agreement Between the Government of the Kingdom of Morocco and the Government of the Federal Republic of Nigeria (signed on 3 December 2016) <https://investmentpolicy.unctad.org/international-investment-agreements/treaty-files/5409/download>. For analysis, see Krajewski (n 202) 114–115 and citations therein.

[217] Nowrot (n 212) 1162 (remarking, also, that inclusion of direct corporate obligations in international treaties is 'from the point of view of general public international law, undoubtedly a possible and admissible option when discussing potential regulatory techniques aimed at ensuring an appropriate balance in the realm of investment treaty practice between the legal protection granted to foreign investors on the one side and their responsibilities towards the societies in which they operate on the other side'). Similarly, in the ICSID context, see the *Urbaser* tribunal's recognition that, as a general rule, '[i]f the BIT therefore is not based on a corporation's incapacity of holding rights under international law, it cannot be admitted that it would reject by necessity any idea that a foreign investor company could not be subject to international law obligations': *Urbaser and others v The Argentine Republic* (Award) ICSID Case No ARB/07/26 (8 December 2016), para 1194. For further analysis of *Urbaser*, see Section 5.3.2 at nn 255–260.

[218] See analysis supporting this conclusion in Section 5.2.3.1, at text to nn 110–113.

[219] UNCLOS, art 137(1) (emphasis added). See also discussion in Section 5.1.1, at text to nn 7–8.

its application to all corporate actors, 'the mere fact that the language of a provision appears to apply directly to private entities may not be dispositive'.[220] In keeping with the rules of treaty interpretation, one must also afford 'due consideration for the context of the instrument'.[221]

In this respect, the overall context of Article 137 of UNCLOS, and the circumstances of its adoption, lend further support to an interpretation of that provision as applying to all persons, irrespective of nationality. As this chapter has already addressed, the Convention's drafters agreed that deep seabed mining activities should be regulated within an international regime, and that unilateral mining activities outside of that regime should be prohibited.[222] On that basis, there are grounds to argue that Article 137 intended to bind all persons, including corporate actors external to the regime.

Moreover, state practice and commentary augments the notion that, in certain circumstances, treaty parties may impose direct treaty law rights and obligations on nationals of third states, even absent the home state's involvement in the treaty, or other form of consent.[223] For example, in *Steiner and Gross*, the Upper Silesian arbitral tribunal considered the reach of the German–Polish Convention of 1922, concluding that a national of a state that was not a party to the Convention (Czechoslovakia) could bring a claim against one of the Convention's parties (Poland).[224] As Meyersfeld describes, the tribunal allowed the Czechoslovakian national's claim partly 'on the basis that a guiding aspect of the Convention was respect for private rights. Therefore, it would be incompatible with the tenor of the Convention to exclude a claim solely because of the nationality of the claimant.'[225]

Similarly, in the US case of *Glenn et al v Compania Cubana de Aviacion SA*, the Florida district court allowed a Cuban corporation to rely upon certain rules within the Warsaw Convention 1929 concerning international transportation by air, notwithstanding the fact that the corporation was a national of a state which was not a party to that Convention.[226] The court reached this conclusion on the basis that:

> [T]he Convention was designed to provide an international code declaring the rights and liabilities of parties to international carriage contracts by air ... And this is true regardless of the citizenship of either carrier or passenger. I, therefore,

[220] Vázquez (n 197) 940; see also 934–935, 947–948. Similarly, see Portmann (n 205) 20.

[221] Karavias (n 56) 13; VCLT, art 31(1).

[222] See analysis at Section 5.2.3.2; see, generally, Virginia Commentary 103–111 on the drafting history of UNCLOS, art 137.

[223] See, e.g. Jennings and Watts (n 15) 1253, fn 2 citing, inter alia, *Steiner and Gross v Polish State* (1927–28) 4 ADIL 291 and *Glenn et al v Compania Cubana de Aviacion SA et al* 102 F Supp 631 (1952).

[224] *Steiner* (n 223).

[225] Bonita Meyersfeld, *Domestic Violence and International Law* (Hart Publishing 2010) 202 (citations omitted).

[226] *Glenn* (n 223).

> hold ... that the provisions of the Convention apply irrespective of the Cuban citizenship of the defendant carrier.[227]

Accordingly, in certain circumstances, treaty provisions may confer upon a third state's national both direct rights and obligations.

In the deep seabed mining context, a factor that strengthens the conclusion that Article 137 of UNCLOS imposes direct obligations on NSP nationals is the objective status of the ISA. This chapter has already assessed the impact of the Convention in harnessing the will of 'the vast majority of members of the international community', in order to 'bring into being an entity possessing objective international personality' – the ISA – to regulate deep seabed mining.[228] Given that the ISA has international legal personality, and that its existence is opposable against external actors, such as NSP nationals, this supports an interpretation of Article 137 of the Convention as applying directly to all corporate actors, regardless of nationality.

Furthermore, by analogy, principles of state jurisdiction at international law also bolster this conclusion. Typically, principles of state jurisdiction are employed to determine the extent of a state's regulatory competence *under domestic law*, as defined in, and limited by, international law. However, extrapolating from this, the principles of jurisdiction can be read across to apply to a state's competence to enact treaty provisions of a certain scope in the first place.[229] The primary grounds of state regulatory competence are rooted in territory and nationality.[230] When negotiating and agreeing a treaty, states are free to legislate in respect of their territory, and with regard to their nationals.[231]

However, in certain circumstances, international law recognises that a state can exercise regulatory jurisdiction on bases extending beyond nationality and territory.[232] For example, international law recognises universal jurisdiction for certain criminal and civil matters of serious concern to the international community.[233]

[227] *Glenn* (n 223) 633–634.

[228] cf *Reparation* (Advisory Opinion) (n 44) 185. See discussion at Section 5.1.2.

[229] Milanovic (2011a) (n 203) 41 and citations therein (recognising that 'states can collectively do on the international plane what they can do individually on the domestic plane, through the doctrine of legislative or prescriptive jurisdiction'); see also 47ff.

[230] Alex Mills, 'Rethinking Jurisdiction in International Law' (2014) 84 BYIL 187, 188 and 194; see also Bernard H Oxman, 'Jurisdiction of States' in Rüdiger Wolfrum (ed), *The Max Planck Encyclopedia of Public International Law* (OUP 2007) para 11.

[231] *Banković and others v Belgium and others* App no 52207/99 (ECtHR, 12 December 2001), para 59; see also Oliver Dörr, 'Nationality' in Rüdiger Wolfrum (ed), *The Max Planck Encyclopedia of Public International Law* (OUP 2006) paras 44–46.

[232] See analysis in Mills (n 230) 196; Marko Milanovic, *Extraterritorial Application of Human Rights Treaties: Law, Principles, and Policy* (OUP 2011) 24–25; and (on state criminal jurisdiction), see Harvard Research Draft Convention on Jurisdiction with Respect to Crime (1935) 29 AJIL 439.

[233] On universal criminal jurisdiction, see Roger O'Keefe, 'Universal Jurisdiction: Clarifying the Basic Concept' (2004) 2 JICJ 735. As regards universal jurisdiction in the civil context, see *Case concerning the Arrest Warrant of 11 April 2000 (Democratic Republic of the Congo v Belgium)* (Joint Separate Opinion of Judges Higgins, Kooijmans and Buergenthal) [2002] ICJ Rep 63, para 48 ('[i]n civil matters we already see the beginnings of a very broad form of extraterritorial jurisdiction').

This lends support to the contention that states can agree treaties that confer direct rights and obligations upon non-state actors, including nationals of third states, in certain circumstances.[234] Moreover, to the extent that imposition of the Convention's Article 137 prohibition on unilateral mining activities to nationals of NSPs goes beyond the prescriptive jurisdiction of the UNCLOS States Parties, 'this might not invalidate the prescription itself'.[235] Rather, as Milanovic notes, an 'exorbitant' exercise of prescriptive jurisdiction may violate the sovereignty of third states, but the treaty provision at issue could, nevertheless, remain directly applicable to third state nationals.[236]

On the basis of the preceding analysis, one can interpret Article 137 of UNCLOS as imposing direct obligations upon corporate actors irrespective of nationality. Returning to Karavias's three essential tests for the presence of a corporate obligation,[237] Article 137 would, thus, satisfy the first test (i.e. presence of an international law rule directly binding corporations).

Further, as discussed in Chapter 1, with an international law rule comes international responsibility.[238] If a corporate actor began mining the deep seabed outside of the UNCLOS regime, that actor would violate Article 137 and be responsible, as a matter of international law, for this violation. This scenario would satisfy Karavias's second key test (international responsibility) for the presence of a direct corporate obligation.

Finally, as regards the third test (international enforcement), this is, as noted previously, merely good evidence of the presence of a corporate obligation at international law. In the instant case, international law affords no direct means of enforcing corporate responsibility for an external actor's violation of Article 137 on the international plane. However, the fact that there is not a direct means of enforcement does not undermine the presence of the underlying corporate obligation.[239] Consequently, there are sufficient grounds to argue that Article 137 binds corporate actors, including nationals of NSPs, directly, as a matter of treaty law. The

[234] See, e.g. Milanovic (2011a) (n 203) 49–50 assessing, in the context of the Rome Statute of the International Criminal Court, the extent to which state parties had sufficient universal jurisdiction to directly bind 'every single individual in the world' and noting that this possibility 'cannot be excluded', although 'it should not lightly be presumed either, particularly not in the absence of explicit language in the treaty to that effect'. Similarly, see analysis by Peters (n 204) 89–90, concluding that such a practice may be legitimate where 'it protects global legal goods' (at 90) (notably, in the instant case, protection of the common heritage could be construed as constituting a 'global legal good').

[235] Milanovic (2011a) (n 203) 50.

[236] Milanovic (2011a) (n 203) 50; see also Peters (n 204) 90.

[237] Karavias (n 56) 16. See also Chapter 1, Section 1.2.4 of the present study.

[238] See Chapter 1, text to nn 172–176.

[239] See, e.g. Andrew Clapham, *Human Rights Obligations of Non-state Actors* (OUP 2006), 266–267 (concluding (at 267) that '[l]ack of international jurisdiction to try a corporation does not mean that a corporation is under no international legal obligation'). Similarly, see Peters (n 204) 122 ('existence of direct international individual obligations is not coupled to the availability of international enforcement mechanisms').

following section will consider whether the same conclusion can be reached on the basis of customary law.

5.3.2 Obligations upon External Corporate Actors as a Matter of Customary Law

Does the customary law prohibition on unilateral mining activities apply to corporate actors, preventing them from mining outside of the UNCLOS system? As this section will demonstrate, this query can be answered in the affirmative. As a general rule, a customary norm will bind all subjects of international law.[240] However, this merely resurrects the question raised at the outset of this book, as to whether corporations constitute subjects of international law.[241] Contested issues of international legal personality and subjecthood aside, it is clear that general customary law may bind various other actors as well as states. For example, international organisations,[242] armed opposition groups,[243] individuals[244] and, in some cases, corporations,[245] may be subject to direct rights or obligations under customary law.

Regarding individuals, as Milanovic emphasises, 'since World War II at the latest, the community of states has accepted that their creation, international law, can bind individuals. It is universally accepted that it can do so as custom'.[246] This

[240] See *Interpretation of the Agreement of 25 March 1951 between the WHO and Egypt* (Advisory Opinion) [1980] ICJ Rep 73, para 37 (where the ICJ held that '[i]nternational organizations are subjects of international law and, as such, are bound by any obligations incumbent upon them under general rules of international law'). See also analysis in Section 5.2.1, at text to nn 73–76 (addressing limitations on general application of customary law to states).

[241] Karavias (n 56) 68. See, e.g. Portmann (n 205) 24 (noting that one's position on whether non-state actors are directly bound by customary law 'is predicated on the conception of international personality employed'). See also the present study's previous analysis on international legal personality of corporations in Chapter 1, Section 1.2.3.

[242] *WHO/Egypt* (Advisory Opinion) (n 240) para 37.

[243] Tullio Treves, 'Customary International Law' in Rüdiger Wolfrum (ed), *The Max Planck Encyclopedia of Public International Law* (OUP 2006) para 34; Andrew Clapham, 'The Rights and Responsibilities of Armed Non-state Actors: The Legal Landscape and Issues Surrounding Engagement' (2010) Geneva Academy of International Humanitarian Law and Human Rights, Ownership of Norms Project 10–11, 20–22 <https://papers.ssrn.com/sol3/papers.cfm?abstract_id=1569636>; Anthea Roberts and Sandesh Sivakumaran, 'Lawmaking by Nonstate Actors: Engaging Armed Groups in the Creation of International Humanitarian Law' (2012) 37 Yale J Int'l L 107, 108–109; Karavias (n 56) 10, fn 28, citing *Prosecutor v Sesay, Kallon and Gbao* (Decision on Challenge to Jurisdiction: Lomé Accord Amnesty) SCSL-04-15-PT-060 (13 March 2004); Jordan J Paust, 'Responsibilities of Armed Opposition Groups and Corporations for Violations of International Law and Possible Sanctions' in Noemi Gal-Or, Cedric Ryngaert and Math Noortmann (eds), *Responsibilities of the Non-state Actor in Armed Conflict and the Market Place* (Brill 2015) 106–108.

[244] Portmann (n 205) 280; Milanovic (2011a) (n 203) 47; Kate Parlett, *The Individual in the International Legal System* (CUP 2011) 359–362; Peters (n 204) 90–91, 147ff.

[245] Clapham (2006) (n 239) 79; Portmann (n 205) 280; Karavias (n 56) 68–69; Peter T Muchlinski, 'Corporations in International Law' in Rüdiger Wolfrum (ed), *The Max Planck Encyclopedia of Public International Law* (OUP 2014) para 47.

[246] Milanovic (2011a) (n 203) 47. See also the famous statement in the *Nuremberg Judgment* of 1946, '[t]hat International Law imposes duties and liabilities upon individuals as well as upon States has

phenomenon is most manifest in the field of international criminal law, in which individuals have been held individually criminally responsible for violations of international humanitarian law (*IHL*) primarily on the basis of customary law.[247] Extrapolating from this, in relation to customary law, Portmann argues that:

> With respect to international crimes and fundamental human rights ... there is a presumption for their direct application towards individuals. In so far as analogy with individual human beings is not precluded on logical grounds, this also holds true for other non-state actors, for example private corporations.[248]

As regards the existence of direct obligations on corporations under customary law, a certain degree of support can, again, be drawn from the field of international criminal law. For example, Muchlinski cites the *IG Farben* case at Nuremberg[249] as endorsing the proposition 'that a corporate actor could be liable for war crimes'.[250] Moreover, in drafting the Rome Statute of the International Criminal Court (*ICC*), the decision to exclude a draft provision that would have brought legal persons within the ICC's jurisdiction was based mainly upon time constraints and domestic law considerations, rather than any deep-seated conceptual objection to the capacity of non-state actors, such as corporations, to be subject to direct customary law obligations.[251]

State practice also supports the conclusion that customary law may bind corporate actors directly. A recent example can be found in the Canadian Supreme Court's decision in the *Nevsun* case, concerning claims by Eritrean mine workers that a Canadian corporation had breached its customary law obligations not

long been recognized': *Judgment of the Nuremberg International Military Tribunal 1946* (1947) 41 AJIL 172, 220.

[247] Dapo Akande, 'Sources of International Criminal Law' in Antonio Cassese and others (eds), *The Oxford Companion to International Criminal Justice* (OUP 2009) 48; Milanovic (2011a) (n 203) 29, 39, 43. See, e.g. *Prosecutor v Tadić* (Decision on Defence Motion for Interlocutory Appeal on Jurisdiction) ICTY-94-1 (2 October 1995), para 94 (in which the Appeals Chamber of the International Criminal Tribunal for the former Yugoslavia held, inter alia, that individuals could be prosecuted on the basis of IHL violations under customary law (or treaty law, subject to certain conditions), provided that 'violation of the rule must entail, under customary or conventional law, the individual criminal responsibility of the person breaching the rule'). See also Karavias (n 56) 90–91; Peters (n 204) 90–91, 117ff.

[248] Portmann (n 205) 280 (citation omitted); see also Clapham (2010) (n 243) 11.

[249] In the *IG Farben* case, the defendants were prosecuted for their role as directors of IG Farben, a German corporation which had, amongst other activities, manufactured toxic gas (Zyklon B) used in Nazi concentration camps: *US v Carl Krauch et al* (Judgment of 30 July 1948) VIII Trials of War Criminals before the Nuremberg Military Tribunals under Control Council Law no 10.

[250] Muchlinski (n 245) para 9; see also para 47. See, further, Vázquez (n 197) 939, noting that corporations could not be prosecuted directly at Nuremberg (as jurisdiction was limited to natural persons), but recognising the argument that 'the Nazi corporations were themselves guilty of violating the primary [customary] norms and escaped prosecution only because of a jurisdictional limitation of the tribunal'. cf Karavias (n 56) 95–97. See also Karavias (ibid) 92–94 on the concept of 'criminal organizations' at Nuremberg.

[251] Clapham (2006) (n 239) 30–31, 244–246; Muchlinski (n 245) para 47. cf Karavias (n 56) 99–101.

to engage in forced labour, slavery, torture and crimes against humanity.[252] In February 2020, the Canadian Supreme Court held that this claim should be allowed to proceed, dismissing Nevsun's appeal concerning a motion to strike. In the course of this decision, the court acknowledged that, while 'certain norms of customary international law, such as norms governing treaty making, are of a strictly interstate character and will have no application to corporations, others prohibit conduct regardless of whether the perpetrator is a state'.[253] On that basis, the court opined that 'it is not "plain and obvious" that corporations today enjoy a blanket exclusion under customary international law from direct liability for violations of "obligatory, definable, and universal norms of international law"'.[254]

Similarly, in *Urbaser*, an ICSID tribunal indicated that certain obligations of general international law may be applicable directly to corporations.[255] This investment dispute was commenced by a Spanish claimant against Argentina, in relation to provision of water supply services. In response, Argentina raised a counterclaim, arguing that the claimant had failed to provide sufficient investment in the project, thereby violating its contractual obligations and the human right to water.[256] In dismissing Argentina's counterclaim, the *Urbaser* tribunal found that the human right to water imposed an 'obligation to perform' on states, but not on corporate actors (absent 'a contract or similar legal relationship of civil and commercial law').[257] However, the tribunal recognised that, in theory, a general international law 'obligation to abstain, like a prohibition to commit acts violating human rights' could be of 'immediate application, not only upon states, but equally to individuals and other private parties'.[258] Although this decision has been controversial,[259] subsequent ICSID tribunals and arbitrators have provided a degree of support for the *Urbaser* tribunal's approach.[260]

[252] *Nevsun Resources Ltd v Araya* 2020 SCC 5. See analysis in Julianne Hughes Jennett and Marjun Parcasio, 'Corporate Civil Liability for Breaches of Customary International Law: Supreme Court of Canada Opens Door to Common Law Claims in *Nevsun v Araya*' (*EJIL: Talk!*, 29 March 2020) <www.ejiltalk.org/corporate-civil-liability-for-breaches-of-customary-international-law-supreme-court-of-canada-opens-door-to-common-law-claims-in-nevsun-v-araya/>.

[253] *Nevsun* (n 252), para 105 (citation omitted).

[254] *Nevsun* (n 252), para 113 (quoting Harold Hongju Koh, 'Separating Myth from Reality about Corporate Responsibility Litigation' (2004) 7 J Int'l Econ Law 263, 267). cf dissent in *Nevsun* (ibid) by Justices Moldaver and Côté (arguing at paras 268–269 against direct applicability of customary international law obligations to corporations).

[255] *Urbaser* (n 217).

[256] *Urbaser* (n 217), paras 36, 1156–1164.

[257] *Urbaser* (n 217), para 1210.

[258] *Urbaser* (n 217), para 1210. For analysis of this decision, see, generally, Crow (n 213).

[259] See, e.g. Edward Guntrip, 'Private Actors, Public Goods and Responsibility for the Right to Water in International Investment Law: An Analysis of *Urbaser v Argentina*' (2018) 1 Brill Open Law 37, 60 (critiquing *Urbaser* for recognising binding human rights obligations for foreign investors that the existing human rights regime is incapable of accommodating, in terms of responsibility and enforcement); see further critique in Krajewski (n 202) 122–125.

[260] See, e.g. *David Aven et al v The Republic of Costa Rica* (Final Award) ICSID Case No UNCT/15/3 (18 September 2018), paras 738–742 (relying on the *Urbaser* approach when deciding to exercise jurisdiction over the respondent state's counterclaim, in order to take account of *erga omnes* environmental protections to which it held the claimant could be subject). cf *Bear Creek Mining Corporation v*

Accordingly, through the medium of customary law, corporations may be subject to direct international legal obligations. The process by which this may occur is the same as the formation process for any customary norm. States may, through practice and *opinio juris*, create obligations that are directly binding upon non-state actors.[261] By this means, 'customary international law binds those entities that states intend to bind'.[262] Therefore, '[t]he foundation of customary corporate obligations remains the consent of States, which may elect to submit corporations to obligations derived from [customary international law]'.[263]

Determining whether a customary norm binds non-state actors, such as corporations, depends on the content of the norm. For example, US federal courts have epitomised this process in action, when determining whether individuals or corporations are directly subject to specific norms of customary law in relation to tort actions for violations of the law of nations, pursuant to the US Alien Tort Claims Act.[264] As the US has argued, in such circumstances, 'a court must conduct a norm-by-norm assessment to determine whether the actor being sued is within the scope of the identified [customary] norm'.[265] The *Urbaser* tribunal recommended a similar approach to determining whether a norm is binding on corporate actors in the ICSID context, noting that '[t]he focus must be ... on contextualizing a corporation's specific activities as they relate to the human right at issue in order to determine whether any international law obligations attach to the non-State individual'.[266]

In the deep seabed mining context, is the customary norm prohibiting unilateral mining activities directly applicable to corporate actors? As this chapter has already

Republic of Perú (Award) ICSID Case No ARB/14/21 (30 November 2017), Partial Dissenting Opinion of Philippe Sands, especially paras 10–11 (relying on *Urbaser* to argue that international law protections for indigenous rights, although not directly applicable to corporate investors, should be taken into account in determining claimant damages). See discussion of these decisions in Krajewski (n 202) 125–127.

[261] Milanovic (2011a) (n 203) 39–40. See also Parlett (n 244) 361, recognising that it is 'increasingly common for individuals to be given rights and obligations' directly under international law. Parlett (ibid) notes, where these norms have a customary law basis, 'that custom is the consequence of state practice – or at least failure of states to persistently object to the formation of a customary rule'. Roberts and Sivakumaran (n 243) 115 acknowledge Parlett as forming part of the 'mainstream theories' in this regard, according to which 'nonstate entities may enjoy rights, obligations, and enforcement capacities under international law, but only if, and to the extent that, those rights, obligations, and capacities are created or recognized by states'.

[262] Clapham (2010) (n 243) 12; Karavias (n 56) 68–69 ('one may explain the application of a CIL rule to a corporation on the basis of an analogy to the operation of treaty law: States may enter an international treaty with the intention to create international obligations binding upon persons other than States and this proposition applies with equal force to rules of [customary law]').

[263] Karavias (n 56) 69.

[264] Alien Tort Claims Act (28 USC §1350); see also Parlett (n 244) 325; Karavias (n 56) 105–111.

[265] *Kiobel et al v Royal Dutch Petroleum Co et al, US Brief as amicus curiae supporting petitioners* (21 December 2011) at 18; see also William S Dodge, 'Corporate Liability under Customary International Law' (2012) 43 Geo J Int'l L 1045, 1047.

[266] *Urbaser* (n 217), para 1195.

addressed in detail (in Section 5.2.3), the extensive participation within and recognition of the ISA system throughout the international community, coupled with the absence of contrary deep seabed mining practice outside of the UNCLOS regime, supports the proposition that a corporate actor undertaking unilateral deep seabed mining activities would violate customary law. Indeed, if the customary prohibition were to except corporate actors from its scope, that would defeat the purpose of what is intended to be a universal prohibition on unilateral deep seabed mining activities.

On the basis of the preceding analysis, the customary prohibition on unilateral deep seabed mining activities constitutes an international law rule which is directly binding upon corporate actors. This satisfies Karavias's first essential test for the presence of a direct corporate obligation.[267] Moreover, for the reasons already explored (in relation to the direct treaty norm on corporate actors),[268] if a corporate actor began mining the deep seabed unilaterally, that actor would violate the customary norm prohibiting this activity and, consequently, would be responsible, as a matter of international law, for this violation (thereby satisfying Karavias's second test). Finally, as discussed previously, the absence of international enforcement for any such violation does not preclude the existence of the underlying corporate obligation under customary law.[269]

5.4 Conclusion

The Convention creates a procedural framework for deep seabed mining that operationalises the common heritage's key components, and is binding on actors both inside and outside of the regime, including corporate actors. All actors, both internal and external, are prohibited from engaging in unilateral mining activities (thereby realising Step 2 of this study's framework of analysis (as per Chapter 3, Section 3.3)).

Perhaps one of the most notable aspects of the UNCLOS global system for deep seabed mining is the varying means by which state and non-state actors are brought within it, depending on factors such as their treaty-party status or nationality, respectively. Table 5.2 below illustrates this study's conclusions on the means by which aspects of the UNCLOS deep seabed mining regime have the potential to bind different actors in the international community (subject, of course, to the more detailed analysis within this chapter, explaining the extent of the various obligations upon these differing actors).

[267] On these tests, see Karavias (n 56) 16. See also this book, Chapter 1, Section 1.2.4.
[268] See Section 5.3.1, text to n 238.
[269] See Section 5.3.1, text to n 239.

Table 5.2 Means by which Certain UNCLOS Deep Seabed Mining Obligations (or Equivalent Customary Obligations) are Binding upon Actors within the International Community

	POTENTIAL MEANS OF OBLIGATION				
ACTOR SUBJECT TO OBLIGATION	**Internationalised Functional Contract**	**Direct Treaty Obligation***	**Third-state Treaty Obligation**	**Indirect Treaty Obligation (via Domestic Law)***	**Obligation under Customary Law**
INTERNAL ACTORS					
UNCLOS States Parties	Yes (if State Party is ISA contractor)	Yes	Not applicable	Not applicable	Yes
Non-state Actor ISA Contractors	Yes	Yes	Not applicable	Yes	Yes
Other State-Party Nationals	Not applicable	Yes	Not applicable	Yes	Yes
EXTERNAL ACTORS					
Non-States Parties to UNCLOS (NSPs)	Not applicable	Not applicable	No	Not applicable	Yes
Nationals of NSPs	Not applicable	Yes	Not applicable	Yes (if operating within State Party jurisdiction)	Yes

*On the distinction between 'direct' and 'indirect' corporate obligations under international law, see Chapter 1, Section 1.2.4, especially citations and analysis at nn 162–164 and accompanying text.

PART III

THE COMMON HERITAGE'S SUBSTANTIVE CORE – NAVIGATING CONFLICT BETWEEN REGULATORY AUTHORITY AND CORPORATE PARTICIPATION

No, no dredging of the sea-bottom here. That would defeat one's purpose. The sea does not reward those who are too anxious, too greedy, or too impatient. To dig for treasures shows not only impatience and greed, but lack of faith. Patience, patience, patience, is what the sea teaches. Patience and faith. One should lie empty, open, choiceless as a beach – waiting for a gift from the sea.

(Anne Morrow Lindbergh, 'The Beach', *Gift from the Sea*, 1955[1])

Introduction to Part III

As Part II has established, UNCLOS creates a procedural framework for deep seabed mining that operationalises the common heritage's key components and constrains both internal and external actors. Part III will now turn to assess the extent to which this regime bestows the common heritage with material content and balances its competing aims of community and autonomy. To that end, Chapter 6 will evaluate whether the ISA's developing regulatory framework (and accompanying implementation and enforcement powers) may be on course to secure the common heritage's main material components of benefit sharing and marine environmental protection, in the face of increasing corporate activity. By so doing, Chapter 6 will address Step 3 of this study's framework of analysis (as set out in Section 3.3).

Thereafter, Chapter 7 will address Step 4 by determining whether the regime strikes an appropriate balance between the common heritage's dual goals of community and autonomy.[2] In order to do so, Chapter 7 will focus on reconciling the ISA's regulatory regime with investment protection rights for deep seabed miners. As Chapter 7 will explain, the extent to which the UNCLOS regime incorporates investment protection rights for deep seabed mining investors will be crucial for the commercial viability of the regime, and the presence of such rights is likely to be a key driver in securing corporate investment in the Area. However, to what extent can these rights be balanced alongside the communitarian aspects of the common heritage?

[2] See Chapter 3, text to nn 72–75, 104–111 and Section 3.2.7. See also Martti Koskenniemi, *From Apology to Utopia: The Structure of International Legal Argument* (CUP 2005) 476; and see 488–493.

6

Does the Regime Secure the Common Heritage's Benefit-sharing and Marine Environmental Protection Components?

This study has already set out the means by which the Convention enshrines within its procedural framework the common heritage goals of benefit sharing and marine environmental protection.[1] However, as noted previously, while incorporating these material goals in a 'formal-procedural way', the regime engages in a 'strategy of referral', deferring their ultimate realisation to further institutional procedures.[2] The substance of these matters awaits further resolution within the ISA's regulatory regime. As the ISA's regulatory regime is still being constructed, this chapter cannot offer a definitive conclusion on the extent to which the regime will fully achieve the common heritage's benefit-sharing and marine environmental protection goals. However, this chapter will provide an interim assessment of whether the emerging regulatory regime is proceeding towards realising benefit sharing (Section 6.1) and marine environmental protection aspects (Section 6.2). Given the immaturity of the deep seabed mining industry, a key measure of the regulatory regime's ability to secure the common heritage is likely to be the extent to which it retains flexibility to adapt to new challenges, as Section 6.3 will consider. Ultimately, substantive rules on benefit sharing and marine environmental protection will operate within the regime's existing framework for implementation, responsibility and enforcement. This chapter will, in Section 6.4, assess the position of corporate actors in terms of each of these aspects, as robust implementation options will, in practice, be vital for achievement of benefit sharing and marine environmental protection.

[1] See discussion in Chapter 4, at text to nn 23–40.

[2] Martti Koskenniemi, *From Apology to Utopia: The Structure of International Legal Argument* (CUP 2005) 492–493; see also David Kennedy, *International Legal Structures* (Nomos Verlagsgesellschaft 1987) 201–245. See, further, this book's analysis in Chapter 3, text to nn 180–182.

International Law and Corporate Actors in Deep Seabed Mining. Joanna Dingwall, Oxford University Press. © Joanna Dingwall 2021. DOI: 10.1093/oso/9780192898265.003.0007

6.1 Developing the Regime's Benefit-sharing Aspects in Financial Terms

The benefit-sharing principle is enshrined within the UNCLOS framework.[3] The regime seeks to secure twin goals of equal participation in deep seabed mining and equitable sharing of benefits derived from such activities. The ISA's licensing process already integrates various benefit-sharing elements. These include features such as the parallel approach, with its system of reserved areas (and, for sulphide and cobalt crust mining, the equity interest/joint venture option), and the potential role of the Enterprise, together with constraints on monopolisation and encouragement of technology and skills transfers.[4]

As Chapter 4 demonstrated, the evolving operation of the licensing regime (with its increased role for private corporate actors in reserved areas, the growing popularity of the joint venture/equity interest option as regards sulphides and cobalt crusts, and the continuing postponement of the Enterprise) has uncertain implications for the realisation of the common heritage.[5] Amidst this uncertainty, much more is riding on the regime's financial mechanisms to secure and deliver benefit-sharing aspects.[6] These financial aspects will be the focus of this section. The financial system for deep seabed mining requires two key components: a payment system for the Authority to collect revenues from contractors, plus a mechanism by which it can then distribute surplus revenues on an equitable basis (collectively, these elements may be described as forming the 'payment mechanism'). As activities in the Area progress towards commercial exploitation, to what extent is the ISA's regulatory regime moving towards concretisation of these financial benefit-sharing aspects?

The underlying Convention regime, as modified by the 1994 Agreement, provides guidance to the ISA on developing financial terms for deep seabed mining.[7] This includes the objective of 'ensur[ing] optimal revenues' for the ISA from mining proceeds, while 'attract[ing] investments and technology to the exploration and exploitation of the Area'.[8] In particular, the 1994 Agreement provides that the payment system 'should not be complicated and should not impose major

[3] See, e.g. UNCLOS, arts 140(1), 148, 150, 152(2), 153, 157(1) and Annex III generally. See also Chapter 4 at text to nn 23–28 and Section 4.2.3.2 on key benefit-sharing elements within the ISA licensing process.

[4] For thorough analysis of all of these aspects, see Chapter 4, Section 4.2.3.2.

[5] See discussion in Chapter 4, at text to nn 295–310.

[6] Feichtner critiques this as a move from 'participation' to compensation, arguing that 'the participation objective has given way to a focus on market supply and revenue generation'; Isabel Feichtner, 'Sharing the Riches of the Sea: The Redistributive and Fiscal Dimension of Deep Seabed Exploitation' (2019) 30 EJIL 601, 603.

[7] Guiding principles that the ISA must take into account when developing rules concerning financial terms of contracts are contained in 1994 Agreement, Annex, s 8(1); see also UNCLOS, Annex III, art 13(1) (cf art 13(3)–(10) disapplied by the 1994 Agreement, Annex, s 8(2)).

[8] UNCLOS, Annex III, art 13(1)(a)–(b).

administrative costs on the Authority or on a contractor', and may contain 'a royalty system or a combination of a royalty and profit-sharing system'.[9] It should also be flexible, so that it may be 'revised periodically in light of changing circumstances'.[10] Rates of payment should be comparable with those applicable to land-based mining (to avoid giving a competitive advantage to deep seabed miners).[11]

These matters are developed within the DERs, with Part VII addressing financial terms of exploitation contracts. The Council is charged with 'ensur[ing] equality of financial treatment and comparable financial obligations for Contractors' (reg 62). Nevertheless, the Council may bestow financial incentives upon contractors in certain circumstances: for example, to entice contractors into entering joint ventures with the Enterprise (reg 63). Once a contractor begins commercial production,[12] it will be liable to pay royalties (reg 64).[13] DERs, Appendix IV provides for determination of royalty liability in relation to exploitation activities. The present draft sets out a methodology for calculation of royalty payments but this is 'indicative and presented for discussion only at this time'.[14] Currently, Appendix IV provides for an *ad valorem* royalty system, envisaging that a different value-based royalty rate will apply to each type of mineral extracted (nodules, sulphides or cobalt crusts) on the basis of the value of the metal components contained within. Commercial production for each mineral type will be classified as occurring over two periods, with different rates applicable during each period. All relevant rates have still to be determined.

Part VIII of the DERs provides for application fees, annual fees and other types of contractor fees. As with applications for exploration, there is an application fee (of an amount to be provided for in Appendix II).[15] Like exploration contracts, exploitation contractors must pay annual reporting fees (of an amount to be determined by Council decision 'from time to time').[16] Once a contractor commences

[9] 1994 Agreement, Annex, s 8(1)(c).

[10] 1994 Agreement, Annex, s 8(1)(e).

[11] 1994 Agreement, Annex, s 8(1)(b).

[12] Exploitation includes stages of pre-feasibility, feasibility, construction and commercial production. For a tabular overview of key stages and potential duration, see Foreign and Commonwealth Office and the Royal Society, 'Report of a Workshop on the Draft Regulations for the Exploitation of Mineral Resources in the Area: Policy, Legal and Institutional Considerations' (February 2018) 29 <www.isa.org.jm/files/documents/EN/Regs/2018/RegsWShop.pdf>. Commercial production begins 'where a Contractor engages in sustained large-scale recovery operations which yield a quantity of materials sufficient to indicate clearly that the principal purpose is large-scale production rather than production intended for information-gathering, analysis or the testing of equipment or plant', in accordance with DERs, sch (echoing UNCLOS, Annex III, art 17(2)(g) while acknowledging that, ultimately, '[a] clearer definition of commercial production will be needed').

[13] See also DERs, regs 66–73 for further details on the royalty returns system, and regs 77–78 on measures to prevent contractors from avoiding royalty liability.

[14] DERs, Appendix IV.

[15] DERs, regs 7(3)(j), 86 and Appendix II. The equivalent application fee for an exploration contract is US$500,000: see Chapter 4, n 143.

[16] DERs, reg 84 and Appendix II. Section 10.5 of the standard clauses to exploration contracts (contained in fourth annex of Nodules, Sulphides and Cobalt Regulations) provides for an equivalent annual overhead charge.

commercial production, it will be liable to pay an annual fixed fee (of an amount to be established by the Council).[17] As the LTC has described, this annual fee is 'part of a transition phase to bridge the period of funding prior to the receipt of royalties from commercial production'.[18] Once the ISA adopts a regime for the financial aspects of exploitation, it will be subject to periodic ISA review,[19] and the ISA may issue guidelines in respect of royalty payments.[20]

Although the ISA is beginning to develop its framework for collection of royalties and fees, it has not yet finalised its underlying basis of payment and financial model, nor has it begun to design a mechanism for equitable sharing of revenues in accordance with Article 140(2) of UNCLOS. In practice, revenues available to the ISA for distribution will be curtailed, to some extent, by the ISA's underlying financial arrangements. In the first instance, the Authority is to use available funds (including revenues from mining activities) to cover its expenses.[21] Moreover, its remaining revenues also need to go towards an economic assistance fund for developing land-based producer states,[22] and towards funding the Enterprise (once operational).[23] However, the Authority may also share remaining revenues on an equitable basis, through an appropriate mechanism, which it is yet to devise.[24] The Authority's development of this mechanism for equitable sharing of benefits remains at the very preliminary stages.[25]

[17] DERs, reg 85. For the definition of commercial production, see n 12 above. Within the original UNCLOS regime, the fixed annual fee was to be set at US$1 million: UNCLOS, Annex III, art 13(3). This was modified by the 1994 Agreement, Annex, s 8(1)(d), pursuant to which an unspecified annual fixed fee would be payable from 'the date of commencement of commercial production'. The DERs follow the latter approach, providing that '[t]he amount of the fee shall be established by the Council as required under [the 1994 Agreement, Annex, s 8(1)(d)]' (reg 85(1)).

[18] ISBA/25/C/18, para 33. Accordingly, the annual fixed fee for any given year 'may be credited against any royalty or other amount payable under Part VII' of the DERs (reg 85(4)).

[19] DERs, reg 107; see also regs 81–82 (ISA review of system and rates of payments) and 88(1) (providing for regular review of contractor fees).

[20] DERs, regs 65 and 95.

[21] See UNCLOS, art 173(2) (expenses of the Authority); see also art 171 (on funds of the Authority). See, further, ISA, 'Financial Regulations of the International Seabed Authority', reg 5.7 <www.isa.org.jm/files/documents/EN/Regs/FinRegs.pdf>.

[22] UNCLOS, arts 151(10), 173(2)(c), read with 1994 Agreement, Annex, s 7(1); see also ISA, Financial Regulations (n 21), reg 5.7(c).

[23] UNCLOS, arts 170(4), 173(2)(b); see also ISA, Financial Regulations (n 21), reg 5.7(b).

[24] See UNCLOS, art 173(2)(a), read with arts 140 and 160(2)(g); see also ISA, Financial Regulations (n 21), reg 5.7(a).

[25] See ISA Finance Committee, 'Rules, Regulations and Procedures on the Equitable Sharing of Financial and Other Economic Benefits Derived from Activities in the Area – Report of the Secretary-General' (18 May 2018) ISBA/24/FC/4. For preliminary Finance Committee discussions in this regard, see, e.g. ISA Assembly, 'Report of the Finance Committee' (12 July 2019) ISBA/25/A/10, paras 26–33; ISA Assembly, 'Report of the Finance Committee' (25 September 2020) ISBA/26/A/10, paras 19–23. On difficult questions of distributive justice with which the ISA will need to engage in designing the mechanism for equitable distribution, including intergenerational and environmental considerations, see Michael W Lodge, Kathleen Segerson and Dale Squires, 'Sharing and Preserving the Resources in the Deep Sea: Challenges for the International Seabed Authority' (2017) 32 Int'l J Marine Coastal L 427, especially at 431–442.

Ultimately, the Assembly will adopt rules on financial aspects of the regime on the basis of Council recommendations (which, in turn, will be based upon LTC and Finance Committee input).[26] Developing these financial aspects will be an integral part of the ISA's realisation of the common heritage principle. This matter is 'very much a legacy issue for the ISA in terms of its contribution to ocean governance'.[27] ISA development of the payment mechanism is ongoing, through a series of workshops and related stakeholder activities. The ISA enlisted Massachusetts Institute of Technology (*MIT*) to assist in developing these economic aspects.[28] The ISA's latest initiative has been to establish an open-ended working group (*OEWG*) on financial terms of contracts, and this group had its fourth meeting in October 2020.[29]

In determining a basis for payment, Council members have agreed that 'no option for a payment system should be ruled out' at this stage.[30] The OEWG is focusing on the payment regime for polymetallic nodules for the time being, 'pending further studies on the other types of resources'.[31] Presently, the OEWG has narrowed its focus to four financial systems, and it has 'not fully endorse[d] nor discard[ed] any of the options'.[32] These potential options are a fixed-rate *ad valorem* royalty mechanism, a two-stage *ad valorem* royalty mechanism, a progressive or variable *ad valorem* royalty system or a combined *ad valorem* royalty and profit-based system.[33] The first three approaches are value-based royalty

[26] See Section 4.2.2 for an overview of this process. See also UNCLOS, arts 160(2)(f)(i), 160(2)(g), 162(2)(o)(i) and 165(2)(f); 1994 Agreement, Annex, s 9(7)(f).

[27] Jan-Stefan Fritz, 'Deep Sea Anarchy: Mining at the Frontiers of International Law' (2015) 30 Int'l J Marine Coastal L 445, 475.

[28] See, e.g. Randolph Kirchain and others, 'Update: Report to the ISA on the Development of an Economic Model and System of Payments for the Exploitation of Polymetallic Nodules in the Area Based on Stakeholder Feedback' (Materials Systems Laboratory, MIT, October 2020) <https://isa.org.jm/files/files/documents/Nodule%20Financial%20Payment%20System%20Report%20October%202020%20V3.pdf>.

[29] See ISA, 'Documents from the Fourth Meeting of the Open-ended Working Group of the Council in Respect of the Development and Negotiation of the Financial Terms of a Contract' (October 2020) <https://isa.org.jm/files/files/documents/4thMeet-DocList_3.pdf>. On Council establishment of the OEWG, in response to Germany's proposal, see ISA Council, 'Statement of the President on the Work of the Council during the Second Part of the Twenty-fourth Session, Addendum' (25 July 2018) ISBA/24/C/8/Add.1, para 12 and Annex II.

[30] ISA Council, 'Statement by the President of the Council on the Work of the Council during the First Part of the Twenty-sixth Session' (26 March 2020) ISBA/26/C/13, para 18.

[31] ISA Council, 'Report of the Chair on the Outcome of the Third Meeting of the Open-ended Working Group of the Council in Respect of the Development and Negotiation of the Financial Terms of a Contract under Article 13, Paragraph 1, of Annex III to UNCLOS and Section 8 of the Annex to the Agreement Relating to the Implementation of Part XI of UNCLOS' (17 February 2020) ISBA/26/C/8, para 14.

[32] ISBA/26/C/8, para 15(c).

[33] ISBA/26/C/8, paras 2–3 (for OEWG review of these options, see paras 5–10). For an overview of these options and considerations underpinning them, see slides of MIT's presentation at the third OEWG meeting: MIT, 'ISA: Financial Payment System Working Group Meeting' (Kingston, Jamaica, 13–14 February 2020) <https://isa.org.jm/files/files/documents/cost_workshop-ppt.pdf>. By way of comparison, the payment system for exploitation of the continental shelf beyond 200 nautical miles is on an *ad valorem* royalty basis, with an increasing rate over the lifetime of the project: UNCLOS, art 82(2).

systems, whereas the fourth option incorporates a profit-based component.[34] Both of the fixed-rate *ad valorem* systems would apply a fixed rate to the value of the relevant metals (applying either a flat rate for the entire period (one-stage), or with a change in rate for the second stage (two-stage)).[35] The variable *ad valorem* approach proposes to apply a value-based fixed rate for the first stage and a variable rate for the second stage, which could rise progressively, in line with rising metal prices and on the basis of certain trigger points.[36] Finally, the combined system would also retain a value-based fixed rate for the first stage, with a blended second stage, combining a fixed *ad valorem* rate with a profit-based approach where contractors would pay a percentage of their profits.[37] MIT has pointed out that, in theory, each of these approaches 'can be designed to yield the same revenue to the ISA under baseline conditions'.[38]

Notably, 'different systems bring with them varying amounts of potential income as well as risk'.[39] For example, while royalty-based mechanisms may be low-risk in allowing the ISA to collect income in the face of unprofitable mining operations or a depleted metals market, by the same token, a royalties-only mechanism deprives the ISA of the opportunity to share the profits of a buoyant market or a reduction in operating costs (as this could only be attained by inclusion of a profit-share component).[40] At the other end of the spectrum, reliance on a purely profit-based approach increases the risk of 'creative accountancy [which] could easily minimize the official profits of mining companies, resulting in less income for the Authority and, therefore, mankind as a whole'.[41] Following the OEWG's recommendation, the ISA sought further stakeholder comments for the purpose of refining the assumptions within these models,[42] and, in April 2020, it released the responses that it had received.[43]

[34] Notably, these bases of payment are consistent with the direction in the 1994 Agreement, Annex, s 8(1)(c) that '[c]onsideration should be given to the adoption of a royalty system or a combination of a royalty and profit-sharing system', rather than a purely profit-based system.

[35] MIT (2020) (n 33) 14.

[36] MIT (2020) (n 33) 14.

[37] MIT (2020) (n 33) 14–15.

[38] MIT (2020) (n 33) 14.

[39] Aline Jaeckel, Jeff A Ardron and Kristina M Gjerde, 'Sharing Benefits of the Common Heritage of Mankind – is the Deep Seabed Mining Regime Ready?' (2016) 70 Marine Pol'y 198, 200. For analysis of key features of the main financial systems and various considerations that would need to be addressed for their application in the deep seabed mining context, see Kris van Nijen and others, 'The Development of a Payment Regime for Deep Sea Mining Activities in the Area through Stakeholder Participation' (2019) 34 Int'l J Marine Coastal L 1, 14ff.

[40] See, e.g. analysis by Jaeckel, Ardron and Gjerde (2016) (n 39) 200; Feichtner (n 6) 626–627.

[41] Klaas Willaert, 'Effective Protection of the Marine Environment and Equitable Benefit Sharing in the Area: Empty Promises or Feasible Goals?' (2020) 51 OD Int'l L 175, 185.

[42] ISBA/26/C/8, para 15(b); ISBA/26/C/13, para 19.

[43] ISA, 'Comments on Refining Assumptions of the Financial Model' (6 April 2020) <www.isa.org.jm/node/19595>. MIT responded to these stakeholder comments by updating its report: see Kirchain and others (n 28).

In light of the current push towards commercialisation of the deep seabed, commentators are paying increasing attention to financial aspects of the regime.[44] Certain broad themes are emerging. In offering an economic perspective on the underlying foundations of the deep seabed mining regime, Posner and Sykes caution that, '[d]espite its imperfections, the UNCLOS regime may be significantly better than none at all'.[45] Nevertheless, other commentators have critiqued the assumptions inherent within the financial aspects of the common heritage as reifying a market-based perspective.[46]

As this study has examined, the mid-1990s modification of the deep seabed regime did indeed tilt the balance within the common heritage in favour of 'market-oriented approaches'.[47] The common heritage includes the goals of community and autonomy, and can only be realised successfully, within the regime's own terms, to the extent that it provides a balance between these goals.[48] Therefore, the focus of the remodelled regime is to allow commercial actors to participate within the regime on competitive terms, in pursuit of economic gain, and a key role of the ISA is to collect revenues from mining activities and ensure their equitable distribution. Underlying this narrative is the assumption that investment by private actors, in particular, could be a significant factor for the longer-term success of the deep seabed mining industry.[49] To this extent, the UNCLOS regime, as modified by the

[44] See, e.g. Mara Ntona and Mitchell Lennan, 'An Early Reflection on Benefit-sharing Negotiations at the International Seabed Authority' (*BeneLex Blog*, 30 August 2018) <https://benelexblog.wordpress.com/2018/08/30/an-early-reflection-on-benefit-sharing-negotiations-at-the-international-seabed-authority/>; Kris van Nijen, Steven van Passel and Dale Squires, 'A Stochastic Techno-economic Assessment of Seabed Mining of Polymetallic Nodules in the Clarion Clipperton Fracture Zone' (2018) 95 Marine Pol'y 133; Gaute Voigt-Hanssen, 'Current "Light" and "Heavy" Options for Benefit-sharing in the Context of the United Nations Convention on the Law of the Sea' (2018) 33 Int'l J Marine Coastal L 683; Feichtner (n 6); van Nijen and others (2019) (n 39); Klaas Willaert, 'The Financial Aspects of Deep Sea Mining: Common Heritage of Mankind or First-come-first-served?' (2019) 25 JIML 387; Willaert (2020c) (n 41); Torsten Thiele, Hans-Peter Damian and Pradeep Singh, 'A Comprehensive Approach to the Payment Mechanism for Deep Seabed Mining' (January 2021) Institute for Advanced Sustainability Studies Policy Brief <https://publications.iass-potsdam.de/rest/items/item_6000737_2/component/file_6000738/content>.

[45] Eric A Posner and Alan O Sykes, 'Economic Foundations of Law of the Sea' (2010) 104 AJIL 569, 592 (and see 587–592 for general economic analysis of the deep seabed mining regime and critique of its inefficiencies).

[46] See, e.g. Feichtner (n 6) 623 (suggesting that international law-making projects, such as the 1994 Agreement, 'plausibly could be interpreted as an instantiation of an economic theory that holds that efficiently functioning markets will be welfare enhancing') and 626 (warning that 'the design of the payment mechanism is likely to become a function of the profit expectations of commercial contractors'). See also Ntona and Lennan (n 44) (noting that the principal assumption underlying the MIT models is that 'investors will only engage in exploitation if they will get enough of a return on their investment costs, risks, and advantages of different economic options').

[47] 1994 Agreement, preamble. See also discussion in Chapter 3, at text to nn 104–111 and Section 3.2.7.

[48] On this, see Chapter 3, Section 3.2.7.

[49] See, e.g. ISA Secretary-General's remarks, in 2006, that '[i]t has always been my belief that until the private sector gets involved, the prospects for commercial mining of minerals from the deep seabed will remain uncertain': UNGA '71st Plenary Meeting' (61st Session) (8 December 2006) UN Doc A/61/PV.71 at 5. See also discussion in the introduction to this book, at text to nn 31–36.

1994 Agreement, presents 'greater "market orientation" as a win-win situation'.[50] By this reasoning, Feichtner critiques the 1994 Agreement's turn towards the market, arguing that it recasts the benefit-sharing component within the common heritage as 'a turn towards individualized benefits to be derived by consumers from economic growth'.[51] Flowing from this, the profit expectation of commercial investors becomes a 'guiding concern' for the design of the payment regime.[52]

This underlying balance is reflected in payment discussions so far. For example, the ISA's financial consultants, MIT, have identified, as the philosophy of their analysis, the need to '[i]dentify payment systems that *maximize* the return to the common heritage of mankind'.[53] At the twenty-fourth session of the ISA, Richard Roth of MIT emphasised that '[t]he right balance has to be found between how much money will remain with investors and how much money will be financing the common heritage for this to be an economically attractive endeavour for investors'.[54] From the outset of its recent work on the payment mechanism, the ISA has kept this balance at the forefront of its mission, citing, as key objectives, the need '[t]o ensure optimum revenues for the Authority from the proceeds of commercial production' and the need '[t]o attract investments and technology to the exploration and exploitation of the Area'.[55]

[50] Feichtner (n 6) 614 (citing the 1994 Agreement, preamble).

[51] Feichtner (n 6) 614; see also 621 ('[a]ccording to this reformulation, greater market orientation will ensure that effective exploitation takes place'. This will, in turn, 'generate revenue for distribution'). In this regard, see Posner and Sykes (n 45) 589–592 (highlighting economic inefficiencies of the regime's equal participation aspects (such as anti-monopoly rules, reserved area requirements and the planned role of the Enterprise) and noting that, from an efficiency perspective, cash transfers should be preferred by developing states instead of other, indirect, forms of subsidisation and restrictions on the market). However, cf recent stakeholder comments by private corporate contractors GSR, NORI and UKSRL, which recognise receipt of revenue as an important part of the realisation of the common heritage (at 11), while listing other non-monetary 'returns' on the common heritage which may be achieved through commercial activity, including securement of a supply stream of raw metals needed for global sustainability and clean energy technology (at 10): GSR, NORI and UKSRL, 'Industry Position Paper – ISA Royalty Regime' (March 2020) 10–11 <https://isa.org.jm/files/files/documents/assumptions-tab_0.pdf>.

[52] Feichtner (n 6) 624; see also 626, 632.

[53] MIT (2020) (n 33) 2 (emphasis in original).

[54] IISD Reporting Services, 'Summary of the Twenty-fourth Annual Session of the ISA (Second Part): 16 to 26 July 2018' (29 July 2018) 25:168 Earth Negotiations Bulletin 3–4, 17 <http://enb.iisd.org/download/pdf/enb25168e.pdf>. See also MIT (2020) (n 33) 9 (noting the '[n]eed to find constraint to find ISA maximum return', on the basis that, while higher rates of return may appear to raise more revenue for the ISA, eventually a high rate becomes prohibitive to investors, and the '[r]eturn goes to zero'). See also comments by GSR, NORI and UKSRL (n 51) 12, that 'the returns required by investors in first-movers, which will necessarily take greater technical and economic risk, will be higher than those for followers'.

[55] These goals originate within the guiding objectives for financial terms of contracts in UNCLOS, Annex III, art 13(1)(a)–(b), as reiterated in ISA, 'Discussion Paper on the Development and Implementation of a Payment Mechanism in the Area' (March 2015) 10 <www.isa.org.jm/files/documents/EN/WorkingPapers/DiscussionPaper-FinMech.pdf> (accordingly, 'the financial return to the [common heritage of mankind] from its mineral resources must be set in a manner that does not act as a disincentive to investors').

Arguably, resolving this tension poses the 'main difficulty' to agreeing a payment mechanism.[56] There are mounting concerns, amongst developing states in particular, as vocalised by the African Group, that the proposed economic models may not be sufficient to achieve 'fair compensation to mankind for the loss of resources to common ownership'.[57] The African Group has critiqued the ISA's focus on contractor rates of return, querying 'whether first-movers should be encouraged', on the basis that '[l]and-based mining is capable of supplying the world with necessary minerals and if deep-sea mining is a more expensive and less efficient way of supplying metals it should not be subsidised to be competitive'.[58] As Jaeckel has recognised, this matter is complicated further, when calculating economic costs and benefits of mining activities, by the need to consider mining impacts on 'the natural capital of the seabed', provided through 'ecosystem services, such as climate regulation', the value of which is not readily quantifiable.[59]

Ultimately, in light of these tensions and concerns, the payment regime that emerges from ongoing ISA processes will need to be subject to detailed and sustained examination, in order to ensure that it strikes an appropriate balance and realises common heritage goals. Moreover, as the ISA has cautioned, the 'real economics of the industry' may not become apparent until much further down the line, in light of commercial activities on the ground.[60]

[56] Feichtner (n 6) 625.

[57] Algeria, 'Statement on Behalf of the African Group to the ISA Council – Agenda Item 11: Financial Model' (25 February 2019) 13 <https://isa.org.jm/files/files/documents/1-algeriaoboag_finmodel.pdf>. Similarly, see critique in Deep Sea Conservation Coalition, 'Deep-sea Mining: Who Stands to Benefit?' (June 2020) <www.savethehighseas.org/wp-content/uploads/2020/07/DSCC_FactSheet6_DSM_WhoBenefits_4pp_web.pdf>.

[58] Algeria (n 57) 12 (see also 13, citing particular concerns for developing states which are land-based mineral producers).

[59] Aline Jaeckel, 'Benefitting from the Common Heritage of Humankind: From Expectation to Reality' (2020) 35 Int'l J Marine Coastal L 660, 667 (another factor, as Jaeckel recognises, at 674, when considering security of mineral supplies, is that 'availability of metals may be regarded as a benefit in its own right'). See also Thiele, Damian and Singh (n 44) 6 (calling for 'comprehensive assessment of natural capital and ecosystem services' when calculating financial benefits of deep seabed mining, including assessment of carbon footprints of such activities). Another aspect, which it would be 'imprudent to ignore' is the benefit that may be reaped from marine genetic resources of the deep seabed (unanticipated at the time of UNCLOS negotiation); Jaeckel (ibid) 679.

[60] ISA, 'Discussion Paper' (n 55) 9. See also comments by GSR, NORI and UKSRL (n 51) 11 (arguing that the payment regime applicable to the early stage of the industry must take account of the fact that 'operators will be taking on the greatest technological risk and highest cost of capital', while in the longer term, '[o]nce the industry is mature and established, and there is greater knowledge around the actual profitability of the industry, an updated royalty regime can then be adopted by the ISA that is more appropriate to a mature industry'). cf Feichtner (n 6) 625 (critiquing the ISA's cautious, incremental approach to development of financial aspects as, inter alia, 'miss[ing] the opportunity that this law-making process offers for deconstructing notions of competitiveness, commercial viability and value').

6.2 Developing the Regime's Protection of the Marine Environment

The UNCLOS deep seabed mining regime is premised on the principle of marine environmental protection.[61] The 'marine environment' is defined, broadly, as including:

> [T]he physical, chemical, geological and biological components, conditions and factors which interact and determine the productivity, state, condition and quality of the marine ecosystem, the waters of the seas and oceans and the airspace above those waters, as well as the seabed and ocean floor and subsoil thereof.[62]

The ISA is working towards development of an overall environmental policy for the Area.[63] This is part of the ISA's strategic vision for marine environmental protection, through which it seeks to further the UN's sustainable development goal of ocean sustainability.[64] The ISA intends to implement a series of regional environmental management plans (*REMPs*) within the Area, to protect areas of particular environmental interest (*APEIs*) from mining.[65] Through implementation of REMPs and creation of APEIs, the ISA could 'make a significant contribution towards establishing networks of marine protected areas'.[66] To date, the ISA has adopted one such REMP: it is located within the CCZ, and designates nine APEIs as being protected from mining activities but open for marine scientific research.[67] The ISA is also working towards the establishment of REMPs in other areas.[68]

[61] See analysis in Chapter 4, at text to nn 30–40.

[62] Nodules, Sulphides and Cobalt Regulations, reg 1(3)(c) (for an equivalent definition, see DERs, sch). See also UNCLOS, art 145.

[63] See, e.g. ISA Council, 'Statement by the President of the Council on the Work of the Council during the First Part of the Twenty-fourth Session' (13 March 2018) ISBA/24/C/8, para 40(c).

[64] See, generally, ISA Assembly, 'Decision of the Assembly of the ISA Relating to the Strategic Plan of the Authority for the Period 2019–2023' (27 July 2018) ISBA/24/A/10. See also UNGA Res 70/1 (25 September 2015) UN Doc A/RES/70/1 (Transforming Our World: The 2030 Agenda for Sustainable Development), goal 14 ('[c]onserve and sustainably use the oceans, seas and marine resources for sustainable development').

[65] For analysis of the ISA's innovative use of its powers in this regard, see Aline Jaeckel, 'An Environmental Management Strategy for the International Seabed Authority? The Legal Basis' (2015) 30 Int'l J Marine Coastal L 93 and Aline L Jaeckel, *The International Seabed Authority and the Precautionary Principle – Balancing Deep Seabed Mineral Mining and Marine Environmental Protection* (Brill 2017) 169–173 (analysing the novel legal basis of this approach). See, further, Petra Drankier, 'Marine Protected Areas in Areas beyond National Jurisdiction' (2012) 27 Int'l J Marine Coastal L 291; Kristina M Gjerde and Anna Rulska-Domino, 'Marine Protected Areas beyond National Jurisdiction: Some Practical Perspectives for Moving Ahead' (2012) 27 Int'l J Marine Coastal L 351.

[66] Jaeckel (2017) (n 65) 169; see also 166–169 (analysing the extent to which this improves on fragmented attempts to create marine protected areas in areas beyond national jurisdiction).

[67] ISA LTC, 'Environmental Management Plan for the Clarion-Clipperton Zone' (13 July 2011) ISBA/17/LTC/7; ISA Council, 'Decision of the Council Relating to an Environmental Management Plan for the Clarion-Clipperton Zone' (26 July 2012) ISBA/18/C/22. For analysis, see Michael Lodge and others, 'Seabed Mining: International Seabed Authority Environmental Management Plan for the Clarion-Clipperton Zone. A Partnership Approach' (2014) 49 Marine Pol'y 66; Jaeckel (2017) (n 65) 202–209.

[68] See, e.g. ISA Council, 'Implementation of the Authority's Strategy for the Development of Regional Environmental Management Plans for the Area – Report of the Secretary-General' (28 January 2019) ISBA/25/C/13.

The Convention empowers the ISA to adopt rules, regulations and procedures in order to prevent, reduce and control pollution and other marine environmental hazards in relation to activities in the Area.[69] The exploration regulations give substance to the principle of marine environmental preservation.[70] The regulatory provisions addressing marine environmental preservation 'were among the most controversial to be addressed during the negotiation of the Regulations'.[71] As Lodge notes, the regime for environmental protection already fleshed out in the Mining Code is 'a very significant advance upon Article 145 of the Convention and provides a firm basis for the elaboration of a comprehensive code of environmental regulation'.[72] Pursuant to the Mining Code, the Authority must keep its environmental rules 'under periodic review' to 'ensure effective protection for the marine environment from harmful effects which may arise from activities in the Area',[73] so the anticipation is that the rules will continue to evolve to address new challenges.

Prospective deep seabed miners are subject to various environmental requirements before obtaining an exploration contract. In their applications, they must include a preliminary environmental impact assessment (*EIA*), together with 'a description of a programme for oceanographic and baseline environmental studies'.[74] Once granted permission to explore, contractors must abide by various obligations in relation to marine environmental protection. Contractors must 'take necessary measures to prevent, reduce and control pollution and other hazards to the marine environment arising from [their] activities in the Area as far as reasonably possible' and, in order to do so, they must apply a precautionary approach and best environmental practices.[75] The Mining Code also obliges the Authority and sponsoring

[69] See, e.g. UNCLOS, arts 145, 162(2)(w), 162(2)(x), and Annex III, art 17(1)(b)(xii) and 17(2)(f). As per UNCLOS, art 1(1)(3), 'activities in the Area' includes 'all activities of exploration for, and exploitation of, the resources of the Area': for analysis of the scope of this, see ITLOS AO, paras 82–97.

[70] Michael W Lodge, 'International Seabed Authority's Regulations on Prospecting and Exploration for Polymetallic Nodules in the Area' (2002) 20 J Energy Nat Res L 270, 287–289; see also, generally, Rüdiger Wolfrum, 'The Contribution of the Regulations of the International Seabed Authority to the Progressive Development of International Environmental Law' in Michael W Lodge and Myron H Nordquist (eds), *Peaceful Order in the World's Oceans* (Brill 2014); Jaeckel (2017) (n 65).

[71] Lodge (2002) (n 70) 287 (writing in relation to original version of the Nodules Regulations, adopted in 2000 (ISBA/6/A/18); the current version, revised in 2013 (ISBA/19/C/17), contains significantly improved environmental protections).

[72] Lodge (2002) (n 70) 289.

[73] Nodules Regulations, reg 31(1); Sulphides Regulations, reg 33(1); Cobalt Regulations, reg 33(1). See also Nodules Regulations, reg 42; Sulphides Regulations, reg 44; Cobalt Regulations, reg 44 (subjecting these regulations, as a whole, to the Council's general periodic review). On ISA periodic review powers more generally, see discussion in Chapter 4, at text to nn 111–112. For an overview of previous amendments to the Mining Code, see Jaeckel (2017) (n 65) 150.

[74] 1994 Agreement, Annex, s 1(7); see also Nodules Regulations, reg 18; Sulphides Regulations, reg 20; Cobalt Regulations, reg 20.

[75] Nodules Regulations, reg 31(5); Sulphides Regulations, reg 33(5); Cobalt Regulations, reg 33(5).

states to 'apply a precautionary approach, as reflected in principle 15 of the Rio Declaration, and best environmental practices'.[76]

The content of the contractor's duty to 'take necessary measures' is detailed further within the Mining Code. A contractor must gather oceanographic and environmental baseline data in order to establish baselines against which to assess the likely effects of its activities.[77] The contractor must also participate in an ongoing monitoring programme to evaluate these effects, including through submission of annual reports detailing implementation and results of the monitoring programme.[78] If required by the Council, this monitoring programme may include designation of 'impact reference zones' (areas to be mined) and 'preservation reference zones' (areas in which no mining may occur), for comparison purposes.[79] The monitoring obligations are complemented by the requirement that a contractor must submit a full EIA before undertaking certain activities, such as test mining.[80] To assist in contractor adherence to these obligations, the ISA has issued detailed recommendations giving content to the environmental obligations. These recommendations include information on requirements for environmental baseline studies, EIA processes, data collection and reporting, and measures for cooperative research.[81] If a contractor's exploration activities cause or pose a threat of serious harm to the marine environment, the ISA may adopt emergency orders, in accordance with the process provided in the Mining Code.[82]

Thus far, the Mining Code only regulates exploration activities in the Area. However, exploitation poses increased environmental risks.[83] Within the DERs,

[76] Nodules Regulations, reg 31(2); Sulphides Regulations, reg 33(2); Cobalt Regulations, reg 33(2). Principle 15 of the Rio Declaration provides that, '[i]n order to protect the environment, the precautionary approach shall be widely applied by States according to their capabilities. Where there are threats of serious or irreversible damage, lack of full scientific certainty shall not be used as a reason for postponing cost-effective measures to prevent environmental degradation.': Rio Declaration on Environment and Development, UN Conference on Environment and Development (12 August 1992), UN Doc A/CONF.151/26 (vol I). On ISA implementation of the precautionary approach, see, generally, Jaeckel (2017) (n 65); ISA Secretariat, 'Implementing the Precautionary Approach to Activities in the Area' (9 January 2019) ISBA/25/C/8.

[77] Nodules Regulations, reg 32(1); Sulphides Regulations, reg 34(1); Cobalt Regulations, reg 34(1).

[78] Nodules Regulations, regs 31(6), 32; Sulphides Regulations, regs 33(6), 34; Cobalt Regulations, regs 33(6), 34. See also contractor environmental monitoring obligations in Nodules, Sulphides and Cobalt Regulations (s 5, standard clauses, fourth annex).

[79] Nodules Regulations, reg 31(6); Sulphides Regulations, reg 33(6); Cobalt Regulations, reg 33(6). For analysis, see Jaeckel (2017) (n 65) 211–214; ISA, 'Technical Study no 21: The Design of "Impact Reference Zones" and "Preservation Reference Zones" in Deep-sea Mining Contract Areas' (2017) <https://isa.org.jm/files/files/documents/Technical%20Study%2021%20-%20ebk_0.pdf>.

[80] See Nodules, Sulphides and Cobalt Regulations (s 5, standard clauses, fourth annex). For helpful analysis of EIA obligations in relation to deep seabed mining, see Jaeckel (2017) (n 65) 159–164; see also Alex G Oude Elferink, 'Environmental Impact Assessment in Areas beyond National Jurisdiction' (2012) 27 Int'l J Marine Coastal L 449; Jennifer M Durden and others, 'Environmental Impact Assessment Process for Deep-sea Mining in "the Area"' (2018) 87 Marine Pol'y 194.

[81] The current version of these recommendations is contained in ISBA/25/LTC/6/Rev.1.

[82] Nodules Regulations, reg 33; Sulphides Regulations, reg 35; Cobalt Regulations, reg 35. See also UNCLOS, arts 162(2)(w) and 165(2)(k).

[83] See discussion in Chapter 2, Section 2.3.2. See also Jaeckel (2017) (n 65) 152.

the ISA is developing detailed marine environmental protections.[84] They enshrine marine environmental protection as a fundamental principle of the regime (reg 2(e)–(g)). This end is also evident, for example, within the overriding duty to cooperate and exchange information (reg 3). Contractors must 'use their best endeavours'[85] to cooperate with each other, and with States Parties and national and international scientific bodies, to share environmental information and identify gaps in knowledge (reg 3(f)); and they must cooperate in the establishment of marine environmental monitoring programmes (reg 3(e)).

When applying for exploitation contracts, contractors must submit environmental data, including an environmental impact statement, an environmental management and monitoring plan and a closure plan which includes EIA components;[86] collectively, these are known as the *Environmental Plans*.[87] In addition, a contractor must provide an emergency response and contingency plan, including details of planned prevention of marine pollution and other marine environmental hazards.[88]

The DERs put in place a consultation process for the Environmental Plans, to allow members of the Authority, and interested stakeholders, to comment upon them (reg 11). Taking into account the results of this consultation process, the LTC has a key role in determining whether Environmental Plans provide for 'effective protection of the Marine Environment in accordance with the rules, regulations and procedures adopted by the Authority' (reg 13(4)(e), read with reg 11(5)), and ultimately recommending to the Council whether it should approve the plan of work (reg 15). Once a contractor has secured an exploitation contract, but before commencing commercial production,[89] it must lodge an environmental performance guarantee with the Authority (reg 26). Pursuant to this guarantee, the contractor undertakes to pay certain amounts in respect of anticipated costs of premature or final closure of mining sites, decommissioning, and post-closure monitoring and management of the mining site for residual environmental effects.[90]

[84] Previously, the ISA considered implementing dedicated environmental regulations covering the entire life cycle of deep seabed mining activities for all resources types: see tentative first draft in ISA, 'Discussion Paper on the Development and Drafting of Regulations on Exploitation for Mineral Resources in the Area (Environmental Matters)' (January 2017) <www.isa.org.jm/files/documents/EN/Regs/DraftExpl/DP-EnvRegsDraft25117.pdf>. It remains to be seen whether the ISA will progress this draft, as many aspects of it are now covered in the DERs: see discussion in ISA, 'Technical Study no 17: Towards an ISA Environmental Management Strategy for the Area' (2017) 1 <https://isa.org.jm/files/files/documents/berlinrep-web.pdf>.

[85] Stakeholders have criticised inclusion of this phrase as 'weaken[ing] the relevant obligations': see, e.g. ISBA/26/C/2, Annex, para 3.

[86] See DERs, regs 7(3)(d), 47 and Annex IV (environmental impact statement); regs 7(3)(h), 48 and Annex VII (environmental management and monitoring plan); and regs 7(3)(i), 59 and Annex VIII (closure plan).

[87] DERs, sch.

[88] DERs, reg 7(3)(e) and Annex V.

[89] For the definition of 'commercial production', see DERs, sch; see also previous discussion in Section 6.1 at n 12.

[90] DERs, reg 26(2) (providing, also, that further details and amounts are to be specified in guidelines, which the ISA has still to develop).

Overall, the DERs impose on contractors a range of marine environmental protection obligations, including to reduce the risk of certain incidents (such as incidents of serious marine environmental harm) 'as much as reasonably practicable' (reg 32), and to prevent and respond to these incidents (reg 33), including by notifying the Secretary-General (reg 34), together with ongoing environmental reporting obligations within contractor annual reports (reg 38(2)(g)).

Moreover, Part IV of the DERs is dedicated to protection and preservation of the marine environment. It imposes general obligations upon the Authority, sponsoring states and contractors to take steps to ensure 'effective protection for the Marine Environment from harmful effects in accordance with the rules, regulations and procedures adopted by the Authority in respect of activities in the Area', including by application of the precautionary approach, best available techniques and best environmental practices, and through use of best available scientific evidence (reg 44).[91] The contractor must maintain an environmental management system (details to be developed in guidelines) (reg 46). Part IV of the DERs includes information on the environmental impact statement (reg 47) and the environmental management and monitoring plan (regs 48, 51–52), provision for pollution control (reg 49), restrictions on mining discharges (reg 50) and requirements concerning the emergency response and contingency plan (reg 53).

Notably, Part IV of the DERs provides for establishment of an environmental compensation fund (reg 54), to assist in remediating environmental damage in the Area, and to be used to promote and fund certain research, education and training programmes (reg 55). This fund is to be financed partly through a percentage of fees and penalties paid to the Authority by contractors (reg 56).[92]

As the ISA has noted, the key challenge 'is to adopt a policy and regulatory framework for environmental management that achieves the effective protection of the marine environment, under circumstances of considerable scientific, technical and commercial uncertainty'.[93] Such a framework 'should be adaptive, practical and technically feasible'.[94] This is especially true within the exploitation context, which poses greater risks and challenges for environmental management.

As Section 6.3 will assess in more detail, the DERs leave some room for the regime to continue to evolve, particularly in environmental terms. For example, Regulation 1(5) provides that '[t]hese Regulations are supplemented by Standards

[91] For definitions of best available techniques, best environmental practices and best available scientific evidence, see DERs, sch. For analysis of these terms, see ISA Secretariat, 'Key Terms: Distinguishing between Good Industry Practice and Best Practices under the Draft Regulations on Exploitation of Mineral Resources in the Area' (15 January 2019) ISBA/25/C/11.

[92] By inclusion of this fund, the ISA seeks to address the potential liability gap identified by the Chamber in ITLOS AO, paras 203–205 (this potential gap could arise in circumstances where a contractor is liable for damage but unable to pay in full, and where the sponsoring state is not otherwise liable). On extent of contractor and sponsoring state liability, see Section 6.4.2.

[93] ISBA/24/A/10, para 14.

[94] ISBA/24/A/10, para 14.

and Guidelines ... as well as by further rules, regulations and procedures of the Authority, in particular on the protection and preservation of the Marine Environment'.[95] Additionally, the DERs, once adopted, are subject to future ISA review (reg 107), including in light of 'improved knowledge or technology' (reg 107(2)). These functions, assisted by the ISA's ongoing monitoring of the impacts of deep seabed mining activities, may allow the Mining Code to deploy an adaptive management approach, facilitating adjustment of the regime to address emerging challenges.[96]

Overall, the ISA has made substantial progress in developing its environmental mandate, by creating a detailed regime for marine environmental protection in relation to exploration activities in the Area. This goes some way towards operationalising the common heritage's marine environmental protection component. However, as set out above, the regime applicable to the more invasive exploitation phase remains a work in progress, requiring further development to ensure sufficient environmental protection.

There is already a wealth of critique and commentary concerning the ongoing development of the ISA's marine environmental protection regime.[97] Areas that have been highlighted as requiring further work include: full operationalisation of an ecosystems-based, spatial management approach for deep seabed mining, which could involve implementation of further REMPs; development of overall environmental standards for each resource type; and adoption of clear definitions of serious harm, and distinct thresholds for determining acceptable harmful effects.[98] In addition, further work is required to achieve a suitable EIA process for deep seabed mining exploitation.[99] There is also room for improvement in clarifying the

[95] See, further, DERs, regs 45 (development of environmental standards), 94 (adoption of standards) and 95 (issuance of guidelines).

[96] See, e.g. Durden and others (n 80) 195 (defining adaptive management as 'a deliberate process of staging an activity with planned monitoring, followed by a review of the monitoring results to improve understanding of the environmental impacts of the activity and the re-evaluation and alteration of the activity for the future'): ISA, 'Technical Study no 17' (n 84) 4–5, 63–68. cf critique in Aline Jaeckel, 'Deep Seabed Mining and Adaptive Management: The Procedural Challenges for the International Seabed Authority' (2016) 70 Marine Pol'y 205, 210.

[97] See, e.g. Kristina M Gjerde, 'Challenges to Protecting the Marine Environment beyond National Jurisdiction' (2012) 27 Int'l J Marine Coastal L 839; ISA, 'Technical Study no 17' (n 84); Aline Jaeckel, Kristina M Gjerde and Jeff A Ardron, 'Conserving the Common Heritage of Humankind – Options for the Deep-seabed Mining Regime' (2017) 78 Marine Pol'y 150; Jaeckel (2017) (n 65); Durden and others (n 80); Willaert (2020c) (n 41).

[98] See, e.g. Jaeckel (2015) (n 65); Lisa A Levin and others, 'Defining "Serious Harm" to the Marine Environment in the Context of Deep Seabed Mining' 74 (2016) Marine Pol'y 245; ISA, 'Technical Study no 17' (n 84) 2–3, 10, 13–15, 43–47; Jaeckel (2017) (n 65) 189, 258; Jaeckel, Gjerde and Ardron (2017) (n 97) 150–151; Kristina Gjerde, 'Deep Seabed Mining in the Area: Emerging Legal, Environmental and Economic Challenges' (Brodies Lectures on Environmental Law, University of Edinburgh, Scotland, 19 March 2018).

[99] See, e.g. ISA, 'Technical Study no 17' (n 84) 3–4, 54–63; Jaeckel (2017) (n 65) 240ff; Durden and others (n 80) 200–201.

'ambiguous' relationship between the REMP for the CCZ and the binding obligations upon contractors operating within that region.[100]

As various commentators have acknowledged, to implement its environmental powers fully, the ISA would require enhanced capabilities and increased resources. At present, much of the review of environmental matters falls to the LTC, which has a heavy workload and limited dedicated environmental expertise.[101] To address this, the ISA could benefit from a new organ dedicated to environmental matters, or a specialist environmental unit within one of its existing organs.[102] The Council already raised many of these difficulties when requesting the LTC to further elaborate the DERs.[103] As a step in the direction of addressing this, the Secretary-General highlighted, in February 2019, that the Secretariat had been 'strengthened' with the addition of an environmental management team, focused particularly on the development of REMPs.[104]

Another significant critique of the ISA's marine environmental protection mandate is in systemic terms. When exploitation begins, in what manner will the ISA's regulatory regime maintain consistency with other systems and rules, including the developing regime for conservation and sustainable use of BBNJ? There is no straightforward answer to this question. A notable example of apparent system conflict occurred in relation to Poland's application to explore for polymetallic sulphides on the Mid-Atlantic Ridge. In a move that some commentators have criticised, the ISA approved Poland's application in 2017,[105] notwithstanding the fact that the planned exploration area included parts of the Lost City site (a hydrothermal vent field with unique features, designated as an 'ecologically and biologically significant area' under the Convention on Biological Diversity 1992[106]).

[100] Jaeckel (2017) (n 65) 256; as Jaeckel notes, it is 'difficult to judge' whether a REMP 'could create new obligations for existing contractors' (256–257). In the exploitation context, the ISA has been considering what consequences REMPs should have: see, e.g. ISA Secretariat, 'Relationship between the Draft Regulations on Exploitation of Mineral Resources in the Area and Regional Environmental Management Plans' (20 December 2018) ISBA/25/C/4.

[101] See, e.g. ISA, 'Technical Study no 17' (n 84) 31; Jaeckel (2017) (n 65) 289ff; Durden and others (n 80) 198, 200; Gjerde (2018) (n 98).

[102] For similar suggestions, see ISA, 'Technical Study no 17' (n 84) 2; Durden and others (n 80) 198, 200–201; Gjerde (2018) (n 98). See also Jaeckel (2017) (n 65) 294–297 (suggesting creation of an ISA Environmental Commission).

[103] ISBA/24/C/8/Add.1, Annex I, para 2ff.

[104] Michael Lodge, ISA Secretary-General, 'Opening Remarks to the ISA Council' (25 February 2019) at 1 <https://isa.org.jm/files/files/documents/councilopen_0.pdf>.

[105] ISA Council, 'Decision of the Council of the ISA Relating to an Application by the Government of Poland for Approval of a Plan of Work for Exploration for Polymetallic Sulphides' (10 August 2017) ISBA/23/C/14.

[106] Convention on Biological Diversity (opened for signature 5 June 1992, entered into force 29 December 1993) 1760 UNTS 79. For details on Lost City's designation and status, together with criticism of the ISA's approach, see letter from Inger Andersen, Director General of the International Union for Conservation of Nature to the ISA (12 March 2018) <www.iucn.org/sites/dev/files/let_mr_michael_lodge_isa-jm-2018-03-12-f.pdf>.

Clearly, there is room for improvement in creating a more integrated ISA approach, taking greater account of other systems for marine environmental protection.[107] The ISA is cognisant of this. Mindful of the risk of fragmentation in the application of marine environmental protections, the first of the ISA's strategic directions is to '[r]ealize the role of the Authority in a global context'. This includes enhancing its 'strategic alliances and partnerships with relevant subregional, regional and global organizations with a view to more effective cooperation in the conservation and sustainable use of ocean resources', and working to '[s]trengthen cooperation and coordination with other relevant international organizations and stakeholders' to protect competing interests in the marine environment.[108]

Many stakeholder comments on the DERs include detailed critique of environmental aspects, and the ISA is working to develop a final version in light of these concerns.[109] For example, to ameliorate the systemic critique, the Deep Ocean Stewardship Initiative suggests that the ISA's process for approval of a plan of work for exploitation 'could include a requirement for the applicant to provide a statement confirming whether the area(s) under consideration have received specific attention by another international organization or treaty regime', in order to avoid a repeat of the conflict concerning Lost City.[110]

Given the emergent nature of the deep seabed mining industry, new environmental challenges are certain to arise, particularly as the industry moves towards the more challenging exploitation phase of activities. Therefore, a key factor in the regulatory regime's ability to secure the common heritage (in terms of both marine environmental protection and also benefit sharing) will be the extent to which it can evolve to address new challenges. The following section will now consider this.

[107] On the challenges of attaining an integrated framework for marine environmental protection at international law more generally, see James Harrison, *Saving the Oceans through Law: The International Legal Framework for the Protection of the Marine Environment* (OUP 2017). For an overview of bodies with overlapping areas of interest with the ISA, see ISA, 'Secretary-General Annual Report' (2020) 29 <https://isa.org.jm/files/files/documents/ISA_Annual_Report_2020_ENG.pdf>.

[108] ISBA/24/A/10, 8–9. The ISA has entered into memorandums of understanding with various bodies, available on the ISA website <www.isa.org.jm/legal-documents>. cf UNCLOS, arts 162(2)(f), 169.

[109] See overview of various environmental concerns in ISBA/26/C/2, especially at paras 18–22 and Annex, paras 4, 21, 23, 26–32. For underlying stakeholder critique, see, particularly, comments by Advisory Committee on Protection of the Sea, Deep-Ocean Stewardship Initiative, Deep Sea Conservation Coalition and the Pew Charitable Trusts, respectively, in ISA, 'Compilation of the Proposals and Observations sent by other Member States of the Authority, Observers and Stakeholders on the Draft Regulations in Response to Paragraphs 7 and 8 of ISBA/25/C/37' (January 2020) <https://isa.org.jm/files/files/documents/comments-jan2020a_final.pdf>.

[110] Deep-Ocean Stewardship Initiative, 'Commentary on Draft Regulations on Exploitation of Mineral Resources in the Area' (October 2019) at 6 <https://isa.org.jm/files/files/documents/DOSI%20Comment%20on%20ISA%20Draft%20Exploitation%20Regulations%20October%202019.pdf>.

6.3 Developing the Regime through Ongoing Regulatory Adaptability

The ISA is developing the common heritage's benefit-sharing and marine environmental protection aspects through a remarkable iterative process involving stakeholder participation across the international community. In that sense, the UNCLOS framework provides a 'shared surface'[111] on which participants (such as the ISA and its constituent organs, States Parties, observer states, ISA contractors (including corporate actors) and civil society more generally) are working together to devise a regulatory regime which aims to achieve common heritage ends while remaining viable in practice. Perhaps the most striking feature of this ongoing regulatory development is the extent to which the Mining Code aims to retain flexibility, and an ability to adapt and grow in response to emerging challenges and difficulties. It does so via two main mediums.

Firstly, the ISA must keep its regulations under periodic review, and can amend the Mining Code in light of developments and new challenges.[112] Contractor consent is required for contract revision, so while regulatory amendments bind *future* contractors, *existing* contractors continue to be bound by the rules in force at the time that they entered the contract.[113] The contractor's right to security of tenure underpins this need for consent.[114] As Le Gurun describes, this right of security of tenure 'is so strong that it prevails over the automatic entry into force of amendments to regulations in respect of existing contracts at the time of such amendments'.[115] This has resulted in 'contractors that obtained their respective exploration contracts in different years [being] bound by different clauses'.[116] For example, in 2013, when the ISA introduced an annual overhead fee by inserting

[111] Martti Koskenniemi, 'What is International Law for?' in Malcolm D Evans (ed), *International Law* (5th edn, OUP 2018) 46.

[112] See, e.g. general review powers at Nodules Regulations, reg 42; Sulphides Regulations, reg 44; Cobalt Regulations, reg 44; DERs, reg 107. See also UNCLOS, art 165(2)(g). See, further, Jaeckel (2017) (n 65) 150, 253–254 (for examples of previous regulatory amendments). See also this book's further discussion in Chapter 7, at text to nn 35–36.

[113] Nodules Regulations, reg 42(3)–(4); Sulphides Regulations, reg 44(3)–(4); Cobalt Regulations, reg 44(3)–(4) (providing that regulatory amendments 'shall be without prejudice to the rights conferred on any contractor with the Authority under the provisions of a contract entered into pursuant to these Regulations in force at the time of any such amendment' (para 3), and subjecting contract revision to section 24 of the standard clauses to the contract (para 4), requiring contractor consent for contract revision, including in circumstances of regulatory amendment (Nodules, Sulphides and Cobalt Regulations, fourth annex, s 24.2)); see also UNCLOS, Annex III, art 19(2) (also requiring contractor consent for revision).

[114] The contractor's right to security of tenure is reflected in: UNCLOS, art 153(6) and Annex III, art 16; Nodules Regulations, reg 24(1); Sulphides Regulations, reg 26(1); Cobalt Regulations, reg 26(1); s 2.1 of the standard clauses in the fourth annex of each of these regulations; DERs, reg 18(4), Annex X, s 4.1.

[115] Gwenaëlle Le Gurun, 'Annex III' in Proelss Commentary 2235. See also Jule Siegfried, 'Article 153' (ibid) 1089.

[116] Jaeckel (2017) (n 65) 150.

new standard clauses into exploration contracts,[117] in order to apply this fee to existing contracts, the ISA had to seek contract revision on the basis of contractor consent.[118] Nevertheless, notwithstanding the potential for divergence in contract terms, the ISA's regulatory adaptability 'clearly demonstrates the flexibility incorporated into the regulatory design, to ensure the seabed mining regime develops alongside new realities in ocean sciences, mining standards, social values, and international (environmental) law'.[119]

Interestingly, although the exploration regulations emphasise the importance of contractor consent to revised regulatory terms, the Chamber of ITLOS has hinted that previous versions of regulations should be interpreted in light of developments to the regulatory regime. When comparing the original version of the Nodules Regulations (adopted in 2000),[120] with the Sulphides Regulations (adopted in 2010 with enhanced standards of environmental protection), the Chamber indicated that '[i]n the absence of a specific reason to the contrary, it may be held that the Nodules Regulations should be interpreted in light of the development of the law, as evidenced by the subsequent adoption of the Sulphides Regulations'.[121]

Perhaps influenced by this, the DERs suggest a more nuanced approach to the impact of regulatory amendment on existing contracts. On the basis of the current version, section 3.3(a) of the draft standard clauses to the exploitation contract appear to support an ambulatory approach, which would allow the contract to keep pace with updated regulatory requirements by requiring the contractor to '[c]omply with the regulations, as well as other Rules of the Authority, *as amended from time to time*, and the decisions of the relevant organs of the Authority'.[122] Moreover, the 'Rules of the Authority', which the contractor for exploitation must comply with (as per section 17.1 of the draft standard clauses[123]), are defined as including 'these regulations and other rules, regulations and procedures of the Authority as may be adopted *from time to time*'.[124]

[117] See ISBA/19/A/12 (inserting s 10.5 and 10.6 into the standard clauses to exploration contracts contained in fourth annex of the Nodules, Sulphides and Cobalt Regulations).

[118] By the time of the Secretary-General's annual report on the status of exploration contracts in 2017, all existing contractors had either accepted the new fee, incorporated it into the terms of their extended contracts and/or begun to pay the fee: see ISA Council, 'Status of Contracts for Exploration and Related Matters – Report of the Secretary-General' (5 June 2017) ISBA/23/C/7, Annex II. See also Gwenaëlle Le Gurun, 'Annex III' in Proelss Commentary 2235, 2260.

[119] Jaeckel (2017) (n 65) 150.

[120] ISBA/6/A/18.

[121] ITLOS AO, para 137.

[122] DERs, Annex X, s 3.3(a) (emphasis added). cf s 13.2(b) of the standard clauses contained as fourth annex to Nodules, Sulphides and Cobalt Regulations, which does not include an ambulatory approach, providing instead that the contractor undertakes '[t]o comply with the applicable obligations created by the provisions of the Convention, the rules, regulations and procedures of the Authority and the decisions of the relevant organs of the Authority'.

[123] DERs, Annex X, s 17.1.

[124] DERs, sch (emphasis added).

Some stakeholders have criticised this approach, arguing that it would undermine the stability of the exploitation contract.[125] NORI has warned that 'this essentially removes the certainty of the [c]ontract because it compels the [c]ontractor to comply with unknown rules and regulations that the Authority may bring in to force any time after the [c]ontract is signed'.[126] It is also unclear how the proposed ambulatory approach would comport with the exploitation contract's grant of security of tenure to the contractor and the stated process for contract revision, neither of which are expressly subject to regulatory amendment.[127] Nevertheless, the ambulatory approach of the standard clauses to exploitation contracts, as reflected in section 3.3(a), does imply that there is some room for an evolutionary interpretation of a contractor's regulatory requirements, perhaps allowing them to be read 'in light of the development' of any new regulations (although stopping short of revision of a contract, as such).[128]

Secondly, and equally significantly, the ISA envisages that the exploitation regime will be augmented by standards and guidelines.[129] In practice, such instruments may provide crucial technical or administrative detail for contractors to enhance the operation of the regime, and can be adapted on a flexible basis.

By comparison, in the exploration context, a similar end is achieved through the role of LTC recommendations in augmenting the exploration regime.[130] The LTC has exclusive competence to issue recommendations, and it must merely report them to the Council.[131] The Council, in turn, can request their modification or withdrawal, but cannot annul or amend them directly.[132] LTC recommendations

[125] See overview in ISBA/26/C/2, para 13 (noting that stakeholder comments emphasised the 'importance of protecting contractors' rights and ensuring the stability of exploitation contracts and of the regulations ... with concerns expressed that the current text of the regulations allowed the Authority to change the regulations and that certain provisions defeated the principle that the contract may be revised only with the consent of the contractor and the Authority').

[126] NORI, 'Comments by Nauru Ocean Resources Inc on the Draft Regulations on Exploitation of Mineral Resources in the Area issued by the LTC in 2019' (October 2019) at 2 <https://isa.org.jm/files/files/documents/2019-10-15%20NORI%20Comments%20on%20Draft%20Exploitation%20Regs.pdf>. See also comments by Japan, recommending revision of the DERs to ensure that 'any amendments to the Regulations, especially those which have significant negative impact on the viability, shall not be applied retroactively to the detriment of the [c]ontractors that have already signed an exploitation contract with the Authority': Japan, 'Comments on the Draft Regulations on Exploitation of Mineral Resources in the Area (ISBA/25/C/WP.1)' (October 2019) 25 <https://isa.org.jm/files/files/documents/201910%20Japan%27s%20comments%20on%20draft%20regulations.pdf>.

[127] See DERs, Annex X, ss 4.1 (security of tenure) and 16 (contract revision).

[128] cf ITLOS AO, para 137.

[129] See DERs, regs 94 (adoption of standards) and 95 (issuance of guidelines); see also regs 45 (development of environmental standards) and 65(1) (guidelines concerning administration and management of royalties). See also discussion in ISA Secretariat, 'Draft Regulations on Exploitation of Mineral Resources in the Area – Note by the Secretariat' (15 May 2018) ISBA/24/LTC/6, para 18.

[130] Nodules Regulations, regs 31(3), 39; Sulphides Regulations, regs 33(3), 41; Cobalt Regulations, regs 33(3), 41. See also UNCLOS, art 165(2)(e) (providing LTC with the general power to 'make recommendations to the Council on the protection of the marine environment, taking into account the views of recognized experts in that field').

[131] Nodules Regulations, reg 39; Sulphides Regulations, reg 41; Cobalt Regulations, reg 41.

[132] Nodules Regulations, reg 39(2); Sulphides Regulations, reg 41(2); Cobalt Regulations, reg 41(2). On this, see James Harrison, *Making the Law of the Sea* (CUP 2011) 142.

are not legally binding on contractors, but they do have an ambulatory effect. Contractors must 'observe, as far as reasonably practicable' the LTC's recommendations, as issued 'from time to time'.[133] The LTC has issued various recommendations, including on environmental matters.[134] Despite their non-binding nature, LTC recommendations 'form the basis of an acceptable code of conduct for contractors'.[135] In practice, 'they carry significant weight', and one of their key benefits is that the LTC can develop them on a flexible basis, allowing them to keep pace with changing circumstances.[136] For example, the environmental recommendations by the LTC are 'kept under review regularly to keep abreast with scientific and technological advances'.[137]

Building on this approach, the DERs envisage a significant role for both standards and guidelines.[138] Standards are intended to address technical matters and performance and process requirements, including marine environmental protection.[139] For example, contractors must comply with the Authority's standards in relation to matters of safety, labour and health (reg 30(2)), pollution control (reg 49) and review of activities under a plan of work (reg 58(2)). Standards will be of particular importance in relation to environmental matters, as reflected in regulation 45, which provides for the adoption of environmental standards, including in relation to environmental quality objectives, monitoring procedures and mitigation measures.

The Council is responsible for approving standards (reg 94(2)), on the basis of LTC recommendations, which must take into account views by experts, stakeholders and 'relevant existing internationally accepted standards' (reg 94(1)). Standards are to be 'legally binding' on contractors and the ISA, and they will be subject to periodic review, which may lead to revision 'in the light of improved knowledge or technology' (reg 94(4)). Given their binding but adaptable nature, the use of standards is likely to be an important mechanism through which the exploitation regime can continue to adapt to new environmental and technical challenges.

[133] See Nodules, Sulphides and Cobalt Regulations (s 13.2(e), standard clauses, fourth annex); cf s 13.2(b) (discussed at n 122 above), pursuant to which ISA regulations are binding on contractors, but only to the extent that they were in force at the time the contract was concluded.

[134] See, e.g. ISBA/25/LTC/6/Rev.1. For an overview of other LTC recommendations, see Jaeckel (2017) (n 65) 151–152; Gwenaëlle Le Gurun, 'Annex III' in Proelss Commentary 2249.

[135] Satya Nandan, 'Administering the Mineral Resources of the Deep Seabed' in David Freestone, Richard Barnes and David Ong (eds), *Law of the Sea – Progress and Prospects* (OUP 2006) 88.

[136] Jaeckel (2017) (n 65) 151, see, generally, 150–152, 254–255; see, further, Harrison (2011) (n 132) 141 (describing recommendations as 'an important indication of what is expected of contractors by the Authority', especially given that they are drafted by the same body that initially assesses contractor compliance with its obligations, which 'could influence a contractor in deciding whether or not to abide by the recommendations').

[137] Gwenaëlle Le Gurun, 'Annex III' in Proelss Commentary 2249. See also Jaeckel (2017) (n 65) 255.

[138] See, e.g. DERs, reg 1(5), providing that the DERs 'are supplemented by Standards and Guidelines'.

[139] DERs, reg 94(1) and sch.

Guidelines are the ISA's other intended tool for managing exploitation activities. The LTC plans to issue guidelines to provide guidance on technical and administrative matters to support implementation of the exploitation regulations.[140] The LTC is empowered to issue guidelines 'from time to time', taking stakeholder views into account, and they are to be kept under review 'in the light of improved knowledge or information'.[141] Unlike standards, guidelines are not legally binding, although they can still play an important role in providing guidance to contractors on matters of a technical and administrative nature.[142] Guidelines also have an important role to play concerning the detail of various marine environmental aspects.[143] Moreover, regulation 65(1) envisages that the Secretary-General may issue guidelines 'in respect of the administration and management of royalties'.

The intended far-reaching role for standards and guidelines within the exploitation process has met with comment, and some controversy.[144] For example, private corporate contractors, such as NORI and GSR, have criticised the intended role of standards. NORI has objected to the binding nature of standards, arguing that standards and regulations are 'effectively the same', and recommending that 'the process for adopting [s]tandards should go through a rigorous review process in which [c]ontractors are heavily involved to ensure that the [s]tandards are indeed commercially viable and practicably achievable'.[145]

140 DERs, reg 95(1) and sch.

141 DERs, reg 95(1) and (3), respectively; see also reg 95(2), providing that guidelines do not need Council approval, although the Council can request modification or withdrawal of guidelines (in a process similar to the adoption process for LTC recommendations; on which, see text to nn 131–132 above).

142 For example, the DERs envisage guidelines assisting with preparation of feasibility studies ahead of commercial production (reg 25(1)), development of safety management systems (reg 30(6)) and concerning various contractor obligations, such as those relating to insurance (reg 36), training commitments (reg 37), reporting requirements (reg 38), modification of plans of work (reg 57(2)), review of activities under plans of work (reg 58(2)) and electronic monitoring of mining vessels (reg 102).

143 For example, the DERs provide that guidelines are to set out 'the required form and amount' of the contractor's environmental performance guarantee (reg 26(2)), and contractors must act consistently with guidelines in carrying out exploitation activities with reasonable regard for other activities in the marine environment (reg 31(1)), reducing the risk of incidents (reg 32), maintaining environmental management systems (reg 46(1)), preparing environmental impact statements (reg 47(3)(d)) and ensuring pollution control (reg 49). Guidelines will also address contractor environmental management and monitoring plans (reg 48(3)(c), 51(c), 52), emergency response and contingency plans (reg 53) and closure plans (reg 59(4)).

144 See, e.g. ISBA/26/C/2, para 39 for an overview of stakeholder comments concerning standards and guidelines. Regs 94 and 95 (addressing standards and guidelines, respectively) are two of the most annotated provisions of the DERs, in the collated version of Council Member drafting suggestions in ISBA/26/C/CRP.1. See also critique in Code Project, 'Fifth Report, Part One: Small Papers on Big Issues' (*Pew Charitable Trusts*, 1 June 2019) 8–9 <www.pewtrusts.org/-/media/assets/2019/08/fifth_report_of_the_code_project_p1.pdf> (calling for greater clarity on the consequences of non-compliance with standards, and arguing that the DERs 'move some important aspects of the regulatory regime away from Standards and into Guidelines', which could lead to 'imprudent' over-reliance on voluntary guidelines).

145 NORI (n 126) 11. Similarly, see GSR, 'Comments by Global Sea Mineral Resources to the Draft Regulations on Exploitation of Mineral Resources in the Area – ISBA/25/C/WP.1' (October 2019) at 2 <https://isa.org.jm/files/files/documents/1510-2019-GSR-Comments_to_ISBA-25-C-WP.1.pdf>.

The ISA has noted the need to strike a balance between the regulatory regime's flexibility to adapt and the competing desire for standards and guidelines to 'remain stable and avoid frequent changes in contents, so as not to increase arbitrarily the burden on contractors'.[146] At present, the ISA is engaging with stakeholders further, in order to develop standards and guidelines for the exploitation stage.[147] Although there is much work to be done, standards and guidelines look set to play an important role in ensuring that the regulatory regime remains sufficiently flexible, while aiming to give contractors an appropriate level of regulatory certainty and predictability.

Finally, in addition to these two important mechanisms, there are certain other means by which a mining contract can evolve in light of changing circumstances. For example, the Mining Code's periodic review process of the implementation of a plan of work, and the extension process for mining contracts may both offer opportunities for 'other kinds of revision', taking account of regulatory developments within the regime.[148]

Turning to the first of these methods, the Mining Code provides for a process of periodic review in relation to implementation of a contractor's plan of work. The exploration regulations require the Secretary-General and the contractor to undertake this periodic review 'jointly', on a five-yearly basis.[149] This joint review may result in changes to the contractor's plan of work. In light of the review, the contractor is to 'indicate its programme of activities for the following five-year period, making such adjustments to its previous programme of activities as are necessary'.[150]

As part of this process, the Secretary-General reports to the LTC and the Council, including in relation to contractor compliance with obligations of marine environmental protection.[151] The DERs incorporate a process of periodic review of

[146] ISA Council, 'Statement by the President of the Council on the Work of the Council During the First Part of the Twenty-fifth Session' (18 March 2019) ISBA/25/C/17, para 16.

[147] See, e.g. LTC recommendations in relation to development of standards and guidelines in ISA LTC, 'Report of the Chair of the Legal and Technical Commission on the Work of the Commission at the Second Part of its Twenty-fifth Session' (11 July 2019) ISBA/25/C/19/Add.1, Annex. See also the recent stakeholder consultations: ISA, 'Stakeholder Consultations on Draft Standards and Guidelines to Support the Implementation of the Draft Regulations for Exploitation of Mineral Resources in the Area' <www.isa.org.jm/stakeholder-consultations-draft-standards-and-guidelines-support-implementation-draft-regulations>.

[148] Gwenaëlle Le Gurun, 'Annex III' in Proelss Commentary 2258.

[149] Nodules Regulations, reg 28(1); Sulphides Regulations, reg 30(1); Cobalt Regulations, reg 30(1). For an overview of this process in action, see ISA Council, 'Status of Contracts for Exploration and Related Matters, including Information on the Periodic Review of the Implementation of Approved Plans of Work for Exploration – Report of the Secretary-General' (17 December 2019) ISBA/26/C/4, paras 4–18.

[150] Nodules Regulations, reg 28(2); Sulphides Regulations, reg 30(2); Cobalt Regulations, reg 30(2). See also Nodules, Sulphides and Cobalt Regulations (s 4.4, standard clauses, fourth annex); see, further, s 4.3 of the standard clauses, permitting contractors to adjust their programmes of activities at any time, with ISA consent.

[151] Nodules Regulations, reg 28(3); Sulphides Regulations, reg 30(3); Cobalt Regulations, reg 30(3).

contractor activities under the plan of work, in similar terms.[152] This process provides for joint review of activities by the Secretary-General and the contractor, and discussion as to whether 'any modifications to the Plan of Work are necessary or desirable'.[153] On the basis of this review process, a contractor may seek to amend its plan of work.[154] Although periodic review is a joint process, requiring adjustments to the contractor's plan of work to be 'agreed by both parties',[155] the process does incorporate a degree of flexibility into mining contracts, offering an opportunity for adjustment in light of changing conditions.[156]

The possibility of extension of a mining contract provides further opportunity for the ISA to agree new terms with the contractor, particularly in light of any regulatory updates. The original Convention regime did not provide a fixed time limit for duration of mining contracts.[157] However, the 1994 Agreement set a fifteen-year term for exploration contracts, with the possibility of extension.[158] This is captured in the exploration regulations, which allow for fifteen-year duration, subject to extensions for five-year periods.[159] The standard clauses to the exploration contract make clear that a contract extension will be subject to newly agreed terms.[160]

Interestingly, when addressing duration of exploitation operations, UNCLOS specified that they should be of 'sufficient duration to permit commercial extraction of minerals' and should include 'a reasonable time period for construction of commercial-scale mining and processing systems'; however, 'the total duration of exploitation ... should also be short enough to give the Authority an opportunity to amend the terms and conditions of the plan of work at the time it considers renewal in accordance with the rules, regulations and procedures which it has adopted subsequent to approving the plan of work'.[161] This gives a clear indication that the renewal process was always intended to be an opportunity to revise

152 See DERs, reg 58 (providing for review of contractor activities under the plan of work at five-yearly intervals, or due to certain changes of circumstances listed in reg 58(1), including, at reg 58(1)(f) and (g), changes in best available techniques and best available scientific evidence, respectively.

153 DERs, reg 58(1).

154 The process for making material changes to a plan of work is provided in DERs, reg 58(3) (see also regs 25 and 57 for other means by which contractors may seek to modify plans of work).

155 Gwenaëlle Le Gurun, 'Annex III' in Proelss Commentary 2259. See also Jaeckel (2017) (n 65) 256 (noting that the periodic review process 'does not allow the ISA to *require* the contractor to incorporate certain environmental standards into the next programme of activities').

156 See, e.g. ISA, 'Technical Study no 17' (n 84) 4 (noting that periodic review of the plan of work may have value as 'an additional tool ... through which to consider new knowledge, information and experiences', particularly in environmental terms).

157 cf UNCLOS, Annex III, art 17(2)(b), which merely set out various considerations in relation to contract duration.

158 1994 Agreement, Annex, s 1(9).

159 Nodules Regulations, reg 26; Sulphides Regulations, reg 28; Cobalt Regulations, reg 28; see also Nodules, Sulphides and Cobalt Regulations (s 3, standard clauses, fourth annex). Procedural details of this extension process were set by Council decision ISBA/21/C/19*.

160 See s 3.2 of the standard clauses (contained as fourth annex to Nodules, Sulphides and Cobalt Regulations), which provides that contracts may be extended 'on such terms and conditions as the Authority and the Contractor may then agree in accordance with the Regulations'.

161 UNCLOS, Annex III, art 17(2)(b)(iii).

contract conditions. The DERs reflect this, providing for a thirty-year term for exploitation contracts, with the possibility of renewals of ten years each, on the basis of revised terms.[162]

On the whole, as this section has addressed, the ISA's regulatory regime is 'not static'.[163] Rather, it contains an inherent flexibility in order to keep pace with new challenges and developments in the nascent deep seabed mining industry which it regulates. As Chapter 7 will consider further, the ISA aims to strike a balance between retaining sufficient regulatory flexibility and ensuring an appropriate level of stability and predictability to allow contractors to conduct mining activities.[164] Before turning to that consideration, the following section will address the means by which the ISA implements the regulatory regime against corporate contractors.

6.4 Securing the Regime's Substantive Aspects in Practice: Implementation, Responsibility and Enforcement against Corporate Actors

6.4.1 ISA Implementation Powers

In order to secure the material aspects of the common heritage principle, the deep seabed mining regime relies on robust mechanisms for implementation, responsibility and dispute resolution, which the following sections will address. Turning firstly to matters of implementation, the ISA is endowed with broad oversight and enforcement powers concerning deep seabed mining activities, including those conducted by corporate contractors.[165] The Council plays a particular role in this regard, as it is empowered to 'exercise control over activities in the Area' in accordance with the UNCLOS regulatory regime.[166]

Key aspects of Council powers of control include the power to supervise and coordinate implementation of Part XI of UNCLOS, and to invite the Assembly to consider instances of non-compliance; to issue emergency orders, including orders for suspension or adjustment of deep seabed activities to prevent serious harm

[162] DERs, reg 20(1), (7)–(8) and see also Annex X, s 9 (especially s 9.3, which provides that the contract 'shall be renewed on the terms and conditions of the standard exploitation contract that are in effect on the date that the Council approves the renewal application').

[163] Jaeckel (2017) (n 65) 187.

[164] See analysis in Chapter 7, Section 7.2.3.

[165] See, e.g. UNCLOS, arts 153(4)–(5) (ISA to exercise control over activities to ensure compliance, including by taking measures to induce compliance, and by inspecting installations), 157 (general and incidental powers); Annex III, art 18 (penalties upon contractors); 1994 Agreement, Annex, s 1(1). See also previous discussion in Chapter 4, at text to nn 90–93, 165. See the Secretary-General's overview of ISA compliance powers in ISA Council, 'Report by the Secretary-General – Information Relating to Compliance by Contractors with Plans of Work for Exploration' (16 January 2018) ISBA/24/C/4. See, further, Jaeckel (2017) (n 65) 106–108, 272–277, 286–302 (on ISA monitoring and compliance powers).

[166] UNCLOS, art 162(2)(l).

to the marine environment; and to disapprove exploitation applications due to serious risk of environmental harm.[167] In exercising each of these functions, the Council can seek LTC assistance. For example, upon Council request, the LTC may supervise activities in the Area.[168] In addition, the LTC may make recommendations to the Council concerning matters such as: establishment of a monitoring programme for marine environmental pollution from activities in the Area; issuance of emergency orders; or disapproval of areas for exploitation, to prevent serious marine environmental harm.[169] The LTC is also empowered to prepare assessments concerning the environmental implications of activities in the Area, giving it an important role in the EIA process.[170]

Significantly, the Council may establish mechanisms to direct and supervise an inspections team in monitoring and inspecting deep seabed mining activities, in order to ensure compliance with the UNCLOS regime and ISA contractual terms.[171] Ultimately, in cases of contractor non-compliance, the Council may commence dispute resolution proceedings, on behalf of the ISA, at the Chamber (as Section 6.4.3 will address).[172]

The Authority's implementation powers are further fleshed out by its regulatory regime. For example, as explored in Section 6.3, the Mining Code makes provision for the Authority's periodic review of a contractor's plan of work for exploration, which allows the Authority to monitor contractor conduct, particularly in relation to marine environmental protection.[173] Equally, the standard clauses to exploration contracts oblige contractors to make annual reports to the Authority, and permit the Authority to inspect the contractor's vessels and installations to monitor compliance, and to suspend, terminate or apply penalties in respect of a contract, in certain circumstances.[174]

On the basis of the current version, the DERs will further extend and tailor the ISA's supervisory powers to address the exploitation phase of mining. The draft includes annual reporting requirements (reg 38); joint periodic review of plans of

[167] UNCLOS, art 162(2)(a), (2)(w) and (2)(x), respectively. On emergency orders in relation to exploration activities, see Nodules Regulations, reg 33; Sulphides Regulations, reg 35; Cobalt Regulations, reg 35.

[168] UNCLOS, art 165(2)(c).

[169] UNCLOS, art 165(2)(h), (k)–(l). On LTC powers concerning marine environmental monitoring recommendations, see also Nodules Regulations, reg 31; Sulphides Regulations, reg 33; Cobalt Regulations, reg 33.

[170] UNCLOS, art 165(2)(d).

[171] UNCLOS, art 162(2)(z); see also art 165(2)(m) (allowing the LTC to make recommendations to the Council in this regard).

[172] UNCLOS, art 162(2)(u); see also art 165(2)(i) (which permits the LTC to recommend to the Council that such proceedings should be instituted).

[173] Nodules Regulations, reg 28; Sulphides Regulations, reg 30; Cobalt Regulations, reg 30.

[174] See ss 10, 14 and 21, respectively, of the standard clauses (contained as fourth annex to the Nodules, Sulphides and Cobalt Regulations). For analysis of grounds of lawful termination, see Chapter 7, text to nn 30–31. See also discussion in Markos Karavias, *Corporate Obligations under International Law* (OUP 2013) 148–149 (suspension and termination of contract), 154–155 (monetary penalties).

work by the contractor and the ISA (reg 58); powers to audit and inspect contractor records (reg 75); powers to impose monetary penalties, including in respect of improper financial conduct by the contractor (reg 80); together with broad powers to inspect contractor offices, vessels and installations and to issue instructions to remedy contractor violations (regs 96-100). Importantly, given the sheer size of the Area, the ISA intends to institute a remote monitoring system, pursuant to which certain details of mining activities will be recorded electronically (reg 102). Ultimately, the Secretary-General may issue a compliance notice to the contractor, impose monetary penalties, terminate the exploitation contract (reg 103) or take remedial action (reg 104). The draft standard contractual clauses for exploitation also specify the ISA's power to suspend or terminate the contract in certain circumstances.[175]

Accordingly, under the UNCLOS framework, augmented by the Mining Code, the ISA has various, far-reaching means of inducing contractor compliance. These means are being tailored to apply more specifically in the exploitation context. As the Secretariat has recognised, '[d]esigning a robust and transparent inspection programme will be key to the successful implementation of the Authority's regulatory framework'.[176]

However, despite the significant arsenal of powers the ISA has at its disposal, it does not yet have the capacity and means to implement these powers effectively.[177] Conducting an inspection programme for exploitation activities, in respect of multiple contractors, will require a significant outlay of resources. Indeed, to some degree, these implementation powers are tied to the payment mechanism for deep seabed mining: the system of payments must provide sufficient revenues to fund the ISA's monitoring programme.[178] The operational challenges are considerable, given the vastness of the Area, and the fact that 'a physical inspection of the mining area is a practical impossibility' due to the depths involved.[179] In light of some of these challenges, the ISA has heeded calls for it to incorporate remote monitoring methods into its compliance mechanisms.[180] As noted, the DERs envisage an electronic monitoring system for mining activities (reg 102). However, such a programme would also have cost and resource implications.[181]

175 DERs, Annex X, s 12. See, further, Chapter 7, text to n 31.

176 ISA Secretariat, 'Implementing an Inspection Mechanism for Activities in the Area' (20 December 2018) ISBA/25/C/5, para 5.

177 See, e.g. critique by Jaeckel (2017) (n 65) 175–176, 297–300.

178 1994 Agreement, Annex, s 8(1)(a); on the expenses of the Authority, see also UNCLOS, art 173.

179 ISBA/25/C/5, para 14.

180 ISBA/25/C/5, para 15.

181 See, e.g. Jaeckel (2017) (n 65) 298 (cautioning that 'monitoring compliance using satellite data, video footage, or other technology would require teams of technical experts within the Secretariat to oversee the implementation of the technology and evaluate the data'). For further details on remote monitoring, see ISA Council, 'Submission by the Delegation of Belgium: The Use of Electronic Monitoring Systems as an Effective Way to Remotely Monitor the Activities in the Area' (3 May 2019) ISBA/25/C/21.

To enhance its compliance powers for the forthcoming exploitation phase, the ISA is considering how best to implement an inspection mechanism to monitor contractor compliance and perform inspections.[182] One approach would be to establish a permanent mining inspectorate.[183] Another option, which the Secretariat has suggested for consideration, is the creation of an inspection mechanism administered by the Secretariat, and comprising a roster of inspectors nominated by States Parties, recommended by the LTC and approved by the Council.[184] Pursuant to such a model, the Secretariat suggested that 'inspectors would remain subject to the jurisdiction of the member States of which they are nationals (to promote independence) and to the rules of the Authority, including a code of conduct for inspectors and an inspection manual (to promote consistency)'.[185] Evidently, further work is needed to develop an appropriate inspection mechanism in time for the exploitation phase.[186] Therefore, although the ISA has strong compliance powers, its enforcement capacity remains subject to considerable development.

6.4.2 Responsibility for Deep Seabed Mining Activities

In addition to ISA implementation powers, another important aspect for successful realisation of benefit-sharing and marine protection aspects will be the extent to which the regime secures responsibility for their violation. This element will, in practice, have a vital bearing on achievement of these common heritage goals.

The Convention's regime for responsibility and liability exists in tandem with equivalent rules of international law. For example, within the deep seabed regime, Article 139(2) of UNCLOS affirms that the responsibilities and liabilities of states

[182] See, e.g. discussion in ISBA/25/C/5, paras 5–14.

[183] This approach was recommended in ISA, 'Technical Study no 11: Towards the Development of a Regulatory Framework for Polymetallic Nodule Exploitation in the Area' (26 February 2013) 78 <https://isa.org.jm/files/documents/EN/Pubs/TStudy11-Final.pdf>. Similarly, see Jaeckel (2017) (n 65) 297–300, drawing on precedents for inspectorates in international organisations in the disarmament context, such as the Organisation for the Prohibition of Chemical Weapons and the International Atomic Energy Agency.

[184] ISBA/25/C/5, para 12 (in making this suggestion, the Secretariat draws comparison with the inspection system of the Commission for the Conservation of Antarctic Marine Living Resources (*CCAMLR*), pursuant to which 'inspectors designated by members of the Commission operate under its terms and conditions, [and] they remain subject to the jurisdiction of the contracting party to the Convention (national authority) of which they are nationals': ibid, para 11). In its stakeholder comments on the DERs, Norway also supported development of a system of inspection modelled upon the 'well-established' CCAMLR approach: Norway, 'General Comments from Norway on Draft Regulations on Exploitation of Mineral Resources in the Area' (October 2019) at 2 <https://isa.org.jm/files/files/documents/191011%20Comments%20Norway%20Draft%20Mining%20Regulations.pdf>.

[185] ISBA/25/C/5, para 12.

[186] For a useful overview of various issues requiring consideration and resolution, see report of a July 2019 workshop on inspection mechanisms organised by some stakeholders: Pew Charitable Trusts and RESOLVE, 'ISA Inspections and ISA Inspectorate: What will be Needed?' (20 September 2019) <www.resolve.ngo/docs/2019_jamaica_workshop_-_isa_inspections_and_isa_inspectorate_-_summary_final.pdf>.

and international organisations are '[w]ithout prejudice to the rules of international law'.[187] The general rules of international law 'supplement' the Convention's system of responsibility and liability.[188]

In relation to state responsibility, the rules of general international law are codified in the ILC's Draft Articles on Responsibility of States for Internationally Wrongful Acts (*ILC Draft Articles*).[189] Many of these rules have the status of customary international law,[190] and the Chamber has recognised that they must be taken into account in the deep seabed mining context.[191] Pursuant to these rules, a state is responsible for internationally wrongful conduct that is attributable to it under international law.[192] Conduct is internationally wrongful if it 'constitutes a breach of an international obligation of the State'.[193] General international law contains similar rules of responsibility in relation to international organisations.[194]

Despite the continuing relevance of the general international law of responsibility and liability, the Convention develops its own rules in this regard in relation to deep seabed mining.[195] These rules are tailored to reflect the differing participants and scenarios in the deep seabed mining context, as compared to more traditional paradigms of state (or international organisation) responsibility. For example, within the present international legal system, private corporate actors do not typically attract international responsibility in respect of their actions.[196] Moreover, as

[187] See also UNCLOS, art 304.

[188] ITLOS AO, para 171.

[189] ILC, 'State Responsibility – Text of the Draft Articles on Responsibility of States for Internationally Wrongful Acts' in 'Report of the International Law Commission on the Work of its 53rd Session' (23 April to 1 June and 2 July to 10 August 2001) UN Doc A/56/10.

[190] See, e.g. *Armed Activities on the Territory of the Congo (Democratic Republic of Congo v Uganda)* (Judgment) [2005] ICJ Rep 168, para 160; *M/V 'SAIGA' (No 2) (Saint Vincent and the Grenadines v Guinea)* (Judgment of 1 July 1999) ITLOS Reports 1999, 10, para 171; ITLOS AO, para 169.

[191] ITLOS AO, para 169.

[192] ILC Draft Articles (n 189), arts 1 and 2.

[193] ILC Draft Articles (n 189), art 2(b). Circumstances in which conduct is attributable to a state at international law are also set out in the ILC Draft Articles. Generally, 'the only conduct attributed to the State at the international level is that of its organs of government, or of others who have acted under the direction, instigation or control of those organs, i.e. as agents of the State': ILC, 'State Responsibility – Draft Commentaries' in 'Report of the International Law Commission on the Work of its 53rd Session' (23 April to 1 June and 2 July to 10 August 2001) UN Doc A/56/10 (*ILC Commentaries*) 38 (citation omitted). Thus, forms of conduct attributable to a state at international law include conduct of state organs (ILC Draft Articles, art 4), conduct of persons or entities exercising elements of governmental authority (ibid, art 5) and conduct directed or controlled by a state (ibid, art 8).

[194] ILC, 'Text of the Draft Articles on the Responsibility of International Organizations' in 'Report of the International Law Commission on the Work of its 63rd Session' (26 April to 3 June and 4 July to 12 August 2011) UN Doc A/66/10. On development of the notion of responsibility of international organisations under international law, and elements of that responsibility, see Matthias Hartwig, 'International Organizations or Institutions, Responsibility and Liability' in Rüdiger Wolfrum (ed), *The Max Planck Encyclopedia of Public International Law* (OUP 2011).

[195] See also UNCLOS, arts 235, 263 (concerning state responsibility and liability for protection and preservation of the marine environment, and in relation to conduct of marine scientific research, respectively).

[196] This is by virtue of the fact that most obligations upon corporations are not direct obligations of international law and, therefore, their breach cannot attract international responsibility (on which, see Chapter 1, Section 1.2.4 and Chapter 5, Section 5.3).

a general rule, conduct of non-state actors, such as private corporate actors, is not attributable to the state under international law, absent certain circumstances, such as the existence of a nexus of control[197] or a failure of due diligence, on the part of the state, to 'prevent the violation or to respond to it' appropriately.[198]

Within the deep seabed context, in respect of both the direct responsibility of private actors and the due diligence obligations of states, the Convention regime advances and adapts the existing rules of responsibility. Considerations of responsibility in relation to deep seabed mining can be divided into three categories of actor. As noted by the Chamber, 'distribution of responsibilities for deep seabed mining activities [is] between the contractor, the Authority and the sponsoring State'.[199] This tripartite distribution of responsibility is reflected within the Convention regime.[200]

At the heart of the regime is the premise that a contractor will be liable for its wrongful conduct. As the Virginia Commentary explains, if a contractor commits wrongful acts during the conduct of its deep seabed mining activities, then 'the contractor is, *prima facie*, liable for damage'.[201] Notably, such responsibility and liability attaches to a contractor irrespective of whether that contractor is a state, state enterprise or private actor.[202] Equally, if the Authority commits wrongful acts in the exercise of its powers and functions, the Authority is, prima facie, liable for the resultant damage.[203] This dual arrangement is reflected in Article 22 of Annex III of UNCLOS, which provides that:

[197] ILC Commentaries (n 193) 52: '[t]he general principle, drawn from State practice and international judicial decisions, is that the conduct of a person or group of persons not acting on behalf of the State is not considered as an act of the State under international law' (see also 38: 'the conduct of private persons is not as such attributable to the State' and 47: '[a]s a general principle, the conduct of private persons or entities is not attributable to the State under international law').

[198] *Velásquez Rodríguez Case* (Judgment) Inter-American Court of Human Rights Series C No 4 (29 July 1988), para 172 (finding that a human rights violation 'not directly imputable to a State (for example, because it is the act of a private person or because the person responsible has not been identified) can lead to international responsibility of the State, not because of the act itself, but because of the lack of due diligence to prevent the violation or to respond to it as required by the [Inter-American Convention on Human Rights]'); see also ILC Commentaries (n 193) 38.

[199] ITLOS AO, para 200. Note that where the state is engaged directly in deep seabed mining operations, the state itself will constitute the contractor: there will be no sponsoring state in this scenario.

[200] ITLOS AO, para 171.

[201] Virginia Commentary 127, on the basis of UNCLOS, Annex III, arts 4(4) and 22; see also Karavias (n 174) 144–147.

[202] Moreover, if the contractor is a state (or entity whose conduct is attributable to the state under the ILC Draft Articles (n 189)), UNCLOS provides an additional route for direct responsibility. In such circumstances, that state would also be responsible for ensuring that any conduct attributable to it was carried out 'in conformity' with Part XI of UNCLOS (as per UNCLOS, art 139(1)). Failure to do so would attract state liability (UNCLOS, art 139(2)). In any event, in this scenario, the state would be responsible for its wrongful acts in the conduct of its operations, and liable for any damage which results, in accordance with general international law (see ILC Draft Articles, ibid; see also this section's previous discussion at text to nn 192–193).

For analysis of the operation of UNCLOS, art 139 in relation to activities by state-sponsored entities whose actions are not attributable to the state, but in relation to which the state retains certain responsibilities, see this section's forthcoming analysis at text to nn 209–213.

[203] UNCLOS, Annex III, art 22.

> The contractor shall have responsibility or liability for any damage arising out of wrongful acts in the conduct of its operations, account being taken of contributory acts or omissions by the Authority. Similarly, the Authority shall have responsibility or liability for any damage arising out of wrongful acts in the exercise of its powers and functions, including violations under article 168, paragraph 2, account being taken of contributory acts or omissions by the contractor. Liability in every case shall be for the actual amount of damage.[204]

Therefore, in the deep seabed mining context, primary liability for damage in the Area rests with the contractor, and with the Authority, in relation to any wrongful conduct which either of these respective actors commit. The Chamber recognised this when it acknowledged that:

> [T]he main liability for a wrongful act committed in the conduct of the contractor's operations or in the exercise of the Authority's powers and functions rests with the contractor and the Authority, respectively, rather than with the sponsoring State.[205]

However, to what extent is the sponsoring state responsible for wrongful activities by an entity which it has sponsored? In keeping with the position under general international law, a private actor's wrongful conduct in the Area is not attributable to the sponsoring state, absent a nexus of control.[206] The Chamber confirmed this when it remarked that 'the liability regime established in Annex III to the Convention and related instruments does not provide for the attribution of activities of sponsored contractors to sponsoring States'.[207] Nevertheless, the Convention places certain obligations on sponsoring states in respect of the entities that they sponsor. Determining the extent of a state sponsor's responsibility and obligations in this regard was the key focus of the Chamber's advisory opinion in 2011.[208]

[204] See also Nodules Regulations, reg 30; Sulphides Regulations, reg 32; Cobalt Regulations, reg 32. These provisions emphasise contractor liability for marine environmental damage by providing that '[t]he contractor shall continue to have responsibility for any damage arising out of wrongful acts in the conduct of its operations, in particular damage to the marine environment, after the completion of the exploration phase'. See also Nodules, Sulphides and Cobalt Regulations (s 16, standard clauses, fourth annex) on responsibility and liability. In the exploitation context, see DERs, Annex X, s 7. See also Virginia Commentary 755.

[205] ITLOS AO, para 200.

[206] ITLOS AO, para 182.

[207] ITLOS AO, para 182.

[208] For thorough analysis of the ITLOS AO, see David Freestone, 'Responsibilities and Obligations of States Sponsoring Persons and Entities with Respect to Activities in the Area' (2011) 105 AJIL 755; Ilias Plakokefalos, 'Seabed Disputes Chamber of the International Tribunal for the Law of the Sea, Advisory Opinion' (2012) 24 J Env L 134; Ximena Hinrichs Oyarce, 'Sponsoring States in the Area: Obligations, Liability and the Role of Developing States' (2018) 95 Marine Pol'y 317; Keith MacMaster, 'Environmental Liability for Deep Seabed Mining in the Area: An Urgent Case for a Robust Strict Liability Regime' (2019) 33 Ocean YB 339.

Pursuant to Article 139(1) of UNCLOS, States Parties have the 'responsibility to ensure' that any activities in the Area conducted by them, or by state-sponsored entities, are performed consistently with Part XI of UNCLOS.[209] In the event that a State Party fails to discharge this responsibility, it will be held responsible at international law and incur liability for damage caused as a result of its failure.[210] However, a State Party will be absolved of liability for damage caused by an entity that it has sponsored if the State Party has taken 'all necessary and appropriate measures to secure effective compliance' by the sponsored entity, in accordance with Article 139(2) of UNCLOS.[211] In order to satisfy this obligation, sponsoring states have:

> [The] responsibility to ensure, within their legal systems, that a contractor so sponsored shall carry out activities in the Area in conformity with the terms of its contract and its obligations under this Convention. A sponsoring State shall not, however, be liable for damage caused by any failure of a contractor sponsored by it to comply with its obligations if that State Party has adopted laws and regulations and taken administrative measures which are, within the framework of its legal system, reasonably appropriate for securing compliance by persons under its jurisdiction.[212]

In its advisory opinion, the Chamber found that this obligation upon the state sponsor 'to ensure' compliance is a due diligence obligation 'to deploy adequate means, to exercise best possible efforts, to do the utmost, to obtain this result'.[213]

Consequently, pursuant to the Convention's deep seabed mining regime, a state's responsibility may be engaged in respect of activities of private entities that they have sponsored, in certain circumstances. However, as the Chamber has emphasised, 'not every violation of an obligation by a sponsored contractor automatically gives rise to the liability of the sponsoring State. Such liability is limited to the State's failure to meet its obligation to "ensure" compliance by the sponsored contractor.'[214] In such circumstances, 'the sponsoring State's liability arises not from a failure of a private entity but rather from its own failure to carry out its responsibilities'.[215] In order for the state's liability to be triggered, a causal link must

[209] This principle of responsibility applies equally to international organisations in relation to activities which they undertake in the Area: UNCLOS, art 139(1).

[210] UNCLOS, art 139(2).

[211] See also UNCLOS, arts 138 and 153(4) and Annex III, art 4(4). See, further, ITLOS AO, para 110.

[212] UNCLOS, Annex III, art 4(4).

[213] ITLOS AO, para 110; see also paras 108–116. In addition to this obligation 'to ensure', state sponsors are subject to direct obligations, including duties to apply the precautionary approach and best environmental practices (ibid, para 122).

[214] ITLOS AO, para 109; see also paras 172 and 182.

[215] ITLOS AO, para 182.

be established between the failure of the state and the damage caused by the sponsored contractor.[216]

Therefore, pursuant to the liability regime within UNCLOS, a sponsoring state may be liable for 'its own failure to carry out its responsibilities', while the contractor's liability 'arises from its own non-compliance'.[217] Crucially, 'both forms of liability exist in parallel'.[218] The potential liability of a contractor and a sponsoring state (arising out a contractor's non-compliance and a sponsoring state's failure to meet its responsibilities, respectively), is not joint and several.[219] In circumstances where a contractor has insufficient funds to make full reparations for damage caused, the Convention regime 'leaves no room for residual liability' of the sponsoring state.[220] This means that a liability gap may arise in circumstances where 'a contractor does not meet its liability in full while the sponsoring State is not liable under article 139, paragraph 2, of the Convention'.[221] However, in accordance with the Chamber's suggestion, the ISA plans to establish a fund to address this gap by compensating for damage not covered.[222]

As the preceding analysis has demonstrated, the Convention implements a sophisticated and carefully tailored regime for international responsibility in respect of deep seabed mining activities. Pursuant to this, a deep seabed mining contractor is primarily responsible for its wrongful conduct in relation to its deep seabed mining activities.[223] In practice, this will be especially significant in relation to the achievement of the material core of the common heritage concept. If, for example, a corporate actor engages in deep seabed mining in violation of the regime's benefit-sharing or marine environmental protection aspects, then direct liability for these violations will rest with that corporate actor. As the following section will briefly address, this responsibility regime is underpinned by binding dispute resolution options within the Convention itself.

216 ITLOS AO, paras 181–182 and 184.

217 ITLOS AO, para 201.

218 ITLOS AO, para 201.

219 ITLOS AO, para 201. See also Jean d'Aspremont and others, 'Sharing Responsibility between Non-state Actors and States in International Law: Introduction' (2015) 62 NILR 49, 56 (noting the UNCLOS deep seabed regime as a rare example of an institutional regime that could potentially lead to forms of shared responsibility involving non-state actors).

220 ITLOS AO, para 204.

221 ITLOS AO, para 205.

222 ITLOS AO, para 205. As described in Section 6.2, at n 92, the ISA intends to rectify this liability gap by establishing an environmental compensation fund in the DERs (see regs 54–56).

223 UNCLOS, Annex III, arts 4(4) and 22; see also Virginia Commentary 127; Karavias (n 174) 144–147. On the argument that the UNCLOS approach to contractor liability is 'out of step with international practice' by requiring fault, see Neil Craik, 'Liability for Environmental Harm from Deep Seabed Mining: Towards a Hybrid Approach' (2019) 33 Ocean YB 315, 326; see also Neil Craik, 'Determining the Standard for Liability for Environmental Harm from Deep Seabed Mining Activities' (October 2018) Liability Issues for Deep Seabed Mining Series, Paper no 2 <www.cigionline.org/sites/default/files/documents/Deep%20Seabed%20paper%20no.2_2.pdf>. See further critique by MacMaster (n 208).

6.4.3 Initial Note on Dispute Resolution in Respect of Deep Seabed Mining Activities

A final important consideration is the extent to which the regime has a binding and enforceable dispute resolution system, permitting challenge of deep seabed miners for failure to adhere to the regime's common heritage aspects, such as benefit sharing and marine environmental protection. Detailed consideration of this is deferred to Chapter 7, which balances this end against the right of deep seabed mining contractors to pursue international investment protection in relation to their activities in the Area. However, this section will introduce the Convention's dispute resolution system for deep seabed mining disputes.

UNCLOS contains a dispute resolution system of considerable detail and complexity. During negotiation of the Convention, the dispute resolution mechanisms constituted part of the 'package deal' that states had to accept, in order to benefit from the other provisions within the regime.[224] The Convention's main dispute resolution scheme is contained within Part XV of UNCLOS, which addresses settlement of disputes under UNCLOS as a whole. Part XV, section 1 contains the fundamental principles of dispute settlement which apply to all Convention disputes, including those concerning deep seabed mining.[225] For example, the overriding principle is that disputes must be settled by peaceful means of the parties' own choosing.[226]

In addition to the general Part XV dispute settlement system, the Convention contains a dedicated dispute resolution system focused on deep seabed mining disputes.[227] Part XI of UNCLOS established the Chamber as a special chamber of ITLOS, to deal with disputes relating to the deep seabed.[228] The Chamber has contentious and advisory jurisdiction over deep seabed mining.[229] The Chamber's contentious jurisdiction extends to particular categories of 'disputes with respect to activities in the Area', including certain types of deep seabed mining disputes between States Parties, or between a State Party and the ISA.[230]

In a notable departure from many international dispute settlement regimes, standing before the Chamber is not restricted to States Parties or the regulatory body. As well as the right of States Parties and the ISA to appear before the Chamber, the Convention permits contractors (be they states, state enterprises or

[224] Alan Boyle and Christine Chinkin, 'UNCLOS III and the Process of International Law-making' in Tafsir Malick Ndiaye and Rüdiger Wolfrum (eds), *Law of the Sea, Environmental Law and Settlement of Disputes* (Martinus Nijhoff Publishers 2007) 380. See also Chapter 3 of the present book, text to n 85.

[225] UNCLOS, art 285.

[226] UNCLOS, arts 279–280.

[227] UNCLOS, Part XI, s 5 (arts 186–191); see also Annex VI, s 4 (arts 35–40).

[228] UNCLOS, art 186 and see also Annex VI, art 14 and s 4 (arts 35–40).

[229] UNCLOS, art 187, 191. Thus far, the Chamber has not decided any contentious cases, but it exercised advisory jurisdiction when delivering the ITLOS AO.

[230] UNCLOS, art 187. For fuller analysis of categories of contentious dispute over which the Chamber has jurisdiction, see Chapter 7, Section 7.2.1.

natural or juridical persons[231]) to participate directly in claims concerning certain types of disputes.[232] As Chapter 7 will assess in more detail, the Chamber's jurisdiction encompasses settlement of disputes involving contractors (or prospective contractors) in the Area, in certain circumstances.[233] As Wolfrum explains, the Chamber's far-reaching competence with regard to deep seabed mining disputes 'upholds the rule of law as far as the management of the deep seabed and its resources is concerned'.[234]

As Karavias notes, the 'extended jurisdiction *ratione personae* of the Chamber is exceptional, taking into consideration the global reach of the instrument'.[235] Arguably the most remarkable feature of the system is that 'corporations can act both as plaintiffs and defendants'.[236] Consequently, pursuant to the Convention's dispute resolution system for deep seabed mining disputes, corporate contractors are in the unusual dual position of being both entitled to enforce rights, *and* subject to enforcement of obligations, on the international plane. While it is rare for private entities, such as corporate actors, to have direct international law rights enforceable at the international level, it is rarer still for such entities to be subject to international law enforcement mechanisms in respect of direct international legal obligations.[237]

Accordingly, within the UNCLOS regime, corporate contractors will be responsible for wrongful conduct in relation to deep seabed mining, and this responsibility is enforceable by virtue of the regime's dispute settlement options. For example, the Chamber has jurisdiction over parties to a contract in connection with the interpretation or application of that contract, and in relation to 'acts or omissions of a party to the contract relating to activities in the Area and directed to the other party or directly affecting its legitimate interests'.[238] The broad scope of these grounds gives the Chamber jurisdiction over corporate contractor violations of material obligations in relation to benefit-sharing and marine environmental protection. In this manner, the common heritage's benefit-sharing and marine protection components are directly enforceable against a corporate contractor as a matter of international law, which may be an important practical factor in their realisation.

231 As per UNCLOS, art 153(2)(b).
232 UNCLOS, art 187 and Annex VI, art 37.
233 UNCLOS, art 187(c)–(e); see also Annex VI, art 37.
234 Rüdiger Wolfrum, 'Legitimacy of International Law and the Exercise of Administrative Functions: The Example of the International Seabed Authority, the International Maritime Organization (IMO) and International Fisheries Organizations' in Armin von Bogdandy and others (eds), *The Exercise of Public Authority by International Institutions – Advancing International Institutional Law* (Springer 2010) 934.
235 Karavias (n 174) 156, citing Louis B Sohn, 'Settlement of Law of the Sea Disputes' (1995) 10 Int'l J Marine Coastal L 205, 211.
236 Karavias (n 174) 157.
237 See, further, Chapter 1, Section 1.2.4.
238 UNCLOS, art 187(c)(i)–(ii).

6.5 Conclusion

The ISA is making progress towards developing a common heritage regime for deep seabed mining which enshrines both benefit sharing and marine environmental protection as key elements. As this chapter has addressed, notable challenges lie ahead for the ISA, not least in devising a workable payment mechanism which will deliver tangible benefits to humanity while also ensuring sufficient protections to the marine environment. Notwithstanding the need for considerable development on both of these fronts, the scope of the ISA's regulatory regime is shaping up to be increasingly comprehensive, endeavouring to regulate these paramount substantive elements, while also including mechanisms for the regime to continue to evolve in light of new challenges. On balance, Step 3 of this study's framework of analysis (Chapter 3, Section 3.3) is on course to being achieved. Substantive obligations are being put in place for these two material common heritage components, and these obligations may be realised against corporate contractors via a sophisticated system of implementation, responsibility and enforcement.

However, this begs the question as to whether the regime strikes an appropriate regulatory balance between realising benefits to humanity and respecting market principles. As demonstrated, these two competing elements underpin the common heritage, and realisation of both is essential for the common heritage's achievement. This will be the focus of the following, final chapter.

7

Balancing Community and Autonomy – To What Extent Does the Regime Reconcile ISA Regulatory Authority and Investment Protection for Corporate Actors?

Does the UNCLOS deep seabed mining regime strike an appropriate regulatory balance between the dual common heritage goals of community and autonomy?[1] This chapter will confront Step 4 of this study's framework of analysis (as per Chapter 3, Section 3.3) by addressing this query. In order to do so, it will focus on reconciling the ISA's right to regulate on behalf of humanity with investment protection rights for deep seabed miners.[2] Lodge describes the UNCLOS regime as providing 'a stable environment for investors in deep-seabed minerals under a market-oriented regime'.[3] However, for corporations investing in deep seabed mining, whether the regime is sufficiently 'market-oriented' will depend upon whether it affords suitable investment protection rights.[4] Section 7.1 will address this.

As Section 7.2 will consider thereafter, a vital element of the utility of investment protection rights is the extent to which they are backed by binding and enforceable dispute resolution options. Can corporate contractors enforce deep seabed mining investment protection rights within the UNCLOS regime? If so, can these rights

[1] See Chapter 3, text to nn 72–75, 104–111 and Section 3.2.7. See also Martti Koskenniemi, *From Apology to Utopia: The Structure of International Legal Argument* (CUP 2005) 476, and see 488–493.

[2] Elements of this chapter are also addressed in Joanna Dingwall, 'International Investment Protection in Deep Seabed Mining beyond National Jurisdiction' (2018) 19 J World Investment Trade 890.

[3] Michael W Lodge, 'International Seabed Authority's Regulations on Prospecting and Exploration for Polymetallic Nodules in the Area' (2002) 20 J Energy Nat Res L 270, 272 at fn 8. See also DERs, reg 2(c), designating as a fundamental principle of the regime that 'Resources of the Area are Exploited in accordance with sound commercial principles'.

[4] Other crucial factors in the 'marketability' of the regime will include its licensing process (already assessed in Chapter 4, Section 4.2.3) and its financial parameters (such as financial terms of exploitation contracts and the ultimate system for distribution of financial benefits from mining). As Chapter 6, Section 6.1 has addressed, the financial elements are still under construction. Therefore, this chapter has chosen to focus on investment protection rights, in particular, as a key barometer of the commercial viability of the regime, in market terms.

International Law and Corporate Actors in Deep Seabed Mining. Joanna Dingwall, Oxford University Press. © Joanna Dingwall 2021. DOI: 10.1093/oso/9780192898265.003.0008

be balanced alongside the ISA's right to regulate concerning the communitarian aspects of the common heritage, thereby achieving an overall balance between community and autonomy? Section 7.2 will answer these questions.

7.1 Investment Protections for Deep Seabed Mining Contractors

The deep seabed mining regime affords various rights to deep seabed mining contractors. As this section will demonstrate, these rights are akin, in some respects, to investment protection rights within the context of international investment law.[5]

Despite the 'novelty' of ISA contracts within the international legal system,[6] certain analogies are apposite, including a comparison with international investment law. As Roberts recognises in relation to investment law (in a finding that could equally be applied in the deep seabed mining context), when a legal field is 'new and undertheorized', it is commonplace for participants to 'draw on comparisons with other legal fields when seeking to fill gaps, resolve ambiguities, or understand the system's nature'.[7] Drawing such comparisons or analogies can, thus, be a vital part of the process of understanding how the Convention's deep seabed mining system will operate, in practice. On that basis, this section will now consider the typical international investment law paradigm, before setting out the key substantive rights that tend to accrue in this context, and assessing the extent to which these have been reconfigured within the Convention regime for the deep seabed context.[8]

The most common means by which to guarantee protection of foreign investments is through an international investment agreement. In the last few decades, such agreements have proliferated.[9] These instruments are often bilateral in nature (in the form of BITs). In addition, many multilateral agreements afford investment

[5] In keeping with this book's focus of analysis, this chapter will explore these rights from the perspective of corporate actors holding ISA mining contracts, although other participants (such as states and state-controlled entities) would also benefit from these rights.

[6] Markos Karavias, *Corporate Obligations under International Law* (OUP 2013) 138.

[7] Anthea Roberts, 'Clash of Paradigms: Actors and Analogies Shaping the Investment Treaty System' (2013) 107 AJIL 45, 46 (see also Roberts, generally, on the phenomenon of choice of analogies, in the course of her analysis of the clash of paradigms underlying the investment treaty system). See also Martins Paparinskis, 'Analogies and other Regimes of International Law' in Zachary Douglas and others (eds), *The Foundations of International Investment Law* (OUP 2014) 74 (acknowledging that 'elaboration of the contours and the content of new regimes that partly borrow and partly diverge from existing practice should be, as it were, the bread and butter of international law, lawyers, and legal process').

[8] This builds on the comparison that this study has already drawn between grounds of qualification for a protected investor under an investment treaty and eligibility requirements for corporate participation as a contractor in the deep seabed regime, both of which tend to be satisfied by formal regulatory control (on which, see Chapter 1, Section 1.2.2 and Chapter 4, Section 4.2.3.3).

[9] On this, see Chapter 1, text to n 96.

protections, typically comprising investment chapters within the broader framework of free trade agreements, or within treaties for regional cooperation.[10] Less commonly, some multilateral treaties devoted to a particular sector include a system of investment protection; one such instrument is the Energy Charter Treaty, which affords a multilateral system for energy cooperation including dedicated investment protections.[11]

Given the sheer number of investment agreements, the range of parties to them and the various contexts of their adoption, there is considerable divergence in content and scope. However, the classic paradigm of the investment agreement is that it bestows investment protections upon a foreign investor directly against a host state, in respect of interference with an investment. Another common feature is that most investment agreements contain a core of substantive entitlements for foreign investors, safeguarding them against host state interference. Although the exact wording and scope of protection varies from treaty to treaty, many are worded in broadly similar terms, and are applied rather similarly to norms of a multilateral legal regime.[12]

Typical substantive protections include the prohibition of unlawful expropriation. This is usually framed in such terms as to prohibit the host state's taking or 'deprivation' of an investment, unless the taking occurs under due process of law, in the public interest, in a non-discriminatory manner and accompanied by payment of full and fair compensation.[13] Other common substantive rights within investment agreements include entitlement of investors to fair and equitable treatment (*FET*) and full protection and security (*FPS*).[14] Overlapping to some extent with FET entitlements, an investment treaty may prohibit the host state from impairing investment activity unreasonably or arbitrarily, or acting in a discriminatory manner.[15]

[10] See, e.g. ch 11 of the North American Free Trade Agreement (adopted 17 December 1992, entered into force 1 January 1994) (1993) 32 ILM 289 (*NAFTA*) (which contains investment protections applicable within NAFTA). Alternatively, see also the investment regime within the Association of Southeast Asian Nations (*ASEAN*), contained in ASEAN Comprehensive Investment Agreement (signed 26 February 2009, entered into force 29 March 2012) <www.asean.org/storage/images/2013/economic/aia/ACIA_Final_Text_26%20Feb%202009.pdf>.

[11] Energy Charter Treaty (adopted 17 December 1994, entered into force 16 April 1998) 2080 UNTS 95, Part III (Investment Promotion and Protection).

[12] For the argument that BITs function similarly to a multilateral regime, see Stephan W Schill, *The Multilateralization of International Investment Law* (CUP 2009).

[13] By way of illustration, see prohibition of unlawful expropriation in the Netherlands Model BIT, art 6: Agreement on Encouragement and Reciprocal Protection of Investments between —and the Kingdom of the Netherlands (March 2004) <https://investmentpolicy.unctad.org/international-investment-agreements/treaty-files/2859/download>. The Netherlands is an attractive gateway for investment structuring, due to its investor-friendly BIT network. The terms of this 2004 version of the Netherlands Model BIT (which formed the basis for many Dutch BITs) illustrates the level of protection which investors have favoured.

[14] See, e.g. Netherlands Model BIT (n 13) art 3(1).

[15] See, e.g. Netherlands Model BIT (n 13) art 3(1).

The UNCLOS deep seabed regime can be distinguished from the usual international investment law paradigm in at least two key respects. Firstly, the central relationship in deep seabed mining is between the ISA contractor, on the one hand, and the ISA as regulator and overseer of deep seabed mining contracts, on the other. To participate within the system, the deep seabed contractor must enter into a dual relationship: with its home state, and with the ISA. Firstly, the prospective contractor must secure sponsorship from its state of nationality and control.[16] Once sponsored, the prospective contractor may apply to the ISA to explore for, or exploit, mineral resources in the Area.[17] If successful, the applicant may formalise its relationship by entering into a mining contract with the ISA.

This division of regulatory control is captured well in Article 153(4) of UNCLOS, which provides that 'the Authority shall exercise such control over activities in the Area as is necessary for the purposes of securing compliance [with the regime]', while States Parties, including the sponsoring state, 'shall assist the Authority by taking all measures necessary to ensure such compliance'. The sponsoring state has a 'subordinate' role to the ISA in the investment relationship.[18] Therefore, within the deep seabed mining context, the ISA's role is most equivalent to the role of a host state, from the perspective of international investment law. This is evident from the central role of the ISA as regulator of deep seabed mining, and as the entity with the power to grant the mining contract, vary its terms, monitor and inspect the contractor's compliance with the terms of the contract and, ultimately, to terminate the contract in certain circumstances.[19]

Secondly, even cursory inspection of the UNCLOS regime reveals that it does not provide for an investment chapter or dedicated section of investment rights for deep seabed miners similar to the core of substantive protections typically featured in investment agreements.[20] Indeed, one could argue that the deep seabed mining regime set out in UNCLOS and its associated instruments has more in common with a domestic law regulatory regime governing particular classes of contracts, such as mining concessionary contracts. Rather than specifying dedicated investment protections for deep seabed miners, the UNCLOS regime is a regulatory regime establishing a framework within which particular activities may be conducted. It operates by imposing obligations and bestowing rights upon contractors

[16] UNCLOS, art 153(2)(b); see also Chapter 4, Section 4.2.3.3.

[17] UNCLOS, art 153(3) and Annex III, art 3; see also 1994 Agreement, Annex, s 1(6)(a)(i).

[18] ITLOS AO, para 102; see also UNCLOS, Annex III, art 22.

[19] See Chapter 6, Section 6.4.1.

[20] See, e.g. Christophe Bondy, 'Intégrer le Droit de la Mer et le Droit International de L'Investissement' (2017) 22 An Dr Mer 15, 24–26 (noting, at 25, that the Convention's deep seabed regime provides 'un modèle bien différent que celui gouvernant typiquement l'activité économique privée' (i.e. the UNCLOS regime provides a very different model than the one that typically governs private economic activity)). See also Lorenzo Cotula and Thierry Berger, '"Blue Economy": Why we should Talk about Investment Law' (*International Institute for Environment and Development Briefing*, April 2020) 3 <https://pubs.iied.org/pdfs/17746IIED.pdf> (recognising that 'UNCLOS and investment protection norms reflect fundamentally different approaches').

within a regulatory framework. This regulatory framework is constrained, in turn, by the terms of the regime, in order to provide appropriate safeguards for contractors against improper conduct by the regulator. Nevertheless, as the following analysis will reveal, the UNCLOS regime affords various protections, to deep seabed mining contractors, that are broadly equivalent in function and scope to more traditional investment law entitlements.

Sections 7.1.1 to 7.1.4 will now address the extent to which each of the key investment standards (prohibition of expropriation; FET standard; prohibition of arbitrary, unreasonable or discriminatory behaviour; and entitlement to FPS, respectively) are incorporated, in some form, within the UNCLOS deep seabed regime. Thereafter, Section 7.1.5 will offer reflections upon the model for investment protection within the UNCLOS deep seabed mining regime, and on its potential scope.

7.1.1 Protection against Unlawful Expropriation

Turning, firstly, to address the investment law prohibition of unlawful expropriation, what is the substantive scope of this proscription, and to what extent does the UNCLOS regime afford any equivalent protection to deep seabed miners? In addition to an outright 'taking' of property, unlawful expropriation may also occur by indirect means, provided that the consequence of such 'covert or incidental interference with the use of property' is to 'depriv[e] the owner, in whole or in significant part, of the use or reasonably-to-be-expected economic benefit of property'.[21] Unlawful expropriation may be conducted against both tangible and intangible rights.[22] In particular, the host state's taking or serious restriction of contractual rights may constitute expropriation.[23] Various measures may lead to expropriation of a contract, for example:

[21] This famous test is set out in *Metalclad Corporation v The United Mexican States* (Award) ICSID Case No ARB(AF)/97/1 (30 August 2000), para 103. Subsequent investment treaty jurisprudence has endorsed this definition: see, e.g. *CME Czech Republic BV (The Netherlands) v The Czech Republic* (Partial Award) UNCITRAL (13 September 2001), para 606 (see also para 150, together with para 604, finding that 'measures that do not involve an overt taking but that effectively neutralize the benefit of the property of the foreign owner, are subject to expropriation claims. This is undisputed under international law').

[22] See, e.g. *Phillips Petroleum v Iran* (1989) 21 Iran-USCTR 79, para 76 (the obligation to pay compensation in respect of expropriation applies whether such property 'is tangible, such as real estate or a factory, or intangible, such as the contract rights involved in the present [c]ase'). See also *Case concerning Certain German Interests in Polish Upper Silesia (Germany v Poland)* (Merits Judgment) [1925] PCIJ Rep Series A No 7, 44 (where the PCIJ held Poland's taking of a factory constituted expropriation of contractual rights); see also *Rudloff Case (American-Venezuelan Commission)* (Interlocutory Decision) (1905) 9 RIAA 244, 250 (for early affirmation that 'taking away or destruction of rights acquired, transmitted, and defined by a contract is as much a wrong, entitling the sufferer to redress, as the taking away or destruction of tangible property'); *Norwegian Shipowners' Claims (Norway v United States)* (Award) (1922) 1 RIAA 307, 325 (where the US 'took, both in fact and in law, the contracts under which the ships in question were being or were to be constructed').

[23] See citations at n 22; see also *Shufeldt Claim (Guatemala v US)* (1930) 2 RIAA 1079, particularly at 1095, 1099, 1101–1102 (finding that Guatemala committed expropriation through termination of

> [T]axation, regulation, denial of due process, delay and non-performance, and other forms of governmental malfeasance, misfeasance, and nonfeasance – may be deemed expropriatory if those measures significantly reduce an investor's property rights or render them practically useless.[24]

In the deep seabed mining context, the availability of protection against unlawful expropriation of the mining contract is particularly critical, as the rights and obligations of deep seabed miners in the Area are based largely on their contractual relationship with the Authority.[25] Arguably, the UNCLOS system provides comparable protection against unlawful expropriation, by virtue of the Convention's guarantee of security of tenure for deep seabed miners.

Security of tenure is a vital feature of the UNCLOS regime.[26] Article 16 of Annex III of UNCLOS provides the contractor with the exclusive right to explore for (or exploit) minerals in the contract area:

> The Authority shall, pursuant to Part XI and its rules, regulations and procedures, accord the operator the exclusive right to explore and exploit the area covered by the plan of work in respect of a specified category of resources and shall ensure that no other entity operates in the same area for a different category of resources in a manner which might interfere with the operations of the operator. The operator shall have security of tenure in accordance with article 153, paragraph 6.

This requirement of security of tenure is reflected within the ISA's regulations to date,[27] and in the standard clauses to the contracts for nodules, sulphides and

a concession contract by legislative decree). In the investment treaty context, see, e.g. *CME* (n 21), para 591; *Mondev International Ltd v United States of America* (Award) ICSID Case No ARB(AF)/99/2 (11 October 2002), para 98; *Eureko BV v Republic of Poland* (Partial Award) Ad Hoc Arbitration (19 August 2005), para 241; *Azurix Corp v The Argentine Republic* (Award) ICSID Case No ARB/01/12 (14 July 2006), paras 53–54; *ADC Affiliate Limited and ADC & ADMC Management Limited v The Republic of Hungary* (Award) ICSID Case No ARB/03/16 (2 October 2006), para 304; *Siemens AG v The Argentine Republic* (Award) ICSID Case No ARB/02/8 (6 February 2007), para 267; *Biwater Gauff (Tanzania) Ltd v United Republic of Tanzania* (Award) ICSID Case No ARB/05/22 (24 July 2008), paras 485, 519.

[24] W Michael Reisman and Robert D Sloane, 'Indirect Expropriation and its Valuation in the BIT Generation' (2004) 75 BYIL 115, 123 (citations omitted).

[25] See discussion in Chapter 4, Section 4.3.

[26] UNCLOS, art 153(6); Annex III, art 16. See analysis in Gwenaëlle Le Gurun, 'Annex III' in Proelss Commentary 2135 ('security of tenure which the contract gives, associated with the requirements of consent prior to any revision to a contract, provides stability and predictability to the contractor. This is important given the high investment made by contractors.')

[27] Nodules Regulations, reg 24(1); Sulphides Regulations, reg 26(1); Cobalt Regulations, reg 26(1); similarly, see DERs, reg 18(1)–(4).

cobalt crusts exploration.[28] As described in the commentary, 'unilateral revision, suspension or termination of contracts would create insecurity of tenure'.[29]

One way in which an expropriation may occur is by termination of a contract. In accordance with the right to security of tenure, the manner in which the Convention regime restricts contractual interference protects a contractor against unlawful expropriation. ISA contracts 'shall not be revised, suspended or terminated', except pursuant to the process provided for within the Convention.[30] In particular, Article 18(1) of Annex III to UNCLOS curtails the circumstances in which the Authority can suspend or terminate a mining contract to situations in which:

(a) [I]f, in spite of warnings by the Authority, the contractor has conducted his activities in such a way as to result in serious, persistent and wilful violations of the fundamental terms of the contract, Part XI and the rules, regulations and procedures of the Authority; or
(b) if the contractor has failed to comply with a final binding decision of the dispute settlement body applicable to him.[31]

If the Authority terminates a contract without just cause, the contractor would have a basis on which to seek appropriate remedies.

Another aspect of the expropriation standard is that, in certain circumstances, the exercise of regulatory powers may constitute expropriation of an investment.[32]

[28] See s 2.1 of the standard clauses (contained as fourth annex to the Nodules, Sulphides and Cobalt Regulations); the guarantee of security of tenure is also included in the standard clauses to exploitation contracts (DERs, Annex X, s 4.1).

[29] Gwenaëlle Le Gurun, 'Annex III' in Proelss Commentary 2234.

[30] UNCLOS, art 153(6); see also Annex III, arts 18–19.

[31] These two grounds are reflected in s 21.1(a)–(b) of the standard clauses to mining contracts contained within the fourth annex of the Nodules, Sulphides and Cobalt Regulations. In addition, s 21 widens the Authority's powers by providing two additional grounds to suspend or terminate the contract: either in situations of contractor bankruptcy (s 21.1(c)) or, in consultation with the contractor, in circumstances of *force majeure* (s 21.2). Similarly, s 12 of standard clauses to exploitation contracts in the DERs, Annex X, contains the four grounds for suspension or termination included in s 21 of the standard clauses for nodules, sulphides and cobalt crusts exploration (see Annex X, ss 12.1(a)–(b), (d) and 12.2). However, Annex X includes a further two grounds for suspension or termination of an exploitation contract, permitting the ISA to suspend or terminate where the contractor knowingly, recklessly or negligently provides the ISA with false or misleading information (Annex X, s 12.1(c)), or if the contractor has not made sufficient, bona fide progress towards commercial production (Annex X, s 12.1(e)).

[32] For analysis, see Ursula Kriebaum, 'Regulatory Takings: Balancing the Interests of the Investor and the State' (2007) 8 J World Investment Trade 717, 721 and citations therein, including *Pope & Talbot Inc v The Government of Canada* (Interim Award) UNCITRAL (26 June 2000), para 99 (recognising that 'much creeping expropriation could be conducted by regulations, and a blanket exception for regulatory measures would create a gaping loophole in international protection against expropriation'); *Metalclad* (n 21), paras 109–112; *Técnicas Medioambientales Tecmed SA v The United Mexican States* (Award) ICSID Case No ARB(AF)/00/2 (29 May 2003), para 122; *Marvin Feldman v Mexico* (Award) ICSID AF Case No ARB(AF)/99/1 (16 December 2002), para 103. See also Benedict Kingsbury and Stephan W Schill, 'Public Law Concepts to Balance Investors' Rights with State Regulatory Actions in the Public Interest – the Concept of Proportionality' in Stephan W Schill (ed), *International Investment Law and Comparative Public Law* (OUP 2010) 88–96.

Notably, by virtue of the UNCLOS regime, deep seabed miners may possess greater insulation from regulatory turbulence than equivalent investors within a host state. Although the ISA is entrusted with progressive development of the regime through regulations, and the operation of the regime is subject to ISA review and amendment, there are restrictions on the extent to which the ISA can interfere with the regulatory environment of a particular contract.

For example, despite the ISA's power to review the regime and suggest improvements to its operation,[33] a contract 'may be revised only with the consent of the parties'.[34] The existing regulations are also subject to ISA review (at five-yearly intervals).[35] However, in the event that the regulations are amended, the contract can only be updated to reflect these new amendments if the contractor consents (as discussed in Chapter 6, Section 6.3).[36] These provisions help to safeguard the contractor against any shifting regulatory approach by the Authority. Indeed, in some respects, regulation by the ISA may lead to a more stable investment environment than in many states, given that the ISA is controlled, ultimately, by the international community as a whole, and is not subject to the whim of purely domestic politics.

7.1.2 Entitlement to Fair and Equitable Treatment

The requirement of FET includes several aspects. Investors may rely on FET entitlements in relation to administrative and regulatory action by host states, including in respect of the granting of contracts and licences, and application of rules and regulations concerning their operation. The standard of FET is an expansive one, making it incumbent on the host state to ensure due process, transparency, consistency and non-arbitrary and non-discriminatory conduct in respect of investments.[37] It also protects the legitimate expectations of the investor,[38] and obliges

[33] UNCLOS, art 154.

[34] UNCLOS, Annex III, art 19(2); see also UNCLOS, art 153(6).

[35] Nodules Regulations, reg 42; Sulphides Regulations, reg 44; Cobalt Regulations, reg 44.

[36] Nodules Regulations, reg 42(4); Sulphides Regulations, reg 44(4); Cobalt Regulations, reg 44(4), read with s 24 of the standard clauses to mining contracts (which is the fourth annex in all three sets of regulations, and requires contractor consent for contract revision); and see Aline L Jaeckel, *The International Seabed Authority and the Precautionary Principle – Balancing Deep Seabed Mineral Mining and Marine Environmental Protection* (Brill 2017) 150 (noting that 'contractors that obtained their respective exploration contracts in different years can be bound by different clauses'). See also UNCLOS, Annex III, art 19(2) (a contract 'may be revised only with the consent of the parties'). Although, cf the DERs, which, on the basis of the current draft, put the contractor on notice that it must comply with ISA rules 'as amended from time to time' (s 3.3(a) of the standard clauses to exploitation contracts, Annex X); however, contractor consent is still required for contract revision (standard clauses, Annex X, s 16).

[37] See the classic formulation of the FET standard in *Tecmed* (n 32), para 154; see also *Waste Management Inc v United Mexican States* (Award) ICSID Case No ARB/(AF)/00/3 (30 April 2004), para 98. For analysis of the scope of FET generally, see Schill (2009) (n 12) 78–80, including overview of key commentary, fn 78.

[38] *Saluka Investments BV (The Netherlands) v The Czech Republic* (Partial Award) UNCITRAL (17 March 2006), para 302 ('[t]he standard of "fair and equitable treatment" is ... closely tied to the notion of legitimate expectations which is the dominant element of that standard') (citation omitted)); see also

the host state to provide a transparent, stable and predictable legal and business environment.[39] Although the host state's legal framework need not be frozen, 'as it can always evolve and be adapted to changing circumstances',[40] an investor is entitled to expect that the legal framework on which it reasonably depended when making its investment will not be substantially altered to that investor's disadvantage.[41]

As discussed, various provisions within the Convention regime operate to protect a contractor from regulatory change by the ISA. These provisions serve to restrict the extent to which the ISA can alter the regulatory regime which governs a particular contract without contractor consent. However, the regime actually goes further than this, incorporating many limits on the Authority's regulatory powers; it is broadly equivalent, in effect, to a guarantee of FET. For example, the Authority must adopt and apply its regulations 'uniformly'.[42] Therefore, the Authority is not permitted to act in a manner that is arbitrary or grossly unfair. Other provisions require the Authority to 'avoid discrimination in the exercise of its powers and functions',[43] and to fulfil its powers in good faith.[44] Investment arbitral tribunals have regularly held that good faith constitutes an intrinsic characteristic of FET.[45] A pattern of behaviour taken in the absence of good faith may, of itself, amount to a breach of the FET standard.[46]

Tecmed (n 32), para 154; *Eureko* (n 23), para 235; *International Thunderbird Gaming Corporation v The United Mexican States* (Award) UNCITRAL (26 January 2006), para 147; *Rumeli Telekom AS and Telsim Mobil Telekomunikasyon Hizmetleri AS v Republic of Kazakhstan* (Award) ICSID Case No ARB/05/16 (29 July 2008), para 609.

[39] See, e.g. *Occidental Exploration and Production Company v The Republic of Ecuador* (Final Award) UNCITRAL, LCIA Case No UN 3467 (1 July 2004), paras 183–185, 191 (finding (at para 183) that 'stability of the legal and business framework is … an essential element of fair and equitable treatment'); see also *CMS Gas Transmission Company v The Argentine Republic* (Award) ICSID Case No ARB/01/8 (12 May 2005), paras 274–279 (holding (at para 274) that 'a stable legal and business environment is an essential element of fair and equitable treatment' and (at para 276) 'fair and equitable treatment is inseparable from stability and predictability'). See, further, *Metalclad* (n 21), para 99; *PSEG Global Inc and Konya Ilgın Elektrik Üretim ve Ticaret Limited Şirketi v Republic of Turkey* (Award) ICSID Case No ARB/02/5 (19 January 2007), paras 250, 254–255; *LG&E Energy Corp and others v Argentine Republic* (Decision on Liability) ICSID Case No ARB/02/1 (3 October 2006), paras 125, 131; *BG Grp PLC v The Republic of Argentina* (Final Award) UNCITRAL (24 December 2007), paras 307, 310.

[40] *CMS* (n 39), para 277; see also *Saluka* (n 38), para 305.

[41] See *National Grid PLC v Argentine Republic* (Award) UNCITRAL (3 November 2008), paras 178–179 (finding that the host state's substantial modification of the investment framework on which the investor based its investment, along with host state actions in requiring renegotiation of investment contracts, breached the FET standard); see also *Enron Corporation Ponderosa Assets LP v Argentine Republic* (Award) ICSID Case No ARB/01/03 (22 May 2007), paras 265–267.

[42] UNCLOS, Annex III, art 17(1).

[43] UNCLOS, art 152(1).

[44] See s 13.4 of the standard clauses (contained as fourth annex to the Nodules, Sulphides and Cobalt Regulations); this requirement is also reflected in the standard clauses to DERs, Annex X, s 3.1.

[45] See, e.g. *Tecmed* (n 32), para 153 ('fair and equitable treatment … is an expression and part of the *bona fide* principle recognized in international law' (citations omitted)); see also *Rumeli* (n 38), para 609 (recognising that a concrete principle of FET is that 'the State is obliged to act in good faith').

[46] See, e.g. *Frontier Petroleum Services Ltd v The Czech Republic* (Final Award) UNCITRAL (12 November 2010), paras 300–301.

The UNCLOS deep seabed regime may also operate to safeguard the legitimate expectations of investors. This is evident, for example, in relation to the transition from the exploration phase of mining to exploitation activities. When a contractor has completed exploration, it must make a fresh application to the Authority if it wishes to secure approval for exploitation activities. In accordance with the legitimate expectations principle, a contractor seeking to exploit the same type of resources in the same area that it explored previously is given 'a preference and a priority' amongst other applicants, provided that the contractor's performance has been satisfactory.[47]

Moreover, elements of FET are incorporated within the Authority's exercise of specific powers. For example, when considering whether to recommend approval of a plan of work, the LTC must discharge its duties 'in a uniform and non-discriminatory manner'.[48] If the Authority imposes monetary penalties on a contractor in respect of a violation, such penalties must be 'proportionate to the seriousness of the violation'.[49] Similarly, when developing rules to govern the financial terms of mining contracts, the Authority must act 'to attract investments and technology', 'ensure equality of financial treatment and comparable financial obligations for contractors' and provide contractual incentives 'on a uniform and non-discriminatory basis'.[50] Equally, as regards the performance requirements for deep seabed exploitation, the Authority is to require the contractor to maintain commercial production during the contractual period, 'within reasonable limits'.[51]

7.1.3 Protection against Impairment of Investment Activities by Unreasonable or Discriminatory Measures

Closely related to the FET entitlement is the duty of a host state not to impair investment activities in an unreasonable, arbitrary or discriminatory manner. This duty

[47] UNCLOS, Annex III, art 10; see also 1994 Agreement, Annex, s 1(13); Nodules Regulations, reg 24(2); Sulphides Regulations, reg 26(2); Cobalt Regulations, reg 26(2); see also DERs, reg 10(1).

[48] Nodules Regulations, reg 21(12); Sulphides Regulations, reg 23(12); Cobalt Regulations, reg 23(12); see also DERs, reg 12(3). See, further, UNCLOS, Annex III, art 6(3), requiring the Authority to approve plans of work in accordance with 'the uniform and non-discriminatory requirements' in the Mining Code.

[49] UNCLOS, Annex III, art 18(2); this proportionality requirement is echoed in s 21.6 of the standard clauses (contained as fourth annex to the Nodules, Sulphides and Cobalt Regulations), and is also present in the standard clauses to DERs, Annex X, s 12.6.

[50] UNCLOS, Annex III, art 13(1)(b)–(d); and see art 13(14). See also 1994 Agreement, Annex, s 8(1)(a) (requiring the system of financial payments to the Authority to 'be fair both to the contractor and to the Authority'). Such considerations are also reflected in DERs, reg 62 (requiring the ISA to apply provisions concerning financial terms of exploitation contracts 'in a uniform and non-discriminatory manner and [to] ensure equality of financial treatment and comparable financial obligations for Contractors').

[51] UNCLOS, Annex III, art 17(2)(c); see also DERs, reg 29 (allowing the contractor to seek temporary reduction or suspension of production due to market conditions).

features as a stand-alone requirement in many investment treaties.[52] Investment treaty jurisprudence confirms that '[a]ny measure that might involve arbitrariness or discrimination is in itself contrary to fair and equitable treatment'.[53] Aspects of the duty against arbitrariness and discrimination are captured in the UNCLOS deep seabed mining regime, in the protections already discussed in relation to the FET standard.

7.1.4 Entitlement to Full Protection and Security

Finally, many investment treaties afford investors with a right to FPS, which protects investments from a range of interferences which may be physical, and at times also non-physical, in character.[54] The FPS standard may require the host state to afford investors with a 'secure environment' in terms which are 'physical, commercial and legal'.[55] Thus, the standards of FPS and FET are closely related.[56]

By virtue of its obligation to provide FPS, the host state is required to protect an investment from damage, including at the hands of other actors. In this regard, the FPS standard requires host states to exercise due diligence as regards foreign investments.[57] The FPS entitlement imposes an 'obligation of vigilance', pursuant to which the host state must adopt all necessary measures in order to protect the investment.[58]

Although not explicitly included within the Convention as a protection for deep seabed miners, elements of FPS pervade the deep seabed regime. For example, as noted, the Authority must provide the contractor with security of tenure, including against encroachment and interference by other entities.[59] The regime also imposes requirements and constraints upon the Authority, in order to protect the contractor from adverse regulatory change and ensure a stable and secure environment for the operation of the deep seabed mining investment.[60]

[52] See, e.g. *CMS* (n 39), para 290 ('[t]he standard of protection against arbitrariness and discrimination is related to that of fair and equitable treatment').

[53] *CMS* (n 39), para 290.

[54] *Azurix* (n 23), paras 406, 408 (finding (at para 406) that 'full protection and security may be breached even if no physical violence or damage occurs'); see also *Siemens* (n 23), para 303; *National Grid* (n 41), para 189. See also Christoph Schreuer, 'Full Protection and Security' (2010) 1 JIDS 353, 358–362 (concluding (at 362) that 'authorities suggest that the duty of protection and security extends to providing a legal framework that offers legal protection to investors' (citation omitted)).

[55] *Biwater* (n 23) para 729; see also *Frontier* (n 46) para 263.

[56] *Azurix* (n 23) para 408.

[57] This obligation of due diligence is tailored to the particular circumstances of the host state: *Pantechniki SA Contractors & Engineers v The Republic of Albania* (Award) ICSID Case No ARB/07/21 (30 July 2009), para 81.

[58] *CME* (n 21) para 160; see also *Biwater* (n 23) para 730

[59] UNCLOS, art 153(6) and Annex III, art 16; see also Nodules Regulations, reg 24(1); Sulphides Regulations, reg 26(1); Cobalt Regulations, reg 26(1) and Nodules, Sulphides and Cobalt Regulations, s 2 of standard clauses (contained in fourth annex).

[60] See discussion and references in Section 7.1.1, at text to nn 33–36.

7.1.5 Reflections on the Deep Seabed Mining Investment Paradigm and its Opposability

On the basis of the preceding analysis, the UNCLOS regime clearly includes numerous provisions that operate, cumulatively, to safeguard investor rights in deep seabed mining. These protections are predominantly focused on insulating the contractor from wrongful conduct by the main regulator and overseer of the regulatory regime: the Authority. In this regard, as noted previously, in some respects a comparison between the UNCLOS deep seabed mining regime and domestic regulatory regimes governing particular classes of contracts, such as mining concession agreements, may appear more apposite than the comparison between ISA contractor rights and investor BIT entitlements. An ISA contract is a 'commercial contract', within which the ISA and the contractor have a commercial relationship.[61] ISA contracts 'are framed and formulated in a manner which relies heavily on municipal law analogies'.[62] In contrast to the typical investment treaty model, the deep seabed mining regime regulates all aspects of the mining contract, not only investment protection, and the regime is reciprocal, allowing the regulator to bring enforcement claims against the contractor and vice versa (as will be considered further in Section 7.2).

However, regardless of resemblances to domestic regulatory regimes, ISA contracts are firmly entrenched within the international legal system. As noted previously, ISA contracts are internationalised functional contracts; that is, 'contracts made by an international organization in direct implementation of its functions'.[63] As this study has considered, in many respects ISA contracts are a 'novelty' within the international legal system.[64] They boast a clear pedigree within international law: they were created to implement a treaty law system, and they include international law as the express choice of law governing the contract, in a manner which is '*ex lege*, rather than *ex contractu*'.[65] Moreover, as Section 7.2 will explore, the deep seabed regime, in an echo of other subsets of international law, such as the investment treaty system, grants private actors the right to bring claims directly against the ISA on the international plane.

As with international investment law, there are also parallels between the system of ISA contracts and public law systems (both domestic and international).[66] An

[61] Linlin Sun, 'Dispute Settlement Relating to Deep Seabed Mining: A Participant's Perspective' (2017) 18 Melb J Int'l L 71, 81.

[62] Karavias (n 6) 162.

[63] Karavias (n 6) 117; see also 140–143, 161–162. See, further, Chapter 4, Section 4.3.

[64] Karavias (n 6) 138.

[65] Karavias (n 6) 138 (as Karavias explains, the parties to the ISA contract have negligible autonomy in the choice of law; rather 'the choice of international law as the governing law is ultimately provided for *expressly in [UNCLOS] itself*' (emphasis in original); see also 140–143).

[66] For analysis of interaction between public law and investment law, see, e.g. Gus van Harten, *Investment Treaty Arbitration and Public Law* (OUP 2007); Stephan Schill (ed), *International Investment Law and Comparative Public Law* (OUP 2010).

ISA contract 'establishes an administrative relationship between the ISA as a regulator and the contractor'.[67] Aspects of this relationship are 'on an unequal footing', as the ISA exerts administrative powers over the contractor, and the ISA 'can act as a legal regulator even when they are in a legal relationship under the contract'.[68] Therefore, as Sun concludes, the ISA contract 'is of a mixed nature: it is treated as a commercial contract but at the same time involves the exercise of administrative powers by one of the parties'.[69] In this regard, the ISA regime feeds into the existing body of global administrative law or 'international public law'.[70] Wolfrum cites the role of the ISA as a 'prime example' of 'international administration' within the international legal system.[71]

Consequently, the system of ISA contracts has a hybrid nature, combining various public and private elements. In this respect, the ISA regime and the investment treaty system share important parallels, as the latter also has a 'hybrid or *sui generis* character'.[72] Both the deep seabed mining regime and the international investment law system combine the following components: elements of public international law (including an underlying basis in treaty law); domestic or international public law features (concerning the regulatory relationship established between 'the host states [or the ISA] (as governors) and foreign investors (as governed)'[73]); and private international law and commercial arbitration procedural and enforcement aspects (allowing direct claims by investors against the regulatory body – be it host state or ISA –including by way of international arbitration (as Section 7.2 will explore)).

On this basis, the analogies drawn between the deep seabed mining regime and the investment treaty system are appropriate in the context of the present analysis.[74] As the preceding sections have demonstrated, there is considerable

[67] Sun (n 61) 81.
[68] Sun (n 61) 81.
[69] Sun (n 61) 81.
[70] On 'international public law' as a category that includes human rights and international trade law, see Roberts (2013) (n 7) 46, 69–74. On international investment law as part of the regime of global administrative law, see Gus van Harten and Martin Loughlin, 'Investment Treaty Arbitration as a Species of Global Administrative Law' (2006) 17 EJIL 121.
[71] Rüdiger Wolfrum, 'Legitimacy of International Law and the Exercise of Administrative Functions: The Example of the International Seabed Authority, the International Maritime Organization (IMO) and International Fisheries Organizations' in Armin von Bogdandy and others (eds), *The Exercise of Public Authority by International Institutions – Advancing International Institutional Law* (Springer 2010) 934; see also JHH Weiler, 'The Geology of International Law – Governance, Democracy and Legitimacy' (2004) 64 ZaöRV 547 (on the concept of international administration). See, further, Sun (n 61) 87, fn 65.
[72] Zachary Douglas, 'The Hybrid Foundations of Investment Treaty Arbitration' (2003) 74 BYIL 151, 153; see also Roberts (2013) (n 7) 49, demonstrating that the 'investment system exists at the intersection of multiple fields', including 'public international law, international commercial arbitration, domestic public law, and international public law'. See, further, Paparinskis (n 7) 73–75 (on investment law 'as a normative progeny of multiple regimes of international law' (75)).
[73] Roberts (2013) (n 7) 45.
[74] In some respects, the systemic comparison allowing the most potential for overlap may be between ISA contracts, on the one hand, and the subset of investment treaty disputes that involve reliance on an umbrella clause rendering the entirety of the investment contract justiciable under a BIT, on the other.

functional equivalence between the extent of protections afforded to deep seabed miners against the ISA's improper conduct and investment law entitlements which an investor may be able to wield against a host state, under a BIT.

As Section 7.2 will consider, various scenarios could trigger contractor reliance on UNCLOS protections, such as the ISA's wrongful termination of a mining contract, or the ISA's granting of another mining contract in a way that encroaches upon the original contractor's mining site, and interferes with that investment.

Moreover, other forms of dispute could arise between the deep seabed miner and other actors, including the sponsoring state. Various situations could arise in which a contractor or prospective contractor's deep seabed investment is impeded by virtue of its state sponsor's actions or omissions. For example, what would be the consequences of denial of sponsorship by a state at the last minute, in breach of the prospective contractor's legitimate expectations, or of termination of sponsorship by a state during the life of the mining project?[75] Similarly, what would happen in the event that a sponsoring state imposed stricter regulations under domestic law than those provided by the ISA, requiring extra fees or permits?[76]

Many issues concerning the precise workings of the relationship between the contractor and the sponsoring state lie beyond the scope of UNCLOS and, therefore, beyond the present scope of examination.[77] As regards the sponsorship system, UNCLOS is most concerned with two aspects: setting the main parameters of eligibility for sponsorship (namely, nationality and effective control, so that all sponsored contractors will be within the reach of a State Party to the Convention[78]); and defining the circumstances in which the sponsoring state will be liable for the contractor's wrongful conduct (namely, in circumstances where the state sponsor fails to discharge its responsibility to ensure that the contractor's conduct in the Area is compatible with Part XI of UNCLOS[79]). The Convention also places upon

As Roberts notes, such disputes may 'muddy the public/private distinction', as 'the proximate cause of action is a treaty breach (public liability), but it is based on an underlying breach of contract (private action)': Roberts (2013) (n 7) 65.

[75] UNCLOS does not provide a process to regulate circumstances in which a state sponsor can lawfully terminate sponsorship, aside from requiring it to give notice of termination to the ISA and to provide reasons for it (Nodules Regulations, reg 29(2); Sulphides Regulations, reg 31(2); Cobalt Regulations, reg 31(2)).

[76] This example would not necessarily be incompatible with UNCLOS. Pursuant to UNCLOS, Annex III, art 21(3), although '[n]o State Party may impose conditions on a contractor that are inconsistent with Part XI', in the event that a State Party applies 'environmental or other laws and regulations more stringent than those in the rules, regulations and procedures of the Authority', that does not violate the Part XI regime. For analysis, see ITLOS AO, paras 231–232, 240. See also Klaas Willaert, 'On the Legitimacy of National Interests of Sponsoring States: A Deep Sea Mining Conundrum' (2020) 35 Int'l J Marine Coastal L 1.

[77] See Sun (n 61) 82 ('no mechanism for settlement of disputes arising out of the implementation of a sponsoring agreement is described in the [UNCLOS deep seabed mining] framework'). This will be considered in Section 7.2, when addressing the extent of investor dispute resolution mechanisms within the Convention regime.

[78] UNCLOS, art 153(2)(b).

[79] See UNCLOS, arts 139(2) and 153(4) and Annex III, art 4(4); see also ITLOS AO, para 110.

States Parties, including sponsoring states, a duty to fulfil their UNCLOS obligations in good faith, both in relation, specifically, to the deep seabed regime in Part XI[80] and, more generally, as regards UNCLOS as a whole.[81]

However, several nuances in the relationship between a contractor and its sponsoring state fall to be regulated by a combination of applicable domestic law (such as domestic deep seabed mining legislation[82]), any applicable international law (such as any investment treaty that covers the terms of the deep seabed mining investment[83]) and the provisions of any sponsorship agreement between the contractor and the sponsoring state.[84] Therefore, if a contractor wishes to ensure that it has appropriate investment protections in this regard, it needs to satisfy itself at the outset, when structuring its investment and selecting a sponsoring state, that it has sufficient safeguards from interference by the sponsoring state within domestic law, other international law or in the terms of any sponsorship agreement. Detailed consideration of this issue falls outwith the present scope of inquiry.

In conclusion, as this analysis has demonstrated, despite the *sui generis* nature of the Convention's deep seabed mining regime, and its divergence in form and structure from the classic international investment law paradigm, the UNCLOS regime contains various investment protections for deep seabed miners that are broadly equivalent in scope to typical investment rights. Investors in deep seabed mining can exert these protections primarily

[80] UNCLOS, art 157(4).

[81] UNCLOS, art 300.

[82] Depending on the terms of any applicable deep seabed mining legislation, such legislation may contain safeguards on the sponsorship process, such as restrictions on grounds for refusal or termination of sponsorship, breach of which may be subject to judicial remedies (e.g. judicial review at the domestic level).

[83] Whether a sponsoring state's investment treaty would apply to such an investment would depend on the context and the terms of any such treaty. The first potential jurisdictional obstacle may concern the typical investment agreement requirement that to benefit from the treaty, the investor must be a foreign national investing in a host state. In contrast to this, the Convention's sponsorship system applies only to nationals of the sponsoring state or entities falling within that state's effective control (or that of its nationals) (UNCLOS, art 153(2)(b)). If the relevant investment treaty covers indirect investments, it may apply to the investor (in circumstances, e.g. where an investor from one state routes its deep seabed mining investment through a subsidiary with the nationality of another state (the state sponsor)). The second fundamental challenge to application of an investment treaty in this scenario is extent of territorial scope. Although many investment treaties apply within national waters of a coastal state (territorial sea, EEZ and continental shelf), the application of such instruments in the Area is untested, and could raise compatibility issues under UNCLOS, art 137 (prohibiting states from exercising sovereign rights over any part of the Area). On application of investment treaties to seabed activities within national waters, and analysis of issues of territorial extent, see James Harrison, 'International Investment Law and the Regulation of the Seabed' in Catherine Banet (ed), *The Law of the Seabed: Access, Uses, and Protection of Seabed Resources* (Brill 2020) 488 (noting that 'investment treaties generally cannot be interpreted to apply to seabed investments in areas beyond national jurisdiction'). See also Cotula and Berger (n 20); Alberto Pecoraro, 'Law of the Sea and Investment Protection in Deep Seabed Mining' (2020) 20 Melb J Int'l L 530.

[84] A sponsorship agreement is a private agreement concluded between sponsoring state and (prospective) contractor, in accordance with that state's domestic law: ITLOS AO, para 225; see also Sun (n 61) 82.

against undue interference by the Authority. However, to what extent can deep seabed miners enforce these protections via binding and effective dispute resolution options within the Convention regime? And in what manner may the Convention's competing corporate rights and corporate obligations be reconciled? Specifically, do the corporate investment rights considered in this section undermine the Authority's ability to regulate and enforce substantive elements of the common heritage concept? The following Section 7.2 will confront these issues.

7.2 Deep Seabed Mining Disputes – Reconciling Corporate Rights and Obligations through Dispute Resolution

For investors, the practical value of substantive investment protections often depends on the extent to which binding and effective avenues exist by which to enforce them. One of the central features of many investment agreements is that they permit an investor to bring an arbitral claim concerning an investment dispute against a host state directly.[85] As the preceding analysis has established, the UNCLOS regime provides protections to deep seabed mining investors that could be construed as being functionally equivalent to more traditional investment law entitlements. This section will evaluate the extent to which the UNCLOS regime affords investors access to dispute resolution mechanisms to enforce these protections.

To that end, Section 7.2.1 will consider the scope of the Chamber's contentious jurisdiction over deep seabed mining disputes, with a focus on assessing the standing of corporate contractors in connection with disputes relating to the Authority. Following this, to gain a more holistic view of enforcement within the UNCLOS deep seabed regime, Section 7.2.2 will briefly address resolution of disputes between corporate contractors and other actors aside from the Authority. Finally, Section 7.2.3 will conclude this chapter by reflecting upon the Convention's dispute resolution system for the Area, and critiquing the extent to which a balance is likely to be struck between competing corporate rights and obligations within the operation of the regime (thereby realising the common heritage's community/autonomy equilibrium).

[85] Commonly, such provisions allow investors to commence arbitral proceedings against host states under the auspices of dispute settlement bodies such as ICSID, or by ad hoc arbitration pursuant to the United Nations Commission on International Trade Law (*UNCITRAL*) Arbitration Rules (1976) 15 ILM 701; see also ICSID Convention. An example of an investor-state dispute resolution clause favouring ICSID arbitration can be found in the Netherlands Model BIT (n 13) art 9.

7.2.1 The Seabed Disputes Chamber's Contentious Jurisdiction over Deep Seabed Mining Disputes Involving Corporate Contractors

When engaging in deep seabed mining activities, a corporate contractor enters into a web of legal relationships. In addition to the duties it owes to the sponsoring state and ISA, and the rights it derives from its relationship with them, the contractor has duties to others, including coastal states and other users of the marine environment.[86] Throughout the life of a deep seabed mining project, therefore, many possibilities for dispute could arise between various actors. For example, Craik develops a matrix which identifies nine bilateral relationships between participants in deep seabed mining that may be subject to dispute.[87] As Craik illustrates, disputes concerning a contractor's deep seabed mining project could arise between the contractor and any of the following entities: the ISA, the sponsoring state, other contractors, third states or other users of the marine environment.[88] Sun reaches similar conclusions.[89]

In light of this complex array of legal relationships between a host of actors, the Convention implements dispute resolution mechanisms that have been tailored specifically to deal with deep seabed mining disputes.[90] Part XI of UNCLOS establishes the Chamber as a special chamber within ITLOS to address disputes relating to the deep seabed.[91] The Chamber exercises contentious and advisory jurisdiction over deep seabed mining.[92] When exercising its jurisdiction, the Chamber may apply the entire Convention regime, including UNCLOS and the 1994 Agreement, together with the Mining Code and the terms of relevant mining contracts, plus other rules of international law.[93]

The Chamber has contentious jurisdiction in relation to certain categories of 'disputes with respect to activities in the Area'.[94] The Convention restricts the Chamber's contentious jurisdiction in two key respects. Firstly, by virtue of Article

[86] See, e.g. UNCLOS, arts 142 (rights and legitimate interests of coastal states) and 147 (accommodation of activities in the Area and in the marine environment).

[87] Neil Craik, 'ISA Discussion Paper no 4 – Enforcement and Liability Challenges for Environmental Regulation of Deep Seabed Mining' (June 2016) 8 <www.isa.org.jm/files/documents/EN/Pubs/DPs/DP4.pdf> (identifying potential for dispute between any of the following: the ISA, sponsoring state(s), contractor(s), third state(s) and other non-state actors, such as other users of the marine environment).

[88] Craik (2016) (n 87) 8.

[89] Sun (n 61) 78. See also Tara Davenport, 'Responsibility and Liability for Damage Arising out of Activities in the Area: Potential Claimants and Possible Fora' (February 2019) Liability Issues for Deep Seabed Mining Series, Paper no 5 <www.cigionline.org/sites/default/files/documents/Deep%20Seabed%20Paper%20No.5_1.pdf> (analysing actors that may have standing to bring claims in relation to damage caused by deep seabed mining activities, and possible fora for adjudication of such disputes).

[90] UNCLOS, Part XI, s 5 (arts 186–191) and see also Annex VI, s 4 (arts 35–40). See this book's introduction to the Convention's dispute resolution system in Chapter 6, Section 6.4.3.

[91] UNCLOS, art 186 and see also Annex VI, art 14 and s 4 (arts 35–40).

[92] UNCLOS, arts 187, 191.

[93] UNCLOS, art 293 and Annex VI, art 38.

[94] UNCLOS, art 187.

189, the Chamber lacks jurisdiction to judicially review exercise by the Authority of its discretionary powers, including, for example, the Authority's adoption of rules and regulations as part of the Mining Code.[95] In particular, the Chamber must not 'substitute its discretion for that of the Authority'.[96] A key consequence of this is that, during contentious proceedings, the Chamber cannot opine as to whether the Authority's regulations are consistent with the Convention, and cannot declare them to be invalid.[97] This restriction on the Chamber's jurisdiction was tailored to stop the Chamber from interfering overly in the workings of the Authority.[98]

However, within Article 189 there is an 'exception to the exception'.[99] As will be addressed further below, despite the limitation on judicial review by the Chamber, the Chamber is empowered to decide whether the application of the Authority's regulations and rules in an individual case would violate either the Convention or the terms of a particular mining contract. Moreover, in cases of failure, by the ISA or the contractor, to comply with the mining contract or the Convention, the Chamber may decide on damages or other remedies for the wronged party. Finally, the Chamber is entitled to decide claims concerning the Authority's excess of jurisdiction or misuse of power.[100]

The second key limit on the Chamber's contentious jurisdiction is that it applies only in respect of certain specified categories of persons and subject matters.[101] For example, as noted in Chapter 6, Section 6.4.3, the Chamber has jurisdiction over certain types of deep seabed mining disputes between States Parties,[102] or between a State Party and the ISA.[103] Importantly, for the purposes of this section's analysis,

[95] UNCLOS, art 189. See analysis in Natalie Klein, *Dispute Settlement in the UN Convention on the Law of the Sea* (CUP 2005) 329; James Harrison, *Making the Law of the Sea* (CUP 2011) 149–150; Jaeckel (2017) (n 36) 112–113.

[96] UNCLOS, art 189. For analysis and critique of the application of this limitation to dispute resolution options for contractors, see Sun (n 61) 79–81.

[97] UNCLOS, art 189; notably, the same restriction does not apply to the Chamber's exercise of advisory jurisdiction: Virginia Commentary 637. However, as the Chamber's advisory opinions are not binding, the Chamber would lack the power to invalidate any regulations that it deemed incompatible with UNCLOS; see, further, Harrison (2011) (n 95) 51.

[98] See drafting history of UNCLOS, art 189 analysed by Virginia Commentary 635; see also AO Adede, 'The Law of the Sea – The Integration of the System of Settlement of Disputes under the Draft Convention as a Whole' (1978) 72 AJIL 84, 90.

[99] Virginia Commentary 619, 637.

[100] All three of these exceptions are contained within UNCLOS, art 189.

[101] UNCLOS, art 187; see also art 287(2).

[102] The Chamber's jurisdiction pertains to disputes between States Parties concerning interpretation or application of Part XI of UNCLOS and related Annexes: UNCLOS, art 187(a). In the event of such a dispute, States Parties may request it to be heard by a special chamber of ITLOS under Annex VI of the Convention, or by an ad hoc chamber of the Chamber formed under Annex VI (for more details on this, see art 188(1)(a)–(b)).

[103] The Chamber has jurisdiction over disputes between a State Party and the ISA concerning acts or omissions by either of them in violation of the entire UNCLOS deep seabed regime, including the Mining Code (UNCLOS, art 187(b)(i)); and over disputes between a State Party and the ISA concerning ultra vires acts by the ISA (UNCLOS, art 187(b)(ii)). This is in addition to the Chamber's jurisdiction over disputes in which a State Party is a party, or prospective party, to a mining contract within the Area, which will be discussed directly below, from the perspective of a private actor as contractor (see UNCLOS, art 187(c)–(e)).

standing before the Chamber is not restricted to States Parties or the ISA. In addition to the rights of States Parties and the ISA to appear before the Chamber, the Convention also permits contractors to participate directly in claims concerning certain types of disputes.[104] The Chamber's broad competence in this regard gives it remarkable global reach.[105] To reiterate Karavias's point, the exceptional aspect of this system is that 'corporations can act both as plaintiffs and defendants'.[106] Corporate contractors in the Area are in the unusual position of being both entitled to enforce rights *and* subject to enforcement of obligations on the international plane.[107] Moreover, ITLOS permits counterclaims, so parties defending claims before the Chamber will be entitled to initiate a counterclaim, 'provided that it is directly connected with the subject-matter of the claim of the other party and that it comes within the jurisdiction of the Tribunal'.[108]

The Chamber's jurisdiction over settlement of disputes in the Area involving contractors (or prospective contractors) can be divided into four categories,[109] which this section will consider in more detail, and in the following order:

i. Disputes between parties to a mining contract concerning interpretation or application of a contract or plan of work (UNCLOS, Article 187(c)(i));
ii. Disputes between parties to a mining contract concerning acts or omissions of a party to the contract relating to activities in the Area and either

[104] UNCLOS, art 187 and Annex VI, art 37. In the event that a private actor has standing to bring a claim before the Chamber, its sponsoring state has the right to participate in the proceedings too: UNCLOS, art 190(1).

[105] Karavias (n 6) 156. See also Chapter 6, Section 6.4.3 of this book.

[106] Karavias (n 6) 157. See also Chapter 6, Section 6.4.3 of this book.

[107] Dual standing of corporate actors within the deep seabed system has a degree of overlap with the position of investors under international investment law. In the latter scenario, as well as acting as claimant, an investor may be subject to counterclaims by its host state in certain circumstances. For example, in the ICSID context, a respondent state may instigate a counterclaim against an investor, provided that the counterclaim: (i) arises 'directly out of the subject-matter of the dispute'; (ii) is 'within the scope of the consent of the parties'; and (iii) falls 'otherwise within the jurisdiction of the Centre': ICSID Convention, art 46. For recent examples, see *Urbaser and others v The Argentine Republic* (Award) ICSID Case No ARB/07/26 (8 December 2016); *Burlington Resources Inc v Republic of Ecuador* (Decision on Counterclaims) ICSID Case No ARB/08/5 (7 February 2017); *David Aven et al v The Republic of Costa Rica* (Final Award) ICSID Case No UNCT/15/3 (18 September 2018). See, further, Anne K Hoffmann, 'Counterclaims in Investment Arbitration' (2013) 28 ICSID Rev – Foreign Investment LJ 438; Thomas Kendra, 'State Counterclaims in Investment Arbitration – A New Lease of Life?' (2013) 29 Arb Int'l 575. However, counterclaims against investors remain the exception to the rule. Moreover, host state counterclaims typically involve enforcement of *domestic law* obligations against investors. This can be contrasted to dispute resolution within the deep seabed mining context, which may involve enforcement of direct *international law* obligations against corporate entities.

[108] ITLOS Rules of the Tribunal (as amended on 25 March 2021) ITLOS/8, art 98(1).

[109] UNCLOS, art 187(c)–(e); see also Annex VI, art 37. See, further, 1994 Agreement, Annex, s 8(1)(f) (specifically applying the Convention's dispute settlement procedures to '[d]isputes concerning the interpretation or application of the rules and regulations' relating to the financial terms of contracts). ISA regulations also incorporate the dispute resolution mechanisms in Part XI of UNCLOS: Nodules Regulations, reg 40; Sulphides Regulations, reg 42; Cobalt Regulations, reg 42; Nodules, Sulphides and Cobalt Regulations, s 25, standard clauses, fourth annex; DERs, reg 106 and Annex X, s 18.

directed towards the other party or directly affecting its legitimate interests (UNCLOS, Article 187(c)(ii));

iii. Disputes between a contractor and the ISA concerning ISA liability for damage arising out of the ISA's wrongful acts in the exercise of its powers and functions (UNCLOS, Article 187(e)); and

iv. Disputes between a prospective contractor and the ISA relating to the refusal of a contract or in connection with a legal issue arising during negotiation of a contract (UNCLOS, Article 187(d)).[110]

As will be explored, while the first two grounds (i and ii) provide opportunities for either the contractor or the ISA to act as plaintiff or defendant, respectively, the final two grounds (iii and iv) are dedicated to allowing the contractor or prospective contractor to bring a claim against the ISA. The details of each of these grounds are set out below.

Firstly, and perhaps most crucially, the Chamber has jurisdiction over parties to a mining contract (be they 'States Parties, the Authority or the Enterprise, state enterprises and natural or juridical persons') concerning interpretation or application of a contract or plan of work.[111] By virtue of the contract, the entire UNCLOS deep seabed mining regime – with its various investment protections, including the ISA's regulations – is imported into the contractual relationship between the contractor and the ISA.[112] Therefore, this first ground of jurisdiction would encompass various types of dispute which a contractor may have against the ISA concerning enforcement of the contractor's investment protection rights. Equally, this ground would permit the ISA to bring a wide variety of claims against a contractor, including in relation to a contractor's failure to fulfil its direct obligations. This would encompass the full range of common heritage protections, such as those relating to financial terms and protection of the marine environment set out in Chapter 6. Indeed, this is where the importation of the entire deep seabed mining regime into the deep seabed mining contract may have its most significant impact: as a means by which to bind corporate contractors via directly enforceable obligations.

Notably, as regards this class of dispute, the contractor and/or the ISA is entitled to request that the claim be submitted to binding commercial arbitration conducted pursuant to the UNCITRAL Arbitration Rules.[113] However, the arbitral tribunal has no jurisdiction to decide any question of interpretation of the

[110] Although sequentially within UNCLOS, this is the third ground of standing for an ISA contractor, this book will consider it as the final ground, as it is more distinct from the rest, due to involving only *prospective* contractors.

[111] UNCLOS, art 187(c)(i).

[112] See Chapter 4, Section 4.3.

[113] UNCLOS, art 188(2)(a) and (c) (see also Annex III, art 13(15), which emphasises that this right to request binding commercial arbitration also applies to disputes between the ISA and the contractor specifically concerning 'interpretation or application of the financial terms of a contract').

Convention.[114] If such a question arises, the arbitral tribunal is obliged to refer it to the Chamber for a ruling.[115] Once it receives that ruling, the arbitral tribunal must deliver its award in a manner which is consistent with the ruling.[116]

Although this process has not yet been tested in practice, one could envisage that it would have similarities with the EU's preliminary reference procedure, which enables national courts to refer questions on interpretation or validity of European law to the Court of Justice of the EU.[117] However, the reference procedure for seabed disputes 'may prove a cumbersome procedure in the context of essentially commercial disputes', given that 'all States parties to the Convention have a right to intervene in such proceedings before the Chamber'.[118] In practice, whether any States Parties would choose to intervene in such proceedings remains to be seen.

Secondly, the Chamber's jurisdiction over parties to a mining contract extends to disputes in relation to 'acts or omissions of a party to the contract relating to activities in the Area and directed to the other party or directly affecting its legitimate interests'.[119] In practice, as the Virginia Commentary describes, disputes under this head can be submitted to the Chamber, but, in line with Article 189 of UNCLOS, the Chamber's jurisdiction is limited to the following three categories of claim:

> (a) [C]laims that the application of any rules, regulations, and procedures of the Authority in the claimant's case would be in conflict with the contractual obligations of the parties to the dispute or their obligations under the Convention; (b) claims concerning excess of jurisdiction or misuse of power; or (c) claims for damages to be paid or other remedy to given to the party concerned for the failure of the other party to comply with its contractual obligations or its obligation under this Convention.[120]

Nevertheless, this ground could present another important ground of challenge for a contractor, permitting scrutiny of actions or omissions by the ISA that interfere adversely with the contractor's deep seabed mining operations. Conversely, the ISA could rely on this provision to bring an action against a contractor in respect of a breach of its obligations.

[114] UNCLOS, art 188(2)(a).

[115] UNCLOS, art 188(2)(a)–(b).

[116] UNCLOS, art 188(2)(b).

[117] Consolidated Version of the Treaty on the Functioning of the European Union 2007 [2012] OJ C 326/47, art 267; see also John Collier and Vaughan Lowe, *The Settlement of Disputes in International Law – Institutions and Procedures* (OUP 1999) 89; see, further, Karavias (n 6) 158; Ciarán Burke, 'Article 189' in Proelss Commentary 1266.

[118] Robin R Churchill and A Vaughan Lowe, *The Law of the Sea* (3rd edn, Manchester UP 1999) 459, citing UNCLOS, Annex VI, arts 32, 40.

[119] UNCLOS, art 187(c)(ii).

[120] Virginia Commentary 619–620; see also UNCLOS, art 189, which is the source of these limitations. See the present section's analysis of this subject, at text to nn 95–100.

The final two grounds of the Chamber's jurisdiction in which corporate actors have standing both act as a means by which a contractor or prospective contractor can challenge the Authority. Under the third ground, the Chamber may decide disputes between the ISA and a contractor concerning ISA liability for any damage arising out of the ISA's wrongful acts in the exercise of its powers and functions.[121]

The final ground of standing for private actors allows a prospective contractor to raise an action against the ISA before the Chamber in circumstances where the prospective contractor has secured state sponsorship and complied with the other requisite conditions for issuance of a mining contract,[122] but the ISA has either refused to grant a contract, or else a legal issue has arisen during the negotiation of the contract.[123] This ground permits the ISA to be challenged for its unreasonable refusal to grant a mining contract.[124] This could be viewed as a means by which the prospective contractor's legitimate expectations are protected, in the event that it has satisfied the Convention's conditions for the granting of a contract, yet the ISA has refused to grant one.

As the preceding analysis has addressed, the Chamber's contentious jurisdiction is limited by Article 189 of UNCLOS to prevent it from conducting judicial review of any exercise by the ISA of its discretionary powers.[125] However, by virtue of the operation of the exceptions noted above, in respect of any of these four grounds of private actor standing, the Chamber may still decide whether there has been a violation of the Convention or the mining contract in a particular case, what damages or remedy should apply in the event of a breach of contract, or whether the ISA has acted ultra vires.[126] Therefore, although the Chamber does not function to 'provide a check on the law-making activities of the Authority',[127] the Chamber nevertheless retains competence to decide on many potential instances of ISA interference with a mining contract.[128]

[121] UNCLOS, art 187(e) and Annex III, art 22.

[122] On these conditions, see UNCLOS, Annex III, arts 4, 13(2).

[123] UNCLOS, art 187(d); see also 1994 Agreement, Annex, s 3(12).

[124] In addition to this means of challenge, the contractor has opportunities to amend its application, or make representations to the LTC, ahead of any potential refusal: see Nodules Regulations, reg 21(9); Sulphides Regulations, reg 23(9); Cobalt Regulations, reg 23(9), which all contain a process similar to an internal administrative appeals mechanism. See also DERs, reg 15(4).

[125] In contrast, for a conceptualisation of the investment treaty system as a form of judicial review see Federico Ortino, 'The Investment Treaty System as Judicial Review' (2013) 24 Am Rev Int'l Arb 437. However, as Ortino notes (at 457), there are 'outer boundaries' to the nature and intensity of the investment tribunal's review: the tribunal 'does not stand in the shoes of the primary decision-maker or does not have an open-ended mandate to second-guess government decision-making'. On levels of deference and standards of review generally, within the investment treaty system, see Roberts (2013) (n 7) 66–68; see also Stephan W Schill, 'Deference in Investment Treaty Arbitration: Re-conceptualizing the Standard of Review' (2012) 3 JIDS 577; Ortino (ibid) 458ff.

[126] UNCLOS, art 189; see discussion by Virginia Commentary 619–620.

[127] Harrison (2011) (n 95) 151.

[128] Although, see Sun (n 61) 79–81 (arguing that the limitation on judicial review in Article 189 weakens the effectiveness of the judicial remedies available to contractors, by creating a gap in the dispute resolution mechanism, particularly with regard to the bases of jurisdiction discussed in this section as grounds ii (i.e. UNCLOS, art 187(c)(ii)) and iv (art 187(d)).

7.2.2 Resolution of Disputes between Corporate Contractors and other Actors aside from the International Seabed Authority

As the preceding analysis has demonstrated, the UNCLOS deep seabed mining regime affords binding and enforceable dispute resolution mechanisms for contractors in relation to a range of disputes, and these mechanisms are primarily enforceable against the ISA. Equally, by virtue of these mechanisms, the ISA is entitled to enforce deep seabed mining obligations against contractors in the Area. However, given the array of actors within the Area, does the Convention include other routes for enforcement of corporate obligations (or rights)? For completeness, the following section will briefly assess the extent to which the Convention's deep seabed system applies to disputes between contractors and other parties aside from the Authority. If it does, this could be another important route by which to enforce common heritage obligations against corporate contractors (or, conversely, to implement contractor investor protections).

At first assessment, the four grounds (set out in Section 7.2.1) under which contractors have standing in relation to claims before the Chamber all appear to allow actions only between the contractor and the ISA, either as the other party to the contract (as per grounds i and ii[129]), or else because the ground of jurisdiction applies expressly between the contractor and the ISA (ground iii[130]) or the prospective contractor and the ISA (ground iv[131]). Curiously, in respect of the first and second grounds of jurisdiction under consideration here, and contained in Article 187(c)(i)–(ii) of UNCLOS, Article 190(2) provides that:

> If an action is brought against a State Party by a natural or juridical person sponsored by another State Party in a dispute referred to in article 187, subparagraph (c), the respondent State may request the State sponsoring that person to appear in the proceedings on behalf of that person. Failing such appearance, the respondent State may arrange to be represented by a juridical person of its nationality.

This provision implies in that, in certain circumstances, a private actor acting under Article 187(c) could be involved in an action with a State Party to UNCLOS, and that the latter may request the former's sponsoring state to appear in the proceedings on the private actor's behalf.

[129] Grounds i and ii in this chapter's analysis are contained within UNCLOS, art 187(c)(i)–(ii), which provides the Chamber with jurisdiction over specified 'disputes between parties to a contract, being States Parties, the Authority or the Enterprise, state enterprises and natural or juridical persons referred to in article 153, paragraph 2(b)'.

[130] UNCLOS, art 187(e) (covering 'disputes between the Authority and a State Party, a state enterprise or a natural or juridical person sponsored by a State Party as provided for in article 153, paragraph 2(b)').

[131] UNCLOS, art 187(d) (applying to 'disputes between the Authority and a prospective contractor').

However, Article 187(c) limits standing to apply only 'between parties to a contract, being States Parties, the Authority or the Enterprise, state enterprises and natural or juridical persons referred to in article 153, paragraph 2(b)'. Therefore, an action could be brought by a private actor against another State Party under Article 187(c) only in the narrow circumstances that both of them are parties to the same ISA mining contract. This could be the case, for example, in the event that various entities form a consortium to enter a contract with the ISA. As Brown describes:

> [I]t follows from Articles 187(c) and 188(2), and is confirmed by Article 190(2), that actions may be brought by a natural or juridical person of State A nationality against State B in the Sea-bed Disputes Chamber or, in relation to category (i) disputes, before a commercial arbitral tribunal. Of course, in both cases, such opportunities would be available only on the assumption that both of the disputing parties are contracting parties to the same contract. Thus, if a contract is concluded between the Authority on the one hand and State A and a company registered in State B (Company B) on the other hand, it would be possible for Company B to sue State A before the Sea-Bed Disputes Chamber.[132]

Only in circumstances such as these would the State Party's right under Article 190(2) be triggered.[133] Accordingly, under Article 187(c), contractors have standing to bring claims against their co-contractors. This provides a ground by which a contractor (be it a state, state enterprise or corporation) could challenge failure by its co-contractor to adhere to its common heritage obligations. However, the utility of this mechanism is likely to be limited, in practice, especially given that, at present, all ISA contracts are between the ISA and a single contractor.

This limited instance of co-contractor action aside, the UNCLOS dispute resolution system does not provide standing to private actors to bring claims before the Chamber against their sponsoring state, other contractors operating independently in the Area (be they state or private actors), coastal states or third states conducting activities in the Area, or vice versa. During the drafting of the Convention, arguments were made that 'there should be provision covering disputes between contractors who had independent contracts with the Authority although they did not have a contract between themselves'.[134]

[132] ED Brown, *Sea-bed Energy and Minerals: The International Legal Regime*, vol 2 (Martin Nijhoff Publishers 2001) 145.

[133] As Brown notes, the 'distinctly odd provision' contained in UNCLOS, art 190(2) was a result of a drafting compromise to appease the socialist state negotiating bloc's reluctance for proceedings to be brought directly against a state by a private actor sponsored by another state: see Brown (2001) (n 132) 370; see also Virginia Commentary 639–640.

[134] See 'Report by the Chairman of the Group of Legal Experts on the Settlement of Disputes Relating to Part XI' (29 August 1979) UN Doc A/CONF.62/91, 92; see also Brown (2001) (n 132) 145.

However, this suggestion was not reflected in the final text of the Convention.[135]

However, the ISA's existing exploration regulations do provide a mechanism by which coastal states can raise concerns with the ISA about a contractor's activities, if the coastal state believes that these activities may cause serious harm to the marine environment within its national jurisdiction.[136] This could be a useful means by which a state could initiate a formal process in respect of a contractor's potential breach of common heritage obligations. Pursuant to this process, the Secretary-General must allow the contractor and its sponsoring state a reasonable time to examine and respond to the evidence. Ultimately, the ISA can resort to emergency measures in response to the unfolding environmental situation.[137]

From a corporate contractor's perspective, the lack of a means within the UNCLOS regime by which a contractor can bring a claim against its sponsoring state in relation to wrongful suspension or termination of sponsorship is, arguably, a key gap in the system. However, in any event, suspension or termination of sponsorship by the state sponsor would not extinguish the contractor's ongoing deep seabed mining operations. The Convention regime allows the contractor six months in which to make alternative sponsorship arrangements.[138] Therefore, in contrast to the typical investment law paradigm, whereby host state interference with an investment may spell the end of the project, within the deep seabed mining context the investment may be rerouted, and the project continued under the auspices of alternative sponsorship arrangements.

In addition, to a certain extent there are indirect routes within the UNCLOS system for resolution of disputes between a contractor and either other contractors, third states or the state sponsor. For example, one such indirect route may be open in circumstances where the sponsoring state has violated its sponsorship undertakings in a way that constitutes a flagrant breach of UNCLOS. States Parties are obliged to fulfil their obligations under the deep seabed mining regime 'in good

[135] Earlier iterations of the draft Convention included broader grounds of jurisdiction for the Chamber, encompassing '[d]isputes brought by a State Party against a national of another State Party, or *between nationals of different States Parties*, regarding the interpretation or application of any contract between them, *or in respect of their activities in the Area*' (emphasis added) (this previous version of what was then Article 189, and now forms part of Article 187, is reproduced and analysed in Virginia Commentary 616). The italicised words in this quotation appear to suggest that a contractor would have standing to bring an action against another independent contractor in respect of their activities in the Area. However, this version was amended to ultimately become the current, more restrictive draft within UNCLOS, art 187(1)(c); see Virginia Commentary 609–619 on the drafting process of this article.

[136] Nodules Regulations, reg 34(2); Sulphides Regulations, reg 36(2); Cobalt Regulations, reg 36(2); similarly, see DERs, reg 4(3).

[137] Nodules Regulations, reg 34(3); Sulphides Regulations, reg 36(3); Cobalt Regulations, reg 36(3); see also DERs, reg 4(4).

[138] Nodules Regulations, reg 29(3); Sulphides Regulations, reg 31(3); Cobalt Regulations, reg 31(3). See also DERs, reg 21(2) (extending this grace period to twelve months for a state sponsor's termination of an exploitation contract, except in relation to termination for contractor non-compliance, which must take effect within six months).

faith'.[139] As the Chamber emphasised when commenting on the application of this good faith obligation in relation to sponsoring states:

> Reasonableness and non-arbitrariness must remain the hallmarks of any action taken by the sponsoring State. Any failure on the part of the sponsoring State to act reasonably may be challenged before this Chamber under article 187 (b) (i) of the Convention.[140]

The jurisdictional grounds in Article 187(b)(i) of UNCLOS are a two-way street, empowering the Chamber to decide actions brought by either a State Party or the ISA concerning violations of the Convention regime by the other. Therefore, if a sponsoring state breaches its sponsorship undertaking in bad faith, circumstances could arise in which the ISA may bring an action against that state, which could include seeking provisional measures for the state to halt its violations. Nevertheless, the contractor, in this scenario, would remain unable to raise a direct claim against its state sponsor under UNCLOS. However, as discussed in Section 7.1.5, it does not necessarily follow from the absence of such mechanisms within UNCLOS that alternative avenues do not exist. For example, a contractor may have access to direct dispute resolution methods against its sponsor state on the basis of domestic law, the sponsorship agreement itself or other international law arrangements.[141] However, a contractor would be likely to face significant jurisdictional obstacles if it sought to apply an investment treaty against its state sponsor in relation to a deep seabed mining dispute.[142]

Another indirect means of dispute resolution may be available if a contractor faces encroachment or interference in its mining contract area by another contractor. In these circumstances, the original contractor may be able to commence proceedings directly against the ISA for failing to guarantee security of tenure. In some respects, this would be conceptually similar to investment arbitration proceedings against a host state for failing to guarantee FPS to an investment, against the actions of other actors.

Overall, as this section has demonstrated, the possibility of using the Convention's dispute resolution mechanisms to resolve disputes between corporate contractors and other actors, aside from the ISA, remain limited at best. Article 187(c) of UNCLOS allows for direct actions between contractors to the same mining contract. Where the contract is between the ISA and more than one miner (including any combination of states, state enterprises or private contractors), Article 187(c) allows these co-contractors to bring claims against each other.

[139] UNCLOS, art 157(4); see also art 300.

[140] ITLOS AO, para 230 (see also paras 179–180, concerning compensation for such a claim).

[141] See previous discussion on this point in Section 7.1.5 at text to nn 82–84. As noted, this issue is beyond this book's consideration.

[142] See previous discussion in Section 7.1.5, at n 83.

In practice, this possibility is unlikely to be utilised. Alternatively, in accordance with the exploration regulations, coastal states can raise environmental concerns with the ISA, in relation to a contractor's activities.[143] This process augments the potential for enforcement of corporate contractors' common heritage obligations of marine environmental protection. However, outside of these two examples, the UNCLOS dispute resolution provisions do not give standing before the Chamber to private actors in relation to disputes involving their sponsoring state, other contractors operating independently in the Area (be they state or private actors), coastal states or third states conducting activities in the Area. Consequently, the main route for enforcement of corporate obligations in relation to the Area is by means of ISA action.

7.2.3 Concluding Reflections: Can Corporate Rights and Obligations be Reconciled?

Throughout the life cycle of a deep seabed mining operation, the ISA plays a role functionally equivalent to that of a host state in the context of international investment law. Therefore, the Convention's focus on direct dispute resolution mechanisms that involve the ISA (as both enforcer and defendant) is unsurprising. As the preceding analysis has demonstrated, the UNCLOS dispute resolution system affords deep seabed mining contractors the opportunity to take direct action against the ISA, in the event of various categories of disputes relating to the operation or implementation of a mining contract or in the face of wrongful acts or omissions by the ISA. Equally, the ISA may bring proceedings against contractors in relation to breaches of contract or other acts and omissions in respect of their activities in the Area. This will be a vital means by which the ISA can seek to further the common heritage by holding contractors to account for violations of their obligations.

Significantly, either the ISA or the contractor may elect to submit disputes concerning the interpretation or application of a mining contract or plan of work to binding commercial arbitration under the UNCITRAL Rules.[144] As regards contractor dispute settlement before the Chamber, the Chamber's decisions are binding and enforceable in much the same way as the award of an international arbitral tribunal.[145] Also consistent with the mechanisms typically available within international arbitration is the fact that contractors are entitled to seek provisional

[143] Nodules Regulations, reg 34(2); Sulphides Regulations, reg 36(2); Cobalt Regulations, reg 36(2); similarly, see DERs, reg 4(3).

[144] UNCLOS, art 188(2)(a) and (c).

[145] See UNCLOS, Annex VI, art 39, which, in terms comparable to ICSID Convention, art 54, provides that 'decisions of the Chamber shall be enforceable in the territories of the States Parties in the same manner as judgments or orders of the highest court of the State Party in whose territory the enforcement is sought'; see also Collier and Lowe (n 117) 89.

measures in relation to a deep seabed mining dispute before the Chamber.[146] As noted previously, counterclaims are permitted before the Chamber.[147] In all of these respects, the UNCLOS deep seabed mining regime again shares similarities with the investment treaty arbitration system.

Ultimately, the Chamber's approach to any claim by a contractor that the Authority has violated investment protections inherent within UNCLOS has not yet been tested. As this chapter has discussed, the terms of contractor rights within the Convention differ from those commonly found in international investment agreements. However, to some extent the substance of both types of protections is comparable. Therefore, when deciding on particular disputes involving contractor rights that are akin to international investment entitlements, the Chamber may draw on, and further develop, the existing body of investment treaty jurisprudence.[148]

In practice, the Chamber's approach may require a balancing exercise similar to that deployed by investment arbitral tribunals when evaluating the appropriate exercise of regulatory authority by the host state (or, in this case, the Authority) versus rights of the investor, in a particular case. This key tension point within international investment law inevitably entails a delicate balance of competing entitlements. Indeed, Ortino goes so far as to designate this as the fundamental debate underpinning the investment law system.[149]

As Chapter 6 has demonstrated, one notable aspect of the deep seabed mining regime is its evolutionary design. It incorporates an inherent regulatory flexibility, permitting the ISA to refine and develop the regime through further regulations (which may be amended periodically), and to issue recommendations or, as regards exploitation, standards and guidelines.[150] For example, built into both the exploration regulations and the current DERs is the ability of the ISA to

[146] UNCLOS, art 290; see also Annex VI, art 25.

[147] ITLOS Rules of the Tribunal, art 98(1).

[148] cf ICJ dismissal of the relevance of investment arbitration jurisprudence when ruling that Bolivia was not entitled to rely on the doctrine of legitimate expectations (as 'found in arbitral awards concerning disputes between a foreign investor and the host State that apply treaty clauses providing for fair and equitable treatment') as against Chile, because this doctrine does not give rise to a principle of general international law 'that would give rise to an obligation on the basis of what could be considered a legitimate expectation': *Obligation to Negotiate Access to the Pacific Ocean (Bolivia v Chile)* (Judgment) [2018] ICJ Rep 507, para 162. However, this finding can be distinguished for present purposes as, in that case, Bolivia was seeking to rely on a principle of investment protection that did not apply to its relationship with Chile. Whereas, within the deep seabed context, there are contractor rights within the regime with some functional equivalence to typical investment protections, rendering reliance on investment arbitration jurisprudence more apposite.

[149] Ortino (n 125) 437 ('[a]t a more fundamental level, it seems that the debate about the nature of the system revolves around the following two key values: granting maximum protection to foreign investors and safeguarding host States' ability to regulate in the public interest'). See also Anthea Roberts, 'Triangular Treaties: The Extent and Limits of Investment Treaty Rights' (2015) 56 Harv Int'l LJ 353, 378–382.

[150] See discussion in Chapter 6, Section 6.3.

subject these rules to continued, periodic review.[151] In addition, particularly in the exploitation context, ISA standards and guidelines are likely to play a key role in providing a sufficiently detailed exploitation regime that is capable of evolving to meet new challenges and demands.[152] However, what is the outer limit of the regime's flexibility in the face of a contractor's claim for regulatory certainty?

As this study has already addressed,[153] if the ISA amends its exploration regulations, a contract under the amended regulations can only be updated if the contractor consents.[154] However, on the basis of the current DERs, a contractor is put on notice that it must comply with the ISA's rules 'as amended from time to time'.[155] As such, the ISA has identified that one of the key challenges facing it is to strike an appropriate '[b]alance between certainty and predictability, as well as flexibility and adaptability'.[156] As the LTC has elucidated:

> [It] is conscious of the need to develop a regulatory framework that provides certainty, predictability and stability for the contractor base and other stakeholders, while at the same time providing flexibility and adaptability to adjust the framework as the industry develops and new knowledge becomes available. That balance, at times, is a delicate one.[157]

Accordingly, in the deep seabed mining context, perhaps the most challenging tension point to confront the Chamber will be determination of the permissible extent of the ISA's right to regulatory freedom versus the contractor's right to certainty. Such a dispute may arise, in particular, in relation to the ISA's future regulatory developments concerning the regime's benefit-sharing or marine environmental protection aspects.

In this event, the Chamber may be guided by the approach of investment arbitral tribunals in comparable circumstances. The approach of such tribunals varies as to whether state regulation for public purposes (e.g. for environmental or public health goals) constitutes a breach of investor rights.[158] As Roberts notes, '[n]o

[151] See, e.g. general review powers at Nodules Regulations, reg 42; Sulphides Regulations, reg 44; Cobalt Regulations, reg 44; DERs, reg 107.

[152] See DERs, regs 1(5), 45, 65(1), 94–95.

[153] See Chapter 6, Section 6.3 and Section 7.1.1, at text to nn 35–36.

[154] Nodules Regulations, reg 42(4); Sulphides Regulations, reg 44(4); Cobalt Regulations, reg 44(4), read with s 24 of the standard clauses to mining contracts (which forms the fourth annex in all three sets of regulations, and requires contractor consent for contract revision).

[155] DERs, Annex X, s 3.3(a) (albeit, as per ibid, s 16, contractor consent is still required for actual contract revision).

[156] ISA LTC, 'Draft Regulations on Exploitation of Mineral Resources in the Area – Note by the Legal and Technical Commission' (10 July 2018) ISBA/24/C/20, para 22.

[157] ISBA/24/C/20, para 22.

[158] See, generally, analysis and case law citations within Thomas Waelde and Abba Kolo, 'Environmental Regulation, Investment Protection and "Regulatory Taking" in International Law' (2001) 50 ICLQ 811; Kriebaum (n 32); Kingsbury and Schill (n 32); Rahim Moloo and Justin Jacinto, 'Environmental and Health Regulation: Assessing Liability under Investment Treaties' (2011)

single formula exists for determining the precise balance that should be struck between these goals'.[159] To some extent, a tribunal's approach depends on the particular investment standard at issue.[160] Different tribunals have adopted different methodologies.[161] Nevertheless, within investment treaty jurisprudence, one can glean certain common factors which, when present, mitigate in favour of the permissibility of state regulatory conduct.

For example, in *Fireman's Fund v Mexico,* the tribunal held that, in order 'to distinguish between a compensable expropriation and a non-compensable regulation by a host State', factors that a tribunal may take into account include:

> [W]hether the measure is within the recognized police powers of the host State; the (public) purpose and effect of the measure; whether the measure is discriminatory; the proportionality between the means employed and the aim sought to be realized; and the bona fide nature of the measure.[162]

Similarly, again in the expropriation context, when considering a case under NAFTA concerning US environmental regulation, the *Methanex* tribunal held that:

> As a matter of general international law, a non-discriminatory regulation for a public purpose, which is enacted in accordance with due process and, which affects, *inter alios*, a foreign investor or investment is not deemed expropriatory and compensable unless specific commitments had been given by the regulating government to the then putative foreign investor

29 Berkley J Int'l L 1; Jorge E Viñuales, *Foreign Investment and the Environment in International Law* (CUP 2012); Jason Haynes, 'The Evolving Nature of the Fair and Equitable Treatment (FET) Standard: Challenging its Increasing Pervasiveness in Light of Developing Countries' Concerns – The Case for Regulatory Rebalancing' (2013) 14 J World Investment Trade 114; Daniel Behn and Malcolm Langford, 'Trumping the Environment? An Empirical Perspective on the Legitimacy of Investment Treaty Arbitration' (2017) 18 J World Investment Trade 14; Harrison (2020) (n 83) 496–501. See also Graham Mayeda, 'Integrating Environmental Impact Assessments into International Investment Agreements: Global Administrative Law and Transnational Cooperation' (2017) 18 J World Investment Trade 131.

[159] Roberts (2015) (n 149).

[160] See, e.g. analysis of tribunal approaches in relation to claims that regulatory action infringed expropriation, FET and discrimination standards, in Moloo and Jacinto and Viñuales (both n 158). See, further, Kriebaum (n 32) (on expropriation) and Haynes (n 158) (on FET).

[161] On tribunal use of police powers, proportionality and margin of appreciation analysis in such circumstances, see Kriebaum (n 32); Kingsbury and Schill (n 32); Moloo and Jacinto (n 158). See also Viñuales (n 158) for detailed analysis of the scope of the police powers doctrine (367–376) and margin of appreciation doctrine (376–381), including considerations of proportionality in respect of both doctrines.

[162] *Fireman's Fund Insurance Company v The United Mexican States* (Award) ICSID Case No ARB(AF)/02/1 (17 July 2006), para 176(j) (citations omitted).

> contemplating investment that the government would refrain from such regulation.[163]

More recently, in the public health context, the *Philip Morris* tribunal held that Uruguay's restrictions on the tobacco industry were a legitimate exercise of state regulatory powers, on the basis that these measures were 'taken *bona fide* for the purpose of protecting the public welfare [and were] non-discriminatory and proportionate'.[164] Overall, in circumstances where state regulation is a proportionate measure for legitimate purposes, backed by scientific evidence (where relevant), adopted pursuant to due process and not in violation of any specific assurances to the investor, tribunals have been inclined to view it as a permissible exercise of a state's regulatory powers rather than a breach of investment rights.[165]

As regards deep seabed mining, any such regulatory change would be likely to satisfy these factors. For example, the ISA intends that the regime should keep pace with legitimate, science-based developments in marine environmental protection. In the event of evolution of the regime, and in keeping with due process, the LTC considers that '[a]ny amendments to the regulations, adoption of standards or the issue of guidelines having a material impact on contractor operations should be consulted on in advance of any amendments or adoption'.[166]

Moreover, there are specific features within the UNCLOS regime that may strengthen the ISA's basis to regulate flexibly. Firstly, as this chapter has already addressed, in light of the constraint within UNCLOS, Article 189, the Chamber lacks jurisdiction to judicially review the Authority's exercise of its discretionary powers, such as the Authority's amendment of the Mining Code. If a contractor instigates a challenge to such an amendment, the Chamber would only be able to assess the extent to which the ISA has breached the contractor's contract by its actions.

Secondly, the contractor's rights must be interpreted in the context of the Convention's deep seabed regime as a whole, including the provisions of the Mining Code.[167] The deep seabed system includes various common heritage protections, including those relating to benefit-sharing and marine environmental protection, and it provides for their ongoing protection and development.[168] Indeed, in this respect, to some extent the UNCLOS deep seabed mining regime is most akin to

[163] *Methanex Corporation v United States of America* (Award) UNCITRAL (3 August 2005), Part IV, ch D, para 7.

[164] *Philip Morris Brands Sàrl, Philip Morris Products SA and Abal Hermanos SA v Oriental Republic of Uruguay* (Award) ICSID Case No ARB/10/7 (8 July 2016), para 305 (citation omitted).

[165] See overview in Harrison (2020) (n 83) 497–501 (considering the balance between investment protection and coastal state environmental regulation in the context of seabed investments). See also Moloo and Jacinto (n 158) 24–33, 60–62.

[166] ISBA/24/C/20, para 22.

[167] See previous analysis and citations in Chapter 4, text to nn 319–322, on means by which the entire UNCLOS deep seabed regime is transposed to apply directly to contractors by operation of the contract.

[168] See analysis in Chapter 6, in Sections 6.1, 6.2 and 6.3, respectively.

the subset of investment treaties that carve out express protection for public purposes (such as the environment and public health) within their text.[169] As Moloo and Jacinto note, where an investment treaty 'expressly addresses matters relating to health and the environment, it will be important to interpret the substantive [investment] protections contained therein within the context of the relevant health and environmental provisions'.[170] Equally, as regards deep seabed mining, the contractor's protections must be read in light of the regime's common heritage provisions. These provisions enshrine benefit sharing and marine environmental protection, and reserve the ISA's ability to continue to regulate and evolve the regime in an evolutionary manner to further these purposes.

Thirdly – and following on from this – as is evident from the preceding analysis, deep seabed mining contractors have chosen to participate within a system that is subject to continuous review, ongoing monitoring and evolution.[171] On this basis, deep seabed mining contractors are comparable to investors in other industries that are subject to evolving, and often increasingly stringent, regulatory systems (e.g. the tobacco and energy industries, to name but two).[172] To participate within the deep seabed mining regime, the ISA contractor must accept that the regime will be subject to a certain degree of continuous evolution. This is part of the ordinary commercial investment risk that the contractor assumes by investing within this industry.[173] Indeed, as regards the exploitation phase, arguably the room for regulatory evolution is more expansive, as the contractor will be expressly on notice that it must abide by rules 'as amended from time to time'.[174]

[169] See detailed overview and examples in Moloo and Jacinto (n 158) 8–11. On environmental 'carve-outs', see also Waelde and Kolo (n 158) 814ff; Kathryn Gordon and Joachim Pohl, 'Environmental Concerns in International Investment Agreements: A Survey' (2011) OECD Working Paper on International Investment 2011/01 <www.oecd.org/daf/inv/investment-policy/WP-2011_1.pdf>; Viñuales (n 158) 311ff.

[170] Moloo and Jacinto (n 158) 10.

[171] See, generally, Chapter 6.

[172] See, e.g. tribunal finding in *Philip Morris* (n 164), para 430 that 'in light of widely accepted articulations of international concern for the harmful effect of tobacco, the expectation [of the investor] could only have been of progressively more stringent regulation of the sale and use of tobacco products'. This finding could be read across to the deep seabed mining industry, where, arguably, miners 'can have no expectation that new and more onerous regulations will not be imposed', in the environmental context especially (ibid, para 429). Equally, see *Antaris GmbH and Dr Michael Göde v The Czech Republic* (Award) PCA Case No 2014-01 (2 May 2018) concerning host state amendments to an incentive regime for renewable energy, as regards which the tribunal held that the claimant's actions 'were essentially opportunistic, and that the investment protection regime was never intended to promote and safeguard those who, in the words of the Respondent, "pile in" to take advantage of laws which they must know may be in a state of flux caused essentially by investors of that type' (para 435), noting also that the claimant 'should have been aware that other legislative changes, especially with regard to tax, were in the air' (para 433), as this 'would have been obvious to anyone who participated in industry discussions, or paid attention to warnings by specialist professionals, or read the local press' (para 434).

[173] See, e.g. Viñuales (n 158) 312. See also Moloo and Jacinto (n 158) 24–25, fn 126. For a comparable argument in the deep seabed mining context, see Jaeckel (2017) (n 36) 259, proposing that, 'while a regulatory framework should protect contractors from arbitrary obligations imposed during the lifetime of a contract, the regulatory framework also needs to reflect the frontier nature of seabed mining including the financial risks and potential profits that accompany frontier activities'.

[174] DERs, Annex X, s 3.3(a).

Accordingly, as the previous analysis has demonstrated, contractor investment protections should, in the event of a dispute, be capable of being applied in a manner that does not inhibit the ISA's continuing ability to regulate. In theory, this should allow the ISA to continue to develop its regulatory regime in a flexible manner, in response to evolving challenges, while offering corporate contractors sufficient comfort to secure their investment in deep seabed mining.

Concluding Remarks on Corporate Entity Involvement in Deep Seabed Mining

'Doesn't it seem to you,' asked Madame Bovary, 'that the mind moves more freely in the presence of that boundless expanse, that the sight of it elevates the soul and gives rise to thoughts of the infinite and the ideal?'
(Gustave Flaubert, *Madame Bovary*, 1857)

'The world is watching and we have to deliver': so remarked the Council President when opening the ISA's 2018 Session.[1] Now is, indeed, a pivotal time for deep seabed mining beyond national jurisdiction. After decades of anticipation and uncertainty, there are indications that exploitation of deep seabed minerals may begin in the coming years. With commencement of this new phase will come great legal challenges, not least in terms of the need to implement a commercially viable system which includes robust environmental safeguards and an equitable system for distribution of mining profits. Above all, the regime must further its founding principle: that the Area and its mineral resources constitute the common heritage of mankind.

For the deep seabed mining industry to flourish, investment by private corporate actors looks set to be a driving force. Only private investment is likely to afford sufficient capital and requisite technical expertise to achieve a viable deep seabed mining industry in the longer term. Therefore, the purpose of this book has been to examine the role of corporate actors as participants within the deep seabed mining regime, with an emphasis on the implications of this participation for the common heritage's realisation.

To this end, Part I provided the essential backdrop to this analysis by evaluating both the rise of mining activities in the Area, including by non-state actors, and the pivotal role of the common heritage concept in the deep seabed mining context.

[1] IISD Reporting Services, 'Summary of the Twenty-fourth Annual Session of the ISA (First Part): 5–9 March 2018' (12 March 2018) 25:157 Earth Negotiations Bulletin 12 <http://enb.iisd.org/download/pdf/enb25157e.pdf>.

International Law and Corporate Actors in Deep Seabed Mining. Joanna Dingwall, Oxford University Press. © Joanna Dingwall 2021. DOI: 10.1093/oso/9780192898265.003.0009

In particular, as Chapter 3 established, the modern-day common heritage concept can be distilled into four central components: the common management principle, the prohibition of unilateral mining activities, the benefit-sharing principle and the principle of marine environmental protection. Moreover, as Chapter 3's historical analysis of the concept's evolution revealed, the common heritage is premised on a delicate balance between securing benefits for humankind while also fostering commercial participation in line with market principles. To achieve its common heritage goals, the regime must satisfy both of these objectives and, accordingly, attain a balance between 'community and autonomy'.[2]

Consequently, this study has sought to determine the extent to which the UNCLOS regime operationalises the four common heritage components, while maintaining a balance between humanity's interests and commercial market principles. In order to do so, this study applied a four-step analysis (as illustrated in Chapter 3, Section 3.3, Table 3.1). This analysis, set across Parts II and III, served to evaluate the achievement of the common heritage concept in relation to corporate deep seabed mining activities.

Part II focused on process: seeking to determine whether the UNCLOS deep seabed mining regime creates an institutional system constraining actors both inside and outside of it. Firstly, Chapter 4 addressed Step 1, by establishing that the UNCLOS regime provides a procedural, institutional architecture for common management of the deep seabed, and that this framework applies to all participants within the regime, including corporate actors (thereby achieving the first common heritage component).

Thereafter, Chapter 5 answered Step 2, by determining that the prohibition of unilateral deep seabed mining activities prevents external actors, including corporate actors, from acting incompatibly with the UNCLOS regime (thus securing the second common heritage component). Indeed, as Chapter 5, Section 5.4, summarised in Table 5.2, perhaps one of the most complex and interesting aspects of the regime's global reach is the varying means by which state and non-state actors are brought within it, depending on factors such as treaty-party status or nationality, respectively.

Thus, as Part II concluded, the UNCLOS deep seabed mining regime operationalises the common heritage in a manner that has global implications: it creates a procedural framework for common management, and prohibits external actors from conducting unilateral mining activities outside of it. After arriving at this positive conclusion on the procedural reach of the Convention's common heritage principle, Part III progressed to consider the key material goals of the common heritage ideal: benefit sharing and marine environmental protection.

[2] Martti Koskenniemi, *From Apology to Utopia: The Structure of International Legal Argument* (CUP 2005) 476, and see 488–493.

As Chapter 6 addressed, while incorporating these material goals in a 'formal-procedural way', the UNCLOS regime engages in a 'strategy of referral', deferring their ultimate realisation to further institutional procedures.[3] The substance of these matters, therefore, requires resolution within the ISA's regulatory regime. In large part, the achievement of the substantive core of the common heritage concept will be dependent on the ISA's effective institutional workings, for example through enactment and enforcement of appropriate regulations.

To that end, Chapter 6 addressed Step 3, by providing an initial assessment of the extent to which the ISA's developing regulatory framework (and accompanying implementation and enforcement powers) are on track to yield benefit-sharing and marine environmental protection aspects. As Chapter 6 concluded, this appraisal can, at present, be only an interim one. Currently, the ISA is facing significant challenges, especially in its attempts to devise a workable payment mechanism that will deliver tangible benefits to humanity, while also ensuring that the overall regime delivers sufficient marine environmental protections. However, although considerable work is necessary, the regulatory regime is developing in a direction that should, at least, have the capacity to safeguard the common heritage's key material components from corporate infringement (thereby achieving the third and fourth common heritage components). The scope of the ISA's existing draft regulatory regime is shaping up to be increasingly comprehensive, endeavouring to regulate the paramount substantive elements of benefit sharing and marine environmental protection, and leaving room for the rules to adapt to new challenges, while securing a sophisticated system of implementation, responsibility and enforcement.

Perhaps most notably, within this process, the Convention's deep seabed mining system provides a 'shared surface'[4] on which participants (such as the ISA and its constituent organs, States Parties, observer states, ISA contractors (including corporate actors) and civil society more generally) can work together to develop a regulatory regime that aims to achieve common heritage ends while remaining viable in practice. On this basis, Chapter 6 delivered another positive conclusion for the reconciliation of the Convention's common heritage goals with corporate actor participation.

However, the final strand of analysis required to address Step 4. It did so by determining whether the UNCLOS regime strikes an appropriate balance between realising benefits to humanity and respecting market principles. Specifically, does the regime strike a suitable regulatory balance between benefit of humanity concerns and investment protection rights for deep seabed miners? This issue was selected as the crucial barometer of the community/autonomy equilibrium

[3] Koskenniemi (2005) (n 2) 492–493; see also David Kennedy, *International Legal Structures* (Nomos Verlagsgesellschaft 1987) 201–245.

[4] Martti Koskenniemi, 'What is International Law for?' in Malcolm D Evans (ed), *International Law* (5th edn, OUP 2018) 46.

because investment protection rights are likely to be a key driver in securing corporate investment in the Area. They serve as an important indicator of the extent to which the regime is sufficiently 'market-oriented' (in the words of the preamble to the 1994 Agreement).

Chapter 7 answered Step 4 in the affirmative, by demonstrating that the UNCLOS regime affords protections to corporate actors (and other deep seabed miners) that are broadly equivalent in scope to more traditional investment law entitlements. Within the Convention regime, there are numerous provisions that operate cumulatively to safeguard investor rights in deep seabed mining. These protections are focused primarily on insulating the investor from undue interference by the main regulator and overseer of the regime: the Authority. Moreover, these investment rights are backed by binding and enforceable dispute resolution options. Significantly, as Chapter 7 demonstrated, contractor investment protections should be capable of being applied in a manner that does not hamper the ISA's continuing ability to regulate concerning the benefit-sharing and marine environmental aspects of the regime. In theory, this should allow the ISA to continue to develop and enhance the regulatory regime in a flexible manner to respond to evolving challenges, while offering corporate contractors sufficiently robust investment protection guarantees to secure their investment in deep seabed mining.

In conclusion, the UNCLOS deep seabed mining regime has come a long way since its tentative beginnings. From its belated inception in the mid 1990s, after years of polarised, Cold War stalemate, it has evolved to become the sleek system of today: a true example of international administration, unrivalled and effectively universal. In that sense, the regime affords a unique opportunity to engage with what Reisman describes as the true purpose of law:

> [Law] is really about making decisions for the future: about maintaining an appropriate constitutive structure within which all decisions are taken, about maintaining, and hopefully enhancing minimum order and, within those constraints, about identifying the most efficient ways of shaping all the productive processes of social life and about the ways of sharing their fruits within a sustainable ecology.[5]

Operating within this framework, the practical realisation of the regime's common heritage purpose may seem within touching distance. Nevertheless, considerable challenges remain. Achievement of the common heritage will be dependent on the ISA's regulatory regime fulfilling its potential, and implementing a comprehensive Mining Code to govern the entire life cycle of deep seabed mining operations. As the ISA works to implement its regulations and enhance the Mining Code through

[5] W Michael Reisman, *The Quest for World Order and Human Dignity in the Twenty-first Century* (Brill 2013) 22.

detailed consultation with stakeholders, this next phase will be a fundamental step towards long-term attainment of a workable commercial industry in the Area, and the operationalisation of the common heritage.

On balance, it is the conclusion of this study that the UNCLOS deep seabed mining regime is evolving in a manner which, with careful development, may render it capable of realising its common heritage goals of securing communitarian benefits to humanity, alongside market-focused objectives. In this sense, one could argue that corporate participation in the regime is not merely compatible with the common heritage; rather, such participation may assist in the achievement of the common heritage by providing the commercial means to allow deep seabed mining to commence within a globally accepted framework. Indeed, notwithstanding the very real challenges that lie ahead in devising an appropriate system for exploitation, one triumph of the deep seabed mining regime is that it represents the first time in history that common resources have been recognised as such, safeguarded, and regulated on an intensive, global basis *before* the commencement of commercial activities has begun. Moreover, one of the most striking elements of the UNCLOS deep seabed mining regime is that it demonstrates the potential for international law to create sophisticated, enforceable systems of direct rights and obligations upon private corporate actors, where the international community has the willingness to do so.

APPENDIX 1

Types of Contractors Participating in Exploration Activities in the Area

This table provides an overview of the existing ISA contractors holding exploration contracts in the Area, while Appendix 2 provides details of their exploration contracts.

Contractor	Type of Entity (and State Sponsor, if Applicable)
States	
India	State Party
Poland	State Party
Russia	State Party
South Korea	State Party
Consortiums	
Interoceanmetal Joint Organization	consortium of States Parties (Bulgaria, Cuba, Czech Republic, Poland, Russia and Slovakia)
State enterprises, State institutions and other State-controlled entities	
Beijing Pioneer Hi-Tech Development Corporation	state enterprise (China)[1]
China Minmetals Corporation	state enterprise (China)[2]

[1] ISA LTC, 'Report and Recommendations of the Legal and Technical Commission to the Council Relating to an Application for Approval of a Plan of Work for Exploration for Polymetallic Nodules by the Beijing Pioneer Hi-Tech Development Corporation' (28 June 2019) ISBA/25/C/30, para 26; see also ISA Press Release, 'Beijing Pioneer Hi-Tech Development Corporation Submits Plans for Exploration of Polymetallic Nodules in the Western Pacific Ocean' (23 January 2019) <www.isa.org.jm/news/beijing-pioneer-hi-tech-development-corporation-submits-plans-exploration-polymetallic-nodules>.

[2] ISA LTC, 'Report and Recommendations of the Legal and Technical Commission to the Council of the ISA Relating to an Application for the Approval of a Plan of Work for Exploration for Polymetallic Nodules by China Minmetals Corporation' (5 March 2015) ISBA/21/C/2, para 9.

Contractor	Type of Entity (and State Sponsor, if Applicable)
China Ocean Mineral Resources Research and Development Association	state enterprise (China)[3]
Companhia de Pesquisa de Recursos Minerais SA	state enterprise (Brazil)[4]
Cook Islands Investment Corporation (*CIIC*)	state enterprise (Cook Islands)[5] In order to undertake its ISA contract, CIIC entered into a joint venture agreement with private Belgian corporation Global Sea Mineral Resources NV (*GSR*).[6] GSR also holds a separate ISA contract in its own right (sponsored by Belgium).
Deep Ocean Resources Development Company Ltd (*DORD*)	state-controlled corporation (Japan) DORD is over 75% majority-owned by Japanese state enterprise Japan Oil, Gas and Metals National Corporation (*JOGMEC*) (with minority holdings held by private-sector investors).[7] JOGMEC holds a separate ISA contract in its own right (also sponsored by Japan).
Federal Institute for Geosciences and Natural Resources of Germany	public institution (Germany)[8]

[3] ISA LTC, 'Report and Recommendations to the Council of the ISA Relating to an Application for Approval of a Plan of Work for Exploration for Polymetallic Sulphides by the China Ocean Mineral Resources Research and Development Association' (8 July 2011) ISBA/17/C/11*, paras 11, 22; ISA LTC, 'Report and Recommendations of the Legal and Technical Commission to the Council of the ISA Relating to an Application for the Approval of a Plan of Work for Exploration for Cobalt-rich Ferromanganese Crusts by China Ocean Mineral Resources Research and Development Association' (25 February 2013) ISBA/19/C/2, para 9.

[4] ISA LTC, 'Report and Recommendations of the Legal and Technical Commission to the Council of the ISA Relating to an Application for the Approval of a Plan of Work for Exploration for Cobalt-rich Ferromanganese Crusts by Companhia de Pesquisa de Recursos Minerais' (9 July 2014) ISBA/20/C/17, para 9.

[5] ISBA/20/C/18, para 9.

[6] ISBA/20/C/18, para 19; Michael Henry, 'International Seabed Authority Contract Signing' (*Cook Islands Investment Corporations Online News*, July 2016) <http://ciiconline.com/latestnews/international-seabed-authority-contract-signing/>.

[7] See DORD's website <www.dord.co.jp/english/about/index.html>.

[8] ISA LTC, 'Report and Recommendations to the Council of the ISA Relating to an Application for Approval of a Plan of Work for Exploration by the Federal Republic of Germany Represented by the German Federal Institute for Geosciences and Natural Resources' (18 August 2005) ISBA/11/C/7, para 16; ISA LTC, 'Report and Recommendations of the Legal and Technical Commission to the Council of the ISA Relating to an Application for the Approval of a Plan of Work for Exploration for Polymetallic Sulphides by the Federal Institute for Geosciences and Natural Resources on Behalf of the Federal Republic of Germany' (9 July 2014) ISBA/20/C/16, para 15.

Contractor	Type of Entity (and State Sponsor, if Applicable)
Institut Français de Recherche pour L'Exploitation de la Mer	public institution (France)[9]
JOGMEC	state enterprise (Japan)[10]
Marawa Research and Exploration Ltd (*Marawa*)	state enterprise (Kiribati)[11] In relation to its ISA contract, Marawa has a partnership arrangement in place with Singaporean company DeepGreen Engineering Pte Ltd.[12] This company is a wholly owned subsidiary of DeepGreen Metals Inc (*DeepGreen*) (formerly known as DeepGreen Resources Inc), a Canadian mining start-up company.[13] Together with its arrangement with Marawa, DeepGreen holds two ISA contracts indirectly, through wholly owned subsidiaries (and sponsored by Nauru and Tonga, respectively). On its website, DeepGreen lists Kiribati as effectively forming its 'sponsoring state' (in relation to Marawa's ISA contract), in addition to its sponsors Nauru and Tonga (in respect of DeepGreen's other interests).[14]
Yuzhmorgeologiya	state enterprise (Russia)[15]

[9] ISA LTC, 'Report and Recommendations of the Legal and Technical Commission to the Council of the ISA Relating to an Application for Approval of a Plan of Work for Exploration for Polymetallic Sulphides by the Institut Français de Recherche pour L'Exploitation de la Mer' (18 July 2012) ISBA/18/C/16, para 13.

[10] ISA LTC, 'Report and Recommendations of the Legal and Technical Commission to the Council of the ISA Relating to an Application for the Approval of a Plan of Work for Exploration for Cobalt-rich Ferromanganese Crusts by Japan Oil, Gas and Metals National Corporation' (25 February 2013) ISBA/19/C/3, para 9.

[11] ISBA/18/C/18, para 11.

[12] See DeepGreen's website <https://deep.green/sponsoring-states/>. See also The World Bank, 'Precautionary Management of Deep Sea Minerals' (Pacific Possible Background Paper no 2, 30 June 2017) <http://documents.worldbank.org/curated/en/349631503675168052/pdf/119106-WP-PUBLIC-114p-PPDSMbackgroundfinal.pdf> (see 26, noting that 'DeepGreen prepared and funded Kiribati's application [for an ISA contract] in return for an off-take agreement'). For details of Marawa's arrangement with DeepGreen, see discussion in Chapter 4, at text to nn 229, 231; see also Sustainable Opportunities Acquisition Corp, 'Form S-4, Registration Statement' (US Securities and Exchange Commission, 8 April 2021) ('Form S-4') 131, 167–168 <https://sec.report/Document/0001213900-21-020731/fs42021_sustainableoppacq.htm>.

[13] See Form S-4 (n 12) 131; see also DeepGreen Resources Inc, 'DeepGreen Resources Inc Announces Partnership with Maersk Supply Service A/S in Deepsea Metals Industry' (22 March 2017) <www.newswire.ca/news-releases/deepgreen-resources-inc-announces-partnership-with-maersk-supply-service-as-in-deepsea-metals-industry-616799114.html> (which describes that DeepGreen is conducting activities in Marawa's contract area through its wholly owned subsidiary, DeepGreen Engineering Pte Ltd).

[14] See DeepGreen's website <https://deep.green/sponsoring-states/>.

[15] ISA Assembly, 'Plans of Work for Exploration of the Government of India, Institut Français de Recherche pour l'Exploitation de la Mer (IFREMER)/Association Française pour L'Etude et la

Contractor	Type of Entity (and State Sponsor, if Applicable)
Private corporate actors	
Blue Minerals Jamaica Limited (*BMJ*)	private corporate entity (Jamaica) Jamaican corporation, BMJ, holds the most recently approved ISA contract.[16] BMJ's shareholder and operational partner is 'a multinational enterprise engaged for more than 35 years in carrying out challenging marine projects in the offshore oil and gas industry and currently engaged in the deep seabed mining sector'.[17] The identity and nationality of BMJ's partner has not been publicly disclosed.
GSR	private corporate entity (Belgium) Belgian corporation GSR is the deep sea exploratory division of the Belgian corporate group Dredging, Environment and Marine Engineering NV (*DEME*), a world leader in dredging, marine engineering and environmental remediation.[18] GSR was originally G-TEC Sea Mineral Resources NV, a Belgian corporation owned by Belgian geotechnical investigation company G-TEC.[19] However, in 2014, DEME acquired G-TEC Sea Mineral Resources NV and renamed it GSR.[20]
Nauru Ocean Resources Inc (*NORI*)	private corporate entity (Nauru) When NORI submitted its exploration application to the ISA in 2008, it was a wholly owned subsidiary of Canadian mining company Nautilus Minerals Inc (*Nautilus*).[21] By the time of its renewed application in 2011, NORI had ended its relationship with Nautilus.[22] NORI is now a wholly owned subsidiary of Canadian mining company DeepGreen.[23]

Recherche des Nodules (AFERNOD) (France), Deep Ocean Resources Development Co Ltd (DORD) (Japan), Yuzhmorgeologiya (Russian Federation), China Ocean Mineral Resources Research and Development Association (COMRA) (China), Interoceanmetal Joint Organization (IOM) (Bulgaria, Cuba, Czech Republic, Poland, Russian Federation and Slovakia) and the Government of the Republic of Korea' (2 September 1998) ISBA/4/A/1/Rev.2, 17.

[16] ISBA/26/C/27/Rev.1, para 2.

[17] ISBA/26/C/22, para 25.

[18] See DEME's website <www.deme-gsr.com/>.

[19] ISBA/18/C/19, paras 9, 20.

[20] Greenpeace, 'Annex: DEME/GSR Response to Opportunity to Comment' (December 2020) 3 <www.greenpeace.org/static/planet4-international-stateless/95828963-greenpeace-reply_271120.pdf>.

[21] ISBA/17/C/9, para 17.

[22] ISBA/17/C/9, para 17.

[23] DeepGreen holds NORI indirectly through its wholly owned Singaporean subsidiary, DeepGreen Engineering Pte Ltd, as illustrated in the DeepGreen corporate chart within Form S-4 (n 12) 134; see also DeepGreen Metals Inc, 'Copper, Nickel, Cobalt & Manganese Derived from Polymetallic Nodules' (DeepGreen Press Release, April 2020) <https://deep.green/deepgreen-derives-metal-from-polymetallic-nodules/>.

Contractor	Type of Entity (and State Sponsor, if Applicable)
	Founded in 2011, by Nautilus's former CEO, DeepGreen has agreements in place to support its deep seabed mining activities with British commodity trading and mining giant Glencore, Danish offshore marine services company Maersk Supply Service A/S and Swiss offshore engineering company Allseas Group SA.[24] DeepGreen plans to go public on the NASDAQ stock exchange, and it is in the process of a reverse merger with Sustainable Opportunities Acquisition Corporation (a special purpose acquisition company, incorporated in the Cayman Islands and listed on the New York Stock Exchange), to trade as The Metals Company.[25]
Ocean Mineral Singapore Pte Ltd (*OMS*)	private corporate entity (Singapore) OMS is majority-owned by Keppel Corporation, a Singaporean corporation and one of the world's largest offshore and marine groups. Minority shares in OMS are held by Lion City Capital Partners Pte Ltd, a Singaporean private investment company, and UK Seabed Resources Ltd (*UKSRL*).[26] OMS is collaborating with UKSRL in the performance of its contract.[27] As described below, UKSRL is a private British corporation, which also holds separate ISA contracts in its own right (sponsored by the UK).
Tonga Offshore Mining Limited (*TOML*)	private corporate entity (Tonga) Previously, the Tongan corporation TOML was a wholly owned subsidiary of Canadian mining company Nautilus.[28] However, following the financial collapse of Nautilus, DeepGreen acquired TOML, affording it exploration rights in relation to a third ISA contract (in addition to its interests in contracts held by Marawa and NORI, as noted above).[29]

[24] Maersk Supply Service, 'Deep Sea Mineral Exploration' <www.maersksupplyservice.com/wp-content/uploads/2019/08/DeepGreen-Fact-Sheet_140818.pdf>; Peter Koven, 'DeepGreen Strikes Deal with Glencore for Undersea Mining Metals' *Financial Post* (Toronto, 15 June 2012) <https://business.financialpost.com/commodities/mining/deepgreen-strikes-deal-with-glencore-for-undersea-mining-metals>; DeepGreen Metals Inc, 'DeepGreen and Allseas Partner to Harvest Deep Sea Metals to Meet Skyrocketing Growth in Electric Vehicle Demand' (10 June 2019) <www.prnewswire.com/news-releases/deepgreen-and-allseas-partner-to-harvest-deep-sea-metals-to-meet-skyrocketing-growth-in-electric-vehicle-demand-300864716.html>.

[25] See Form S–4 (n 12) (indicating (at 8) that if this merger proceeds, DeepGreen would continue to function as a wholly owned subsidiary of The Metals Company).

[26] ISBA/20/C/7, paras 10, 14. See also Keppel Corporation, 'Joint Venture Agreement with UK Seabed Resources Ltd and Lion City Capital Partners Pte Ltd' (Press Release, April 2013) <www.kepcorp.com/en/download.ashx?id=4877>.

[27] ISBA/20/C/7, para 20.

[28] ISBA/17/C/10, para 15.

[29] DeepGreen Metals Inc, 'DeepGreen Acquires Third Seabed Contract Area, with the Potential to Solve the Supply Bottleneck of Critical Battery Metals' (Press Release, April 2020) <https://deep.green/deepgreen-acquires-third-seabed-contract-area-to-explore-for-polymetallic-nodules/>. For a corporate chart of TOML's holding structure, see Form S–4 (n 12) 134.

Contractor	Type of Entity (and State Sponsor, if Applicable)
UKSRL	private corporate entity (UK) UKSRL is a wholly owned subsidiary of Lockheed Martin UK Holdings Ltd, which is the UK-based component of Lockheed Martin Corporation (a US corporation specialising in aerospace, defence, arms, security and advanced technologies).[30]

[30] ISBA/18/C/17, paras 9, 13; ISBA/20/C/5, paras 9, 13.

APPENDIX 2

Status of Contracts for Exploration in the Area

The following three tables provide an overview of the current status of exploration contracts in respect of each of the three mineral types currently regulated (polymetallic nodules, polymetallic sulphides and cobalt-rich ferromanganese crusts).[1] As the figures in these tables demonstrate, the portion of the deep seabed that the ISA has allocated to contractors for exploration amounts to 1,474,001 km^2. In total, contractors have contributed reserved areas equalling 1,392,833 km^2, some of which are now being explored. Table entries relating to exploration activities within reserved areas are shaded in grey.

[1] The information contained in these tables was derived primarily from ISBA/26/C/4, Annex I: ISA, 'Policy Brief 01/2019 – Current Status of the Reserved Areas with the ISA' (January 2019) <www.isa.org.jm/files/files/documents/statusofreservedareas-01-2019-a.pdf>, as supplemented by ISA approval documentation in respect of each contract (typically comprising a report and recommendation by the LTC, followed by a Council decision in respect of each contractor application: all available on the ISA's website <www.isa.org.jm>). See also ISA, 'Contractors for Seabed Exploration' <https://isa.org.jm/files/files/documents/isacont-update.pdf>.

A Status of Contracts and Approved Applications for Exploration for Polymetallic Nodules

Contractor	Type of Entity	Sponsoring State(s)	Date(s) of Entry into Force	Date(s) of Expiry	Location of Exploration Area	Final Size of Area Allocated to Contractor*	Size of Reserved Area Contributed (if Applicable)[†]
Interoceanmetal Joint Organization (*IOM*)[‡]	consortium of States Parties	Bulgaria, Cuba, Czech Republic, Poland, Russia and Slovakia	29 March 2001 29 March 2016[§]	28 March 2016 28 March 2021[¶]	Clarion-Clipperton Fracture Zone (*CCZ*)	75,000 km^2	150,000 km^2
Yuzhmorgeologiya[‡]	state enterprise	Russia	29 March 2001 29 March 2016[§]	28 March 2016 28 March 2021[¶]	CCZ	75,000 km^2	132,328 km^2
Government of South Korea[‡]	State Party	–	27 April 2001 27 April 2016[§]	26 April 2016 26 April 2021[¶]	CCZ	75,000 km^2	150,000 km^2
China Ocean Mineral Resources Research and Development Association (*COMRA*)[‡]	state enterprise	China	22 May 2001 22 May 2016[§]	21 May 2016 21 May 2021[¶]	CCZ	75,000 km^2	150,000 km^2
Deep Ocean Resources Development Company Ltd (*DORD*)[‡]	state-controlled corporation	Japan	20 June 2001 20 June 2016[§]	19 June 2016 19 June 2021[¶]	CCZ	75,000 km^2	150,000 km^2

Institut Français de Recherche pour L'Exploitation de la Mer (*IFREMER*)[‡]	public institution	France	20 June 2001 20 June 2016[§]	19 June 2016 19 June 2021[¶]	CCZ	75,000 km^2	155,440 km^2
Government of India[‡]	State Party	–	25 March 2002 25 March 2017[‖]	24 March 2017 24 March 2022	Central Indian Ocean Basin	75,000 km^2	150,000 km^2
Federal Institute for Geosciences and Natural Resources of Germany (*BGR*)	public institution	Germany	19 July 2006	18 July 2021[¶]	CCZ	77,271 km^2	72,746 km^2
Nauru Ocean Resources Inc	private corporate entity	Nauru	22 July 2011	21 July 2026	CCZ (in an area formed from portions of reserved areas contributed by BGR, IOM and Yuzhmorgeologiya)	74,830 km^2	–
Tonga Offshore Mining Limited	private corporate entity	Tonga	11 January 2012	10 January 2027	CCZ (in an area formed from portions of reserved areas contributed by BGR, DORD, IFREMER and South Korea)	74,713 km^2	–
Global Sea Mineral Resources NV (*GSR*)	private corporate entity	Belgium	14 January 2013	13 January 2028	CCZ	76,728 km^2	71,937 km^2

Continued

Table A Continued

Contractor	Type of Entity	Sponsoring State(s)	Date(s) of Entry into Force	Date(s) of Expiry	Location of Exploration Area	Final Size of Area Allocated to Contractor*	Size of Reserved Area Contributed (if Applicable)†
UK Seabed Resources Ltd (*UKSRL*)	private corporate entity	United Kingdom	8 February 2013	7 February 2028	CCZ	58,620 km^2	58,280 km^2
Marawa Research and Exploration Ltd	state enterprise	Kiribati	19 January 2015	18 January 2030	CCZ (in a reserved area contributed by South Korea)	74,990 km^2	–
Ocean Mineral Singapore Pte Ltd	private corporate entity	Singapore	22 January 2015	21 January 2030	CCZ (reserved area) (in a reserved area contributed by UKSRL)	58,280 km^2	–
UKSRL	private corporate entity	United Kingdom	29 March 2016	28 March 2031	CCZ	74,919 km^2	74,904 km^2
Cook Islands Investment Corporation	state enterprise	Cook Islands	15 July 2016	14 July 2031	CCZ (in a reserved area contributed by GSR)	71,937 km^2	–
China Minmetals Corporation	state enterprise	China	12 May 2017	11 May 2032	CCZ (in an area formed from portions of reserved areas contributed by COMRA, IOM and Yuzhmorgeologiya)	72,745 km^2	–

Beijing Pioneer Hi-Tech Development Corporation	state enterprise	China	18 October 2019	17 October 2034	Western Pacific Ocean	74,052 km^2	74,198 km^2
Blue Minerals Jamaica Limited (*BMJ*)	private corporate entity	Jamaica	4 April 2021	3 April 2036	CCZ (in an area formed from portions of reserved areas contributed by UKSRL, South Korea and IOM)	74,916 km^2	–
						Total contract area: 1,389,001 km^2	**Total reserved area:** 1,389,833 km^2

* The total area allocated under a contract for exploration for polymetallic nodules is subject to a schedule for relinquishment (in accordance with Nodules Regulations, reg 25).
† The requirement to provide a reserved area does not apply to applications in respect of reserved areas (UNCLOS, Annex III, art 8; Nodules Regulations, reg 15).
‡ These contractors were registered pioneer investors, obtaining approval of plans of work for exploration under the special expedited procedure in 1994 Agreement, Annex, s 1(6)(a)(ii).
§ Five-year extension of contract granted at the ISA's 22nd Session (2016); ISBA/22/C/L.4 – L.9.
‖ Five-year extension of contracted granted at the ISA's 23rd Session (2017); ISBA/23/C/15.
¶ Contractor is seeking five-year extension of contract; ISBA/26/LTC/6.

B Status of Contracts for Exploration for Polymetallic Sulphides

Contractor	Type of Entity	Sponsoring State	Date of Entry into Force	Date of Expiry	General Location of Exploration Area	Size of Exploration Area*	Did Contractor Provide Reserved Area or Equity Interest in Joint Venture Arrangement?†
COMRA	state enterprise	China	18 November 2011	17 November 2026	Southwest Indian Ridge	10,000 km^2	equity interest in joint venture arrangement
Ministry of Natural Resources and Environment of Russia	State Party	–	29 October 2012	28 October 2027	Mid-Atlantic Ridge	10,000 km^2	equity interest in joint venture arrangement
Government of South Korea	State Party	–	24 June 2014	23 June 2029	Central Indian Ridge	10,000 km^2	equity interest in joint venture arrangement
IFREMER	public institution	France	18 November 2014	17 November 2029	Mid-Atlantic Ridge	10,000 km^2	equity interest in joint venture arrangement
BGR	public institution	Germany	6 May 2015	5 May 2030	Central Indian Ridge and Southeast Indian Ridge	10,000 km^2	equity interest in joint venture arrangement
Government of India	State Party	–	26 September 2016	25 September 2031	Indian Ocean Ridge	10,000 km^2	equity interest in joint venture arrangement
Government of Poland	State Party	–	12 February 2018	11 February 2033	Mid-Atlantic Ridge	10,000 km^2	equity interest in joint venture arrangement
						Total contract area: 70,000 km^2	**Total reserved area:** 0 km^2

* The total area allocated under a contract for exploration for polymetallic sulphides is subject to a schedule for relinquishment (in accordance with Sulphides Regulations, reg 27).

† An applicant may elect to contribute a reserved area or offer an equity interest in a joint venture arrangement (in accordance with Sulphides Regulations, regs 16, 19).

C Status of Contracts for Exploration for Cobalt-rich Ferromanganese Crusts

Contractor	Type of Entity	Sponsoring State	Date of Entry into Force	Date of Expiry	General Location of Exploration Area	Size of Exploration Area*	Did Contractor Provide Reserved Area or Equity Interest in Joint Venture Arrangement?†
Japan Oil, Gas and Metals National Corporation	state enterprise	Japan	27 January 2014	26 January 2029	Western Pacific Ocean	3,000 km^2	equity interest in joint venture arrangement
COMRA	state enterprise	China	29 April 2014	28 April 2029	Western Pacific Ocean	3,000 km^2	equity interest in joint venture arrangement
Ministry of Natural Resources and Environment of Russia	State Party	–	10 March 2015	9 March 2030	Magellan Mountains in the Western Pacific Ocean	3,000 km^2	reserved area of 3,000 km^2
Companhia de Pesquisa de Recursos Minerais SA	state enterprise	Brazil	9 November 2015	8 November 2030	Rio Grande Rise in the South Atlantic Ocean	3,000 km^2	equity interest in joint venture arrangement
Government of South Korea	State Party	–	27 March 2018	26 March 2033	Western Pacific Ocean	3,000 km^2	equity interest in joint venture arrangement
						Total contract area: 15,000 km^2	**Total reserved area:** 3,000 km^2

* The total area allocated under a contract for exploration for cobalt-rich crusts is subject to a schedule for relinquishment (in accordance with Cobalt Regulations, reg 27).

† An applicant may elect to contribute a reserved area or offer an equity interest in a joint venture arrangement (in accordance with Cobalt Regulations, regs 16, 19).

Index

For the benefit of digital users, indexed terms that span two pages (e.g., 52–53) may, on occasion, appear on only one of those pages. For page references to cases, treaties and related documents, please consult the relevant tables at the beginning of this monograph.

Tables and figures are indicated by *t* and *f* following the page number

1994 Agreement:
- impact of 84–86, 91, 103–4, 108, 110–15, 118, 124, 126–28, 130–31, 145
- 'market-oriented' approach 85–86, 95, 96, 97*t*, 112, 129, 175, 205–6, 235, 271–72
- negotiation of 84
- relationship with UNCLOS 103–4

activities in the Area:
- definition 3n.22, 121n.139, 209n.69
- *see also* deep seabed mining; exploitation; exploration

African Group 143–45, 207
analytical framework of this book 95–99
Antarctica 48–49, 73–75, 156
Area, the:
- boundaries 48–49
- Clarion-Clipperton Fracture Zone 54, 55*f*, 62–63n.107, 66, 67, 128, 131–34, 177, 208, 213–14, 282–84*t*
- common management of 9, 72, 77, 82, 87–89, 95–96, 97*t*, 103–6, 110–11, 144–45, 149, 269–70
- definition 2n.9, 45, 48
- extent 49
- geology/geomorphology 48, 51–56
- Lost City 214–15
- map of 50*f*
- Peru Basin 54
- Prime Crust Zone 54, 58n.75
- prohibition of unilateral claims/activities 1–2, 9, 72, 77–78, 82, 84n.99, 88–89, 95–97, 105–6, 110, 149, 151–54, 159, 166–67, 169, 171, 175, 179–80, 182–83, 186–90, 193–94, 269–70
- reservation for peaceful purposes 72–73, 77, 78–79, 87, 93–94, 109–10
- *see also* marine biodiversity; mineral resources

Authority *see* International Seabed Authority

BBNJ *see* marine biodiversity
benefit sharing:
- distributive justice 90–91, 93, 202n.25
- economic assistance fund 130n.212, 202
- equal participation 82–83, 90–91, 92n.150, 104n.6, 106–7, 110, 125, 128, 130–31, 135, 200, 206n.51
- equity interest in joint venture 128–30, 144, 200, 286*t*, 287*t*
- financial aspects *see* payment mechanism
- interests of developing states 1–3, 7, 70–71, 74–75, 78–82, 90, 106–7, 125–31, 134, 135, 142–44, 202, 206n.51, 207
- monopolisation 90, 106–7, 123–25, 130–31, 142–44, 200, 206n.51
- production policies 80–83, 85, 94, 98n.182, 130n.212
- reserved areas 3, 32n.125, 90, 106–7, 123–31, 134, 135, 136, 137, 141–44, 200, 206n.51, 281, 282–84*t*, 286*t*, 287*t*
- as a spectrum 91
- transfer of technology 72–73, 80–83, 85, 89–90, 94, 126n.183, 130, 141n.292, 200
- *see also* developing states; Enterprise

China 3–4, 52, 57, 69n.6, 128, 151n.5, 275, 282–84*t*, 286*t*, 287*t*
climate change 61, 64–65, 75–76
coastal state rights 45–48, 51, 53, 251, 259–61
cobalt regulations *see* Mining Code
Cold War 93–94, 272
Commission for the Conservation of Antarctic Marine Living Resources 226n.184
Commission on the Limits of the Continental Shelf 18n.42, 47–49
common concern of humankind 76–77
common heritage of mankind:
- ambiguity of 86–87, 95, 105, 162
- central components 86–93
- customary status 161–62
- development of 68–73, 77–86
- disputed aspects 80, 82–84, 94–95
- diverging interpretations 78–80, 86–87, 162
- future generations 72–73, 87, 92, 129n.204, 202n.25

common heritage of mankind (*cont.*)
as *jus cogens* 104
Pardo proposal 71–73, 77–78, 82, 87
tension between community/autonomy 80, 82–83, 85–86, 95, 97*t*, 205–6, 235, 250, 269–70, 271–72
use in other treaty regimes 73–77
continental shelf:
boundary with the Area 48–49, 109–10
definition 46–47
'extended' continental shelf 45, 47
geology/geomorphology 46–47, 51–52
resources 47–48, 52
contract *see* mining contracts
Cook Islands 6n.33, 21n.59, 53n.48, 54, 58–59, 67n.132, 67n.134, 128, 133–34, 275, 282–84*t*
corporate actors:
chartered companies 33
definition 21–23
diplomatic protection 23–28, 30–32, 33n.129, 34n.137, 36–37n.155, 140–41
international legal personality 32–36, 39, 190
nationality 23–32
see also corporate obligations under international law; corporate participants; corporate rights under international law
corporate obligations under international law:
concept 37–38
conditions 36–40, 146, 189–90, 194
distinction between direct/indirect obligations 37–38, 148, 183–84, 195*t*
enforceability 39–40, 146, 148, 189–90, 194
responsibility for violation 38–39, 146, 148, 189, 194
under customary law 38, 183, 190–94, 195*t*
under internationalised functional contracts 38, 146–48, 183, 195*t*, 246
under treaty law 38, 183–90, 195*t*
under UNCLOS regime 146–48, 183–94, 195*t*, 233
corporate participants:
Blue Minerals Jamaica Limited 65n.124, 132–33, 275, 282–84*t*
collaboration with developing states *see* developing states: corporate collaboration
DeepGreen Metals Inc 4, 64–65, 120, 131–36, 275
DEME 4, 132, 275
financial and technical requirements 121–23
Global Sea Mineral Resources NV 132–34, 142–43, 177n.162, 206n.51, 206n.54, 207n.60, 220, 275, 282–84*t*
Lockheed Martin Corporation 4, 132, 136, 177–79, 275
Nauru Ocean Resources Inc 131–32, 134n.232, 136–37, 142–43, 206n.51, 206n.54, 207n.60, 218, 220, 275, 282–84*t*
Nautilus Minerals Inc 53, 60n.96, 64–65, 127, 131–32, 136–37, 275
Ocean Mineral Singapore Pte Ltd 132–34, 142–43, 275, 282–84*t*
origin of capital 140
participation within reserved areas 127–28, 130–31, 134, 135, 136, 137, 141–44, 200, 282–84*t*, 286*t*, 287*t*
role of nationality/effective control 2–3, 29–32, 121–22, 126–28, 131, 134–44, 150, 248–49
state sponsorship *see* state sponsorship
The Metals Company *see* DeepGreen Metals Inc
Tonga Offshore Mining Limited 132, 134n.232, 136–37, 142n.293, 142–43, 275, 282–84*t*
UK Seabed Resources Ltd 57n.72, 132–37, 142–43, 179, 206n.51, 206n.54, 207n.60, 275, 282–84*t*
corporate rights under international law 36–37, 185–86, 187–88
COVID-19 pandemic 51n.36, 63n.110, 119–20
customary international law:
applicability to corporate actors 38, 183, 190–94, 195*t*
Baxter paradox 168–69
formation 159–61
persistent objector rule 84n.99, 161, 180–83, 193n.261
see also law of treaties: relationship to customary law

deep seabed *see* Area, the
deep seabed mining:
calls for moratorium 53n.48, 61
contrast with land-based mining 59, 64–65
corporate opposition 61
increasing corporate involvement 1, 3–4, 6–8, 65–67, 131–44
within national jurisdiction 53, 58–61
see also corporate participants; exploitation; exploration; prospecting
deep seabed mining regime *see* UNCLOS regime for deep seabed mining
developing states:
corporate collaboration 7, 128, 133–35, 136–37, 142–44
decolonisation 70–71
G77 71, 82–84, 114, 169n.127
historical distinction between developed/developing states 69n.6

land-based producer states 70–71, 114, 130, 202, 207n.58
NIEO movement 80–81, 91, 94
see also benefit sharing
diplomatic protection *see* corporate actors: diplomatic protection

Economic Planning Commission 113
Enterprise 3, 82–83, 85, 90, 106–7, 112–13, 121–22, 125–31, 141n.292, 144–45, 167, 200, 201, 202, 206n.51, 254, 257n.129, 258
environment *see* marine environmental protection
erga omnes obligations 108, 155, 158, 192–93n.260
European Union 1–2, 57, 60–61, 171–72, 185n.205, 255
exploitation:
commercial production 3, 6–7, 118, 201–2, 206, 211, 220n.142, 241n.31, 244
emerging technology 1, 3–5, 59–61, 68–69, 96, 207n.60, 212–13, 218–19
environmental concerns 3, 56, 61–65, 92–93, 213–15
see also deep seabed mining; Mining Code; mining contracts
exploration:
current activities 3–4, 21, 65–67, 131–34, 282–84*t*, 286*t*, 287*t*
see also deep seabed mining; Mining Code; mining contracts
expressio unius est exclusio alterius 141

Finance Committee 113, 117n.110, 202n.25, 203
flag state jurisdiction 30–32, 140–41
formalism 12–16, 18–20, 31–32
fragmentation of international law 17–18, 48n.25, 215
freedom of the high seas 69–71, 75, 79, 83–84, 178n.170

General Assembly 49–51, 71, 77–80, 81n.77, 87, 163, 169–70, 172
global commons 1–2, 70–71, 74–76

HMS Challenger expedition 68–69
hydrocarbons 52

Intergovernmental Working Group on Transnational Corporations and Other Business Enterprises with Respect to Human Rights 184
International Atomic Energy Agency 226n.183
International Centre for Settlement of Investment Disputes 29, 35n.147, 36–37n.155, 186n.217, 192, 193, 250n.85, 253n.107
international investment law:
approach to nationality 26–30, 31–32, 141–42
basic features 26–27, 185–86, 236–37, 246–47, 250
bilateral investment treaties 27, 185–86, 236–37
comparison with deep seabed mining regime 30–32, 141–42, 198, 236–45, 246–50, 253n.107, 256n.125, 260–67, 272
corporate obligations under 185–86, 192–93
counterclaims 192, 253n.107, 261–62
crisis of legitimacy 185–86
dispute resolution 250, 253n.107, 256n.125, 261–62
expropriation 237, 239–42, 264–65
fair and equitable treatment 237, 242–45, 264n.160
full protection and security 237, 245, 260
protected investor 23–24n.74, 26–30, 141, 249n.83
right to regulate 262–66
umbrella clause 247–48n.74
unreasonable or discriminatory treatment 237, 242–43, 244–45, 264n.160
within international agreements 26–27, 236–37
see also mining contracts: investment protection rights
International Law Commission 25–26, 34n.137, 39, 81–82, 155–57, 165, 168–69, 180–81, 227
International Seabed Authority:
balance of power 82–83, 111–16, 144–45
evolutionary approach 112, 126–27
financing 202, 225
international legal personality 111–12, 158–59, 188
law-making powers 2, 16, 18–20, 53–54, 110–11, 116–21, 144–45, 216–23
membership 111
monitoring, inspection and enforcement powers 112–13, 115, 124, 144–45, 221–22, 223–26, 238
observers 111, 157n.47, 158, 171–72, 173*t*, 175–76, 181–82, 216, 271
organs of 113
provisional membership 150n.3, 172–76, 181–82
remote monitoring system 224–25
responsibility 226–31
role in licensing process 2–3, 53–54, 121–44

International Seabed Authority (*cont.*)
  role of the Assembly 113–15, 117–18, 120–21, 145, 203, 223–24
  role of the Council 113–21, 122, 123–24, 126–27, 145, 201–4, 210–11, 214, 218–19, 221–22, 223–26
  role of the LTC 113–19, 123–25, 127, 129–30, 139, 203, 211, 214, 218–22, 223–26, 244
  see also Economic Planning Commission; Enterprise; Finance Committee; Mining Code; mining contracts; Secretariat, Secretary-General of ISA
internationalised functional contract 38, 147–48, 183, 195*t*, 246
Interoceanmetal Joint Organization 21, 67n.130, 275, 282–84*t*

Jamaica 1–2, 111, 128, 275, 282–84*t*
Japan 6–7n.36, 21, 52–53, 56–59, 69n.6, 218n.126, 275, 282–84*t*, 287*t*
jus cogens obligations 104, 158n.58, 161, 181n.182
jus dispositivum 161

Kiribati 6n.33, 21n.59, 64–65, 67n.132, 67n.134, 128, 133–34, 275, 282–84*t*
Kosovo 171–72, 173*t*

landlocked states 69, 78–79, 161n.72, 171–72, 173*t*
law of treaties:
  extraterritorial application 188–89
  objective regimes 154–59, 188
  pacta sunt servanda 152
  pacta tertiis principle 152–54, 158n.58, 184n.204
  relationship to customary law 153, 163–65, 167–69, 175
  third state obligations 151–56, 195*t*
  third state rights 152–56
  travaux préparatoires 13–14, 71n.18, 105, 105n.15, 137–38
  treaty interpretation 13–14, 28n.106, 105, 137–38, 141, 152, 185–87
licensing *see* mining contracts

marine biodiversity 18n.42, 49–51, 61–63, 75–76, 214
marine environmental protection:
  adaptive management 212–13
  areas of particular environmental interest 208
  critique of safeguards 213–15
  environmental impact assessment 209–11, 213–14, 223–24
  precautionary approach 91–93, 107–8, 209–10, 212, 230n.213
  regional environmental management plans 208, 213–14
  see also exploitation: environmental concerns; Mining Code: environmental protections
marine genetic resources *see* marine biodiversity
marine scientific research 3, 109–10, 208, 227n.195
maritime zones:
  baselines 45, 46nn.5–6, 47
  contiguous zone 45–47
  exclusive economic zone 45–48, 53–54, 58–59, 249n.83
  resource definitions 45–51
  territorial sea 45–47, 249n.83
  see also Area, the; continental shelf
methane hydrates 52
methodological approach of this book 11–20
Minami-Torishima 58–59
mineral exploitation *see* deep seabed mining; exploitation; mining contracts
mineral exploration *see* deep seabed mining; exploration; mining contracts
mineral resources:
  cobalt-rich ferromanganese crusts 53–54, 55*f*, 56
  critical metals 59, 60
  definition of 2n.17, 49
  demand for 1, 4, 56–61
  map of distribution 55*f*
  polymetallic nodules 53–54, 55*f*
  polymetallic sulphides 53–56, 55*f*
  potential role in energy transition 56, 64–65nn.117–18
  rare earth elements 1, 56–60
Mining Code:
  amendment of 117–18, 129–30, 209, 216–18, 222–23, 242, 262–63, 265–66
  development of 2, 53–54, 114–15, 116–21, 144–45, 216–23
  environmental protections 208–15
  financial terms 200–7
  interpretation of 138n.263
  regulatory flexibility 209, 216–23, 241–43, 245, 262–67
  role of recommendations 118–19, 210, 218–19, 262–63
  role of standards and guidelines 201–2, 211n.90, 212–13, 218–21, 262–63, 265
  stakeholder participation 18–19, 119, 143–44, 171–72, 203–4, 206n.51, 211n.85, 211, 215–21, 226nn.184–86, 263, 272–73
  'two-year rule' 120–21
  see also mining contracts

mining contracts:
- application process 121–24
- duration 2–3, 124, 222–23
- extension 66, 221–23, 282–84*t*
- fees 121–22, 201–2, 212
- as internationalised functional contracts 147–48, 183, 195*t*, 246
- investment protection rights 236–50
- penalties, suspension or termination 115n.90, 124n.165, 212, 223–25, 240–41, 244
- periodic review process 221–22, 224–25
- plan of work 120–27, 211, 215, 219, 221–23, 224, 244, 253, 254, 261–62
- responsibility and liability 226–31, 233
- security of tenure 177n.164, 178–79, 216–18, 240–41, 245, 260
- state sponsorship *see* state sponsorship
- *see also* corporate participants; International Seabed Authority: monitoring, inspection and enforcement powers; Mining Code; seabed mining disputes

National Oceanic and Atmospheric Administration 177–79
Netherlands, the, 237n.13
Nauru 7, 64–65, 128, 131–32, 136, 142–43, 275, 282–84*t*
New Approaches to International Law 19
New Haven approach 19, 34n.137
New International Economic Order *see* developing states: NIEO movement
nodules regulations *see* Mining Code
non-state actors:
- applicability of customary law 190–91
- armed opposition groups 39, 190
- definition 21
- individuals 21, 23–25, 32–35, 35n.147, 36–37, 38n.166, 39, 40n.186, 184n.203, 185, 188–93
- international legal personality 32–35, 190
- international organisations 21, 34–35, 39, 116, 156–57, 190, 227–28
- *see also* corporate actors

Organisation for the Prohibition of Chemical Weapons 226n.183
outer space 73–75

package deal approach 81–82, 103–4, 170, 232
Papua New Guinea 53
payment mechanism:
- critique of 205–7
- development of 200–7
- Massachusetts Institute of Technology involvement 203–4, 205n.46, 206
- open-ended working group 203–4
- profit-sharing 2–5, 89–91, 106–9, 110, 114–15, 117n.108, 117n.110, 144, 200–2, 205–6, 235n.4, 269
- *see also* benefit sharing

plate tectonic theory 51–52
Poland 67nn.130–31, 127, 187, 214, 275, 282–84*t*, 286*t*
process/substance distinction 89n.132, 92n.153, 97–98
prospecting 2n.14, 3, 118–19, 121n.139

reciprocating states regime 83–84, 163–64, 169–71, 176, 178n.170
res communis see freedom of the high seas
res nullius 69, 70
resources *see* mineral resources
Russia 3–4, 21, 67nn.130–32, 69n.6, 129n.202, 275, 282–84*t*, 286*t*, 287*t*

Seabed Committee 77–78
Seabed Disputes Chamber:
- advisory jurisdiction 232, 251, 252n.97
- applicable law 251
- binding nature of decisions 261–62
- contentious jurisdiction 232, 251–56
- counterclaims 252–53, 261–62
- limits on judicial review 251–53, 256, 265
- provisional measures 260–62
- standing before 110, 148, 232–33, 251–59, 260–61
- standing between co-contractors 257–59, 260–61
- *see also* seabed mining disputes

seabed mining disputes:
- coastal state concerns 48–49, 109–10, 251, 258–61
- commercial arbitration 254–55, 258, 261–62
- dispute resolution mechanisms 232–33, 251, 254–55, 261–62
- matrix of relationships 251
- potential grounds for dispute 233, 248–49, 251–56, 257–62
- *see also* Seabed Disputes Chamber; state sponsorship: potential for dispute

Secretariat 113, 119, 126–27, 140–41, 214, 225–26
Secretary-General of ISA 1, 3, 6–7n.36, 16–17, 59–60, 65, 113, 127, 205n.49, 212, 214, 220–22, 224–25, 259
Singapore 128, 275, 282–84*t*
socio-legal approach 18–19
sources of international law 12–13

South Korea 3–4, 67n.131, 275, 282–84*t*, 286*t*, 287*t*
state-controlled corporations:
  Deep Ocean Resources Development Company 21, 23n.70, 275, 282–84*t*
  distinct from private corporate actors 22–23
  as participants in UNCLOS regime 21, 67
state enterprises:
  China Ocean Mineral Resources Research and Development Association 21, 275, 282–84*t*, 286*t*, 287*t*
  Cook Islands Investment Corporation 133–34, 142–43, 275, 282–84*t*
  Marawa Research and Exploration Ltd 133–34, 275, 282–84*t*
  need for state sponsorship 121n.141
  as participants in UNCLOS regime 2–3, 21, 67, 121–22
state jurisdiction 188–89
state responsibility 23n.68, 39, 40n.186, 140n.284, 226–31
state sponsorship:
  denial of sponsorship 248
  eligibility for sponsorship 29–30, 121–22, 135–42
  generally 2–3, 29–30, 121–22, 150, 238, 248–49
  potential for dispute 248–49, 259–60
  responsibility and liability 138–39, 228–31
  termination 248, 259
sulphides regulations *see* Mining Code

Tonga 64–65, 128, 136–37, 142n.293, 142–43, 275, 282–84*t*
treaty interpretation *see* law of treaties: treaty interpretation
Tropic Seamount 59

UNCLOS III 79–86, 93–94, 103–4, 107, 116, 153–54, 163, 170
UNCLOS regime for deep seabed mining:
  amendment procedures 104, 118
  customary status 162–83, 194
  impact of 1994 Agreement *see* 1994 Agreement
  interpretation of 13
  negotiation of *see* UNCLOS III
  non-parties 150–51, 171–75, 173*t*
  as objective regime 155–59
  overview of 1–4, 103–10
  parallel system 3, 82, 125–30, 142–43, 200
  pioneer investors 83n.93, 282–84*t*
  relationship with general international law 17–18, 107–8, 226–28
  review procedures 82–83, 85, 104n.6, 117–18
  stalemate in ratification 83–84, 272
  States Parties 1–2
  widespread participation within 158, 171–72, 175
  see also International Seabed Authority; Mining Code; mining contracts; Seabed Disputes Chamber; seabed mining disputes
United States:
  domestic licences 177–79
  domestic regime for deep seabed mining 170, 176–79
  opposition to UNCLOS 83
  as persistent objector 181–83
  practice in relation to deep seabed mining 154, 175–83
  provisional membership of ISA 172–75, 181–82